A volume in the series

Anthropology of Contemporary Issues

EDITED BY ROGER SANJEK

A complete list of titles in the series appears at the end of the book.

Creativity/Anthropology

Edited by

Smadar Lavie, Kirin Narayan,
and Renato Rosaldo

Cornell University Press

Ithaca and London

First published 1993 by Cornell University Press.

International Standard Book Number 0-8014-2255-8 (cloth)
International Standard Book Number 0-8014-9542-3 (paper)
Library of Congress Catalog Card Number 92-52765

Printed in the United States of America

*Librarians: Library of Congress cataloging information appears on
the last page of the book.*

⊗ The paper in this book meets the minimum requirements of the
American National Standard for Information Sciences–Permanence
of Paper for Printed Library Materials, ANSI Z39.48-1984.

In memory of Victor Turner

Contents

Contents

[viii]

Contents

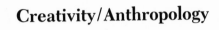

Creativity/Anthropology

Introduction:
Creativity in Anthropology

Renato Rosaldo, Smadar Lavie,
and Kirin Narayan

This volume on creativity is dedicated to the memory of Victor Turner, an extraordinary ethnographer whose life and work exemplified the creative processes he wrote about with passion and insight. He seriously reformulated earlier theories about the human significance of play and ritual, and he pioneered in developing the concepts of communitas and liminality. Turner sought out social situations that enhanced full human encounters and understanding. He found that a range of ritual processes produced transformations that allowed the participants to rework their past and move toward a renewed future. His views of the human condition aspired to universality yet rarely strayed far from the concrete particulars of specific human experiences. He was a consummate ethnographer, and his theoretical writings emerged from and constantly returned to his extended Ndembu field research in central Africa.

In his first book, the classic ethnography *Schism and Continuity in an African Society* (1957), Turner remolded the case history method central to his school of anthropological thought, the Manchester School, by developing the "social drama." Deliberately theatrical, the social drama used a cast of named characters. Its process of unfolding

This brief introduction is a collaborative effort. All three editors shared ideas and bibliography. We also wish to thank Edward Schieffelin and two anonymous reviewers.

[1]

followed characteristic phases: breach, crisis, redressive action, and reintegration or schism. As Turner tells it, the notion of the social drama came to him not in the serious solitude of his study, but in the jocular give-and-take of conversation in a pub. For Turner the most creative human spaces were on the margins or along interstitial zones; these were sites of frolic, play, and joking, as opposed to those of earnest workaday routines. For him—as a person and a theorist— significant human contact and creativity flowed from the margins to the centers more often than the reverse.

In reflecting on human creativity, Turner developed the concepts of communitas and liminality (from the Latin *limen,* threshold). The term "communitas" refers to the potential fullness of human encounters, both within and beyond the social group. Human action in its plenitude embraces cruelty and tenderness, rage and compassion. It involves forms of knowing that are at once cognitive, affective, and ethical. Both cerebral and heartfelt, communitas allows thought to shape feeling and feeling to inform thought. In its full plenitude, communitas encompasses the turbulence of human life as well as the warmth of friendly fellow feeling.

The term "liminality" was first used to refer to transitional states endured by initiates during rites of passage. Liminal states recombine and at times scramble the cultural symbols of workaday life in startling, grotesque, and contradictory ways. Thus a single symbol represents birth and death, a newborn and a corpse in much the manner that initiates exist in a betwixt-and-between state, no longer children and not yet adults. The paradoxes and conundrums that arise in liminal phases force initiates to think again about matters they took for granted. They must reflect on their culture and its conventions. For them, a major reorientation, whether conservative, revolutionary, or somewhere in between, becomes the order of the day.

In his earliest formulation of the concept Turner pointed out that liminality was also a suspended state of awareness. "Liminality," he said, "may be partly described as a stage of reflection. In it those ideas, sentiments, and facts that had been hitherto for the neophytes bound up in configurations and accepted unthinkingly are, as it were, resolved into their constituents" (1967: 105). In his later work, Turner extended his central concept of liminality from rites of passage to historical periods of upheaval and reorientation. He generalized still further and coined the term "liminoid" to designate modern industrial society's notion of leisure, as activities set apart from work. Found in many

[2]

places, from a soccer match to a pilgrimage, these interstitial zones were always the ground for cultural creativity. Turner's processual notion of accepted configurations, their dissolution into constituent elements, and their subsequent reformulation has proven crucial in setting an agenda for the study of creativity in culture.

In a related vein, Turner's biographical portrait of Muchona, a frail and brilliant Ndembu "doctor" endowed with an especially articulate version of traditional wisdom, provides a moving example of the complex relationship between ethnographer and subject. "Muchona the Hornet" appeared in a collection edited by Joseph Casagrande (1960: 334–55) in which seasoned anthropologists portrayed their chief informants. Even in this context Turner stands out by refusing to conform to the canons of his day. His portrait of Muchona creates a space that includes a reflective and socially marginal doctor, an astute and hardened politician, and an Anglicized school teacher named Windson. Educated in a mission school, estranged from his traditions, and troubled by the colonial presence, Windson embodies the jarring historical transformations that shape the encounter between ethnographer and informant. The world, as Turner was well aware, often refuses to be tidy.

Whether speaking of individuals caught in colonial ruptures or exploring notions of liminality, Turner's work highlights the dialectic of innovation and tradition. He brings together odd juxtapositions, unlikely bedfellows, and interactions impossible to anticipate in more neatly compartmentalized theoretical projects. Muchona the man of wisdom, Windson the school teacher, and Turner the ethnographer share overlapping biographies, influencing and being influenced by one another's lives. In his work and in his life, Turner explored complex processes marked by clashes, moments of communion, spontaneity, and insight. Like his subject matter, his writing displays passion, elegance, and aesthetic form. Turner blazed the trail his successors now follow.

In the present collection, Turner's successors range widely in subject matter and geographical area, yet their unifying debt to an inspiring predecessor appears evident in even an epigrammatic description of their essays (readers who desire a fuller discussion of the volume's papers before reading them should immediately turn to Edward Bruner's fine epilogue). James Fernandez describes how Ceferino Suárez uses his poems to play both lovingly and critically, upon village life as he lives it in the mountains of Asturias, Spain. Kirin

[3]

Narayan tells of Swamiji, a Hindu Guru in India, who whimsically reshapes a traditional story so that it comments on contemporary Gurus who offer instant experiences of God, for a goodly fee. Writing about the !Kung of southern Africa, Marjorie Shostak draws biographical portraits of Jimmy, a musician, N!ukha, a healer, and Hwan//a, a bead weaver. Barbara Babcock's analysis of transformation in Pueblo Indian pottery of New Mexico shows how an exceptional woman, Helen Cordero, appropriated and literally remolded dominant male discourse by inventing storytelling dolls. Similarly, Anna Tsing provides an account of how the Indonesian woman shaman Induan Hiling used visual art to scramble and reformulate the performances of male shamans. In depicting the lethal conflicts of field research in the Middle East, Smadar Lavie uses narratives to tell how she used traditional Bedouin story forms to provide the Bedouins an idiom for reflecting, in the midst of jolting changes, on their identities. Donald Handelman uses a deceptively traditional scholarly idiom to insert himself as a character in the drama of how Henry Rupert, a Washo shaman of the northwestern United States, plays with anthropologists' descriptions of his identity.

Victor Turner himself becomes a character in this collection when Edith Turner describes the depth of her late husband's play and creative insight during his participation in an Israeli pilgrimage. The Turners' companion on the Israeli pilgrimage, Barbara Myerhoff, describes how the traditional practice of dreaming reveals personal insight and how she dreamed of her death; shortly thereafter, she died. Richard Schechner reflects on his reading and his experience as a theater director to speak of the connections linking creativity, ritual, and violence. In reflexively depicting his teacher Américo Paredes's balladlike study of a ballad among people of Mexican ancestry in south Texas, José Limón invokes a political vision opposed to Anglo-Texan anti-Mexican sentiment. In exploring the human possibilities afforded by a specific social situation, Renato Rosaldo flips through his field notes to tell how Ilongot visiting in northern Luzon, Philippines, eludes structural definition yet enjoys an open-ended quality that reveals a culturally valued sense of improvisation and social grace. In a related vein, E. B. Schieffelin introduces social complexity into his account of a possession ritual among the Kaluli of Papua New Guinea by writing about how the spirits emerge through the interaction of mediums, audience members, and the ethnographer. Drawing their

[4]

inspiration from many parts of the world, these papers appear in a succession from relatively individual to more collective creativity.

The authors in this collection broadly define creativity as human activities that transform existing cultural practices in a manner that a community or certain of its members find of value. A range of cultures and individuals regard such transformations as, among other things, insightful, wise, divine, inspirational, productive, or fertile. The activities that induce creativity at times are, as Turner saw them, set apart in special spheres, and at times they are, as contributors to this volume would add, integrated into the mundane arenas of everyday life. This book shows that states of liminality and communitas emerge from myriad social contexts; they require less compartmentalization than Turner's initial explorations, which often sought out pure types, seemed to suggest. At once a property of individuals and of social situations, creativity (not unlike laughter) often erupts at unpredictable times and on unexpected occasions.

Creativity, as Roy Wagner (1981) has argued, is always emergent. Members of a society's younger generations always select from, elaborate upon, and transform the traditions they inherit. The healthy perpetuation of cultural traditions requires invention as well as rote repetition. Even decisions to alter nothing received from the past will usually be thwarted because changing circumstances transform the meaning and consequences of dutifully repeated traditional actions. From this perspective, mundane everyday activities become as much the locus of cultural creativity as the arduous ruminations of the lone artist or scientist. In modern societies the succession of generations requires a similar mix of tradition and change. Today's avant-garde, for example, plays a variation on a traditional nineteenth-century romantic theme of bohemian culture. Marginality itself is a cultural category with its own institutional practices and its own space for creative innovation. Creativity often dissolves, or perhaps more precisely redraws, the boundaries of social institutions and cultural patterns.

"Creation," anthropologist Edward Sapir (1924: 418) has aptly written, "is a bending of form to one's will, not the manufacture of form *ex nihilo*." Invention takes place within a field of culturally available possibilities, rather than being without precedent. It is as much a process of selection and recombination as one of thinking anew. Creativity emerges from past traditions and moves beyond them; the

[5]

creative persona reshapes traditional forms. The circumstances of creativity admit to contact, borrowing, and conflict. Regarded as a field of creativity, the zones of interaction among and within cultures more nearly resemble the overlapping strands of a rope than separate beads on a string. Similarly the essays in this collection explore the multifaceted juxtapositions of everyday life. They seek less to separate out social sectors (such as kinship, ritual, politics, economy, ecology) than to render intelligible the complexity with which they come together.

Eruptions of creativity within cultural performances comment upon, just as they often reformulate, the dilemmas a society faces at a particular historical moment. Creative processes emerge from specific people, set in their social, cultural, and historical circumstances. When distinct visions and traditions come together, expressive cultural forms often become politically charged because different actors have unequal chances to make their voices heard. The depiction of situations where cultures mix and blend thus makes both an analytical and a political statement. Similarly, the authors in this volume bring political passions to their studies and move between distance and closeness, detachment and involvement, rather than remaining fixed within the constricted space of detached impartiality. The cultural texts under study here thus often appear as dialogues or conversations rather than monologues.

The ethnographer herself or himself frequently appears as one character among others in the dialogues and conversations of this book. She or he appears not as somebody who has gone native, but as another person (no longer a mere outsider, but not really an insider either) witnessing fellow human beings with sympathy, exasperation, tenderness, distress, and amusement. The sigh, the groan, the caress, the snarl, and the chuckle, all marked by human limitations and insight, inform the ethnographer's perceptions of social life and creativity. The acceptance of one's own role in producing ethnographic writing collapses the infamous dichotomy between Self and Other. The object of analysis also becomes an analyzing subject, and vice versa. What phenomenologist Alfred Schutz (1967: 163–67) called a "We Relation" emerges as ethnographers interact with their subjects. We share time and space, and we grow old together.

In its central subjects and in its style of writing culture, this book celebrates play. The authors find that playfulness erupts in solemn everyday worlds as well as in the circumscribed activities, set apart from work, that Turner or cultural historian Johan Huizinga (1955) would expect. Stepping out of seriousness proves creative, subversive, and innovative. Linguist and literary theorist Mikhail Bakhtin argues that laughter, intertwined with the grotesque and the carnivalesque, breaks the grip of taken for granted realities. "It," he says, "frees human consciousness, thought and imagination for new potentialities. For this reason great changes, even in the field of science, are always preceded by a certain carnival consciousness that prepares the way" (1968: 49). Carnival and laughter thus dissolve the world of earnest necessity into imaginative blueprints and perhaps later realizations of human potentialities. Far from being frivolous, humor in these essays is fundamental to experimentation and politics, for ethnographers and their subjects alike.

This book builds upon recent works of critical anthropology that have called attention to conceptual and political issues involved in writing ethnography. Several significant experimental works that have already appeared have been cited and discussed by Marcus and Cushman (1982) and Marcus and Fischer (1986). In addition, two recent collections, Bruner 1984; and Turner and Bruner 1986, have been landmarks in their graceful bridging of theory and practice in writing engaged social description (see also Clifford and Marcus 1986; Clifford 1989; Rosaldo 1989). The authors here try, through actual ethnographic analyses, to show how circumstantial social descriptions can illuminate and revise theories of cultural creativity.

Like many people in and beyond anthropology, the contributors to this book sorely miss Victor Turner. Turner had a deep grasp of enduring complex processes, such as bereavement, with their maddening blend of sadness, rage, wrenching hurt, and the ludic. The anthropologist's search for meaning, the creative spirit as encountered in its most concrete cultural particularity, animated his work. He thought and lived his ideas about social processes to the fullest, with insight, wit, and a sense of the carnivalesque. We stand diminished without him.

REFERENCES

Bakhtin, Mikhail. 1968. *Rabelais and His World.* Cambridge, Mass.: M.I.T. Press.
Bruner, Edward, ed. 1984. *Text, Play, and Story: The Construction and Recon struction of Self and Society.* 1983 Proceedings of the American Ethnologica

Society. Washington, D.C. (reissued 1988: Prospect Heights, Ill.: Waveland Press).

Casagrande, Joseph, ed. 1960. *In the Company of Man: Twenty Portraits of Anthropological Informants.* New York: Harper and Brothers.

Clifford, James. 1989. *The Predicament of Culture.* Cambridge: Harvard University Press.

Clifford, James, and George Marcus, eds. 1986. *Writing Culture: The Poetics and Politics of Ethnography.* Berkeley: University of California Press.

Huizinga, Johan. 1955. *Homo Ludens: A Study of the Play Element in Culture.* Boston: Beacon Press.

Marcus, George, and Dick Cushman. 1982. "Ethnographies as Texts." *Annual Review of Anthropology* 11: 25–69.

Marcus, George, and Michael Fischer. 1986. *Anthropology as Cultural Critique: An Experimental Moment in the Human Sciences.* Chicago: University of Chicago Press.

Rosaldo, Renato. 1989. *Culture and Truth: The Remaking of Social Analysis.* Boston: Beacon Press.

Sapir, Edward. 1924. "Culture, Genuine and Spurious." *American Journal of Sociology* 29: 401–29.

Schutz, Alfred. 1967. *The Phenomenology of the Social World.* Evanston, Ill.: Northwestern University Press.

Turner, Victor. 1957. *Schism and Continuity in an African Society.* Manchester: Manchester University Press/Rhodes-Livingston Institute.

Turner, Victor. 1967. "Betwixt and Between: The Liminal Period in Rites of Passage." In Turner, *The Forest of Symbols.* Ithaca: Cornell University Press. Pp. 93–111.

Turner, Victor, and Edward Bruner, eds. 1986. *The Anthropology of Experience.* Urbana: University of Illinois Press.

Wagner, Roy. 1981. *The Invention of Culture.* Chicago: University of Chicago Press.

PART I

Creative Individuals
in Cultural Context

[1]

Ceferino Suárez:
A Village Versifier

James W. Fernandez

> Muttering his wayward fancies he would rove.
> —Thomas Gray, *Elegy Written in a
> Country Churchyard*

At a time when anthropologists seek to capture some of the more subtle and emotional aspects of fieldwork in verse of their own, it may be illuminating to evoke the "creative persona" of Ceferino Suárez, a country versifier of the Cantabrian Mountains of Northern Spain. Ceferino was a man of various talents, a sculptor in stone and wood, and something of a musician as well as a poet. His poetry, I discovered, was largely confined to a thick handwritten notebook—a notebook that was misplaced or thrown away at the time of his death. Though I was able to copy out most of Ceferino's verse, I often wondered how many other notebooks were lost in those mountains, for Ceferino was not the only versifier my wife and I heard of, though he may have been one of the most prolific and talented. Thomas Gray in his *Elegy Written in a Country Churchyard* set for us in respect to such unknown talents the pen-

This paper is one product of an ongoing ethnographic project conducted by Renate Lellep and myself on sociocultural change in the Cantabrian Mountains of northern Spain supported over the years by the National Science Foundation and the Spanish American Joint Committee. I am grateful for that support as well as for the very helpful commentary provided for this paper not only by Renate Lellep but by Ruth Behar, Julia Holloway, and Edmund King.

[11]

sive thought: "Full many a Gem of purest Ray serene, / The dark unfathom'd Caves of Ocean bear: / Full many a flower is born to blush unseen, / And waste its sweetness on the desert Air." But this elegiac mood is quite different from the ironic playfulness of Ceferino Suárez himself. And though romantic sentiments animate our anthropology, to be sure, yet our method moves us beyond them to the actual voices of countrymen and women such as Ceferino.

In this essay, then, consulting only several of his more notable poems from a much larger corpus, I will try to evoke the spirit of Ceferino—this village versifier now passed on—such as I came to understand it first in the many hours I spent with him in the early 1970s, taking down his life history on the bench—the *mentidero* or "yarning bench" as it is called—that stood beside his portal. By "evoking the spirit" I mean to indicate trying to recapture Ceferino's particular voice and trying to place it among the village voices and the voices from beyond the village that he heard and to which he had to relate in his time. I use the term "spirit" to denote some essential play of mind of the man that transcends the materials out of which it arises and from which it is made. Probably what we mean by spirit is the lively search for identity—his own identity preoccupied him—but, as pursued in his own work, an identity more adequate to his persona than what can be discovered in the usual categories applied to a man of Ceferino's place and position in life: peasant, countryman, villager. In the several poems out of a larger corpus selected for comment here we see our poet animated by the problem of what we would call individual and generic identity. For Ceferino this was one of the central problems of his life in community, and he addressed it with verve, insight, and poetic resource.

What His Life History Tells Us: "El Habanero"

The life history, it ought to be said, was not Ceferino's particular genre—at least at the time he was asked to recount it—for his telling of it was not a virtuoso performance, an unburdening or release of long withheld memories and treasured experiences. He told it with hesitation and some reiteration, too much influenced by two hectoring elderly women—distant relatives living with him—who loomed over his words in many sessions. As at the time he was plagued by the infirmities of old age, his life history was rather more reminiscent of his misfortunes and frustrations than might have been the case in earlier years. Nevertheless, from it we can learn several important things having to do with his sense of the contrast between the limited possibilities of village life and the "world" opened up by his fifteen years in Cuba in the teens and twenties and by the books he read. For Ceferino was surely one of the villagers who had *mundo* ("world" or "worldliness") as the Spanish say. It was one among other reasons that the villagers called him *el habanero*, the man from Havana.

The phases in Ceferino's life are three. His first thirty years, 1883–1913, were spent in the village, where he was mostly involved in herding and agriculture on family lands. The next fifteen years, 1913–1928, he spent in Cuba. There his *mundo* and its possibilities opened up to him. In the final phase of his life, 1928–1975, he returned to his mountain village, where he took up once again the care of family lands, either those passed directly on to him or those he administered for collateral relatives and particularly nephews, sons of his older siblings, who had gone into the professions. These lands barely provided enough for a modest living.

It is the Cuban period that he remembered most vividly and talked about most animatedly—even though he had been obliged to return to the Asturian Mountains because of a persistent tropical infection of the throat and lungs, even though his attempts like many emigrants' to make his fortune had come to nothing, and even though while in Cuba he confessed that he had thought every day about Asturias and had dreamed frequently about his mother. (His determined bachelorhood, his attachment to his mother, and his timid, symbolic, mostly poetic courtship of women are aspects of his identity I will not comment upon.)

No doubt the frequency with which Ceferino talked about Cuba to his fellow villagers was partly what caused them to nickname *him* the *habanero,* although other villagers had spent years in Cuba and could have claimed the title as well. Perhaps there was something insouciant, breezy, "tropical" in Ceferino as well—something resistant to the severities and sobrieties of village life. When he returned, Ceferino, like many *indianos* (the Spanish word for the emigrant returned from the New World), took a judgmental, usually amused if not ironic, view of that life; it was a view loquacious, even voluble, in expression. Because the vehicle of that judgment was rhyme, verse, and other expressive media, Ceferino became something of a rare bird by village standards. In his life history he recognizes that his mannerisms were a "little strange" (*extraños*) by

[13]

those standards, and he ascribes this to two facets of his character: a desire to know (*deseo de saber*) as much as possible about things of the world and a complete disregard for the long-standing enmities between village families and village factions. Though Ceferino was very adept, even formidable, at *andando cantares*, inventing verses to put up or put down himself or his fellows in the jocularly competitive give-and-take of village life, upon his return he came to regard himself as above all that. Ceferino thus saw in his own character a curious mix of restlessness with respect to knowing the world, *inquietudes*, as the Spanish call it, and tranquility about the challenges of social life. These aspects of his character were reinforced by his years in Cuba, which animated his desire to know and offered him some of the tools to fulfill that desire as they removed him from the day in and day out experience of familial enmities. Ceferino recognized very clearly that his emigration had enabled him to transcend many of the limitations of village life though not, in the end, the nostalgic hold of the village upon him.

Of the first thirty years of his life Ceferino remembered little more than a bad school, a series of nondescript uninterested teachers disgruntled at their rural assignment, and no books except an *abecedario*, a counting book, and a book on Christian doctrine. He learned rapidly, but there was no encouragement. He left the school at the age of twelve to take up the usual tasks of herding, haying, and subsistence agriculture, and in carrying out these tasks, he became like any other villager. He also began gradually, as the youngest child, to take on more and more responsibilities for the care of his parents as his older brothers and sisters married. (I will not comment on the influence on his character of his role as the last and favorite son.) A much older brother, married in Cuba, persuaded him to emigrate in 1913 after the death of his father.

Then began the phase in Ceferino's life that he recalls as his time of opportunity, even though materially speaking and by reference to that yardstick by which the *indiano* is usually measured, it was eventually a bitter failure. He lost all his hard-earned savings in a poor investment in railroad stocks and in a bank failure at the end of the 1920s. But at the same time, there was something lyrical as he evoked his years in Cuba. He found himself transported from the confinements of the village in both a physical and a psychological sense. The possibilities of the world were opened up to him. It was a world, he tells us, about which he wanted to know everything.

[14]

The free public libraries of Havana—and he spent long hours there every weekend—offered him the chance to learn about astronomy, meteorology, music, and the ancients. He took up the violin. It was there that Ceferino began to compose spontaneous verse in honor, one by one, of the various girls working with him in the factory or of his fellow tenants in a rooming house. The tradition of spontaneous *coplas* was certainly part of his own village culture, but it took the transport of his years in Cuba to activate it. And he tried longer poems based on the fables of Samaniego, the nineteenth-century Spanish fabulist.[1] At the same time his roots in Asturias did not cease clutching at him in his dreams. And, as his throat and respiratory problems persisted, he became convinced that he could only become well by leaving the tropics and returning to Asturias—and of necessity to his village, for having no money he had no other alternative.

But Ceferino was a different man when he returned, and psychologically at least he had a hard time accepting the constrictions of village life. In the 1930s and 1940s he composed much verse on that life. In gestures of symbolic courtship, of solidarity or affection, he composed rhymes on spoons or other domestic utensils for favored women or young girls of the village. His *inquietud* was still with him. He embarked on a plan to climb all the mountains in the vicinity, and tried to keep up his astronomical and meteorological studies and his violin. But, as he repeated, there was no appreciation, no stimulation for his "Cuban" ideas and ambitions. Gradually over the decades the *habanero*, Ceferino, relinquished his ambitions in the midst of an ambiance, in his view, so unsuitable and so unsympathetic to them as eventually to dampen them entirely. He fell back slowly into the village round of life, making of his own house by his skills of wood and stone carving a kind of microcosm, which he rarely left. By his final decade he had become a strange bird indeed, seen occasionally muttering to himself, walking the village streets or heard practicing, increasingly ineptly, on an old Havana violin.

The Multitude of Marias and the Abundance of Juans

Ceferino's verse was appreciated more than he knew, particularly a pair of long poems, one celebrating all those named Maria in his

village and the other, all those named Juan in the next village over
the mountains. In the latter poem, *Juan de Juanes,* a native of
Ceferino's valley, an Allerano, goes over the mountain to pay for a
cow sent him by a certain Juan whose other names he has forgotten.
(These other names in this province would not be family names,
which are also very common, but locality names or names or nicknames of spouses, parents, or grandparents.) The poem records in
463 lines and with considerable inventiveness the travail of this
visitor's attempt to find the right Juan in a village that seems to be
made up of nothing but Juans—fifty of them, a veritable "downpour"
of Juans. He finally encounters his man, the fifty-first Juan, who
happens to be called Juan de Juana de la Cuadra, at the very top
of the village. The poet then renames the town, formerly Caliao,
Juanes (or Johnstown).

What is most interesting about this poem is that it is not made up;
the Juans who figure in it were actual residents of the village of Caliao
at the time. What is inventive is that Ceferino effectively builds for
us the visitor's frustration and at the same time gives us a good picture
of the appearance and architecture of the town. He also offers us
humorous capsule commentary on the characters and notable histories
of some of the Juanes who pass in review, for example, Juan de Durán,
a heroic soldier who, on sentinel duty, it is told, shot a mule, mistaking
it for an enemy infiltrator.

The *Marias of Felechosa,* Ceferino's own village, is a poem of 570
lines that proceeds in the same way to make mention of all the Marias,
ninety-six in number, that inhabit the town. The poet organized his
poem as a parade of Marias:

Silencio: suenan campanás	Silence: bells sound
que pasa? Que algo mucho va a pasar,	What's coming to pass? something considerable is coming to pass.
que van a pasar las Marías,	The Marias are going to pass by,
que hay en este lugar.	All of those in this town.
Niñas, mozas, ancianas,	Girls, young ladies, old women
sin una sola quedar.	None will be ignored.
Verán una multitude de Marías	You will see a multitude of Marias,
las que van a presenciar,	Those who will present themselves,

y de todos los matices,	And of all varieties.
hay de Marías la mar.	There is a sea of Marias here.
Hay Marías Magdalenas,	There are Maria Magdalenes,
y de cuerpo virginal,	And of virginal body,
las hay blancas y morenas,	There are white ones and dark ones,
guapas y feas, como la arena	Pretty ones and ugly, like sand
las hay malas, las hay buenas:	There are good ones and bad ones:
altas, medianas, pequeñas,	Tall, medium, and small,
de todas formas las hay.	They come in every form.

As Ceferino knows his fellow villagers, their family lives and foibles, much better than he knows the villagers of Caliao, the anecdotal detail that accompanies the naming of many of the Marias is much richer. Most of these Marias are mentioned in one laudatory way or another, but others are just mentioned and, for some, sharp comments are reserved. Here are some examples:

Sin mover la vista nada	Without shifting your view,
pueden ver a otra señora,	One can see another señora,
que sus plácemes merace,	That merits all your compliments,
María la de Isidora,	Maria she of Isidora,
que an aumentar nuestra especie,	Who in augmenting our species,
ha sido muy productora,	Has been very productive,
También es merecedora,	Also meritorious,
de algo bueno y no vió nada	Of recompense but unrequited,
María la de Gervasio,	Maria she of Gervasio.
que va la pobre olvidada,	Poor one she now goes forgotten,
hasta de los muchos pobres,	Even by the many poor,
que les dió feliz posada.	To whom she gave joyful shelter.
Y María la mocona,	And Maria the snotty one,
esta mujer achatada,	This flat-nosed woman,
va conforme con su chato,	Accepts her flat nose
y a nadie le importa nada.	And is of no bother to anyone.
María del José del Cuadro	Maria of José of the Square.
Ahí veréis también,	There you'll see her also,
que en los mares de amor,	Who in love's seas,

[17]

ha sufrido su vaivén,	Has suffered her ups and downs.
si lo sufrió por su gusto,	If she suffered from her own desire,
nadie importa, hizo bien;	None blames her, she did right;
ella misma se lo quiso,	She herself desired it,
ella misma se lo ten.	And she had what she desired.
Sigue María de Flora	Now follows Maria of Flora,
la pobre ya deflorada.	The unfortunate deflowered one.
y luego otras Marías,	And then come other Marias,
muchas bien aventuradas	Many of innocent felicity,
que en amores e ilusiones	That as far as love's illusions
ni sufren ni piensan nada.	Neither suffer nor aspire.
Una es María del Pesquero	One is Maria of the fisher,
que va sin hablar palabra.	That goes about without a word.
y María la papuina,	And Maria of the little goiter,
Va con ella acompañada.	Who always accompanies her.

As the poem progresses there are so many Marias, such a progression of village women, that the poet despairs of his powers to provide a poetic vehicle for each of them. He also despairs about the "thousand plagues and quarrels" that he may be laying up for himself with these women because he lacks the "clarity of expression" to treat the fair sex with the proper delicacy. But

voy seguir a la que salga	I will continue with each as she appears.
o yo acabo con ellas	Either I will finish with them
o ellas conmigo acaban.	Or they will finish me off.

Periodically during the poem the poet plays upon the identification, more or less intended in village naming practices, between the Virgin and all those who are her village namesakes. Ceferino is sufficiently inventive to end the poem with a playful evocation of the Virgin in a prayer (*oración*) and a *salve* which turns out to be addressed much more to the Marias than to María. I emphasize the term "play" and "playfulness" because this prayer and salutation exploit with tongue in cheek not only the ambiguity existing between the name and the namesake but also the ambiguity between ultimate and immediate blessings—the ultimate blessing that only the Virgin can provide and the immediate domestic and corporeal blessings that only village women can provide to village menfolk. Indeed, as I say, the Blessed

Virgin is much less present in these final "religious invocations" than the real, physically present village women named after her.

Evocación	*Invocation*
He nacido en mala hora,	I was born in a bad time,
de tanta María que hay,	When there are so many Marias,
no hay una que exhale un ay,	Yet not one who will exclaim, Ay!
por el mi bien a deshora.	For my good at a bad moment.
Ya no es merecedora,	Perhaps it does not merit
la mi suerte de este bien,	My fortune such a boon,
de gozar del bello edén,	As to enjoy that lovely Eden
que una María atesora.	That any Maria can treasure up.
Aunque mi alma la llora,	Although my heart cries out to her
ya con santa devoción,	Now with holy devotion,
para las Marías todas	To all the Marias
me encomiendo esta oración.	I dedicate this prayer.

Oración	*Prayer*
Oh! Marías del amor,	Oh! beloved Marias,
que a vuestras divinas plantas,	At whose divine feet
me postro, porque me encantan,	I am prostrate because they enchant me
y les pide por favor.	Beseeching your favor.
Si me veréis con dolor,	If you see me suffering,
y de vos necesitado,	And in need of you,
dadme vuestra protección,	Give me your protection,
dulce consuelo y amparo.	Sweet consolation and comfort.
En nada pongáis reparo,	Let nothing prevent you,
dulces prendas de mi vida,	Sweet treasures of my life,
en darme lo que vos pida,	In granting what I request,
de aquello que bien tenéis,	Of that you so surely possess,
y si vosotras queréis,	And if you should so wish,
hacer algo por my suerte,	To influence my fate,
no temáis por la mi muerte,	Do not fear for my death,
si cayera desmayado,	If I should faint away,
y mi cuerpo abandonado,	And my body be abandoned,
por natural accidente;	By some natural accident;
ya me veréis de repente,	You will see that I quickly
glorioso y glorificado.	Pass to glory glorified.

Salve	*Salutation*
Salve, Marías de gracia,	Hail, Marias full of grace,
y de mil encantos llenar,	You of a thousand enchantments,

Salve bellas azucenas,	Hail beautiful lilies,
y vuestra piedad me salve.	May your mercy be my salvation.
en vuestro pecho se guarde,	Within your breast may you keep
el perdón de mis agravios,	A pardon for my offenses,
no me miréis con resabio,	Do not regard me with distaste,
amorosas criaturas;	Loving creatures;
y dadme vuestras dulzuras,	And grant me your sweet favors
que mis dolores se acaben.	That my sufferings may end.
Por esta bendita salve,	Through this blessed hymn,
les espero el santo bien,	I await a sainted well-being.
me lleváis a vuestra gloria,	Carry me to your glory,
por siempre jamás, Amen!	For ever and ever. Amen!

Beyond giving the anthropologist some idea of what was public knowledge and grist for gossip in the village, these two poems deal with various themes of anthropological interest. One of the themes is that of poetry as symbolic courtship, which is discussed below; Ceferino's employment of this theme derives both from his readings in the literature of courtly love, or even Platonic love, and from franker country traditions of the relation between the sexes. What is, however, most interesting in these two poems and what is at play, it seems to me, is the tension between generic or communal identity and individual identity. For although a given name is, as opposed to a family name, a gesture toward individual identity, the irony that Ceferino observed and played upon is that these individual names are so common that they are no longer individualizing. Since family names are also so very common in these villages (more than half of the villagers may carry the family name of González or Fernández or Rodríguez or García), individuality is given by reference to location, Juan of the Stable; or by reference to peculiarities, Juan the Curly-headed One; or by reference to the names or particularities of spouses or parents, Juan of Juana, Juan of the Lame One, Juan of the One-eyed One, Juan of the Watchmaker.

Such naming practices have been well studied in the literature, but this poem is revelatory in its exploration of the communal identity–individual identity dynamic. Ceferino explored this dynamic in other poems as well, as, for example, in *The Marriage of the Villages* (*Los casamientos de los pueblos*) in which he assigns male and female characters to pairs of villages and marries them off. Such a poem follows the logic of *Juan de Juanes* or *Las Marías* in which a village is assigned an identity ("Juanes," for example) by reference to the name and sex most widely represented.

Atención noble auditorio!	Attention, noble audience!
si podéis estar atentos:	If you can be attentive:
este vuestro servidor	This your servant
que orgulloso está de serlo,	And proud to be so,
se encuentra en comisión,	Finds himself charged
desde países muy lejos	From very distant lands
con gran autorización,	With the highest authorization,
y sagrado documento,	And by the most sacred document,
para emparejar los pueblos	To pair up the villages
por medio del casamiento.	By means of marriage.
Ahora voy a empezar,	Now I am going to begin,
en cumplir con mi destino,	In fulfilling my charge
en casar a Felechosa	By marrying Felechosa
con el lugarín del Pino.	With the little town of Pino.

Ceferino not only assigns a sex but also a distinct character to each village, mostly according to popular views prevalent in the countryside at the time and by reference to popular metaphors. Of course these views express the sociocentrism characteristic of village life.

Y siguiendo mi carrera,	And following my course,
Tengo que darme a casar,	I must attend to marrying
la chancla de Casomera,	The old worn-out shoe of Casomera
con el chiribitil de Villar.	With hole-in-the-wall Villar.

The poem continues with rhymes to his own village:

Felechosa es buena moza,	Felechosa is a handsome girl,
tiene ganas de comer,	And she wants to eat;
bebe, usa tabaquero,	She can drink and roll cigars,
y café sabe moler.	And she knows how to grind coffee.
Aunque su futuro esposo,	Although her future husband
es mas pequeño y ruin,	Is smaller and less prosperous,

[21]

es un joven provechoso,	He's a worthwhile match,
pues que se vayan al fin.	So let them go all the way and marry.

What this poem does, of course, is project individual identity upon another level, the level of the village. It is a logical outcome, as noted above, of the earlier poems about the Juans and the Marias in which identities at the individual level are aggregated at the community level. Anthropologically it is an instructive poem; in showing the diversity of character among the various villagers, it cautions against our reductionist tendency to generalize about peasant character or provincial character or national character when, in fact, the municipality, the valley, and the province from the local point of view are made up of congeries of individual Marias and Juans.

This tension between generic and individual identity and the ambiguity about what level of conceptualization identity processes are at work on are wonderfully captured in this set of poems— captured in a richer way than could any formal statement of the logic of it. We know that Ceferino felt this tension and this ambiguity very strongly. For, in a sense, his entire life was an attempt to assert his own individual identity and his own talent, his desire to know and to express himself in music and poetry and sculpture in the face of community disinterest, community constriction, and community unwillingness to recognize or encourage the expression of that individuality. So these poems work out in a playfully ironic way the creative Ceferino's own "literati" frustration with the constricting folk culture of his surroundings.

It is, perhaps, a bit more complicated than that. For by subsuming all the individual Juans of Calaio or Marias of Felechosa into one Maria or one Juan, or into a male or female partner apt for marriage, into one collective representation as it were, Ceferino is also expressing his own presumption to possess the generic voice, to speak for the entire community and to moralize in the fabulist's mode. He presumes, as many returned emigrants—*indianos* or *habaneros*—before and after him have presumed, that because of the distancing and the transcendence their emigration gave them, they had the wherewithal to speak for or pass judgment upon the Asturian community. Doubtless that distancing in part gave to Ceferino powers of expression denied to his fellow villagers. But it was also precisely that claim to the generic

[22]

voice, to the right to the collective representation, that his fellow villagers in their insistent egalitarianism, and despite how much they enjoyed some of his poems, denied to this *indiano*, this *habanero*, among them.

Poetry as Symbolic Courtship

I have intended Ceferino's verse to stand at the center and to be the vehicle of the argument here. For he entitles my argument just as he entitles this essay. He gives it its raison d'être. This man and his verse are the sine qua non of what I have written about him. In discussing his life history, for example, I have avoided a psychological analysis that would have displaced, and possibly diminished, him into one or another psychological category or made him a dependent of theories and theorizers of interest to us professionally, but unknown and irrelevant to him. One aspect of Ceferino's psychological life, however, does bear commenting upon in the light of the particular verses presented here. And that is the fact that he never married—a fact that provided, as frustration or impediment, the impulse toward much of his poetry.

I remember, and he remembered well, that in his Havana days the first short verses he composed were in honor of young female co-workers or acquaintances. He remembered, for example, that on the top floor of the building where he lived, in the attic, was an apartment occupied by a beautiful young mulatto woman, Carmen Julia, and her mother. There was a shopkeeper on the street who was something of a womanizer, and one day he pointed out Carmen Julia on her balcony and promised Ceferino a drink if he would recite a verse to her on the spot. "So I asked her permission and on the spur of the moment I recited":

Cuando Usted mira hacia abajo	When you are looking down
E yo mirando hacia lo alto	And I am looking upward
Veo el reflejo de sus ojos	I see the reflection of your eyes
Como dos brillantes astros!	Like two brilliant celestial orbs!

And Ceferino remembered a beautiful young girl who worked in the factory with him and was being courted by a wolf (*lobo*), a formerly married man. He sent her this poem:

[23]

Tú que más parece una niña	You who appear so much a girl
Llena de gracia y hermosura	Full of grace and beauty
No vas, cielito santo,	You are not going, divine heaven,
Echar por el suelo	To throw down to the ground
Todos tus encantos	All your enchantments
Por una cierta basura?	For a certain piece of garbage?

In Cuba Ceferino became a great inventor of rhymed street compliments to the female sex (*piropos*). In his life history, after discussing this phase of his life, he asked rhetorically: "What is the good of such beauty in women if not to be looked upon and praised?" Whatever transpired between him and the women he came across in Cuba, when he returned to Felechosa it appeared that he did not consummate any relationship, and he continued to look upon women from a distance and praise them in poetic courtship. The variety of this verse was considerable. Into the handles of the various domestic utensils he carved, wooden spoons, for example, he would work such verses as:

Soy la cuchara la más feliz	I am the happiest of spoons
a servir la boquita	To be able to serve the little mouth
de una Hurí	Of a Houri.
Soy la cuchara la más hermosa	I am the most beautiful of spoons
a servir la boquita	For I can serve the little mouth
de una rosa.	Of a rose.

Ceferino continued to address throw-away verses, *alabanzas* he called them, to village women, married and unmarried alike. The first two that follow are to married women, and the third is to a girl whom Ceferino considered to be of rather promiscuous character. We note that he carefully maintains third-person reference when referring to married women. The more promiscuous girl he addresses in the second person.

Quisiera ser huracán,	I would be a hurricane
y elevarla hasta los cielos,	To lift her up to the heavens,
para que digan los sabios,	In order that the learned may say
de que hay un astro nuevo.	That there is a new star.

Perdóname Usted señora,	Pardon me, señora,
del respeto que le debo,	Of the respect I owe you,
su hermosura me dió el tema,	Your beauty gave me my theme,
Y a veces callar no puedo.	And at times I cannot be quiet.
Dulce Amada del amor,	Sweet Amada of love,
tierna viola del Abril,	Sweet April violet,
que dichoso es el barón	How fortunate is the man
que la vela en su dormir.	That watches over her in her sleep.
Para escribirte mi cielo,	To write of you, my heaven,
dame tu tintero gloria,	Give me your glorious inkwell,
que mi pluma de modelo,	That my barrel pen
hará letra en tu memoria.	Will write verses in your memory.

When, after the nationalist victory in 1937, a detachment of Civil Guards was stationed in the village to patrol against Republicans who had taken refuge in the hills, Ceferino wrote a poem addressing the courtship relation between the village beauties and these men. (I note only in passing the subliminal sexual imagery that often enough appeared in these efforts.)

Alto! una advertencia!	Halt! A warning!
doy al público sensato,	I give to the prudent public
del peligro y la influencia,	(Notice) of the dangerous influence
de las flores de este patio,	Of the flowers of this patio,
que asaltan la guardia civil	That assault the Civil Guard
y aprisionan la de asalto;	And imprison these assault troops;
tienen armas tan terribles,	They have such terrible arms,
y un calibre de los diablos,	And of such a devilish caliber,
que domenan y fascinan	That they tame and fascinate
al más soberbio y más bravo,	The proudest and the bravest,
y unas espinas tan finas,	And with thorns so fine,
que no se le va ni el gato.	Not even a cat could escape them.
Pero no hay que asustarse,	But there is no reason for alarm,
Porque estos guardias cautos,	Because these wary guards
en un momento propicio	In a propitious moment
ya saben ponerse a salvo	Will know how to save themselves

[25]

disparando sus fusiles,	Discharging their rifles,
contra esos bellos encantos,	Against these beauteous enchantments,
haciendo blancos al punto,	Finding their target instantly,
y al punto dejan en blanco.	And instantly rendering them insignificant.

Ceferino's interest in the opposite sex and his symbolic courtship of women expressed itself in different poetic forms from throw-away verses to long romantic poems, such as the *Vixen's Child*, which is an account of an abandoned orphan girl saved by a fox. The poem is largely devoted to her courtship by a young nobleman.

While there are many poems of courtship in Ceferino's work, there are also poems devoted to the dangers presented by love for the opposite sex. Below is one from a series of short verses which Ceferino called *Refranes con filosofía barata* ("Proverbs offering a cheap philosophy"). Following this poem in his notebook was another which evoked the relationship of all women to the mother figure. This relation seems to have animated Ceferino's symbolic courtship and, perhaps, at the same time, prevented its normal fruition in marriage.

En los mares del amor,	In the seas of love,
todos se quieren bañar	All wish to bathe themselves
sin pensar en el temor	Thoughtless of the fearfulness
de lo que pueda pasar,	Of that which could occur,
ese mar es un traidor	That sea is treacherous
no sirve saber nadar.	It is of no use knowing how to swim.

No hables mal de las mujeres,	Do not speak badly of women,
ni hacia el diablo las compares,	Nor compare them to the devil,
debe de pensar si quieres,	You should be willing to recognize
que una mujer fue tu madre.	That your mother was a woman.

As suggested, a number of themes thread through Ceferino's poetry. But the two major themes, those problems that animate the poet toward poetic solutions, are that of individual and generic identity and that of courtship or the relation between the sexes. A close relationship exists between these two themes. For courtship and marriage are directed toward and effect the creation of a supra-individual or generic identity through the emergence of a married couple—the smallest corporate unit of community. Though Ceferino did not, for whatever reason, bring this about in his own life (if he had, he might not have written so much poetry about it), nevertheless, he courted effectively and effusively in his poetry and brought about many marriages—even marriages between villages. Essentially a lonely, transported individual, Ceferino nevertheless maintained perceptive, if playful, relationships with his fellow villagers and their characters, well captured in his poetry. And ironically, he achieved for them what he could not achieve for himself: a generic (and fully gendered) identity as well as an identification with community.

Conclusion: "Ripeness Is All"—A Poetics for Anthropology

In the late 1960s when I was teaching at Dartmouth College, the college, using a much earlier generation of computers than we have now, was developing the Basic language. A group of us experimented with generating computer verse—randomly recombining, within a constant framework of functors, a large set of subjects and objects, and qualifications and predications upon them. This verse did not rhyme, unlike Ceferino's, but it *was* rather suggestive. I once sent an example of it to the late Victor Turner. He wrote back, with his usual perceptiveness and wit, that he was impressed with how much "poetry" the computer could write and how fast it could write it. But he did not think it could write, "Ripeness is all." Turner, of course, was referring to Shakespeare's "Men must endure / Their going hence, even as their coming hither: / Ripeness is all" (*King Lear* 5.2.9–11). I think he meant the computer could not write in real time.

It seems to me that this observation can be taken to stand for, to express, a feeling that lies behind much of the "poetics" movement in the social sciences and anthropology, whether we mean those studies derived from hermeneutics and semiotics or the anthropologist's own poetry. It is a feeling that so many of our analyses, or systematic formalizations of our field experience, are not being written in real time. They do not contain that complex and often ambiguous interplay of forces coming into being and forces passing away—of men and women "going hence" and "coming hither"—that makes up the human experience of ripeness.

The computer could suggest, but it could not write like Ceferino in real time. He was a man, in my "real time" with him, far past his

[27]

"ripe" time, though he could remember it and its frustration, which he had expressed in his poetry. He was a man, after all, whose great experiences in life were a "going hence" and a "coming hither" again— struggling to find his voice and his identity between individual and generic identities. He was a man who had long searched for a frustrated and then a lost "ripeness," although in the end his realization of such experience was mainly poetic. In this poetry was a struggle—the poetic struggle and the poetic challenge—to meld the contraries of his career, contraries, perhaps, of the human condition itself. I say "challenge" because Ceferino was clearly aware of the challenges of his life to which he did not or could not respond. In counterpart, in his poetry he did meet these challenges, for the most part with wry irony. And he thus in this register preserved for later memory the ripest, the fullest and the most fleeting, moments of his life.

Somewhere in the middle of his poetic career in the 1930s (the two verses bear no date), Ceferino had enough awareness of the fleetingness of that career to compose his own epitaph.

Yace Ceferino Suárez,
en este sitio enterrado
que vivió en este mundo,
ni envidioso ni envidiado.

Ceferino Suárez lies,
Interred in this place
Who lived in this world,
Neither envious nor envied.

Si no consigo panteón,
para señalar mi tierra;
que me pongan un moyón,
como los que hay en la vega.

If I achieve no pantheon
To mark my piece of earth
Let them put up a fieldstone,
Like those that divide fields in
the valley.

The field marker seems an appropriate metaphor for one (we remember Victor Turner's phrase) so "betwixt and between" childhood and adulthood, "betwixt and between" bachelorhood and marriage, "betwixt and between" the covetousness and envy of his fellow villagers and the disinterestedness of a "transported" personality, "betwixt and between" his barely literate community and the bookishness of the Spanish literary tradition.

When I knew Ceferino and took his life history, he was in his very old age. The bloom was long gone from his cheeks. He might be thinking, but he could not write "ripeness is all." He was living not in real time but in recalled time. But it is our fortune that he preserved and we could retrieve the notebook of his scribbled verse—verse written in his ripe time when his transported intelligence was shot through with the desire to express his feelings about himself, his fellow villagers, and his villages. I can hardly imagine a more authentic document upon which to base an anthropological poetics.

Notes

1. Félix María Samaniego, *Fábulas* (Buenos Aires: Espasa Calpe Argentina, S.A., 1946).

[2]

On Nose Cutters, Gurus, and Storytellers

Kirin Narayan

Salutations to the Goddess who dwells in all beings in the form of intelligence: salutations, salutations, salutations again and again.

—*Durgā Saptashatī*

In anthropological circles, Clifford Geertz's (1966) definition of religion as "a system of symbols" continues to command widespread respect. Yet, work in the fields of philosophy, religious studies, and Christian theology suggests that religion could equally be defined as a system of stories (Braithewaite 1955: 32–33; Goldberg 1982; Hoffman 1986; Slater 1978; Tilley 1985; Wiggins 1975). Narratives, after all, cluster around the dominant symbols, beliefs, and ritual actions of

Though the background knowledge on which this essay is based extends back to 1970, I stayed with Swamiji as a graduate student in anthropology between June and August 1983 and July and October 1985. I am grateful for a National Science Foundation Graduate Fellowship, a University of California–Berkeley Graduate Humanities Research Grant, Robert H. Lowie funds, and a Charlotte W. Newcombe Dissertation Fellowship. My thanks to Didi Contractor, Narayan Contractor, Alan Dundes, "Gulelal," Smadar Lavie, Victor Perera, Renato Rosaldo, Shubhro Sen, and Sayyad Zaidi for reading earlier drafts of this essay. Also thanks to the audiences at the Center for South and Southeast Asian Studies at U.C. Berkeley and the anthropology departments at Swarthmore College, Bowdoin College, and Westchester University for their helpful questions and comments. Above all, my deepest and abiding thanks remain with Swamiji for his endorsement and encouragement of this project.

[30]

religions the world over. Through stories, morals are fleshed out, gods acquire character, saints become exemplars, tenets are made real. As a religion is transmitted across historical eras, what happens to the stories? How are they creatively reinterpreted and retold? In this essay I turn to a religion well known for its sumptuous stories—Hinduism. Examining a folk narrative about false Gurus used by two Gurus separated by almost a hundred years, I argue that the flexibility of a spoken story allows for an improvisation that can capture the religious imagination of different audiences afresh; religious stories can be sprightly yet stern custodians of moral canons, even as creative tellers mold them around changing historical circumstances.[1]

The bulky man who sat cross-legged against the wall had been telling us about his Guru's workshops. One could sign up for initiation, he explained: It was merely a matter of a few hundred rupees, and a mystical experience was guaranteed. These workshops had been developed in America, he said, but now they were even held locally. He, Advani, had helped organize them here in this ancient pilgrimage town of Nasik in Western India.

Swamiji sat listening from his aluminum deckchair, gray head resting against a brilliantly flowered orange pillowcase. To his left was an altar filled with an array of deities. On the floor around him was the usual motley gathering: local people, visitors from other Indian towns, a handful of Westerners. There were perhaps fifteen people present, among them the graduate-student ethnographer poised with her notebook and tape recorder. As Swamiji questioned and Advani talked on, we were all listening or observing according to our varying degrees of Hindi competence. This was Swamiji's *darshan* time: the hours in which he, as an ascetic "renouncer" (*sannyāsī*) and Guru, met with visitors. *Darshan*, (to view) refers to the act of gazing at a more powerful being, whether a respected elder, a holy person, or a deity (Babb 1981; Eck 1981). So though Advani held forth, the group was largely focused on Swamiji.

There was a break in the conversation as a few visitors stood up to leave. "Hail to the Mother of the Universe, hail!" muttered Swamiji as they saluted him. He presented them with bananas. As the screen door creaked behind them, he asked us, "Haven't you heard of the Narayandarsimat?"

"The what?" we said.

"The Nose Cutters (*nāk kātne vāle*)."

[31]

"The *what?*"

"The Nose Cutters," he repeated, looking around the room, where women were seated along the right wall, men along the left. He scanned all our faces. "She's heard it!" he pointed to "Gayatri" of New Jersey who sat at his feet, wearing a sari of light blue silk. She looked to me for clarification; as an Indian-American anthropologist I often served as the culture broker who could translate or elaborate. But I was nonplussed too. Mr. Gupta, who was visiting from North India, though, rolled his head: "The...Nose...Cutters," he slowly repeated in Hindi, then added in English, "a group."

Grinning with the pleasure of a story to tell, Swamiji started in. He was still reclining with his legs outstretched, a crumpled, ochre cloth wrapped around his waist, and several weeks growth of white hair on his genial round face. He wore enormous spectacles which magnified his eyes, a strand of sacred *rudrāksha* beads, and on his forehead, a lopsided, red spot of vermillion (*kumkum*) sacred to the Goddess. Swamiji often referred to himself as a "topsy-turvy holy man" (*agaṟam bagaṟam sādhu*) who spoke a "topsy turvy" and "any-which-way" (*ultā sultā*) language. Indeed, the language in which he now told the story was his own idiosyncratic mixture. Though the basic framework was Hindi, Swamiji put in Kannada case endings (from the place of his birth), Marathi words (from the region in which he now lives), English words (which he has picked up along the way) and Sanskrit terms (from scriptures). Bombay, which is four hours southwest of Nasik, has bred a similar form of hotchpotch Hindi, so most listeners could understand Swamiji. In my translation, which follows—reconstructed through headphones long after the event—I underplay the ways in which the constituent languages interact (cf. Bakhtin 1981) through Swamiji's retellings, marking only English words with an (E).

There was a Guru, like me. He had many devotees. He wasn't really like me...he was greater than I. Consider him to be a little like me. He would tell his disciples, "I'll give you darshan of God." And the disciples spread the word. "Our Guruji reveals God." This was the kind of propaganda they did. This world exists through propaganda. The more advertising you do, the greater a thing becomes. That's why companies(E) all advertise: on the radio(E) on the television(E). The products themselves are nothing much, that's why they must spend so much money advertising them.

[32]

[Swamiji is chuckling, and we all laugh.]

The Guru advertised himself in the same way. Say the disciples meet someone like you—especially the important officials (officer(E) *log*)—they would say, "Our Maharaj gives people darshan of God." Now everyone wishes to see God. You'll say, "Yes, I would very much like to see God."

"If that's so," the disciples would say, "Then you must donate 10,000 rupees."

"All right, I'll give you 10,000 rupees." [Swamiji agreeably rocks his head.] What's it to you if you have a lot of money? Certainly, seeing God is worth the expense. So you would be taken there by the disciples.

The Maharaj was quite handsome. He'd put on a jeweled crown. In his own hands he'd hold a conch and a discus. A disciple hiding behind him would hold a lotus and mace. He'd sit on a throne wearing golden yellow garments and a shawl. He'd sit there, just as Lord Narayan sits, with all the attributes of Narayan.

[Swamiji raises his hands up by his shoulders, then lowers them down by his waist to demonstrate this four-armed form of Vishnu, Preserver of the Universe. Narayan is a common name. As Swamiji calls me just "Kirin Mataji"—Mother Kirin—no one present seems to see this as in any way relating to me.]

This was in a dark room(E). A person would be led in through one door. A small light would be lit.

"Look, you can see God for just one second(E). If you look at him any longer than that, you'll be blinded."

So the person would be led through. The Guruji would do this— [Swamiji straightens up in his chair, fluttering his eyelids, flexing his arms bent at the elbow first upwards, then down.]

And then the person would be led through the other door. "I have seen God," the person would say [in a voice muffled with awe].

In this way, the Guru earned a great deal of money. You've had *darshan*, so you tell someone else. The second person tells a third. And so, there's a lot of advertisement.

[Swamiji pauses. We wait. Over the tape recorder, the voices of a man and a woman interweave with drum and sitar: a fast clip devotional song, bringing together classical North Indian music and contemporary film styles. Outside the room, town traffic putters past.]

One day, the Guru died. He died, leaving a lot of disciples. None

[33]

of them were quite like him. There was one disciple—like me—yes? Wherever he went, he stole.

[We laugh uncertainly.]

The king of that place gave the order(E) that his nose should be cut(E) off. The police(E) cut off his nose. As soon as this was done, he began to dance. He danced(E), then fell at the feet of the man who'd cut off his nose. "You've done me a great service!" he said, and he began to dance once more, to dance away.

[Swamiji bobs from side to side, clicking fingers against his palms.]

The police looked at him, wondering "Why is this man dancing?" [in a baffled voice].

The man danced his way out. Everyone asked [brows weighted with concern], "Why do you dance?" And he said, "I see God everywhere."

"Is that so? You see God?"

"Yes, I can see God."

Then he met someone—like our Gayatri—"Oh Baba, why don't I see God?" she asked.

[Swamiji is grinning at "Gayatri" of New Jersey. Her eyes widen: she seems surprised to find herself in the story.]

"You can see God too. I'll show you God. Come with me."

Gayatri came. He said to her. "Cut off your nose and you'll see God." ["Gayatri" adjusts her blue sari, smiling with an uncomfortable air.] She came. He cut off her nose. "Now you too should dance like me," he said. [Swamiji's white stubbled chin is raised and he exudes droll enjoyment. "Gayatri" 's face folds in mock horror, then, like everyone else, she ends up grinning.]

So Gayatri began to dance. "I see God too!" she said. By then Sarasvati appeared. [Now "Sarasvati" from London, face pale beneath her curly red hair, looks alarmed.]

"Why can't I see God?" she demanded. They told her: "You cut off your nose too, then you'll see Him." Her nose was sliced off. She began to dance too. In this way, the group(E) grew. There were a hundred, there were two hundred, there were a thousand. All people without noses. They danced all the time, cymbals in their hands. They didn't rest for a minute(E) they danced so much. "We're all seeing God!" they cried.

Doing this, they traveled to another kingdom. By then the group had grown to four or five thousand people. They would just camp in a park. They never had to worry about money; the disciples would take care of all that.

[34]

Then once there are so many followers, a religion (*dharma*) should be given a name. They gave themselves the name "Narayandarsimat," the group that gives you *darshan* of Narayan. This was the name. After they gave themselves this title, they began to travel. They went to another kingdom and stayed in a park. They ate rich sweets and fried bread (*halvāh aur pūrī*). And they danced.

Some people came up and asked, "What, *ji*, who are you?"

"We're the people who can show you God."

"Is that so? How come we don't see God?"

"It's because you have a nose, blocking your vision of God."

Those people said, "Who knows, maybe this so. . . . " They sent this news on to their King. The King was the same. He immediately came to the gardens where the visitors had camped.

"Who are you all?" the King asked, "None of you have noses. What does this mean?"

They said. "We are the people who reveal God. Our religion is called Narayandarsimat."

"Is that so? How come I don't see God?"

"Your nose blocks your vision, that's why you can't see God."

"If I cut(E) off my nose, will I see God?" the King asked.

"Yes, certainly you'll see God. We'll show you."

"Fine!" said the King. So he called his Pandit. Every state has a royal Pandit. "Tell me an auspicious time to see God."

The Pandit said, "Tomorrow at 10 is an auspicious time."

The King said, "You're such a great Pandit, you're the Pandit for the royal family. And you only tell me now that such an auspicious time is coming up tomorrow! Those people had to come here to bring this to your attention. How fortunate we are!"

The King sent his drummers out to announce(E), "Tomorrow at 10 o'clock everyone in this kingdom will see God. Whether they are men or women, everyone can see God. This is the King's order. The auspicious time is tomorrow at 10."

[Swamiji pauses again. Now the singing in the background is slow and reverential. We sit silent, tensed.]

Now a King's Prime Minister is smarter than a King. He thought— like our Gupta Saheb [Gupta Saheb, a dark man with a narrow alert face, sits impassively though all eyes now turn to him]. "No matter how much I reason with the King, he won't listen," he thought. He went home. That evening he met his grandfather. The grandfather asked, "What's new in our kingdom? What's going on?"

[35]

The Prime Minister said, "It's like this. Some people called the Narayandarsimats have come to our kingdom. The King has issued the order that everyone's nose be cut off tomorrow. No matter how much I reason with him, he refuses to listen."

Then the old man said, "Look here, where's the nose and where are the eyes? How can a nose block your vision? There's something fishy going on ("something black in the lentils"). There's some mistake(E). The King is ruining everyone. They'll all be trapped, deceived. We can't let this happen."

"What can I do?"

"Take me to the King."

So the Prime Minister took his grandfather to the King. The old man said, "King, don't do this, there's something wrong here. It's not right."

"What do you know?" asked the king. [impatiently] "You're just an old man. This is a new age. These kinds of things go on these days. These people who've come are all great scientists (*vijñānī*). Your nose blocks your vision. You haven't seen God, you don't know anything. These people have come to show us God. Why do you block their way?"

The grandfather said, "But who in our kingdom has seen the God they show? You're just assuming this is true."

"No, in our kingdom, no one has seen God," the King agreed.

"I won't lie," said the old man, "If you want to do it, do it, but let my nose be cut off first. I'll tell the truth. Don't wantonly cut off your nose and spoil yourself. You're my King and these are all your subjects. Don't ruin them all. Let my nose be cut off first."

"All right," said the King.

The next day, the military(E) surrounded the park on all sides. The Nose Cutters had all their knives ready. Then all the subjects arrived, along with the King. The Guru came in and sat down.

The King said, "Look, Maharaj, this is the most venerable minister in my kingdom. The old must always be respected. That's why he should be shown God first. Then you can give us darshan of God after him."

The Guru thought, "Thousands have had their noses cut off, does one more matter?" He said, "All right, send him on." So the old man was sent to the Guru. The Guru took his nose in one hand. In the other hand he held a knife. [Swamiji tilts back his head, pinching his nose with the left hand and straightening the right hand above it as

though ready to slice. Murmurs of apprehension rise around the room.]
He cut the old man's nose off.

At the time of initiation, a *mantra* should be whispered in a person's
ear, shouldn't it? At that moment, the Guru said, "Look brother, your
nose has now been cut off. The nose that's gone will never come back.
The whole world will make fun of you. The whole world will laugh
on seeing you. That's why you should do as we do: say you've seen
God. The entire world will raise you up, you'll get a lot of reverence
and respect."

[Swamiji notices that the young mother with oiled black braids has
set her bonneted baby down on the carpet beside her. "Pick up your
baby," he advises. "He might pee. This is where everyone sits, and
if he pees there's no one to clean it up." The woman hurriedly lifts
the baby, patting the carpet with her handkerchief. "Has he peed?"
Swamiji asks. "No," says the woman. "No," echoes Prakash Seth, a
local farmer, examining the carpet's orange surface. "Babies don't
know anything," Swamiji gently observes. Then he resumes the story.]

So the old man's nose was cut off. He came out and he said, "I
didn't see God, I didn't see anything. I'm in terrible pain. In one ear
I was told, 'Say what we say, else you'll be mocked by the world.'
These people are just rogues. Round them up."

The army was already there, surrounding the place. They caught
hold of the Nose Cutters and began to thrash them. Then each one
began to cry out. "I don't see anything, I don't see anything! I said I
did because so-and-so said so. So-and-so said so because he was told
by someone else."

[Swamiji's voice has speeded up, he is grinning broadly. We all
laugh. Wrong has been righted: the tension we felt as listeners has
been released.]

This was the Narayandarsimat sect. One King was able to cut them
short. There is a book called *Satyārth Prakāsh* and the story is written
there. I read this as a child. This isn't a lie, this story actually happened
in our India. Finished.

———————

The story was done, the *Durgā Saptashatī* had also run to comple-
tion. We sat silent for a minute, attention still fixed on Swamiji. He
adjusted his spectacles and looked around the room. When he spoke
again, his voice was low and earnest: "The Lord has no form. You
can't see Him with these eyes, but you can perceive Him through

[37]

wisdom. Wisdom is the Lord. Then, if you look into the matter, your own form is the Lord's form. Everyone's true identity is divine. Why don't you understand that everyone is God? People need to stop hating each other, to abandon jealousy, malice, backbiting. For who is it that you attack? No one other than the Lord."

By this time, the hour of darshan was well over. The long-legged little boy who lived downstairs had come and gone, having dropped off a tiffin with Swamiji's lunch inside. The visitors started to surge forward and bow before they left. A man asking for holy water deflected the conversation. As usual, Swamiji put a banana into each person's cupped hands. Then we emerged into the sunshine bright on the terrace outside.

It is well known that Hinduism consists of a plethora of doctrines, deities, and sects. Hinduism has no overarching institutional structure, no unified hierarchical organization. Through history, the Guru or religious teacher has played a vital role in transmitting and making innovations in the diverse branches of the Hindu tradition. The Guru-disciple relationship has been described as the "core of the Hindu devotional attitude," cutting across all sectarian lines (Gross 1979: 219).

According to the *Guru Gītā*, a Sanskrit scripture chanted each morning by Swamiji's altar, "*gu*" stands for darkness, "*ru*" for light: a Guru is one who leads a disciple out of the darkness of ignorance and into the bright light of understanding. Additionally, Sanskritists link *guru* to "weighty"; therefore, a Guru is a person who commands uncommon prestige (Gonda 1965: 237). The term can be used for a teacher of any sort. As Shri Shankar Lal, a Brahman interviewed by G. M. Carstairs, succinctly put it, "A man who teaches something new to anybody is called a Guru" (1961: 223). I have heard Sanskrit teachers, Hindi teachers, music teachers, and dancing masters all referred to as "Guruji," respected Guru. But insight into the nature of reality forms the highest order of understanding, and the holy person freed from attachments and desires is a cultural ideal (Carstairs 1961: 55; Singer 1972: 79; Spratt 1966: 9, Srinivas 1952: 241). Though the role and the meaning of the Guru has been subject to historical variation, the Guru as religious teacher has been and remains a central locus of sacred authority in India (Babb 1986; Gold 1987; Lannoy 1971: 346–72; Miller 1976–77; Mlecko 1982).

Most religious teachers are also ascetics. They are sādhus, holy men, and occasionally *sādhvīs*, holy women. There is a colorful range of costume, initiation, doctrine and practice among ascetics (Ghurye 1953; Oman 1905; Miller and Wertz 1976; Sinha and Saraswati 1978; Tripathi 1978). Swamiji's ochre-wearing order of Dashanami Dandi renouncers (*sannyāsīs*), for example, emphasizes a simple, celibate life; at the other extreme, Aghori ascetics prescribe necrophagy and sex with menstruating prostitutes as part of their practices (Parry 1982). The only unifying features amid this variety may be that all ascetics see themselves as following some path that will release them from the transient world (*samsāra*), and that they all distinguish themselves from householders who are not ascetics (Burghart 1983: 643).

Louis Dumont has popularized a model in which the ascetic who stands outside the categories of caste and kinship is the only individual in an otherwise relationally oriented world. Dumont argues that Hinduism can be viewed as emerging in the dialogue between the renouncer and the man in the world. The liminal renouncer "whose unique position gave him a sort of monopoly for putting everything in question" (1970: 46) is the source of innovation in Hinduism. This argument was rephrased in Victor Turner's (1969) terms by Robert Gross: the sādhu's antistructure and communitas provide an arena for escape from structured caste society, and through interacting with the dominant society, can also trigger change such as the formation of sects (Gross 1979). The liminal renouncer, in short, is in a position to be creative, and it is as a Guru that the effects of his or her creativity have the greatest social impact.

As Dumont observes, most sects have been founded by renouncers who serve as Gurus, initiating other ascetics and also ordinary worldly people: "A majority of Indian heads of families, of all castes—even Muslims—have chosen a guru who has initiated them while whispering a *mantra* in their ears, and who, in principle, visits them once a year. Of course there is scope here for degradation, but by this channel the religion and thought of the sects, that is of the renouncer, penetrate to the great mass of men-of-the-world" (Dumont 1970: 58).

The scope for degradation that Dumont mentions lies in the potential abuse of power in the the Guru-disciple relationship. A sādhu becomes a Guru when chosen by disciples. Thereafter, it is an intense personal relationship with a secret initiation and ongoing submission on the part of a disciple. In order to reveal a transcendent reality, a Guru might strive to throw a disciple's established patterns of thought and action into question. Arbitrary, even humiliating, demands might be leveled on a disciple. It is popularly believed that if the Guru is

[39]

truly wise, any of these actions and instructions can be a source of profound understanding. But if the Guru is a pretender—self-seeking, avaricious, despotic—he or she can wreak chaos in submissive disciples' lives. This is particularly the case since the offerings of disciples are the primary source of material support for a Guru. If extravagant regalia or Rolls Royces are a part of a Guru's lifestyle, it is the disciples who feel the pinch. The two Gurus in the Nose Cutter legend, then, play upon the cultural suspicion that disciples may not only pour support into an unworthy cause, but also harm themselves by following a pretender's commands.

How does a false Guru establish himself or herself? The answer lies partly in the stripping away of identity that asceticism entails. Initiation into an ascetic order involves breaking the ties of caste and kinship. Furthermore, many ascetics are itinerant, traveling through regions in which they are not known. Ascetic costume has long been a means of going underground in India. A range of people who want to conceal their identity—spies, runaways, thieves—adopt the attire of a sādhu of some order and wander about receiving offerings from pious householders. Even the anthropologists Sinha and Saraswati confess that the "best part of their study" of ascetic organization was conducted in ascetic disguise (1978: 25).

A group set apart from ordinary life—living in isolation, holding a peculiar knowledge and, all in all, considered special—tends to generate folklore (Jansen 1959). In the case of sādhus this is certainly true. Folklore exists about these groups and within these groups. Some images in these folklore texts are positive, upholding sādhus as saintly ideals; others depict them as misguided and dangerous people. As so often happens with Indian folklore, oral transmission is intertwined with written texts. The false ascetic, for example, exists not just in legends like the Nose Cutters but also in ancient Sanskrit literature (Bloomfield 1925; Gross 1979: 59–62; O'Flaherty 1971: 276–79; Oman 1905: 68–91), in vernacular texts like the *Satyārth Prakāsh* (Dayananda Saraswati 1963; 1970), and also in the work of contemporary Indian novelists (R. K. Narayan 1958). Narratives keep alive the ever-present possibility that a seemingly wise sādhu embraced by many as Guru may not be exactly what he or she appears to be.

Westerners drawn to Gurus often lack this cultural background of stories. Although Christianity and Judaism carry stories about misguided members of religious orders, it often does not occur to a Western disciple smitten with visions of the "spiritual East" (King 1978;

Singer 1972) to apply these tales by analogy. Swami Vivekananda, who lectured in the United States and Europe between 1893 and 1896, was the first Guru to accept Western disciples. As Joel Mlecko observes in his historical survey of the role of the Guru: "This acceptance of foreign disciples without their integration into the Hindu social fabric is a continuing and developing practice with Hindu gurus" (1982: 53). Gurus have come to the West; Westerners have come to India (Brent 1972; Harper 1972; Mehta 1979). In many cases, the romance with the mystical East has ended with disappointment. After the Guru-struck 1960s, it was possible to encounter a glossy, coffee table book whose avowed aim was "to provide the Western enquirer, sceptic or not, with the means to distinguish the charlatan, whose aim is to deceive him, from the honest teacher, whose only object is to help" (Menen 1974: 8).

This then is the cultural and historical background of Swamiji's telling the Nose Cutter story to an audience composed of both Indians and Westerners in 1983. In telling a story, rather than making a summary statement, he was following the precedent of many sādhus before him (Oman 1905: 157; Gross 1979: 233, 435) and religious teachers—rabbis, Zen monks, Christ, Buddha, Mohammed—more generally. In fact, he acknowledged that he had read this story in *Satyārth Prakāsh*, the collected discourses of Swami Dayananda, a nineteenth-century Guru.

"Swamiji" is itself a generic term for an ascetic, and I use this term at his request. "I don't want publicity(E), Mataji," Swamiji said when I was discussing my plans to write about him. Between an orthodox Hindu grandmother and an intrigued American mother, I had been hauled along on visits to many different holy people through my childhood. Swamiji was one of these. Though I was a shy ten-year-old when we first met, I was captivated by his endless repertoire of stories. Graduate school abroad had given me a scholarly excuse to listen to Swamiji's stories which included reminiscences of his questing past, anecdotes about other holy people, and a profusion of folk narratives. Swamiji treated me with overwhelming generosity and indulgence. He seemed amused that a child should return as a young woman bearing the support of a university to record his "topsy-turvy" pronouncements. I was almost forty years younger than him, yet like all other women I was "mother." During the summer in which I recorded this story, I lived next door to Swamiji with three Western women,

[41]

by his arrangement. So when Swamiji requested, "Just write that some Swamiji told you all this," I felt bound to honor his words.

In making this request, Swamiji was not just ducking publicity; he was also allying himself with an ascetic tradition of Swamis. To him, the issue of ascetic authenticity was personal and deeply felt. He often spoke about the attributes of a true holy man (*sādhu*) and renouncer (*sannyāsī*) as well as Guru. According to him, and the tradition at large, desirelessness and devotion to the indwelling Self are paramount as inner attributes. In terms of behavior, the true ascetic remains celibate, and has no attachment to possessions. He does not sell food, women, or spiritual teachings (*anna vikraya, strī vikraya, dharma vikraya*). He serves all people, treating them as "his own, regardless of caste, nationality or religion." This emphasis on an ascetic's active service in the world rather than on removed renunciation is a nineteenth century construct that Swamiji owes partly to Swami Vivekananda. It also has a source in Swamiji's experience as a disciple of Gandhi's and as a freedom fighter for Indian Independance.

A Guru as well should ideally bear all these qualities. Yet, as Swamiji noted with dismay, being a Guru had through the 1960s and 1970s become a big "bij-ness." He was particularly concerned about what had happened to the Gurus who went abroad, hypothesizing that there was something in the air and water (*havā-pani*) of America which made even the best Gurus crazy about money. He also worried that, rather than serving the world, Gurus now "took slaves." One afternoon in 1983, shortly after he told this story, I found Swamiji lying flat on the cool floor musing over why contemporary Gurus behaved so rapaciously with foreigners. How could there be such injustice in the name of religion? Swamiji explained that according to his "upside down thinking," Americans had previously taken slaves from Africa. Now, the wheel of *karma* had turned and the descendants of the slave owners were being hauled off by Gurus in India. The three of us present, Prakash Seth, "Pagaldas" and I, were speechless with laughter. "Pagaldas" (slave of craziness) was originally from California, but had lived in other ashrams where he learned Hindi and got this name. If anything, he laughed loudest, shaking his frizzy, graying head as the glasses in his wire-rimmed spectacles gleamed. Looking up at us from the floor, Swamiji just grinned.

Though Swamiji allowed people to stay near him for short periods of time, he was adamant that Indians and foreigners alike should continue with their everyday lives. Many of the young men and women from England, America, Australia, and France who found their way to him in the 1980s had in the past been involved in large-scale ashrams. Swamiji sent them home with the advice that God is within and can be found anywhere. Time in the world, he said, is best spent in your own country, caring for your family, working, and, if possible, making jobs for the poor. In his view, the Guru is a principle that exists everywhere: hanging around in an ashram can be a waste of time.

Storytelling is a creative activity; even with a folk narrative that already exists in multiple variants, the gifted teller improvises as he or she goes along (Azadovskii 1974, Degh 1969, Ortutay 1972). Listening to Swamiji retell the same stories on different occasions, I was impressed by the skill with which he altered his tellings according to the situation and audience. As he explained when questioned, "If you tell any story any time, it's not really good. You must consider the time, and shape the story so it's right. All stories are told for some purpose." In his hands, then, folklore became an interactional strategy: "an implement for argument, a tool for persuasion" (Abrahams 1968: 146). Through stories, he "shot" morals at people (cf. Basso 1983) and eased tensions by displacing the problem at hand to a structurally parallel level (Kirshenblatt-Gimblett 1975). For example, rather than criticizing outright Advani's Guru, or the workshops selling instant mystical experience, or the gullibility of Westerners, Swamiji couched his commentary in a narrative form. Telling the Nose Cutter legend, Swamiji adroitly attributed his views to the tradition, the past, a book. He also left the moral of the story and his motive for telling it ambiguous; if people chose to ignore the criticism couched in the story, they could.

The Nose Cutter legend was one of the few in which he acknowledged a written source. In Berkeley, two years later, I finally looked in the library for the book in which Swamiji had read the story. I found it in Hindi as *Satyārth Prakāsh* by Swami Dayananda Saraswati and in English translation as *The Light of Truth*. Swami Dayananda (1824–1883) was the founder of the Arya Samaj, a Hindu religious and social reform movement. Swami Dayanananda, like Swamiji, left his Braham background to wander through India in search of spiritual wisdom, eventually taking the vows of a Dashanāmi sannyāsī. On the orders of his blind Guru, Swami Dayananda campaigned for a return to a pristine Hinduism based on the ancient Vedas. He condemned

[43]

idolatry, emphasized humanitarianism, and bitterly critiqued other religions, Gurus and sects (Jordens 1978). In the *Satyārth Prakāsh* Swami Dayananda synthesized the views that he had delivered orally in lectures throughout North India. The book, issued in two separate editions in 1875 and in 1884, was translated into English in 1908.

Sure enough, there in *Satyārth Prakāsh* was the story that Swamiji had told, though in a very different form (Dayananda 1963 (1884): 503–11; 1970(1908): 367–71) The story appears in chapter 11, "A Refutation and Advocation of Indian Religions," which presents an unabashedly biased history of various sects within Hinduism. There are spirited exposés of the supposed logical absurdity in mythological systems surrounding various deities, tirades against fellow Gurus, and sarcastic descriptions of the average ascetic's conduct. Many parts of the book are in dialogue. When Swami Dayananda is asked about the Swami Narayan Sect, he launches without hesitation into a description of the founder's wiles.

The Swami Narayan sect was founded in Gujarat during the early nineteenth century by Swami Sahajananda, also known because of his devotion to Vishnu (Narayan) as "Swami Narayan." As Raymond Williams (1984) has shown in a historical overview of the sect, this was a period of extreme political instability in the northwest region of India, and Sahajananda's appearance was seen as a fulfillment of the traditional view that in times of turmoil Lord Vishnu himself will come down to earth. One of Sahajananda's major patrons was a landlord called Dada Kachar who provided a residential base from which Sahajananda proceeded on tours. As more devotees gathered, a growing phenomenon was the state of mystical union (*samādhī*) that they claimed to experience through the grace of their Guru.

> What made this unusual was that it did not result from long practice of the yogic path of ascent to higher consciousness—thought by many to be the only path of its attainment; it came immediately through contact with or meditation on Sahajanand Swami. There are hundreds of stories of persons in the trance state, especially from the early part of his ministry. A constant theme in the stories is that the men and women who had such visions saw Sahajanand Swami as the Supreme Being served by other divine figures. (Williams 1984: 15)

Gurus have always judged each other from the vantage of their own teaching tradition (*sampradāya*). Swami Dayananda, writing a few decades later, distrusted these mass visions and did not hesitate to speak his mind. According to his account in *Satyārth Prakāsh*, Swami Sahajananda had dressed up as four-armed Narayan to win over the powerful landlord, Dada Kachar. His disciples led Dada Kachar through the room with a small lamp and allowed the landlord to glimpse the Guru-deity for a brief minute. Swami Dayananda then writes, "a parable is apposite here," and starts in on the story of the criminal whose nose is cut off and claims to see God.

The story of the noseless man who dupes others is an Indic tale type[2] with other recorded variants (Crooke 1894; Robinson 1885: 31–32; Upreti 1894: 50–51). Swami Dayananda used this traditional tale as a comment on what he presents as locatable historical fact. Swamiji, in his retelling, fit together the two sequences into one legend set in an unmarked past. By making the thief whose nose is cut off a disciple of the Guru who decks himself out as a deity, Swamiji linked the two sequences through a Guru-disciple relationship. As the Guru, so the disciple, the link suggests. Fakes breed further fakes.

A detailed comparison of Swami Dayananda's written account and Swamiji's orally performed one is a potentially endless undertaking. There are differences in the use of language, the names of characters, details about when and where events occurred, and even the style of the two English translators. The most intriguing discrepancies, though, involve Swamiji's updating of Dayananda's version so that it speaks to the present: the "historically dialogical" dimension of the text (Bruner and Gorfain 1983). Broad trends in the behavior of Gurus during the latter part of the twentieth century and the immediate details of the gathering on 7 July 1983 are reflected in the shape of Swamiji's story. Both Dayananda and Swamiji describe Gurus who offer instant experiences of God and maintain a front with the help of devotees who cannot admit themselves duped. The Gurus in Swamiji's story though are likened to companies that advertise on radio and television. Members of the sect are upheld as "scientists"; manifestations of a "new age." And foreigners are among the gullible initiates.

More immediately, specific people present when the story was told were drawn into the narrative frame.[3] Swamiji likened himself to both the masquerading Guru and the thieving disciple turned Guru. "Gayatri" and "Sarasvati" became noseless initiates. Gupta Saheb was compared to the prime minister. When these analogies were made, there was a stir among those of us listening. (The baby slept on.) We smiled, exchanged glances, and listened with the added intent of following

[45]

the fates of those present who now found themselves buffeted along by the story's flow. It is difficult to definitively state Swamiji's intention in making these characterizations or telling this tale. Questions rather than a discrete list of answers appear here. Did Swamiji mean to emphasize that he belonged to the category of Guru and disciple; that the story was a reflexive statement of what he was, or craftily could be? Did he mean to mock "Gayatri" and "Sarasvati" for trekking to India in search of a Guru, to chide them for their lack of discrimination in previous involvements with sects? Did he mean to praise Gupta for his levelheadedness? Was he aware that the noses being sliced off could possibly be linked with castration anxiety among celibate ascetics? Through allusions to the present, was he consciously striving to emphasize that life and story are not, after all, too far apart?

Swami Dayananda extracts a moral at the end of the section where the Swami Narayan and Nose Cutter sects are discussed. He writes: "In this same manner, all the opponents of the Vedas are clever in stripping others of their wealth. Such is the imposition of sects" (1963: 511; 1970: 370). Similarly, in another variant of the Nose Cutter narrative recorded by a missionary in his collection of "heathen writings" from South India, the story ends: "It is thus that one of a false religion tries to draw others into it" (Robinson 1885: 32). Swamiji finished with the comment: "This isn't a lie, the story actually happened in our India." Though he did not draw out a moral, I heard this assertion of the story's facticity as implying that deception by Gurus was a real, ongoing possibility in India. I understood the story as stating that instant experiences of God were liable to be phony, that duping disciples was wrong, that sincerity and the courage to admit you had been fooled eventually triumphed over deceit. The Westerners' involvement in the story implied their need for a cultural background of cynicism. Yet, in leaving the moral implied rather than stated outright, Swamiji left the audience a generous space for interpretation. It was up to us to figure out (or forget about) what the story meant and why he chose to tell it when he did.

I did not, at the time, think to elicit "oral literary criticism" (Dundes 1966) from everyone who was slipping on the shoes lined by the door. What had they made of the story? Mr. Advani seemed unruffled. Maybe he had not caught on that there was an analogy between the workshops he was so fervently organizing and the Nose Cutters' initiation. Gupta Saheb, who had been portrayed as the prime minister, nodded goodbye with a grin; but that was no gauge that he was pleased by this characterization, or that he agreed with the story, for he always smiled.

Upstairs, the group of women living together spread newspapers on the floor in preparation for lunch. "Gayatri" and "Sarasvati" made passing reference to the tale. Both seemed amused about having had their noses sliced off. "As though I'd do a thing like that!" "Gayatri" said, grinning and shaking her head. "Am I as gullible as all that?" "Sarasvati" mused in her clear British tones. "He always has a *message*, you know; I wonder why he said *that*." They had both at one time been involved with large religious institutions. Bhavani's comment came a few days later. New to India, she had quite literally absorbed the story as one more insight into the complex civilization. "Far out," she said. "This country is too much. Do you know when this happened? Do you know who the king was who stopped the Nose Cutters?" I burst out laughing, but had to agree when she pointed out that Swamiji had stressed that this was true.

When I returned to Nasik in 1985, having written a preliminary draft of this essay, I was particulary interested in audience interpretation. Swamiji did not retell this legend but, in the course of an interview, "Gulelal" brought it up. "Gulelal" was an American Jew from Pittsburgh who had spent twelve years at various centers of the intercontinental ashram of another Guru. When he became disenchanted with the bureaucratic structure, he had made his way to Swamiji, and had subsequently divided his time between work in America and visits to India. "When I went to America last time, Swamiji told me not to cut off any noses," "Gulelal" said. I grinned, understanding that he had been advised not to set himself up as a bogus Guru. But, he went on to offer a very different explanation: "What he meant was, don't destroy anyone's faith. When you cut a nose, it's the central part of their face and their faith." "Gulelal" felt that Swamiji was referring to his disappointment in the previous Guru; to reveal the loss of faith to disciples who were still involved was equivalent to cutting off their noses. I openly disagreed with him over his interpretation of what Swamiji had meant. In the end, we referred back to Swamiji himself, who said, " 'Don't cut noses' means 'don't deceive others.' "

There is no doubt that we had all heard the story in different ways, that it brought us different insights depending on our own life-experiences and central concerns: "Bhavani," craving more knowledge

[47]

about India, understood it as a history lesson; "Gulelal," who felt betrayed by a Guru, saw it as a statement on the loss of faith; I, the graduate student, strained to set it in a cultural, historical, and theoretical context. Bettelheim's observations on the therapeutic power of fairy tales for children are applicable to the stories Swamiji tells his visitors: "The fairy tale is therapeutic because the patient finds his *own* solutions, through contemplating what the story seems to imply about him and his inner conflicts at this moment in his life" (Bettelheim 1977: 25).

Stories abound in all religious traditions, though the genres that these fall into and the emphasis given to stories over other forms of religious communication may vary. In religions that emphasize a written canon, stories become fixed in texts. The stories remain the same though history flows on. Yet, if a religion is to continue offering meaning to believers, it must necessarily accommodate history and changing human experience. When embedded in written form, scriptural stories require an ongoing tradition of exegesis to bring them into meaningful conjunction with the everyday lives of believers (van Baaren 1972). So, stories are reread from different perspectives. Christ's parables, for example, have been reinterpreted through time as being allegorical, historical, social interactional, and so on. Alternatively, stories may generate a growth of subsidiary stories closer to contemporary concerns; the apocryphal stories deriving from the Koran or Bible are good examples. Received stories may also be rewritten in an updated vernacular language. The Ramayana, for example, exists in multiple variants—sanskritic, vernacular, written, oral (cf. Richman 1991), all of which contain statements not only about religion but also of group identity.

Written scriptures anchor religion in the past, but teachings transmitted orally are made contemporaneous through their retellings. As can be seen in written versions of Dayananda's and Swamiji's oral performances, traditional stories are reshaped as they are retold. In drawing on a story, the storyteller shapes it to accommodate the concerns of a different audience in a changed historical circumstance. Emerging from a collectivity, a folk narrative expresses deep-rooted cultural themes, yet, its telling is effortlessly updated in language, details, and the emphases given to particular themes. The spoken word endows the message of the story with a vital immediacy, binding the teller and audience in a community (Ong 1982: 74–75). Furthermore, the ambiguity of a story, unlike a straightforward proposition, allows listeners to project their own concerns while it links them to the other believers who have heard the story in other moments in history. As Slater writes, "A creative thinker or great teacher in the tradition is one who takes us through the familiar stories. . . . and points us to new conclusions, which we can then see to be congruent with what has gone before" (1978: 165–66).

Swamiji used the story of the Nose Cutters as an example of what living Gurus could but should not be. I now shift from the negative to the positive, presenting Swamiji's conception of how the Guru should be viewed: more as an omnipresent principle than a particular person. In the afternoon of 7 July 1983, before the doors were officially reopened to visitors, Swamiji sat in his room, reflecting. He leaned against the wall, legs stretched out on a stool placed in front of his bed, pink mosquito net looped above him. Light fell through the window on the left side of his face. I sat on the floor, tape recorder by my side. Leaning against the door frame, Dagu Seth listened, too. Swamiji spoke slowly, solemnly.

Swamiji: The entire universe is the Guru. Wherever you tread, you should continue to find the Guru. Every second. Whatever you do, find a Guru in it. When you think over something—"Why is it like that?"—that act of reflection is the Guru. You can gain some wisdom from everything, so the entire universe is the Guru. We learn each thing from this universe, don't we? That's why it should be saluted as the Guru.

Kirin: So the Guru is not one person?

Swamiji: That's what I think. Dattatreya [the Guru of the Gods] made twenty-four Gurus. He learned something from each one of them. He even made a prostitute his Guru, a dog his Guru. Look how honest and faithful a dog is—if you feed it just a bit of bread it doesn't forget you. A human being should be like this, too. That's why Dattatreya made a dog one of his Gurus. Even if you strike a dog after you've fed it, it won't bite you; it rolls at your feet.

He made a python a Guru too. Why? Because it keeps lying in one place. It doesn't go out in search of food. It just leaves its mouth open, trusting that whatever is destined will come its way. When it feels hungry, it inhales deeply and something or the other enters its mouth. At the most it will move ten feet away from where it lives. That's why the python was made a Guru; it's so peaceful, just lying there. . . .

Then Swamiji told another sequence of stories about another group of Gurus. Looking back at Swamiji from the vantage of 1993, the

[49]

respectful, tolerant version of religion that he stood for is increasingly eclipsed by Hindu nationalists' rhetoric of hatred. If he were still alive, might Swamiji tell the story of the Nose Cutter sect to critique political leaders—both lay and ascetic—who today purport to speak for Hinduism?

Notes

1. The material in this essay is largely a condensed and altered version of Chaps. 6 and 11 in K. Narayan 1989. This essay was written first in 1985.

2. Tale Type 1707: *"The Noseless Man:* A man who has lost his nose persuades others that they too can see God if they will cut their noses off. They do so, whereupon he scoffs at them" (Thompson and Roberts 1960). The legend as told by Swamiji contains the following folklore motifs: K1286 Mock initiation for dupe; K1829 Disguise as holy man; J758.1 Noseless man persuades others to cut off their noses; 286 Wisdom of an old man (Thompson 1955–58; Thompson and Balys 1958).

3. For the concept of "frame" as the marker for a shared definition of an activity in progress, see Bateson 1955; Bauman 1977; Goffman 1974.

REFERENCES

Abrahams, Roger D. 1968. "Introductory Remarks to a Rhetorical Theory of Folklore." *Journal of American Folklore* 81: 143–58.

Azadovskii, Mark. 1974. *A Siberian Tale Teller.* Trans. James Dow. Austin: University of Texas Press.

Babb, Lawrence A. 1981. "Glancing: Visual Interaction in Hinduism." *Journal of Anthropological Research* 37: 387–401.

———. 1986. *Redemptive Encounters: Three Modern Styles in the Hindu Tradition.* Berkeley: University of California Press.

Bakhtin, M. M. 1981. *The Dialogic Imagination.* Ed. Michael Holquist. Austin: University of Texas Press.

Basso, Keith H. 1983. " 'Stalking with Stories': Names, Places and Moral Narrative among the Western Apache." In E. Bruner, ed., 1984. Pp. 19–55.

Bateson, Gregory. 1955. "A Theory of Play and Fantasy." *Psychiatric Research Reports* 2: 39–51.

Bauman, Richard. 1977. *Verbal Art as Performance.* Rowley, Mass.: Newbury House.

Bettelheim, Bruno. 1977. *The Uses of Enchantment: The Meaning and Importance of Fairy Tales.* New York: Knopf.

Bloomfield, Maurice. 1924. "On False Ascetics and Nuns in Hindu Fiction." *Journal of the American Oriental Society* 44: 202–42.

Braithwaite, R. B. 1955. *An Empiricist's View of the Nature of Religious Belief.* Cambridge: Cambridge University Press.

Brent, Peter. 1972. *Godmen of India.* London: Allen Lane, The Penguin Press.

Bruner, Edward. 1984. *Text, Play, and Story: The Construction and Reconstruction of Self and Society.* 1983 Proceedings of the American Ethnological Society, Washington, D.C.

Bruner, Edward, and Phyllis Gorfain. 1984. "Dialogical Narration and Paradoxes of Masada." Bruner, ed., 1984. Pp. 56–79.

Burghart, Richard. 1983. "Renunciation in the Religious Traditions of South Asia." *Man* (n.s.) 18: 635–53.

Carstairs, G. Morris. 1961. *The Twice-Born: A Study of a Community of High-Caste Hindus.* Bloomington: Indiana University Press.

Crooke, William. 1894. "The Man without a Nose." *North Indian Notes and Queries* 4: Entry 301.

Dayananda Saraswati, Swami. 1963 (1884). *Satyarth Prakash* (Hindi). Delhi: Govindram Hasanand.

———. 1970 (1908). *The Light of Truth: An English Translation of the Satyarth Prakash.* Trans. Durga Prasad. New Delhi: Gnan Prakashan.

Degh, Linda. 1969. *Folktales and Society: Story Telling in a Hungarian Peasant Community.* Trans. Emily M. Schossberger. Bloomington: Indiana University Press.

Dumont, Louis. 1970. "World Renunciation in Indian Religions." In Louis Dumont, ed., *Religion/Politics and History in India.* The Hague and Paris: Mouton. Pp. 33–60.

Dundes, Alan. 1966. "Metafolklore and Oral Literary Criticism." *The Monist* 60:505–16. Reprinted 1975 in A. Dundes, *Analytic Essays in Folklore.* The Hague: Mouton.

Eck, Diana. 1981. *Darsan: Seeing the Divine Image in India.* Chambersburg, Pa.: Anima Books.

Geertz, Clifford. 1966. "Religion as a Cultural System." In M. Banton, ed., *Anthropological Approaches to the Study of Religion.* London: Tavistock. Pp. 1–46.

Ghurye, Govind Sadashiv. 1953. *Indian Sadhus.* Bombay: Popular Prakashan.

Goffman, Erving. 1974. *Frame Analysis: An Essay on the Organization of Experience.* New York: Harper and Row.

Gold, Daniel. 1987. *The Lord as Guru: Hindi Sants in the North Indian Tradition.* New York: Oxford University Press.

Goldberg, Michael. 1982. *Theology and Narrative: A Critical Introduction.* Nashville: Abingdon.

Gonda, Jan. 1965. *Change and Continuity in Indian Religion.* The Hague: Mouton.

Gross, Robert. 1979. "Hindu Asceticism: A Study of the Sadhus of North India." Ph.D. diss. University of California, Berkeley.

Harper, Marvin Henry. 1972. *Gurus, Swamis and Avataras: Spiritual Masters and their American Disciples.* Philadelphia: Westminister Press.

Jansen, William Hugh. 1959. "The Esoteric-Exoteric Factor in Folklore." *Fabula*

Kirin Narayan

2: 205–11. Reprinted 1965 in A. Dundes, ed., *The Study of Folklore*. Englewood Cliffs, N.J.: Prentice Hall. Pp. 43–51.

Jordens, J. T. F. 1978. *Dayananda Sarasvati: His Life and Ideas*. Delhi: Oxford University Press.

King, Ursula. 1978. "Indian Spirituality, Western Materialism: An Image and its Function in the Reinterpretation of Modern Hinduism." *Social Action* 28 (1): 62–86.

Kirschenblatt-Gimblett, Barbara. 1975. "A Parable in Context: A Social Interactional Analysis of Storytelling Performance." In Dan Ben Amos and Kenneth S. Goldstein, eds., *Folklore: Performance and Communication*. The Hague: Mouton. Pp. 105–30.

Lannoy, Richard. 1971. *The Speaking Tree*. London: Oxford University Press.

Mehta, Gita. 1979. *Karma Cola: Marketing the Mystic East*. New York: Simon and Schuster.

Menen, Aubrey. 1974. *The New Mystics and the True Indian Tradition*. With Photographs by Graham Hall. London: Thames and Hudson.

Miller, David. 1976–77. "The Guru as the Center of Sacredness." *Studies in Religion* 6/5: 527–33.

Miller, David M., and Dorothy C. Wertz. 1976. *Hindu Monastic Life: The Monks and Monasteries of Bhubanesheshwar*. Montreal: McGill Queens University Press.

Mlecko, Joel D. 1982. "The Guru in Hindu Tradition." *Numen* 29: 33–61.

Narayan, Kirin. 1989. *Storytellers, Saints, and Scoundrels: Folk Narrative as Hindu Religious Teaching*. Philadelphia: University of Pennsylvania Press.

Narayan, R. K. 1958. *The Guide*. Mysore: Indian Thought Publications.

O'Flaherty, Wendy. 1971. "The Origin of Heresy in Hindu Mythology." *History of Religions* 10: 271–333.

Oman, J. C. 1905. *The Mystics, Ascetics, and Saints of India*. London: T. Fisher Unwin.

Ong, Walter J. 1982. *Orality and Literacy: The Technologizing of the Word*. New York: Methuen.

Ortutay, Gyula. 1972. "Fedics Relates Tales." In *Hungarian Folklore: Essays*. Trans. Istvan Butyav. Budapest: Akademiai Kiada. Pp. 225–85.

Parry, Jonathan. 1982. "Sacrificial Death and the Necrophagous Ascetic." In M. Bloch and J. Parry, eds., *Death and the Regeneration of Life*. Cambridge: Cambridge University Press. Pp. 74–110.

Richman, Paula, ed. 1991. *Many Rāmāyanas: The Diversity of a Narrative Tradition in South Asia*. Berkeley: University of California Press.

Robinson, E. J. 1885. *Tales and Poems of South India*. From the Tamil. London: T. Woodmer.

Singer, Milton. 1972. "Passage to More than India: A Sketch of Changing European and American Images." In M. Singer, *When a Great Tradition Modernizes*. London: Pall Mall Press. Pp. 11–38.

Sinha, Surajit, and Baidyanath Saraswati. 1978. *Ascetics of Kashi: An Anthropological Investigation*. Varanasi: N. K. Bose Memorial Foundation.

Slater, Peter. 1978. *The Dynamics of Religion: Meaning and Change in Religious Traditions*. New York: Harper and Row.

Spratt, Philip. 1966. *Hindu Culture and Personality*. Bombay: Manaktalas.

Srinivas, M. N. 1952. *Religion and Society among the Coorgs of South India*. New York: Asia Publishing House.

Thompson, Stith. 1955–58. *Motif Index of Folk Literature*. 6 vols. Bloomington: Indiana University Press.

Thompson, Stith, and Jonas Balys. 1958. *The Oral Tales of India*. Folklore Series 10. Bloomington: Indiana University Press.

Thompson, Stith, and Warren E. Roberts. 1960. "Types of Indic Oral Tales: India, Pakistan and Ceylon." *Folklore Fellows Communications* 180. Helsinki: Suomenalainen Tiedakatemia.

Tilley, Clarence W. 1985. *Story Theology*. Wilmington, Del.: M. Glazier.

Tripathi, B. D. 1978. *The Sadhus of India: The Sociological View*. Bombay: Popular Prakashan.

Turner, Victor. 1969. *The Ritual Process: Structure and Anti-Structure*. Chicago: Aldine.

Upreti, Pandit Ganga Datt. 1894. *Proverbs and Folklore of Kumaun and Garhwal*. Lodiana: Lodiana Mission Press.

Van Baaren, T. P. 1972. "The Flexibility of Myth." *Studies in the History of Religions* 22: 199–206.

Wiggins, James. 1974. *Religion as Story*. New York: Harper and Row.

Williams, Raymond. 1984. *A New Face of Hinduism: The Swaminarayan Religion*. New York: Cambridge University Press.

[3]

The Creative Individual in the World of the !Kung San

Marjorie Shostak

> Prophets and artists tend to be liminal and marginal people,
> "edgemen," who strive with a passionate sincerity to rid
> themselves of the cliché associated with status incumbency
> and role-playing and to enter into vital relations with other
> men in fact or imagination.
>
> —Victor Turner

> Art is the means whereby a healthy society manages to put
> to a constructive use man's seemingly least socializable im-
> pulses, and even to augment their ultimate intensity, by
> placing at their disposal the vast resources of culture,
> thereby making them both expressible and culturally
> productive.
>
> —George Devereux

The !Kung San living on the northern fringe of the Kalahari Desert
in Botswana and Namibia in southern Africa are probably the most
well-researched hunting and gathering society in the anthropological
literature. A multitude of research projects have described the !Kung's
subsistence ecology, kinship and social structure, demography, population genetics, health, infant care and child training practices, and
systems of belief and religious orientation. My own research conducted
during approximately two-and-a-half years of field work focused on

[54]

the psychological makeup of the individual as expressed in the oral life history.

Despite what might appear to be an enviable data base, little of it relates to the creative realm. A few outstanding efforts do exist, however: a detailed thesis on !Kung music (England 1968), an analysis of the compositions of a !Kung musician (Biesele 1976) discussed in the latter part of this essay, and some exploratory material on bead design and style (Shostak 1976). Less directly concerned with creativity, but indirectly relevant, is research on the religious realm (Lee 1968; Marshall 1976; Katz 1982) and on !Kung oral traditions (Biesele 1975).

Exploring what creativity means to the !Kung and identifying their more accomplished creative people is nevertheless a tricky task—and not because !Kung artists are not well represented. They are—primarily as musicians, healers, bead-weavers and storytellers. They are the ones who tell and retell the great myths, capturing the nuances of incest, murder, revenge and especially, the war between the sexes that abound in this oral tradition; they sing songs of longing and pain, their voices blending into the fabric of the night air; they heal the sick by uncovering hidden wishes and fears thought to interfere with health; and, exercising their imagination and skill, they create intricate, beautiful bead-weavings.

The !Kung value their artists, for without them, !Kung culture would stagnate: old songs, old renderings of stories, well-known events in the spirit world and bead designs would cease to excite. But their society is also staunchly egalitarian, exerting a strong social pressure against anyone rising in status above others. This attitude can create problems for !Kung artists who, by the sheer power and idiosyncratic nature of their creative expression, are inevitably set apart (at least in relation to that expression). Considerable tension, therefore, exists between encouraging the individual voice of the artist and discouraging an aura of superiority. In order for creative expression to flourish, the protocol followed by the artist must be comparable to that of others who succeed (such as a talented hunter): eschew all appearance of self-importance or expectation of special status accruing from success.

The form these cultural requirements take, however, is not censorship. A popular misconception that small-scale communities demand greater conformity in individuality and creative expression than larger-scale societies finds no validation here. Indeed, the very smallness of !Kung society allows for considerable tolerance of individual differences. People have personal space, literally and figuratively, to

[55]

be themselves. The expectation—even requirement—that individuals contribute to the culture is reflected in a variety of norms (such as the healing dance songs where everyone—from the most gifted to the least talented musician—improvises on standard melodies).

This delicate balance, deftly handled by the !Kung, is troublesome to an outsider gauche enough to inquire who might be the best artists in any one of a variety of !Kung expressive forms. Embarrassment for a person of such poor judgment who asks such an indelicate question is the initial (silent) response; then follows an answer in which all the names of those who participate in that expressive activity are included—offered in no particular order. To rank them would be bad manners.

I confronted this attitude during my second field trip (1975) when I asked people to judge photographs of bead-weavings I had collected during my first field trip (1969–71). Of two dozen photographs I brought with me, a small number reflected high artistic accomplishment—as had been recognized by curators at the Museum of Primitive Art (now part of New York's Metropolitan Museum of Art), where files on the bead-weavings were established, and by curators of a variety of other exhibitions. I had wanted to see how bead-weavers and those who didn't weave among the !Kung would rank the various pieces, especially these most impressive ones.

Since the bead-weavings had originally been collected in different villages and four years had intervened between field trips, I assumed that it would be easy to generate discussions of the beaded works from a purely aesthetic point of view. But an overwhelming reluctance to rank continued to prevail, whether discussed with an individual or with a group. It was not that judgments could not be made: one artist was willing to discuss the superiority of some of the weavings. She also acknowledged in private what I already believed: that she was the best (or, at least, one of the best) among those whose work I had followed. She would never say this to the others, of course, but within herself she knew.

Music, healing, bead-weaving, storytelling and fortune-telling (throwing leather discs and interpreting the resulting pattern) are the most typical avenues of creative expression. Etching on ostrich eggshell water containers or pieces of wood is traditionally less common (except, more recently, for the tourist trade). Healing is primarily the realm of men and bead-weaving the exclusive province of women, but expression in music and storytelling is generally exercised by anyone so inclined. Except for healing (which usually takes place during a medicinal ceremony known to anthropologists as a trance dance), creative expression takes place almost anywhere, during any segment of the day, when time and temperament prevail.

My work led me to interview a number of creative individuals. This essay explores some of the issues concerning the position of artists in !Kung society—the avenues available to them as they negotiate the conflicting demands of self and society, and the nature and content of their creative works. The concept of artists as "liminal" figures (Turner 1969) is valuable to this discussion, as is George Devereux's concept of art as "the harmless social safety valve for the expression of that which is taboo" (Devereux 1961).

My discussion centers on the lives of three creative !Kung individuals: Jimmy, a brilliant musician in his late twenties, who, over a period of years created a thumb piano repertoire that was subsequently adopted by a large percentage of the population; N!ukha, a woman healer in her early forties, who is a pioneer in the new women's drum dance which has increasingly given women a more direct and significant role in healing; and Hwan//a, a woman composer, singer, and bead design artist in her early thirties, whose art plays a more private but very crucial role in her life.

Jimmy

As traditional !Kung musical instruments are made of natural materials, it was only after a critical amount of metal became available that the metal-key Bantu instrument, the thumb piano or *mbira*, was adopted into !Kung musical culture. At the time of my first field trip in 1969, the instrument had been in the study area, *Dobe*, for about ten years. Younger children, adolescents, and young adults played it more frequently than older people, who preferred more traditional music.

Interested in learning the captivating rhythms and melodies that so often filled the air, I went among the young to learn their songs. The name "Jimmy" came up repeatedly. "This is Jimmy's music, Jimmy's compositions," they would say. And not just at Dobe. "Jimmy's" songs were being played everywhere I went.

Jimmy was a man in his late twenties, married with one child. Sullen and outcast in manner, he explained that no one liked him, which,

[57]

given his difficult character, did not seem surprising. Yet when he played, everyone listened. The power of his music affected them. So, too, did his clairvoyance when he entered trance, which he accomplished while playing the thumb piano, instead of during the more traditional healing dance. No one before Jimmy or since has been able to do that. His unusual musical abilities as well as his ambiguous status within the culture made me curious. When I finally interviewed him I asked about his view of himself, his involvement with the thumb piano, and his battles with the world of the spirits.

When Jimmy was about eight years old, he experienced the first of many bouts with extreme illness. In this initial episode, his sickness stayed from one rainy season to the next. "All the !Kung healers tried to cure me, but nothing happened." It was the same when a Bantu healer tried. Then he had a dream in which God came to him. God told him, "Pick up the thumb piano and play." He had never played the instrument before; yet, "I just played." After that the sickness went away.

He was around fifteen at the time of his next encounter. Again, it was the rainy season. Suddenly, there was a clap of thunder, "so loud" and a bolt of lightning "so powerful" that it "picked me up and threw me against the back of my hut. The same clap of thunder made the tree behind my hut crack and fall. It killed four cows." (This incident was corroborated by another man who had been in the hut at the same time and who described Jimmy as having been hit by lightning; Biesele 1976.) This event was followed by a convalescence that lasted around eight months; he had a number of broken ribs, as well as injuries to his lower back and chest. "I stayed in the house the whole time and didn't sit with any woman except my mother."

His health returned only to be forfeited again, this time directly through "God's agency." He was near a well, pouring water into a trough. He spilled some water, slipped, and fell into the well. "I was flying down the well very far . . . when God saw me and saved me. He turned me around so my feet hit the water first." When he hit, he momentarily lost consciousness. When he regained it, he grabbed the side of the well and called to others to throw down a chain and bucket. He got out and lay on the sand, sick. That's when God came to him and told him, once again, to play the thumb piano. He started to play and played beautifully. God then told him that He himself, not a !Kung, had given birth to Jimmy. He confirmed that everyone, except Jimmy's mother and younger sister, hated him. "Yes. People like me if I play . . . but if I live with them long, they don't like me at all."

Jimmy married some time later, but within the year, a new sickness entered his life. This time God informed him that his wife had taken a lover; Jimmy later found the couple together. Not long after, his wife had a child (who lived only three days) by her lover, a fact revealed to Jimmy by God. Jimmy brought the issue to tribal court. The lover was fined and gave Jimmy seven goats, but the situation did not change. In fact, not long after, the lover tried to poison Jimmy: he poured evil medicine through the grass of his hut while Jimmy slept. The medicine fell on his shoulder. While Jimmy was playing the thumb piano, God revealed the lover's role in this new sickness. Jimmy asked another healer to make medicinal cuts on him; within a few months he was better. Barely three days later, his wife complained of a headache. That very night she died. Some time later, Jimmy married again and had a daughter with his new wife. He has not been ill since.

Jimmy acquired his Western name after working on a Bantu cattle post, an experience quite common for younger !Kung men. Yet, he is one of very few in the population to be known by such a name; clearly, both he and others find it fitting. His name reflects a status that is tentative, somewhat foreign and removed; yet, as are most outsiders with such names, he is also elevated and respected. "Crazy Jimmy," as he is often referred to, lives in a bush camp with his immediate family, a few miles apart from a more established group of villages. As such, he is physically and socially separate.

Those of his compositions adopted by others are his shorter songs, ones without words. The music he plays for himself, however, is sometimes expressed in an unintelligible tongue; at other times its language is clear, picturing him as persecuted and unique. He often sings of the fear and the allure of death:

> "Where will I hide from God's death?
> The day when God speaks where will I be. . . .
> The year of my death is known,
> The day of my death is known."

> "I am the one whom death visits first,
> Then it passes by me and goes to all people."

> "Death Year is upon me. . . ."

He makes reference to his exalted position as the offspring of God and to God's having given him his musical gift:

"I am God's son...."

"God spoke, telling me to take up
These metal bits and this scrap of wood
And with them to sing."

"I speak to God in his speech
I cry with God
I tell him to lift me from the earth
God deceives me, yes."

He also sings of his misery:

"Yesterday we sat together and spoke
You said that I was your child.
This piece of wood you gave and said it might be mine.
Why have you changed your mind and now you wish to kill me."

"You said I should sing what we two own between us: our song."

"You, God, said
These bits of metal,
These scraps of wood
Would give me life.
But it was a trick:
My people are dying
And I will die."

"Terrible God deceives, torments.
God's arms descend into my fingers."

"Everyone stop tormenting me.
Stop bringing me misery
Don't bring me any more pain."

[Biesele 1976]

Jimmy embodies the contradictions of life that his music, somehow, both expresses and resolves, touching upon themes that deeply touch those who hear him play. As such, his art expresses the deepest of wishes and fears, ones that have few other culturally sanctioned outlets.

N!ukha

N!ukha is Jimmy's half sister. She comes from a long line of medicinal healers; her mother and father and their respective parents all had the ability to lay on hands and cure. Her own daughter developed, in her early twenties, a form of psychosis that was labeled schizophrenia by a visiting medical team, but other researchers hypothesized it may have been manic-depressive illness.

Unlike Jimmy, and despite her daughter's illness, N!ukha is not an outcast. She lives in a large !Kung village where she is caught up in an active social world. She has three living children all with different fathers. Her first daughter was conceived with her first husband; a second daughter was conceived with her third husband; and a son was conceived with a lover. All three of her husbands are deceased.

After years of being uninvolved in spiritual exploration, N!ukha began to put her energies into healing and earned a reputation as a powerful shaman. She had the ability, not only to enter altered states of consciousness, but to actually lay on hands and heal. Just months after the death of her third husband, I interviewed her about her life and about her experience with healing.

!Kung healers play two fundamental roles. The first, while in trance, is to "discover" the underlying cause of disease. Sometimes "discovery" involves referring to an "obvious" problem in the ill person's life and identifying it as a causal agent. More often, however, the healer must articulate a more subtle conflict within the individual and, by revealing it, help destroy its power to fuel illness. This analysis requires psychological insight, imagination, and physical stamina. Different healers may uncover different causal factors.

The !Kung description of how the healer's soul leaves the body to commune with the world of the spirits is a fitting metaphor for the creative process: peeling off successive layers of consciousness so that the soul is free to wander in the midst of psychic phenomena; then the pieces of the pattern may make sense. For it is only after the healer "sees" the cause (or causes) of a person's illness that the second role—laying on hands and "pulling out" illness—can begin. Each "cure" is a testament to the healer's ability to "listen" to the inner, intuitive voice. Once the pattern is articulated, the success of the cure is measured in its power to weaken the force that subconscious psychological factors play in predisposing a person to disease.

Insofar as the interpretation of illness reflects the ability to delve

[61]

into this subterranean world of the human psyche, to articulate underlying wishes and fears, and to create patterns of meaning and "truth" for the community, this process is a kind of primal creative expression. This is particularly true for women who, traditionally, were less involved than men in the trance experience and who followed a more individualized and circuitous career. According to N!ukha, her own experience in this realm started when she was quite young. She was around eight years old when her mother first introduced her to an alleged herbal hallucinogen, the !gwa root, to teach her about different states of consciousness. Her mother directed her through this experience about four times. N!ukha experienced strange feelings in her stomach and in her back, and she threw up.

Not long after, she went gathering with her mother and saw honey on the ground, as though set down by a person. She looked for the tree it might have come from, or for the tracks of the person who might have gotten it, but did not see anything. She called for her mother, who explained that the honey had come from God, and that she should eat it. They both ate, leaving some behind. Soon after, N!ukha became nauseous and threw up. Her body shook and trembled just as it had done with the !gwa root. Her mother said that this was good; she wanted N!ukha to have strong medicine.

After that, whenever there were curing dances, her mother tutored her. Within a few years she was able to enter a light trance state known as *tada*. It was painful and frightened her, although she had already achieved some power. One time, the pain was so great that her mother told her she should stop her apprenticeship for a while. After that she went to very few dances; she was afraid of the sensations, which she described as, "Your insides are like thorns."

Then, one night, while asleep, she saw God. He was on a horse with white in the middle of its face. He sat in a chair and laughed at her fear. He told her that when she was older, she would have very powerful medicine. She cried out and when her mother heard, she knew what had happened. She told N!ukha not to be afraid. "God just wanted to see you."

God came to her again, another night, and asked why she was not doing what she was supposed to do: learning to trance. She trembled and cried; her back and stomach felt intense pain. Her mother woke and rubbed her stomach until the pain went away. Then she slept. The next morning her mother told people to have a medicine dance so she could help her daughter. They sang the traditional songs while her mother carried N!ukha around on her back. N!ukha felt the medicine surging within her again, and it hurt. When her mother put her down, she threw up. Soon she was tired and they stopped. But she was still afraid; even though her mother wanted her to learn more, she refused.

Her next memory, of a curing dance, dates from when she was around fourteen. Although she had not eaten !gwa for a number of years, the sensations of the spiritual forces once again "struck" her. People said that she could become a powerful healer, but she remained aloof from trancing for years. It was only after her first child was born that she went back to it, because "childbirth hurts so much more than medicine. . . . A child's pain kills you and medicine doesn't." Now past the age of childbearing, she not only "sees" sickness, she has the power to lay on hands and cure: a spiritual and physical purging—a "pulling out" of sickness. Unlike other powerful healers, she does not see the gods. When she goes into trance, "Only my mother helps me; she tells me what is wrong with people."

Since she started laying on hands, people have come to her to be cured. But she will not trance during the men's ceremonial dance; because other women healers rarely do that. "I want to do what most other women do." She trusts a few men who have helped her become stronger, but she worries that others might steal her powers, leaving her without strength. She lets the more experienced male healers cure first, even though she thinks her healing powers are as strong. If their cure does not work, then she tries. People might laugh at her, she explains. "When men are not successful in curing, they aren't afraid of being laughed at . . . because they are men. Everyone knows that women are without strength. Things defeat them all the time. . . . If it's spiritual powers, people will laugh at you for thinking that you have medicine."

Another reason she lets the experienced medicine men try first is to avoid being accused of interfering. "Sometimes God kills someone. He refuses to help the medicine man . . . but God usually helps [me] in the end." She waits and watches. Then she lays on hands and the person gets better. She feels that she is more successful than most of the male healers, and "I may even be more powerful." She does concede, however, that one or two men may be even more powerful than she. But she is quick to point out that she learned to cure long after they did. Because, unlike women, men do not have to put aside their apprenticeship to have babies.

[63]

N!uhka claims she has cured many people, impressing them with the strength of her spiritual powers. Once, for example, there were huge rain clouds nearby. She told everyone that the clouds would not come their way, that they would pass. Others did not believe her. She recalls, "Because they refused to believe [me], the clouds came." It rained heavily that night and the people asked her to make it go away. At first, she refused because "they had not listened to me." But then, she thought "of the children." She spoke to God and the rain left. When God heard what had happened, he said that the others should never dispute her words again. The next morning she told them, "If you do not listen to me, God will bring lightning and everyone will die."

Her relationship to God was not always congenial. Once she angered God and became so sick that she almost died. This happened soon after her husband took her to live at another village, leaving her father behind. Once she had settled there, God visited her. He asked how she was, "just like an ordinary greeting." He wanted to know if she had come to live there. When she told him she had, he said he would kill her. She became very sick; her "heart was like it was swollen." Other healers tried to help, but they could not "see" the cause of the illness. She felt herself drifting away, as a feeling like sleep came over her.

While she lay there, God came to her again. He told her she should not have left the other village. He touched her chest and she threw up all night. She told her husband what had happened, but he did not want to leave, so someone else brought her back. The night she arrived home, God came to her again and thanked her. He blamed her husband, saying it was his fault; and he warned her that, if she ever went back to the other village, "it will be like you are about to sleep, but you will die." She did not go back and soon was better. Her relationship to God has been pleasant ever since. "When I see him, he's happy with me. He greets me when he arrives, and when he leaves."

Unlike her half brother Jimmy, N!ukha does not exude a creative force of such great magnitude that she is set apart from others. Indeed, other than the problems associated with her daughter's illness, she participates in the nexus of !Kung life. True, there is much gossip about her, especially about her having buried three husbands; and there is no doubt that she strives to dampen her effervescent personality, to be more like everyone else. Yet, she is also clearly willing to explore the art of healing, one in which few women participate. In so doing she challenges the more established male healers, offering, in the least threatening way she knows how, her alternative brand of medicine.

As with psychoanalytic training, in which the initiate undergoes self-analysis, !Kung healers are also most effective after having delved into the forces working upon their own lives. N!ukha's own "self-analysis" reflects a recognition of the depth of her connection to her parents, especially to her mother (even as it put her at odds with others, including her husband). Whether her gift is explained as God's voice or her own, her willingness to tap these psychic resources and to use intuition and perception makes her "cures" daring and fuels her creative personality. There is no clear theoretical structure handed down for generations by practitioners as in psychoanalysis. A framework with broad outlines does exist, but it leaves ample room for N!ukha's imagination, especially since her role is a fairly new one for women. Ultimately, she must rely on her own vision of the spiritual forces that cause illness and suffering—to uncover what Devereux called the "eternal nature of the eternally ungratified and therefore eternally challenging wishes underlying it" (Devereux 1961). In a way she is a composer of fictions with psychological insight and moral purpose, much as she is a medical practitioner, and her work gives life to the cliché that art can heal.

Hwan//a

Hwan//a is a woman in her early thirties who does elaborate bead-weavings—one of the few mediums available to the !Kung for the expression of visual form—and who also writes songs and plays musical instruments. Born into the mainstream of traditional !Kung life, she now is something of an outsider. When young and beautiful and full of a sparkling spirit even now in ample evidence, she attracted the handsome son of the local Bantu headman. The ensuing romance was passionate and intense, and soon they married. Yet, as the years passed, Hwan//a had only one pregnancy, and that ended in miscarriage. Probably because of the strength of her husband's love, he never did what most other Bantu men do with a !Kung wife: marry her as a second wife, or bring in another woman to be her cowife. After years

[65]

of remaining childless, however, her husband did start a family—albeit an illegitimate one—with a Bantu woman living in a nearby village.

Hwan//a bemoans her misfortune, mourning the loss of the children she never had and the exclusive relationship she once had with her husband. No one, not even Hwan//a, completely faults her husband—both the !Kung and the Bantu sanction polygyny—yet, jealousy, anger, and resentment still plague her. She wishes that he would end the marriage so that she could return to live with her mother and other relatives. But he will not agree to that. She wavers between thinking that this indicates the depth of his love for her, and thinking that he is using her, wanting a free servant to look after his cattle and household. She complains about how hard she works for him, that he is rarely there, and that he never gives her presents.

Yet Hwan//a's sorrow does constant battle with forces of play and delight. When energized, she can rivet all around her, be it while playing the *tama* melon tossing game or being a lead singer in the traditional healing dance. Her most impressive achievements, however, are when she sits by herself, singing songs she has composed or working out intricate patterns of bead-weavings, choosing colors and design with the skill of an accomplished artist.

I first met Hwan//a soon after her husband had his first child with his mistress. I included her in the life-history study I conducted with seven other women. Once this study was completed, I engaged her, along with others, to sew colorful trade beads. The format was headbands or pubic aprons (coverings worn in front of the genitals underneath a variety of leather skirts). None of the pieces was destined to be worn: these forms were chosen to conform to existing cultural patterns, but I thought of them as resembling blank canvases.

The details of the beadwork are not appropriate to review here, except to remark on the extraordinary creative accomplishments in Hwan//a's pieces. Abstractions called Zebra's Face or Starry Night boldly explored spatial planes and color. Sophisticated variations on a theme were worked out in a composition called Owl Eyes. Stripes rhythmically alternating with triangles (a motif of leaves on water) graciously spanned the breadth of a headband. And there were more.

Her musical talents as composer, singer, and musician were equally impressive, and much appreciated by those who clustered around her when she played. Her most haunting song (and my favorite), "Come here . . . come here, little one of mine," is played on the thumb piano while variations on these words are sung. At times, the longing refers to the child she never had; then it changes color and the enchantress ever so gently calls to her lover. While others may enjoy her music, it is intensely private. Unlike Jimmy and N!ukha, she is seeking neither notoriety nor influence. She seems to be playing to, and for, herself.

Conclusion

The portraits of three individuals show a variety of modes of creative expression available in !Kung life as well as different levels of creative involvement. Jimmy, the farthest from the norm—perhaps even borderline in personality—is by far the most innovative. It is unclear whether he would actually want to alter his "outsider" position, since his fervent belief that he is the son of God as well as God's messenger precludes his reaching out to others as much as it distances them. People flock to hear him play and sing about his tortured life both in the "real" and in the "spirit" world, as much as they ask him to communicate with God about spiritual meddling in earthly concerns.

Jimmy knows, and everyone else agrees, that he is unusually gifted. Yet, unlike the negative feelings that sometimes attach to a successful hunter, gatherer, singer, dancer, healer, or musician—who must outwardly downplay his or her accomplishments—envy and scorn are allayed in Jimmy's case by the anguish and torment that pervade his life. Few could desire his less than appealing personality or his lot in life, even though his talent and music are striking. His isolation helps protect him from residual jealousies even as it helps him keep his paranoia and feelings of persecution in control. For Jimmy, creative expression *is* his life. That he occasionally receives presents for explaining the ways of the spirits, or for pleading with them for specific interventions, is a secondary gain.

N!ukha the healer and Hwan//a the musician and bead designer differ from Jimmy and from each other, offering alternative models of the creative individual in !Kung society. Despite the quirks in their life histories, they partake in the normal range of !Kung life and the avenues of creative expression they explore are trod by many. Creative expression does not rule their lives or define their selves with Jimmy's singleness of purpose. N!ukha excels in a public area usually the province of men; Hwan//a's expression is more private and internal.

Jimmy, N!ukha, and Hwan//a conform to Devereux's concept of the artist as articulator of the taboo, who turns raw feelings and submerged

[67]

interpersonal connections into culturally acceptable expressions that touch upon psychic undercurrents in other people's lives. In terms of "liminal" personalities, Jimmy clearly fits Turner's model of the artist, but both N!ukha and Hwan//a could be considered liminal as well: N!ukha, with her closeness to mental illness (her schizophrenic daughter and "Crazy Jimmy," her half brother), her several marriages ending in the deaths of her husbands, and her willingness to do battle in a predominantly male domain; and Hwan//a, with her Bantu husband and her lack of children. Yet, their liminal position does not seem fundamental to their participation in !Kung creative life, nor to the tolerance accorded them by their society. In fact, contributions like N!ukha's in the spiritual realm are matched, if not to the same degree, at least in kind, by almost half the men and a small percentage of women. True, few people compose songs as Hwan//a does, but a great many do sing and play instruments. The same might be said of the sophisticated bead artistry that, although relatively new (glass beads have been unavailable in adequate supply until recently), still engages a large number of women doing thoughtful and original works.

It might come as a surprise, then, that of the large number of people participating in the creative realm, only a small percentage could be considered truly liminal. This conclusion underscores the relative lack of social restraints, both in physical movement and in personal expression. Males and females, together or apart, leave camp to gather or hunt, walking miles beyond the village and its constraints several times a week. Village life abounds with the ever-present sound of talk—people expressing their point of view, often simultaneously. Individual differences in personality seem to thrive in this environment as does the tolerance for creative expression. Perhaps because no formal change of status ensues and few rewards are received, there is little advantage in being distinctive, other than for oneself. Thus, the egalitarian balance of !Kung society remains unthreatened by creative individuals.

In summary, then, creativity flourishes in !Kung life. There is little material incentive for its exercise, only the gain of the informal respect of others or the pleasure it gives the self. A "liminal" person may be more apt to find comfort in creative expression, but the tolerance and appreciation for the artist applies to those in the mainstream of !Kung life as well. Those who do participate in the creative realm—be it in music, in uncovering the workings of the spirit world, or in weaving stunning bead pieces—clearly fit Devereux's conception of the artist as one who transmutes painful or upsetting truths into beauty, tapping underlying themes that are at once basic and intense. At the same time, despite the prevalence of artistic expression among the !Kung, the lives described here also support Turner's view that the most extreme form of creative expression, as represented by Jimmy, may indeed require a truly and permanently liminal status. Whatever the personality of the artist and whatever form the creative energies take, the richness of their expressive life is itself a testament to the value the !Kung assign to this part of their experience.

REFERENCES

Biesele, Megan. 1975. "Folklore and Ritual of !Kung Hunter-Gatherers." 2 vols. Ph.D. diss., Harvard University.
———. 1976. "Song Texts by the Master of Tricks: Kalahari San Thumb Piano Music." *Botswana Notes and Records,* vol. 7. Gaborone, Botswana.
Devereux, George. 1961. "Art and Mythology." In B. Kaplan, ed., *Studying Personality Cross-Culturally.* Evanston, Ill.: Row, Peterson. Pp. 361–86.
England, Nicholas. 1968. "Music among the Zu/wasi of South Western Africa and Botswana." Ph.D. diss., Harvard University.
Katz, Richard. 1982. *Boiling Energy.* Cambridge: Harvard University Press.
Lee, Richard. 1968. "The Sociology of !Kung Bushmen Trance Performances." In R. Prince, ed., *Trance and Possession States.* Montreal: Bucke Memorial Society.
Shostak, Marjorie. 1976. "Glass Beadwork of the !Kung of Northwestern Gaborone." Gaborone: The Botswana Society.
———. 1981. *Nisa: The Life and Words of a !Kung Woman.* Cambridge: Harvard University Press.
Turner, Victor. 1969. *The Ritual Process.* Harmondsworth, England: Penguin Books.

[4]

At Home, No Womens
Are Storytellers:
Ceramic Creativity and the Politics
of Discourse in Cochiti Pueblo

Barbara A. Babcock

The primitive woman has no choice, and, given the duties
that go with marriage, is therefore seldom able to take much
part in public life. But if she can be regarded as being at a
disadvantage in this respect from our point of view, she
does not regard herself as being at a disadvantage, and she
does not envy her menfolk what we describe as their privileges. She does not desire, in this respect, things to be
other than they are.

—E. E. Evans-Pritchard,
"The Position of Women
in Primitive Societies"

The world man actually lives in, in the sense of his inescapable
necessities and the inevitable conditions of life always bulks
very small in relation to the world he makes for himself.

—Ruth Benedict, "Magic"

Since the late 1960s, Helen Cordero, a Cochiti Pueblo woman who
learned to make pottery at the age of forty-five, has changed the nature

This chapter first appeared as "At Home, No Womens Are Storytellers: Potteries,
Stories, and Politics in Cochiti Pueblo," *Journal of the Southwest* 30 (Autumn 1988);
reprinted with permission.

of Pueblo ceramics (Figure 4.1). When Helen modeled the first "Storyteller" doll in 1964, she made one of the oldest forms of Native American self-portraiture her own, reinvented a long-standing but moribund Cochiti tradition of figurative pottery, and engendered a revolution in Pueblo ceramics comparable to those begun by Nampeyo of Hopi and Maria of San Ildefonso—a revolution that has reshaped her own life as well as that of her family and her pueblo, not to mention the fortunes of innumerable other Pueblo potters (Figure 4.2).[1] She is not, however, without ambivalence about the consequences of her creativity: *See. I just don't know. I guess I really started something. I guess I'm a big Indian artist. But,* she hastens to add, *I don't like to be called famous. My name is Helen Cordero. It's my grandfather, he's giving me these* (Figure 4.3).[2] But, like it or not, Helen, like her grandfather, Santiago Quintana, who was Ruth Benedict's favorite teller of Cochiti tales, is one of those "gifted individuals who have bent the culture in the direction of their own capacities" (Benedict 1932: 26).

I first met this indefatigable women who is always *in a hurry* on a June afternoon in 1978. Fascinated by the Storyteller dolls then becoming popular, I had finally screwed up my courage and driven to Cochiti Pueblo to talk with the inventor herself. That particular day Helen was having a new hardwood floor laid in her pottery room so we sat outside under a cottonwood tree. After we had talked for over an hour about her potteries, her patrons, and her grandfather, she asked me why I was asking her all these questions. I replied that I was thinking about writing an article about Storyteller dolls and without hesitation she responded: *There are three books about Maria* [the famous potter of San Ildefonso Pueblo] *and none about me.* Thus began a complicated and important relationship that has redefined my life and my work. The difficulties as well as delights that Helen and I have had *gathering all these words and pictures together into a big book* about her art and experience have convinced me that representing another woman is a problematic enterprise. Betwixt and between Cochiti Pueblo, museum archives, and the world of dealers and collectors who traffic in Indian art, I have been forced to rethink and revise many assumptions about women's art and creativity, about feminism and crosscultural inquiry, about biography, autobiography, and life history, and about the meaning of things.

When after talking with Helen and many other Pueblo potters who have imitated her invention, I began reading scholars in an attempt

Figure 4.1. Helen Cordero shaping a Storyteller at a Pecos National Monument demonstration in 1974. Photograph

Figure 4.2. The first Storyteller shaped by Helen Cordero in 1964. 8 inches high. Courtesy of the Museum of International Folk Art, Museum of New Mexico, Acc. no. A.79.53-41. Photograph by Glenn Short.

Figure 4.3. Santiago Quintana with one of his many grandchildren. Cochiti Pueblo, ca. 1906. Photograph courtesy of the National Anthropological Archives, Smithsonian Institution, Neg. no. 80-5499.

to understand the dynamics of this revolution in contemporary ceramics, I discovered that, for the most part, discussions of innovation in ethnic and tribal arts have followed an art historical approach, examining the creativity of the artist or performer in relation to the tradition he or she has inherited, and the subsequent changes his or her work has wrought in the aesthetic system (Biebuyck 1969). In contrast to modern Western art, primitive and folk art is generally regarded as subservient to tradition and community values; the assumption that such "art forms reinforce the bonds of the community rather than make manifest and challenge the oppositions within it" is rarely questioned or examined (Firth 1966: 167). Less frequently and more recently (d'Azevedo 1973), innovation has been interpreted from a psycho- or sociobiographical perspective, that is in relation to the life history and motivations of the innovator and the ways in which he or she is already "marginal," "deviant," etc. Unfortunately, this necessary corrective to the myth of anonymous, collective, tradition-bound creativity tends toward a romantic reification of the alienated genius, which says a great deal more about how "we" regard the creative person than about how "they" do. That is beginning to change as scholars move away from these extremes to examine the dialectic of creativeness and constraints, the sociocultural consequences of, and the conditions for creativity, and the politics as well as the poetics of innovation.[3] In insisting on the inseparability of the poetic and the politic, of artistic innovation and social innovation, I am indebted to both Ruth Benedict and Victor Turner, who opposed the separation of the social and the symbolic and the related separation of science and humanism in anthropological analyses. Rather, they insisted on culture as creative process—and on the ways in which performers and performances (verbal, dramatic, or artifactual) not only follow but revise and revitalize accepted rules, acting out and challenging aesthetic conventions and social values.[4]

More than simply reflecting or expressing social structure and worldview, any significant new form reconstructs cultural reality, causing a dislocation in the economy of cultural representations: "A work of art does not substitute, but institutes an original awareness of existence, on the whole; it does not so much reproduce and represent as produce and present a total experience" (Kaufmann 1969: 147). The *Storyteller doll* as conceived and realized by Helen Cordero not only "materializes a way of experiencing" and "brings a particular cast of mind out into the world of objects, where men can look at it" (Geertz 1976: 1478),

[75]

but comments on and expands the premises of Pueblo existence. When Helen Cordero re-created her grandfather in clay, it was one of those "fecund moments" when an artist discovers a structure for her sensibility and experience that "makes it manageable" for herself and "at the same time accessible to others" (Merleau-Ponty 1964: 169). It is, therefore, "in the tenor of its setting," in the discourse that surrounds it, that I have looked for both the sources and the consequences of the powerful generative image that she created, asking, to paraphrase Roy Wagner, how is Helen Cordero's invention related to a Cochiti woman's perception of herself and her world?[5]

All innovation involves a dialectic between convention and invention, and when Helen Cordero began making *little people* over twenty years ago, she continued—with a difference—a centuries-old ceramic tradition. For over a thousand years, Puebloan potters have shaped the clay of the Southwest into representative human and animal forms as well as utility ware. The majority of prehistoric, anthropomorphic figurines are female, and on the basis of contextual archaeological evidence as well as ethnographic data from the past century, archaeologists have conjectured that the Pueblo figurine complex was associated with reproductive ritual—both agricultural fertility cults and rites of human increase.[6] Historic figures such as the mother and child effigy made at Cochiti over one hundred years ago would seem to confirm these connections (Figure 4.4). Her dress is painted front and back with corn plant designs, and here, as throughout Pueblo ritual and religion, the combination of painted and modeled design makes explicit the relationship between human reproduction and other life-giving forms of generation, especially corn.[7] The most sacred of all ritual objects is a perfect ear of corn (*i'ariko* at Cochiti), decorated with beads and feathers, and addressed as "Our Mother" (Parsons 1939: 182, 319–23).

As the Anglo presence increased with the coming of the railroads to New Mexico in the 1880s, the production of figures such as this markedly decreased. Pueblo potters did not, however, hesitate to capitalize on the growing tourist market, and, in addition to bowls and jars, Cochiti women made for sale an abundance of small, desacralized human and animal figures. Anglos bought and sold countless "curiosities," "idols," or "monos," but did not regard them highly or, with the exception of Santa Fe dealer Jake Gold, encourage their production. In the first half of this century, pottery production at Cochiti, as in many other pueblos, declined. As Helen Cordero has

Figure 4.4. Mother and Child Effigy. Artist unknown. Cochiti Pueblo, 1875–80. 7 inches high. This small polychrome figure, collected by Rev. Sheldon Jackson in the late 1870s, is the earliest known Cochiti Singing Mother. Courtesy of the Princeton University Museum of Natural History, Acc. no. P.U.7557. Photograph by J. Bradley Babcock.

said, *For a long time pottery was silent in the pueblo.* Nonetheless, this ancient tradition endured, and among those few figurative forms that continued to be made, the image of a woman holding or carrying a child, or a water jar, or a bowl of bread was the most popular. In the decade before Helen Cordero *started up on little people,* at least three Cochiti potters were still making these *singing ladies, singing mothers,* or *madonnas* (Figure 4.5).

By the late 1950s, the six children that Helen had raised were grown, and like other Cochiti women, she began doing bead and leatherwork to make a little extra money. Unfortunately, most of the profits went for buying more materials, and one day Fred Cordero's aunt, Grandma Juana, asked, *Why don't you girls go back to potteries? You don't have to buy anything. Mother Earth gives it all to you.* And so, Helen *started on pottery* with her kinswoman Juanita Arquero, who had learned to make pottery as a child, and spent six months *under her.* Her bowls and jars were *all crooked* and she despaired of ever *getting it right.* Juanita suggested that she *try figures instead and it was like a flower blooming.* She began with little animals, but was soon shaping countless small standing and seated figures, many of them continuing the Cochiti tradition of pottery mothers and children (Figure 4.6). One of the first times Helen *showed them out* at a Santo Domingo feast day, folk art collector Alexander Girard bought all that she had and asked her to make more and larger figures and bring them to his home in Sante Fe. The first Storyteller (Figure 2) was made in response to his request for a larger seated mother with more children. Helen recalls, *When I went home and thought about it, I kept seeing my grandfather. That one, he was a really good storyteller and there were always lots of us grandchildrens around him.*

In addition to telling stories to his many grandchildren and being esteemed in the pueblo as a gifted storyteller, the leader of one of the clown societies, a *"mucho sabio,"* and the most powerful of the *principales* (the tribal council), Santiago Quintana (Figure 4.3) was the valued friend and collaborator of several generations of anthropologists and observers of Cochiti life: Adolph Bandelier, Frederick Starr, Charles Saunders, Edward Curtis, and Ruth Benedict, who collected many of the *Tales of the Cochiti Indians* (1931) from him and wrote warmly of her "old man" in letters from the field.[8] When Helen Cordero remembered her grandfather's voice and shaped that first image of him telling stories to five grandchildren, she made two significant modifications in the "singing mother" tradition: (1) she made the pri-

[78]

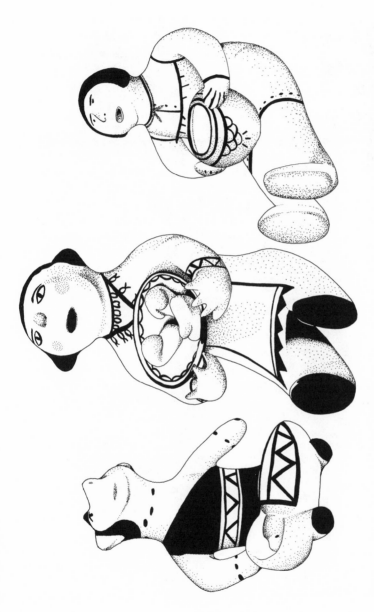

Figure 4.5. Cochiti Singing Ladies. 1955–60. Left to right: Damacia Cordero, 5½ inches high; Teresita Romero, 7¼ inches high; and Laurencita Herrera, 6 inches high. These Pueblo women with a baby on a cradleboard, a bowl of bread, and a water jar, made by three of Cochiti's well-known figurative potters, exemplify the type of figures produced at Cochiti in the decade preceding Helen's invention of the Storyteller. Courtesy, left to right: Laboratory of Anthropology, Museum of New Mexico, Acc. nos. 45967/12 and 25114/129, and Ruth Weber Collection. Drawing by Trudy Griffin-Pierce.

[79]

Figure 4.6. Singing Mother. Helen Cordero. Cochiti Pueblo, 1960–61. 5½ inches high. This figure, characteristic of many small figures Helen Cordero made between 1959 and 1963, is very similar to those made by other Cochiti potters between 1920 and 1960. Marjorie Lambert Collection. Photograph by Glenn Short.

mary figure male rather than female, and (2) she placed more than a realistic number of children on him. In addition to embodying this dialogic relationship between convention and invention, Storytellers are obviously "about" relationships—between generations, between past and future, and between stories and potteries (Figure 4.7).[9] Less obviously, Helen's figures in particular are about the relationship between male and female creativity and the reproduction of the cultural order, for her reinvention of this important mode of cultural production and tradition of representation—pottery-making—controlled by women transformed an image of natural reproduction into a figure of an important mode of cultural reproduction—storytelling—that is controlled by men and both embodies and expresses generativity.

From the body of the Storyteller sprout countless children and grandchildren, and from his open mouth emerges "life for the people" in the shape of stories, testifying yet again to Pueblo culture's instinct for survival and its capacity to revitalize itself.[10] Whether one looks at Pueblo worldview and its dynamics of cultural survival from the perspective of religion, kinship, pottery-making, or narrative traditions, one finds that Pueblo identity and individual and social integration are conceived in terms of fertility and regeneration: "One story is only the beginning of many stories" (Silko 1981: 56); clay images of domestic animals are blessed and buried in the corral "so that there will be more of them" (Parsons 1919: 279) and corn, "the seed of seeds," multiplies itself many times from a single grain (Cushing 1920: 54). The history of the Storyteller is itself an expression of this reproductive dynamic, for the first one was the beginning of countless *little people.* Helen herself has made more Storytellers and won more prizes than she can or will count—*it's like breads, we don't count* (Figure 7). By 1973, when the "What Is Folk Art?" exhibit was mounted at the Museum of International Folk Art in Santa Fe, the success and popularity of the Storyteller was such that at least six other Cochiti potters had imitated her invention (Figure 4.8). A decade later, no less than fifty other Cochiti potters and over a hundred potters throughout the New Mexico Pueblos were shaping Storytellers and related figurative forms. Many of these imitations are female figures, and as far as Helen is concerned, they are empathically *not really Storytellers.* They call them *Storytellers, but they don't know what it means. They don't know it's after my grandfather. At home, no womens are storytellers!*[11]

In the six years that I have known Helen, I have repeatedly heard her insist upon both the ancestral and the masculine attributes of her

Figure 4.7. Storyteller. Helen Cordero. Cochiti Pueblo, 1971, 12½ inches high. This Storyteller with 17 children took first prize at the 1971 Santa Fe Indian Market. In 1976, it was featured on a poster printed by the collectors for Helen's one-woman show at the Heard Museum in Phoenix; in 1982, it appeared on the cover of *National Geographic*. Collection of The Hand and the Spirit Crafts Gallery, Scottsdale, Arizona. Photograph by Glenn Short.

Figure 4.8. Cochiti Storytellers in the "What Is Folk Art?" exhibit at the Museum of International Folk Art, Santa Fe, 1973. Left to right: Helen Cordero, Felipa Trujillo, Aurelia Suina, Juanita Arquero, Frances Suina, Seferina Ortiz, and Damacia Cordero. This is one of very few Storytellers produced by Helen's teacher, Juanita Arquero, whose artistry is primarily expressed in the finest of contemporary Cochiti bowls and jars. Courtesy of the Museum of New Mexico, Neg. no. 70433. Photograph by Arthur Taylor.

figures. Given the fact that both she and her mother (who was Esther Goldfrank's principal informant) tell stories, and that half of Ruth Benedict's narrators were most assuredly female, why this assertion that appears to contradict observed "fact"? And, why, I have asked much more recently, given the obvious economic benefit to the pueblo, did one of its officers try to persuade the tribal council to forbid the well-known Cochiti Storyteller potters—all of whom are women—from having exhibits of their work and from giving pottery-making demonstrations at museums and national parks?

I would like to suggest that these two questions are not unrelated and that answers to them provide clues as to the local significance of Helen Cordero's creativity and to the generative, transformative, and dangerously liminal power of the image she invented. It seemed very strange indeed that in the summer of 1982 the all-male tribal council would have debated whether women potters should demonstrate the making of Storytellers to Anglo tourists when extra income was sorely needed to support summer ceremonials and when Pueblo pottery has been made for an Anglo market for over a century. The more I considered this "social drama," the more entangled I became in a complicated situation involving the politics of reproduction and issues of discourse and authority—of who has the right to represent what to whom. Crises initiate reflexivity and this one forced me to realize that I had naively assumed—as have other scholars of Pueblo ceramics—that pottery and politics have nothing to do with each other. As I contemplated conflict and clay, I began to see that Storytellers as conceived and invented by Helen Cordero were *not just pretty thing made for money* in terms of personal identification (*All my potteries come from my heart. They're my little people,*) but were to be understood in terms of the degree to which they resist and revise discursive constraints.[12]

When Helen Cordero insists upon the ancestral and masculine attributes of her Storyteller, she is doing much more than emphasizing the difference and uniqueness of her potteries. She is both explicitly and implicitly "authorizing" her creation. Explicitly, by invoking ancestral authority and power: *It's my grandfather, he's giving me these. He was a really wise man. He had lots of stories and lots of grandchildrens, and we're all in there, in the clay.*[13] Implicitly, by insisting on the masculinity of her composite figure, and so identifying her pottery with a sacred, masculine activity—a tradition that is both patriarchal and genealogical. Women do tell stories at Cochiti, but

[84]

they do not tell *the* stories—the master fictions by which the people live. As Parsons (1939: 40) and many other Pueblo scholars have pointed out, men and women have differential access to sacred discourse. Origin myths and legends as well as songs and drums and kachinas and kivas and all the other aspects of sacred discourse, including the ceremonial Keresan in which it is spoken, are controlled by men. As Helen's uncle, Joe Trujillo, remarked several decades ago, "Our kivas are like—how you say in English? Yes, like men's clubs. The women are only admitted for certain ceremonies, but most of the time we men are there alone. Religion is man's business with Indians" (Mason 1948: 85).

If women are practically peripheral, they are symbolically central to this "man's business" which involves, among other things, a transcendental appropriation of the female principle. Pueblo religion is elaborated around the idea of fertility and is indigenously described as a vast, interconnected symbolic web at the center of which sits Spider Woman, Thought Woman, the "mother of all" (Parsons 1939: 192–93). Not surprisingly, the practice of religion involves both comic and serious female impersonation. The *cacique*, or religious leader of the pueblo, whose chief functions concern rain and fertility and the well-being of his "children," is not only regarded as the representative of Iyatiku, the Corn Mother; he is, after he is installed in office, symbolically viewed as a woman and referred to in female terms.[14] The *cacique* is responsible for the spiritual and physical welfare of the pueblo and he "takes care of his people by looking after 'his children' just as the Mother (Iyatiku) whom he represents looked after the images in her basket" (Parsons 1939: 336). In Keresan emergence narratives, Spider Woman sends Iyatiku ("bringing to life") and her sister Nao'tsiti ("more of everything in the basket") up into the light, to this earth with baskets crammed full of seeds and little clay images and sacred cornmeal with which they create and pray into being all forms of life.[15] The continued association of clay figures with the creation, maintenance, and reproduction of Pueblo life is this practice of collectively representing Keresan townspeople in male and female clay images which are kept and cared for by the *cacique*.

If Iyatiku's clay figures are regarded as the embodiment of "life for the people," so too are the stories about Iyatiku that are kept and told by men such as Helen's grandfather. Both sacred and secular stories were and are one of the primary modes in which the family, the clan, and the community regenerates itself, for such narratives both describe

[85]

and create "chains" linking generation to generation and back again, and involve what Silko describes as the vital dynamic of "bringing and keeping the people together" (1981: 59).[16] In the words of contemporary Keresan storytellers, Leslie Silko and Simon Ortiz, "you don't have anything if you don't have the stories" (Silko 1977: 2) and "the only way to continue is to tell a story and there is no other way" (Ortiz 1977: 9). What is remarkable about these stories, past and present, oral and written, is that the idea of fertility and the model of reproduction is re-presented again and again—in the language of and about the stories, in their content, and in the embedded style in which they are structured and told. Nowhere is this more manifest than in the images of a grandfather storyteller, his belly full of "life for the people," giving birth to both children and stories that Leslie Silko and Helen Cordero have created in words and in clay. (See, e.g., Figure 4.8 and Silko's title poem in *Ceremony*, 1977: 2.)

Both cosmologically and socially, the Keres world is constructed of a series of oppositions of which male vs. female is primary.[17] Given the facts that woman is ideologically and symbolically central, that clans are matrilineal, and that residence was traditionally matrilocal at Cochiti, it has been fashionable, if not doctrinaire, to describe the distribution of power as complementary and to ascribe to women much more "real" power than they in fact have.[18] Once upon a time, a Cochiti child received his social identity and physical place from his father.[19] But times have changed, and while a child is still of his mother's clan and clans still fulfill a nurturant function, Cochiti clans and "clan mothers" are far less important and powerful than they once were.[20] Wage labor, increased prosperity, and government housing have virtually abolished matrilocal residence—a man who wants his own house builds it. If one's livelihood does not depend on one's fields, the fact that one's wife "owns" them matters little. And with Catholicism in the Rio Grande Pueblos came absolute monogamy, greatly increasing a man's status in the household and his power over his wife.[21] At the same time, the two kiva organizations or moieties—Turquoise and Pumpkin—are larger and more powerful than ever, and they are patrilineal. Upon marriage, women become members of their husband's kivas and assume the role of "helpers"; children take their father's surname and belong to his kiva. Today, kiva membership is a much more significant determinant of Cochiti social identity than clan affiliation.

Man's business at Cochiti is political as well as religious, for the

Pueblo government is a theocracy. Supreme power resides with the *cacique* and the heads of the three medicine societies who annually choose the six major secular officers—governor and lieutenant governor, war captain and lieutenant war captain, and *fiscale* and lieutenant *fiscale*—who belong in equal numbers to the two kivas and who become members of the tribal council for life. While the governor controls secular affairs and the *fiscale* manages the Catholic church, the war captains, who represent the mythic twin war gods, are the "ceremonial police," whose principal duties are preserving traditions and secrets, and leading the fight against tribal enemies.[22]

In sacred discourse and religious practice, in social and political organization, and in domestic and family situations, the relationship between the sexes is a classic example of female power and male dominance.[23] For all their ascribed symbolic significance, Cochiti women are, in Edwin Ardener's terms, a "muted" rather than an "articulate group," excluded from "the dominant communicative system of the society—expressed as it must be through ideology and that 'mode of production' which is articulated with it" (1975: 22). *We don't have any say about that* are words I have heard from women at Cochiti more times than I can count. However, as Ardener and others have pointed out, in a world in which discourse is controlled by men, women's ideas or models of the world about them finds expression in forms other than direct speech. But, as Ardener also notes, far too few ethnographers have talked to women or deemed their modes of expression worthy of investigation. This is true even in Pueblo studies where, despite the fact that a larger than usual amount of ethnography has been done by women, the overwhelming focus has been on male-dominated discourse.

Frank Cushing, who was an iconoclast, and Ruth Bunzel, who was a woman influenced by Boas's insistence on the importance of art, were exceptions to this male bias in their recognition that for generation upon generation of Pueblo women, pottery-making has been a primary and privileged mode of expression.[24] In Pueblo life, *potteries* are one of the few forms of "objective culture" that have been identified with and created almost exclusively by women.[25] Traditionally, men were associated with this mode of production, but excluded from the transformative activities of shaping and firing clay. "In the beginning, Itc'tinaku [Spider Woman] considered how the people should live," and sent her mother and father down to them as "Clay Old Woman and Clay Old Man." Clay Old Woman "began to coil a pot with her

[87]

clay, and Clay Old Man danced beside her singing while she worked"
(Benedict 1981: 12). "He" has continued to dance and sing, and "she"
has continued to shape the flesh of Mother Earth into ceremonial,
utilitarian, and commercial forms, *talking to and thanking Grandma
Clay* at every stage of the creative process.

As archaeologists have demonstrated, as Cushing so finely described
in "Zuni Breadstuff," and as the Cochiti story about the origin of
pottery I have just quoted reflects, settled Pueblo existence as it
developed in the southwestern United States over 2,000 years ago and
was lived until the latter part of the nineteenth century was inconceivable without rain, without the cultivation of corn, and without
pottery to store water and grain. Clay was not only essential to life
but in traditional Pueblo belief was regarded as a living substance. A
pottery vessel was not thought of as an inert object but as a "made
being," acquiring a kind of conscious and personal existence as it was
being made. "As a receptacle for water and food, it held, and was in
turn, a source of life" (Hardin 1983: 33), and the designs with which
it was painted had "one dominant theme, a prayer for rain for the
maturing crops" (Chapman 1950: 6). Moreover, in the Keresan origin
myths I have already cited, innumerable forms of life originate as clay
images. In addition to the descendents of these clay people that the
cacique takes care of, human and animal ceramic figurines are associated, both historically and prehistorically, with the idea of fertility,
with agricultural fertility cults, and with rites of human increase.[26] In
this worldview, the creation of babies and the generation of culture
are not only compatible, they are inseparable; with both their bodies
and their hands, women reproduce the cultural order.

If Pueblo ceramics were once a primary mode of production, they
were also and still are symbolic forms, containers of cultural value and
models of and for reproduction and regeneration.[27] Their potteries,
like their stories, their rituals, and their kinship system, connect the
reproductive aspect of generation with the cultural basis of thought,
transmission, and "in a different voice," clay sings. With the en-
croachment of an Anglo world and the expansion of an Anglo market
for Indian objects, pottery-making has become increasingly important
as mode of cultural survival and as a cultural voice, a statement of
ethnic identity. Potteries are, in Bourdieu's apt phrase, "symbolic
capital," for "in a very real way, the survival of the craft symbolizes
the survival of the people" (Brody 1976: 76). And, although ceramic
scholars have not talked about it in these terms, precisely because it

[88]

is "symbolic capital," Pueblo pottery-making is an institutionalized mechanism for consolidating and preserving female power.[28]

Although women produce these necessary and symbolic vessels, men have traditionally controlled their distribution and marketing, along with other forms of communication with the outside world. This too is reflected in the Cochiti story about the origin of pottery as well as in subsequent ethnographic accounts: after Clay Old Woman shaped the clay, "the old man took the pot and gave a piece of it to everybody in the village" (Benedict 1981: 12). Since at least the fifteenth century, "the exchange of pottery has played a considerable economic role in Rio Grande Pueblo culture" (Snow 1973: 55), and this trading has been the business of men. Matilda Coxe Stevenson recorded the following situation at Zia Pueblo in the late 1880s:

> The Sia women labor industriously at the ceramic art as soon as their grain supply becomes reduced, and the men carry the wares to their unfriendly neighbors for trade in exchange for wheat and corn. As long as the Sia can induce the traders through the country to take their pottery they refrain from barter with their Indian neighbors. The women usually dispose of the articles to the traders, but they never venture on expeditions to the Santa Ana and the Jemez. [1894: 11–12]

After 1880, the railroads and the influx of Anglos to the territory created both an expanding "tourist" market for Pueblo pottery and wage-labor jobs for men; women took increasing responsibility for marketing the products of their labor. Predictably, there was resistance to the latter, and as late as 1925, when Chapman, Halseth, and others at the Museum of New Mexico were encouraging pottery "revivals," they discovered that the Santo Domingo Pueblo council did not want Santo Domingo women to take their pottery to the newly instituted Indian Fair in Sante Fe. Acculturation, automobiles, and the advent of an Anglo "art" market that names and wants to know its Indian artists has changed all that. Women still dominate the manufacture of pottery—for example, of approximately two hundred figurative potters in 1984, only twenty are men—but they have also assumed control of its distribution, and have entered into a cash economy and the business of communicating with the outside world—activities that were once their husbands' prerogatives. While Pueblo pottery has continued to be an important vehicle of identity maintenance, it has also become a means of identity change and a crucial variable in the transition from

[89]

Barbara A. Babcock

a subsistence to a cash economy.[29] Both the fortunes of this ancient craft in this century and the recent "social drama" centering on pottery at Cochiti support the argument of several students of material culture that the objectual aspects of a culture are both more conservative and more innovative as well as more readily diffused than its behavioral and ideological aspects.[30]

In the remarkable revival of figurative pottery that Helen Cordero's Storyteller has engendered in the last twenty years, women potters have done much more than reshape their traditional roles in terms of economics, mobility, and communication.[31] By creating not only Storytellers, but Nightcriers, Drummers, Turtles, and other ceremonial and mythic figures, and by exhibiting and demonstrating their art, they have assumed the right to re-present and interpret to the outside world at least some of the aspects of the very discourse in which they are displaced. Both endorsing and challenging men's ideological hegemony, a clay Storyteller is a woman's visual re-creation of a man's verbal and symbolic representations of a woman's biological experience. It is *her* re-appropriation both of her own symbolic power and *his* right to articulate it. The very gender ambiguity of Storytellers— both presentational and perceptual—is a statement of competing interests in the terrain of symbolic production. *At home, no womens are storytellers*, but women are potters and with the transformative power of their hands, they have contrived to tell stories about storytelling, to subvert masculine discursive control, and profoundly to disturb the distribution of power. In this case, the struggle between the powerless and the powerful has been displaced quite literally onto the surface of things. It would seem, in terms of Bauman's reformulation of the distinction between static and dynamic cultures, that the sociocultural system at Cochiti—and probably in other pueblos as well—is changing from a static one "in which rights to signs are derivative from social position" to a dynamic one "in which social position is derivative from the possession of signs" (Bauman 1971: 287).

Helen Cordero and her sisters are manipulating considerably more than clay. They are reproducing "with a difference," and they are figuratively as well as literally playing with fire. Helen teases me a lot, and on one recent occasion, I couldn't resist the temptation to give her a hard time about her fancy new Frigidaire Harvest Gold ice-dispensing refrigerator. She stopped making tortillas, turned from the stove—which she had also just replaced with a new Magic Chef because the old one's self-cleaning oven had ruined the *potteries* that

[90]

she was preheating before firing them outside *in the old way, the right way*—and said quite seriously, *I'm getting me what I always wanted.* And, she has empowered three generations of other Pueblo women to do the same, to reshape their lives and the roles traditionally allotted to them.

Clearly, Evans-Pritchard talked to very different "primitive women" from the ones that I have—if he talked to them at all—and just as clearly the tribal official's attempt to silence them reflects the highly authoritarian nature of Pueblo society and bespeaks a recognition that continuity over time is a political as well as a biological and cultural problem.[32] Although his motives were reportedly baser, in acting as he did that official was re-asserting the traditional Pueblo male right to mediate with the outside world and protect what he deems sacred discourse as well as attempting to reinvoke an ancient male prerogative to appropriate and control female generativity and creativity. It was, you can almost hear him saying, one thing for old Santiago Quintana to travel to California or to share his culture and its stories with Bandelier and Benedict; it is quite another for his granddaughter to hop a plane in Albuquerque, and to make Storytellers, and to talk about her grandfather and his stories in Denver. Times *have* changed, and this time *he* lost his case against the women, but that's another story. . . .[33]

Notes

1. For discussion and documentation of the Storyteller revolution, see Babcock 1983 and Babcock and Monthan 1986.

2. This statement and others that follow in italic type were made by Helen Cordero in conversations between 1978 and 1984. When we began to work on the story of her life and art, she insisted that she would not spill the beans, and I have not discussed sacred discourse or social and ceremonial organization with her or any other Cochitis. The information about these matters in this essay was obtained from already published accounts by various observers of Cochiti and Keresan life in the past century and from conversations with anthropologists who lived and worked at Cochiti under very different constraints in previous decades.

3. For a general theory of the nature of innovation and the consequences of and conditions for the appearance of novel ideas, see Barnett 1953.

4. Many of these points are made by Judith Modell in her discussion of Zuni Mythology. She argues that Benedict's achievement in this and "other folklore pieces, was to incorporate a notion of imaginativeness into the study of culture" (Modell 1983: 243).

5. Much of my argument, in addition to this statement, is indebted to Roy Wagner's

Barbara A. Babcock

stimulating meditation on culture as creativity, as invention in *The Invention of Culture* (1981).

6. For further discussion of both prehistoric and historic Pueblo figurative pottery traditions, see Babcock and Monthan 1986.

7. For an encyclopedic inventory of Pueblo religion, see Parsons 1939. For discussions of fertility as the root metaphor or master trope of Pueblo culture, see especially Haeberlin 1916, Cushing 1920, and Benedict 1934. See also Black 1984 for an analysis of Hopi corn metaphors.

8. For descriptions of Santiago Quintana, see Benedict's Preface to *Tales of the Cochiti Indians* (1931: xi) and her letter of 5 September 1925 to Margaret Mead (Mead 1973: 300).

9. In his important essay "Style, Grace, and Information in Primitive Art," Bateson argues that it is probably an error to think of art as being about any one matter other than relationship (1973: 254–55).

10. For discussion of the Pueblo capacity for revitalization, the dynamics of cultural survival, and the importance of art therein, see A. Ortiz 1976 and Brody 1976, 1979. The description of stories as "life for the people" is from the title poem of Leslie Silko's novel *Ceremony* (1977: 2).

11. The image of a large composite figure covered with smaller versions of itself · universally connotes reproduction and, by implication, femaleness. Not surprisingly, Helen's Storytellers have been perceived as female both by Anglo consumers and by Pueblo potters who have imitated her invention. In his suggestive essay "Levels of Communication and Taboo in the Appreciation of Primitive Art," Leach argues that punning, particularly sexual ambiguity, is very common in art forms: "My general proposition is that all true artists tend to devote their principal efforts to themes which contain elements of sensory ambiguity and are subject to taboo. . . . When we examine the products of exotic cultures the confusions which first fascinate us are those which have a physiological base, they are the confusions between male and female, between food and not food, between symbols of dominance and symbols of submission" (1973: 230, 234).

12. For discussion of Helen's potteries as autobiographical statements, as shaping and shaped from personal experience, see "Modeled Selves" (Babcock 1985). See Turner 1980 for discussion of social dramas and stories about them.

13. Lange (1968: 232) has this to say about ancestral power: "A fundamental belief in the religious orientation of the Cochiti is that supernatural power is believed to be held by certain individuals at specific times because these powers have been transmitted to cultural predecessors from supernatural beings during various eras of the past. The specific powers vary in accordance with the person's official capacity, or status, and also to the extent to which he is worthy of that status."

14. See especially Fox's discussion of the term *yaya* ("mother"), which is used both for the *cacique* and his stone fetish (1967: 143).

15. For transcriptions, summaries, and interpretations of Keresan emergence narratives, see Benedict 1981, Boas 1928, Dumarest 1918, Forde 1930, Parsons 1939, Sebag 1971, Stevenson 1894, Stirling 1942, and White 1932a, 1932b, 1935, 1942, 1962. The motif of creation through the molding of meal, dust, or clay is not limited to origin myths, but is widely found throughout Pueblo narratives.

16. For a very suggestive Jungian analysis of the importance of "chains" of generations, etc., in creation myths as a way of being linked "with historical continuity, i.e., from the inside, with one's ancestral soul, to be connected with the archetype foundations of the psyche, as counter-magic against dissociation," see von Franz 1978.

17. Pueblo "world structure," as a "relentlessly connected universal whole" in which "men, animal, plants, and spirits are intertransposable in a seemingly unbroken chain

of being," constructed in terms of a series of oppositions (A. Ortiz 1972: 143), is something of a structuralist's dream. For a structural analysis of Tewa worldview, see A. Ortiz 1969; of Keres through their creation myths, see Sebag 1971.

18. The position one ascribes to women in Pueblo society depends significantly on whether one focuses on ideology or on praxis. As Bennett and others have remarked, those interpretations (e.g., Benedict) that center on the ideology, which Bennett calls "organic," view Pueblo culture and society as integrated and harmonious. Those (e.g., Goldfrank) who focus on the praxis, which he calls "repressive," emphasize the tension, conflict, and fear of Pueblo life, and the extent to which the individual (male or female) is suppressed and repressed (Bennett 1946: 361–74). The truth, I suspect, is somewhere in between, and one must look at the position of women in both ideology and praxis. On the basis of crosscultural evidence, including Alice Schlegel's Hopi work, Peggy Sanday argues (1981: 114) that "female economic and political power is ascribed as a natural right due the female sex when a long-standing magico-religious association between maturity and fertility of the soil associates women with social continuity and the social good." I would respond, not necessarily so, especially not in increasingly acculturated situations which have modified both the social and religious position of women, and certainly not among the Keresan Pueblos.

19. For discussion of the "manly/womanly dichotomy" in terms of which the Keres order their world and of the anthropology of Keres identity, see Miller 1972. See also Austin 1983 for discussion of the relationship between house and kiva.

20. For discussion of Cochiti clans, their curing and nurturant functions, their declining importance, and concomitant changes in Cochiti social organization, see Fox 1967, 1973.

21. In discussing Pueblo attitudes toward innovation in 1949, John Collier observed: "With Christianity, in the Rio Grande Pueblos, came the morality and custom of indissoluble marriage. It was a radical innovation, and apparently was welcomed by the males because it increased their status and power: the men no longer dwelt in the kiva, but lived in his [sic] children's home as co-head of the establishment. The absolute prohibition of divorce became a custom, guarded as such by the officials and priests of the ancient Pueblo religions" (1949: 51). For further crosscultural discussion of the decline in indigenous female power with colonialism, see Sanday 1981: chap. 7.

22. For discussions of Cochiti social and ceremonial organization and changes therein between the early 1920s and the early 1950s, see Goldfrank 1927, Lange 1968, and Fox 1967.

23. Here and elsewhere, I am following Friedl's definition of "male dominance" as "a situation in which men have highly preferential access, although not always exclusive rights, to those activities to which the society accords the greatest value, and the exercise of which permits a measure of control over others" (1975: 7).

24. In particular, see Cushing 1886, 1920, and Bunzel 1972 [1929] for discussion of the meanings, uses, and importance of pottery in Pueblo life.

25. Simmel describes "objective culture" as the world of cultural forms and their artifacts that have become independent of individual human existence. Objective culture is the domain of objects that function as instruments for the cultivation of the person, or as conditions under which he can become a cultural being. He observes that objective culture is overwhelmingly a product of male activity and that, with few exceptions, the artifacts of culture represent the objectification of the male spirit. In his insightful discussion of "Female Culture," and the ways in which female psyche "becomes visible," he notes that "we should expect from women a special interpretation and mode of forming phenomena in the plastic arts" (1984: 6–7, 22, 83).

26. See Parsons 1918, 1919, and 1939 for beliefs and practices associated with rites

of increase, and the use of clay figures therein. For further discussion, see Babcock and Monthan 1986.

27. Here and elsewhere, I am indebted to Annette Weiner's "model of reproduction," derived in part from Bourdieu, which she has developed in several essays (1978, 1979, 1980, 1982) and which is based on the premise "that any society must reproduce and regenerate certain elements of value in order for the society to continue. . . . These elements of value include human beings, social relations, cosmological phenomena such as ancestors, and resources such as land, material objects, names, and body decorations" (1980: 71). Within this model, she distinguishes between "reproduction," referring to cultural attention and meaning given to acts of forming, producing, or creating something new, and "regeneration," referring to the cultural attention and meaning given to the renewal, revival, rebirth, or recreation of entities previously reproduced. More recently, she has formulated the notion of "elementary cycling," by which she means "the cultural configuration of the state of affairs that encompass birth, growth, decay, death, and regeneration. . . . The life cycle of individuals, now understood as those processes which attach relations and objects to an ego and detach them at other times from other egos, cannot be separated analytically from the societal configuration wherein the natural phenomena of birth, growth, decay, and death are culturally circumscribed. . . . In this way, the configuration of elementary cycling is the basic logical form out of which integration between the individual and society takes place" (1982: 10). Whatever else it may be, the Storyteller as conceived and created by Helen Cordero is the embodiment of elementary cycling. I am also indebted to Meillassoux's Marxist analysis of precapitalist formation in which he argues that "agricultural self-sustaining formations described here . . . rely less on the control of the means of material production than on the means of human reproduction: subsistence and women. Their end is reproduction of life as a precondition to production. Their primary concern is to 'grow and multiply' in the biblical sense. . . . The relations of production are established between 'those who come before' and 'those who come after' " (1972: 100–102).

28. For further crosscultural discussion of institutionalized mechanisms "for consolidating and conserving female power during colonialization," see Sanday 1981: 37 and passim.

29. For further discussion of the value of Pueblo pottery in the transition from a subsistance to a cash economy and the importance of the Acoma pottery-making tradition for women's economic survival, see Reynolds 1986.

30. See, in particular, Barnett 1953, Graburn 1976, and Dawson, Frederickson, and Graburn 1974.

31. For further discussion of the Storyteller revolution and the development and diffusion of this new genre of Pueblo pottery, see Babcock 1983 and Babcock and Monthan 1986.

32. In addition to Weiner 1978, 1979, 1980, see O'Brien 1981, Paige and Paige 1981, and Zelman 1977 for further discussion of the "politics" of reproduction. There is abundant evidence and discussion of the highly authoritarian nature of Pueblo society and the power exerted by the religious hierarchy, but see especially Goldfrank 1945, Ellis 1953, Dozier 1961, and Fox 1973. See also Meillassoux 1972: 100–102 for a Marxist perspective on the politics of reproduction. He argues that in "agricultural self-sustaining formations [which Pueblo society once was] concern for reproduction becomes paramount . . . [and] reproduction of the unit, both biologically and structurally, is assured through the control of women. . . . The shift from production for self-sustenance and self-perpetuation to production for an external market, must necessarily bring a radical transformation, if not the social destruction of the communities."

33. In conclusion, my thanks to Helen Cordero, who has shared her life and her work with me and changed my life in the process, and to Susan Aiken, with whom I have shared the experience and the interpretation of mutedness. Cochiti Pueblo is not a place where the politics of reproduction are discussed as such, and feminist anthropologists have been rightly cautioned both against projecting our own political concerns and theoretical models onto our analyses of the position of women in other cultures and against using data about women there to buttress arguments about women here. Nonetheless, if we are not attuned to gender dynamics and the politics of discourse in the cultures we are studying, as well as in our own, we will perpetrate such idealistic and projective distortions as the ideas that simpler societies are not contaminated by sexual politics and that potteries and politics have nothing to do with each other. Finally, my apologies for being both unable and unwilling to give a more detailed account of what transpired at the tribal council.

REFERENCES

Ardener, Edwin. 1975 "Belief and the Problem of Women, and The 'Problem' Revisited." In Shirley Ardener, ed., *Perceiving Women*. London: Malaby Press. Pp. 1–27.
Austin, Mary. 1983. *The Land of Journey's Ending* (1924). Tucson: University of Arizona Press.
Babcock, Barbara A. 1983. "Clay Changes: Helen Cordero and the Pueblo Storyteller." *American Indian Art* 8, 2: 30–39.
———. 1985. "Modeled Selves: Helen Cordero's 'Little People.' " In E. Bruner and V. Turner, eds., *The Anthropology of Experience*. Urbana: University of Illinois Press.
Babcock, Barbara A., Guy Monthan, and Doris Monthan. 1986. *The Pueblo Storyteller: Development of a Figurative Ceramic Tradition*. Tucson: University of Arizona Press.
Bandelier, Adolph F. 1890. *The Delight Makers*. New York: Dodd, Mead.
———. 1890–92. Final Report of Investigations Among the Indians of the Southwestern United States, Carried on Mainly in the Years from 1880 to 1885. 2 vols. *Papers of the Archaeological Institute of America*, American Series 3 and 4. Cambridge, Mass.
Barnett, Homer. 1953. *Innovation: The Basis of Cultural Change*. New York: McGraw-Hill.
Bateson, Gregory. 1973. "Style, Grace, and Information in Primitive Art." In Anthony Forge, ed., *Primitive Art and Society*. London: Oxford University Press. Pp. 235–55.
Bauman, Zygmunt. 1971. "Semiotics and the Function of Culture." In Julia Kristeva, J. Rey-Debove, and Donna Jean Umiker, eds., *Essays in Semiotics*. The Hague: Mouton. Pp. 279–91.
Benedict, Ruth. 1932. "Configurations of Culture in North America." *American Anthropologist* 34: 1–27.
———. 1933. "Magic." Reprinted in Mead, ed., 1974. Pp. 105–15.
———. 1934. *Patterns of Culture*. Boston: Houghton Mifflin.

Barbara A. Babcock

——. 1981. *Tales of the Cochiti Indians* (1931). Albuquerque: University of New Mexico Press.

Bennett, John W. 1946. "The Interpretation of Pueblo Culture: A Question of Values." *Southwestern Journal of Anthropology* 2, 4: 361–74.

Biebuyck, Daniel, ed. 1969. *Tradition and Creativity in Tribal Art.* Berkeley: University of California Press.

Black, Mary. 1984. "Maidens and Mothers: An Analysis of Hopi Corn Metaphors." *Ethnology* 23, 4: 279–88.

Boas, Franz. 1928. *Keresan Texts.* Publications of the American Ethnological Society, vol. 8.

Bourdieu, Pierre. 1977. *Outline of a Theory of Practice.* Cambridge: Cambridge University Press.

Brody, J. J. 1976. "The Creative Consumer: Survival, Revival, and Invention in Southwest Indian Arts." In Nelson Graburn, ed., *Ethnic and Tourist Arts.* Berkeley: University of California Press. Pp. 70–84.

——. 1979. "Pueblo Fine Arts." In A. Ortiz, ed., *Handbook of North American Indians,* vol. 9. Washington: Smithsonian Institution Press. Pp. 603–8.

Bunzel, Ruth. 1972. *The Pueblo Potter: A Study of Creative Imagination in Primitive Art* (1929). New York: Dover.

Chapman, Kenneth. 1950. *Pueblo Indian Pottery of the Post-Spanish Period.* Santa Fe: School of American Research.

Collier, John. 1949. *Patterns and Ceremonials of the Indians of the Southwest.* New York: E. P. Dutton.

Cushing, Frank Hamilton. 1886. "A Study of Pueblo Pottery as Illustrative of Zuni Culture Growth." *4th Annual Report of the Bureau of American Ethnology.* Pp. 437–521.

——. 1920. "Zuni Breadstuff." *Indian Notes and Monographs,* vol. 8. New York: Museum of the American Indian.

Dawson, Lawrence E., Vera-Mae Frederickson, and Nelson H. H. Graburn. 1974. *Traditions in Transition: Culture Contact and Material Change.* Berkeley: Lowie Museum of Anthropology.

d'Azevedo, Warren L., ed. 1973. *The Traditional Artist in African Society.* Bloomington: Indiana University Press.

Dozier, Edward P. 1961. "Rio Grande Pueblos." In Edward H. Spicer, ed., *Perspectives in American Indian Cultural Change.* Chicago: University of Chicago Press. Pp. 94–186.

Dumarest, Fr. Noel. 1918. "Notes on Cochiti, New Mexico." *Memoirs of the American Anthropological Association,* no. 23: 135–236.

Ellis, Florence Hawley. 1953. "Authoritative Control and the Society System in Jemez Pueblo." *Southwestern Journal of Anthropology* 9: 385–94.

Evans-Pritchard, E. E. 1965. *The Position of Women in Primitive Societies and Other Essays in Social Anthropology.* New York: Free Press.

Firth, Raymond. 1966. "The Social Framework of Primitive Art." In R. Firth, *Elements of Social Organization.* Boston: Beacon Press. Pp. 155–92.

Forde, C. Daryll. 1930. "A Creation Myth from Acoma." *Folk-Lore* 41: 370–87.

Forge, Anthony, ed. 1973. *Primitive Art and Society.* London: Oxford University Press.

Fox, Robin. 1967. *The Keresan Bridge*. New York: Humanities Press.
——. 1973. *Encounter with Anthropology*. New York: Harcourt Brace.
Friedl, Ernestine. 1975. *Women and Men: An Anthropologist's View*. New York: Holt, Rinehart, and Winston.
Geertz, Clifford. 1976. "Art as a Cultural System." *Modern Language Notes* 91, 6: 1473–99.
Goldfrank, Esther. 1927. "The Social and Ceremonial Organization of Cochiti." *Memoirs of the American Anthropological Association*, no. 33.
——. 1945. "Socialization, Personality, and the Structure of Pueblo Society." *American Anthropologist* 47: 516–39.
Graburn, Nelson H. H., ed. 1976. *Ethnic and Tourist Arts*. Berkeley: University of California Press.
Haeberlin, H. K. 1916. "The Idea of Fertilization in the Culture of the Pueblo Indians." *Memoirs of the American Anthropological Association*, no. 3.
Hardin, Margaret Ann. 1983. *Gifts of Mother Earth: Ceramics in the Zuni Tradition*. Phoenix: The Heard Museum.
Kaufmann, Fritz. 1969. "Art and Phenomenology." In W. Natanson, ed., *Essays in Phenomenology*. The Hague: Martinus Nijhoff. Pp. 144–56.
Lange, Charles H. 1968. *Cochiti: A New Mexico Pueblo, Past and Present*. Carbondale: Southern Illinois University Press.
Lange, Charles H., and Carroll L. Riley, eds. 1966. *The Southwestern Journals of Adolph F. Bandelier, 1880–1882*. Albuquerque: University of New Mexico Press.
——. 1970. *The Southwestern Journals of Adolph F. Bandelier, 1883–1884*. Albuquerque: University of New Mexico Press.
Lange, Charles H., Carroll L. Riley, and Elizabeth M. Lange, eds. 1975. *The Southwestern Journals of Adolph F. Bandelier, 1885–1888*. Albuquerque: University of New Mexico Press.
Leach, Edmund. 1973. "Levels of Communication and Problems of Taboo in the Appreciation of Primitive Art." In Anthony Forge, ed., *Primitive Art and Society*. London: Oxford University Press. Pp. 221–34.
Mason, Edith Hart. 1948. "Enemy Bear." *The Masterkey* 22, 3: 80–85.
Mead, Margaret, ed. 1973. *An Anthropologist at Work: Writings of Ruth Benedict*. New York: Equinox Books.
——. 1974. *Ruth Benedict*. New York: Columbia University Press.
Meillassoux, Claude. 1972. "From Reproduction to Production: A Marxist Approach to Economic Anthropology." *Economy and Society* 1, 1: 93–105.
Merleau-Ponty, Maurice. 1964. "Indirect Language and the Voices of Silence." In M. Merleau-Ponty, *Signs*. Evanston, Ill.: Northwestern University Press. Pp. 39–83.
Miller, Julius. 1972. "The Anthropology of Keres Indentity." Ph.D. diss. Rutgers University.
Modell, Judith Schachter. 1983. *Ruth Benedict: Patterns of a Life*. Philadelphia: University of Pennsylvania Press.
O'Brien, Mary. 1981. *The Politics of Reproduction*. London: Routledge & Kegan Paul.
Ortiz, Alfonso. 1969. *The Tewa World: Space, Time, Being, and Becoming in a Pueblo Society*. Chicago: University of Chicago Press.

Barbara A. Babcock

———. 1972. "Ritual Drama and the Pueblo World View." In A. Ortiz, ed., *New Perspectives on the Pueblo*. Albuquerque: University of New Mexico Press. Pp. 135–61.

———. 1976. "The Dynamics of Pueblo Cultural Survival." Paper presented at the American Anthropological Society Meetings, Washington, D.C.

Ortiz, Simon J. 1977. *A Good Journey*. Berkeley: Turtle Island.

Paige, Karen Ericksen, and Jeffrey M. Paige. 1981. *The Politics of Reproductive Ritual*. Berkeley: University of California Press.

Parsons, Elsie Clews. 1918. "Nativity Myth at Laguna and Zuni." *Journal of American Folklore* 31, 120: 256–63.

———. 1919. "Increase by Magic: A Zuni Pattern." *American Anthropologist* 21: 279–86.

———. 1939. *Pueblo Indian Religion*. 4 vols. Chicago: University of Chicago Press.

Reynolds, Terry R. 1986. "Women, Pottery, and Economics at Acoma Pueblo." In Joan M. Jensen and Darlis A. Miller, eds., *New Mexico Women: Intercultural Perspectives*. Albuquerque: University of New Mexico Press. Pp. 279–300.

Sanday, Peggy. 1981. *Female Power and Male Dominance: On the Origins of Sexual Equality*. Cambridge: Cambridge University Press.

Sebag, Lucien. 1971. *L'invention du monde chez les indiens pueblos*. Paris: François Maspéro.

Silko, Leslie Marmon. 1977. *Ceremony*. New York: Viking Press.

———. 1981. "Language and Literature from a Pueblo Indian Perspective." In Leslie A. Fiedler and Houston A. Baker, Jr., eds., *English Literature: Opening Up the Canon*. Baltimore: Johns Hopkins University Press. Pp. 54–72.

Simmel, Georg. 1984. *On Women, Sexuality, and Love*. Trans. with an introduction by Guy Oakes. New Haven: Yale University Press.

Snow, David H. 1973. "Some Economic Considerations of Historic Rio Grande Pueblo Pottery." In A. Schroeder, ed., *The Changing Ways of Southwestern Indians: A Historic Perspective*. Glorieta, N.M.: Rio Grande Press. Pp. 55–72.

Stevenson, Matilda Coxe. 1894. "The Sia." *11th Annual Report of the Bureau of American Ethnology*. Washington: Smithsonian Institution.

Stirling, Matthew. 1942. "Origin Myth of Acoma and Other Records." *Bureau of American Ethnology Bulletin*, no. 135.

Turner, Victor W. 1980. "Social Dramas and Stories about Them." *Critical Inquiry* 7, 1: 141–68.

von Franz, Marie-Louise. 1978. *Patterns of Creativity Mirrored in Creation Myths*. Zurich: Spring Publications.

Wagner, Roy. 1981. *The Invention of Culture*. Chicago: University of Chicago Press.

Weiner, Annette B. 1978. "The Reproductive Model in Trobriand Society." *Mankind* 11, 3: 175–86.

———. 1979. "Trobriand Kinship from Another View: The Reproductive Power of Women and Men." *Man* 14, 2:328–48.

———. 1980. "Reproduction: A Replacement for Reciprocity." *American Ethnologist* 7, 1: 71–85.

———. 1982. "Sticks and Stones, Threads and Bones: This Is What Kinship Is Made

Of." Paper presented at the conference on Feminism and Kinship Theory, Bellagio.

White, Leslie A. 1932a. "The Acoma Indians." *47th Annual Report of the Bureau of American Ethnology.*

——. 1932b. "The Pueblo of San Felipe." *Memoirs of the American Anthropological Association,* no. 38.

——. 1935. "The Pueblo of Santo Domingo." *Memoirs of the American Anthropological Association,* no. 43.

——. 1942. "The Pueblo of Santa Ana." *Memoirs of the American Anthropological Association,* no. 60.

——. 1962. "The Pueblo of Sia." *Bulletin of the Bureau of American Ethnology,* no. 184.

Zelman, Elizabeth S. 1977. "Reproductive Ritual and Power." *American Ethnologist* 4, 4: 714–33.

[5]

"Riding the Horse of Gaps": A Meratus Woman's Spiritual Expression

Anna Lowenhaupt Tsing

> Adu hai,
> Riding the horse of gaps, babe.
> Swept by the wind,
> Riding the horse of gaps, friend.
> —Induan Hiling

This essay presents several dream-inspired shamanic pictures and associated songs from the Meratus Mountains of Indonesia. They are a woman's work, and I ask in what way that makes a difference.

This essay was originally written for this volume in 1985. A slightly different version was published in 1990 as "The Vision of a Woman Shaman" in Joyce McCarl Nielsen, ed., *Feminist Research Methods* (Boulder: Westview Press), pp. 147–73; reprinted by permission of the publisher.

Research in South Kalimantan was carried out between 1979 and 1981 under the auspices of the Lembaga Ilmu Pengetahuan Indonesia and the sponsorship of Dr. Masri Singarimbun. Support was provided by fellowships from the National Institute of Mental Health and the Social Science Research Council. This article has benefited from readings by Jane Atkinson, James Fernandez, Janet Jacobs, Ann-Marie Mires, Beth Nelson, Renato Rosaldo, Alix Kates Shulman, Lynn Wilson, and Harriet Whitehead. Elizabeth Fischbach drew the portrait of Induan Hiling, which I reproduce with her

My answer has to do with the way these compositions interpret and revise a dominant tradition. I suggest that attention to such pieces as commentary and new addition to discourse, rather than only as fragments of an established text, can break up the false homogeneity of what we tend to present as "culture."

My analysis here is aided by the work of feminist literary critics, and I draw insights from several distinct feminist viewpoints on the sources and shapes of women's creativity. First, some feminist literary critics call attention to common female experiences and connections among women authors as influences on women's creative consciousnesses (e.g., Moers 1976, Showalter 1977). Second, feminist critics emphasize the influence of dominant male traditions on the creative productions of women. They suggest that in writing, women incorporate dominant conventions at the same time as they invert them, resist them, and transform them (e.g., Gilbert and Gubar 1979). Third, some feminist literary critics argue that male dominance is involved in the very conditions of representation—in language and in writing. They show how women's writing refuses the constraints of male structures of signification, thus exposing and challenging these basic conditions of creative production (e.g., Cixous 1980, Kamuf 1982). Each of these frameworks sheds light on the ways that women's creative expression can be shaped by, yet be separate from, the main streams of male-dominant cultural convention.[1]

The best explored intersection between anthropology and literary criticism has taken the metaphor of culture as text to show the systematic nature of cultural logic. Recently, interest has turned as well toward improvisation and negotiation in cultural performances, and multiple "readings" of cultural texts (e.g., Bruner and Gorfain 1984). I propose that it can also be useful to look to multiple "writers" within a single cultural context and the process in which they confront, incorporate, resist, and modify dominant conventions. By attending to the heterogeneity of authors, it is possible to gain a perspective on

---

permission. I am particularly grateful to Induan Hiling for sharing her work with me—and allowing me to share it with others.

Induan Hiling is a pseudonym for a Meratus Dayak woman whose name I have changed to protect her privacy. The lines in the epigraph are from one of her inspired songs. I have translated the entire song in an appendix to show the textual context of the fragment. In order to let some sense of this song come through in my analysis, I have used fragments from it throughout this essay.

the logic of dominant conventions that takes into account the conditions of their dominance. Viewed along the intersection of power and cultural expression, creativity can be seen to sponsor inequality as well as provide channels for improvisation and imagination.

Perspectives from feminist literary criticism also enrich the anthropological analysis of gender and male dominance. Here, the "culture as text" metaphor has pressed anthropologists to focus on what feminist literary critics call "images of women." We have familiarized ourselves with representations of women as sexually voracious whores and selfless mothers, and with gender oppositions that pose female as closer to nature than male or as inside layers of male protection. But this is not always the most useful approach. In my fieldwork among Meratus Dayaks of the mountains of southeast Kalimantan (Indonesian Borneo),[2] I found that more important than images of women was the issue of who had access to politically significant expressive modes; women were disadvantaged not so much by what was said but by who got to speak.[3]

Although the imagery of Meratus ritual is generally gender-balanced or gender-neutral, the star performers and producers of ritual are almost always men. In this context, the questions posed by feminist critics about women who manage to participate in purportedly universal creative traditions dominated by men seem particularly relevant. Under layers of conventional—and sometimes brilliant—compliance, the work of these women can reveal a cutting edge of resistance.

This essay extends this bridge between literary criticism and anthropology by looking at the ritual contributions of the Meratus shaman Induan Hiling. Her songs and pictures—the latter drawn in a context in which any kind of drawing or writing was unusual—offer us a perceptive and challenging interpretation of Meratus shamanic tradition. They also provide a guide to the gendered basis of Meratus modes of expression.

Gendered Resources for Expression

I first learned of Induan Hiling's spiritual work through a connection among unconventional women. Although we had known each other casually for some time, Induan Hiling spoke to me of her inspiration only when she heard of my close ties with another spiritual innovator, a woman named Uma Adang who was leading a religious movement in a Meratus community a day's hike to the east.[4] Both Induan Hiling and I considered Uma Adang a sister, a mentor, and a remarkable leader. On

Figure 5.1. Induan Hiling performing. Portrait by Elizabeth Fischbach.

the strength of this connection, Induan Hiling invited me to share her own spiritual revelations, her curing experiences, and her knowledge of *adat* (customary) law. She took out her pictures, showed me her songs and dances, and urged me to take her message to America.

Uma Adang was the first person to encourage Induan Hiling to take her spiritual calling seriously. When Induan Hiling consulted Uma Adang, Induan Hiling had not been sure of herself: was she crazy or legitimately inspired? Uma Adang confidently directed her to view herself as a shaman in training. But despite her continued respect for Uma Adang's teachings, Induan Hiling never portrayed herself as a purveyor of Uma Adang's message. Her spiritual teachings, she insisted, came from her deceased father, once a well-respected shaman, who visited her in dreams. Although encouraged by women, Induan Hiling was a student of the male-dominated central tradition.

Feminist literary critics have shown how women writers draw from one another even as their work fits neatly within the male-dominated canon. These critics argue that women's creative work often develops from and extends a "female subculture." For anthropologists, this point seems almost commonplace, since anthropological studies of gender divisions in expressive culture have focused on the separation between male and female traditions (e.g., Weiner 1976, Bell 1983, Ardener 1975, Herdt 1981). However, feminist literary critics also show that the "female subculture" of Western literature is neither autonomous from nor complementary to a "male subculture"; each woman's writing is intimately bound up with the *dominant* literary tradition, which rests mainly in the hands of men. This point should remind anthropologists that a separation between male and female cultural spheres cannot be breezily assumed, and, even in ethnographic contexts of gender segregation, it is useful to look at the gender relations upon which segregated expressive modes are predicated. The approach from feminist criticism suggests we explore the dynamic process in which men and women interact differentially with dominant cultural modes.

The Dominant Tradition in Meratus Shamanism

Meratus rituals feature a star performer, the shaman (*balian*), who chants and dances to "bring down" spiritual beings to help with cures, taste the newly harvested rice, or protect the community from spiritual danger. Shamans are almost always men. Women may have a speaking role in ritual performances as *pinjulang*, the accompanist singer paired with each shaman to echo or answer him.[5] Often pinjulang are wives of shamans, and they learn from their husbands. In contrast to the enthusiastic self-presentation of shamans, pinjulang sometimes put a hand or a piece of their skirt over their mouths, muffling their own voices. Although some pinjulang are bolder, and even claim to learn their skills from other women, pinjulang never summon spirits, sponsor ceremonies, or initiate a round of chanting within a ceremony.

Women are also participants in shamanic ceremonies in other ways: both women and men help to prepare the ritual apparatus, bring their rice to be consecrated, and present themselves as patients for shamans to cure. Meratus ceremonies are never gender-segregated, although male shamans dominate center stage. Both women and men are essential in forming the audience, which is the spiritual community that creates the success of the performance.

Shamanic performances are occasions for socializing, eating together, and—in big community festivals—dancing, fighting, arranging love affairs, settling disputes, and visiting relatives. The importance of shamanic expression in the Meratus setting stems in part from its centrality in events in which both women and men reaffirm social and political affiliations. Shamanic performances also involve the recitation of long, poetic chants, which map the shaman's travels through spiritual realms. Many women, as well as men, can knowledgeably discuss this poetic tradition. Unlike the exclusively male rituals of many parts of Melanesia, Australia, and the Amazon, Meratus shamanic ceremonies do not construct gender-segregated ritual spaces or commitments.

Most Meratus I asked would not rule out the possibility that a shaman could be a woman, even if they knew of no examples. But women have less access than men to both formal and informal training. Men are more likely than women to practice and play with ritual expression. Boys sing the drum beats that signify particular spiritual styles as they play by the river;[6] young men call out lines from the chants as they hike through the forest. Young men who want to become shamans can embark on a formal apprenticeship; they learn by sitting next to, and dancing behind, an experienced shaman. The apprentice repeats each line of the shaman's chant, committing it to memory. Some men also learn through dreams or spiritual encounters on lonely mountain tops or on great rocks in the middle of wild rivers.

Becoming a successful shaman involves more than expressive training: a shaman must use personal charisma and theatrical display to draw an audience for his ceremonies. The ability to combine a dramatic self-presentation with articulate knowledge of the tradition is especially important. Shamans can impress their audiences by fainting away from impassioned spiritual dialogue, or, when possessed by dangerous spirits, growling and drinking blood while crouched on all fours. A woman with extensive pinjulang experience may know a great deal about the chants. But knowledge alone cannot draw an audience, and without an audience, she has few opportunities to present herself as a spiritual authority.

The Women's Possession Movement

Since men ordinarily dominate the dramatic center of ritual performances, I was quite surprised at one big festival when a woman jumped up and began a wild dance around the ritual decorations, waving her arms and singing under her breath. As the festival proceeded over the next few days, a number of other women followed her example. I soon learned that episodes of women's possession had been sweeping across the mountains over the past few years, and, people said, they were spreading from one festival to the next. It was said that the women were possessed by the *dewa* spirits who had been invited to the festival. Some women even continued possessed singing and dancing outside the festival context.

Senior shamans and other men described the movement as an epidemic of illness or craziness. They did their best to cure the affected women, noting that otherwise the women might kill themselves by wandering off at night or stepping obliviously into a ravine. Since most of the women danced without a clearly articulated shamanic chant to explain their dancing, it was easy for the senior shamans to classify the possessed women as patients rather than healers. A number of the women, however, spoke later not of being wordlessly possessed but of learning inspired teachings from this spiritual contact.[7]

Induan Hiling first found herself affected by uncontrollable singing and dancing about a year and a half before the episode I have just described. She remembers that her in-laws told her she was crazy. She had tended to agree until she consulted Uma Adang and, as a result, began to take her spiritual training seriously. She then realized that her deceased father was passing on his teachings through her dreams. Slowly, his teaching came to be augmented by other spiritual dream guides. As a shaman in training, Induan Hiling went beyond the women who danced and tranced inarticulately—with whom she originally identified—and her actions challenged standards of gender-appropriateness in new ways.

Induan Hiling's Contribution

Induan Hiling vacillated at times between the labels of "shaman" and "pinjulang." As her influence was not yet great enough that she could claim to be a successful shaman, she avoided presumptuousness by calling herself a pinjulang. But she never meant her talents to serve as accompaniment to a shaman's performance; her innovative work challenged shamans, not their pinjulang support. Her ambivalence about labels reflected her dependence on female resources as she attempted to enter the male tradition.

This ambivalence can be seen throughout Induan Hiling's work. She calls her songs *dunang*, the term used for the love songs and lullabies that both women and men sing and compose freely. But her love songs have a spiritual rather than a romantic message; her songs describe a spiritual flight that puts her in the company of shamans and separates her from the answering counterpoint of pinjulang as well as the teasing admiration of lovers. In the song fragment that begins this essay, Induan Hiling rides a flying horse. In the fragment below, she chooses a flying cobra, a conventional familiar of Meratus shamans. The cobra's scales map her route of spiritual flight, as it extends both forward and back:

> Child of a cobra, babe,
> soaring to the sun.
> If it has scales,
> they cross across each other.
> The scales they point, babe,
> Where do they point, friend?
> They point to its tail,
> They point to its head,
> Those scales, babe.

Pinjulang sometimes describe themselves as supporting the shaman's flight or following him, but they never launch themselves. In contrast, Induan Hiling's is a shaman's song. Yet, the melody and the use of

[107]

line markers like "babe" (*ding*, short for *ading*, "younger sibling," used for romantic partners as well as children) remind us that this is the kind of song a woman could sing.

When I knew her in 1980 and 1981, Induan Hiling was in her mid-thirties, the married mother of three sons, and a central figure in a small cluster of households that included her mother and sister as well as her husband and some of his kin. She was a soft-spoken, graceful woman, with no particular aspirations to a "male" dramatic style. Yet, she had embarked on a route of independent spiritual innovation. Only her close relatives and neighbors knew of her abilities at that point, but all agreed that she was on her way to more important achievements.

Induan Hiling stressed the importance of her creative connections to her deceased father, once an important shaman in the area. (One of the first things she told me about herself was that her father had encouraged her to climb trees as a child, endowing her with an admired talent few women possess.) Yet the development of her skills and influence depended on the support of her mother and younger sister, who both lived next door. Both mother and sister were well-respected pinjulang with a thorough knowledge of ritual. Within the social cluster of which their households formed a central part, Induan Hiling's spiritual innovations provided a basis for aspirations to autonomy from the larger encompassing neighborhood.[8] There were no shamans within the cluster; instead, the women explored their own spiritual authority.

Induan Hiling's sense of her spiritual antecedents and mentors reflects her ability to use female resources while inserting herself within a male tradition. Of necessity, she uses conventions created by male shamans and appeals to male sources of authority for inspiration and legitimation. However, she also draws inspiration and support from other creative women.

Inversions and Revisions

Induan Hiling's contributions proceed in dialogue with dominant conventions of shamanism. At the time of my research, her work had not sparked a prairie fire of change; however, an analysis that began with the assumption that her work merely reproduces social categories and reenacts cultural values would miss the tensions and break-throughs of her innovations.

Unsubmissive, inspired women have made other appearances in

the anthropological literature. A number of analysts have shown how women use possession, or other ritual participation, as an "oblique strategy" of protest (Lewis 1971: 117, Kessler 1977). Yet, because most anthropologists focus on predictably repetitive, nondisruptive female protest, their accounts too often take for granted the stability of local discourses of male dominance. Thus, although functionalist and psychoanalytic analyses have highlighted women's defiance of male authority in ritual (e.g., Gluckman 1963, Freeman 1968), these analyses ultimately dismiss women's challenges as a reaffirmation and restabilization of women's subordination through the expression of tensions. Interpretive approaches have looked more closely at local discourse on gender; for example, Kapferer (1983) discusses Sinhalese beliefs that women are "natural" victims of possession and perpetrators of disorder. But because his analysis shows women as objects of cultural interpretation rather than as positioned subjects, Kapferer obscures the possessed women's role in negotiating new understandings of gender and inspiration. In such analyses, we watch the women through the eyes of conservative male elders—like those senior Meratus shamans who denied women's spiritual initiative by saying the women were victims of an epidemic illness. In contrast, my approach avoids assumptions of social or cultural stability by exploring how an inspired woman's work contributes to a continually evolving discourse.

Induan Hiling's work draws eclectically from a set of familiar metaphors and genre conventions. As she uses pieces from one tradition to revise others, she creates products that, like the writings of Western women novelists and poets, seem open to multiple and sometimes contradictory interpretations. The following sections explore some of Induan Hiling's revisions and innovations, showing how her work contests conventional Meratus expectations of the links between gender and expression. Indeed, although her work builds from the dominant Meratus tradition, it also interprets this tradition in a new way that is linked to her status as a woman creator.

Induan Hiling's Innovations: The Songs and Dances

> What shall be used, babe?
> Forging spurs,
> Finished in a day.

[109]

Induan Hiling inverts and revises both male and female expressive traditions in her song and dance repertoire. For example, male shamans use hand-held rattle bracelets to control rhythm and cue the drummer; Induan Hiling puts rattling bells on her ankles, thus setting the rhythm with her steps without appearing to control it.[9] Her dance movements, featuring small, circumscribed steps and graceful body and arm movements, bear some resemblance to the secular women's dance done at festivals. (Male shamans tend to include much more prancing and stomping.) But, diverging from the slow, mincing gait of the women parading at festivals, she moves to a lively and energetic rhythm, responding to her own inspired singing. Whereas women at festivals normally dance with their faces away from the audience, Induan Hiling dances with her face to the audience, thus dramatically unmuffling her voice.

As I mentioned earlier, Induan Hiling uses the melodic structure and refrains of love songs (*dunang*)—a comfortable, familiar medium for women. But she fills her songs with sacred imagery from the repertoire of shamans. One song she sang for me traces spiritual travel in a form almost identical to that found in conventional shamans' chants. In other songs, however (including the one I translate in the Appendix and quote throughout this essay), she forges a hybrid genre.

Induan Hiling's songs refer to the gendered metaphors of conventional love songs, but transform them in gender-free spiritual directions. Thus, like ordinary love songs, her songs are filled with metaphorical references to vegetation. In love songs, shining, golden, healthy but passive plants represent the beautiful women pursued by male suitors, who are portrayed as birds, wandering soldiers, and tree-cutters. In Induan Hiling's songs, the lovely but passive vegetation is transformed into an extremely active element: she sings of "swaying" fig trees and "singing" bamboos. Removing vegetation even further from the love song context, she omits the male half of the tree/bird and tree/tree-cutter contrast. The result is that vegetation becomes a metaphor for various aspects of *human* spiritual expression rather than for *women*.

The following fragment shows one complex set of associations for bamboo:

> There is a planting:
> A cut bamboo
> A bamboo that plays the flute

A bamboo that sings.
We cut it off,
Touching the shoulders,
The scissored bamboo
Touching the waist.
Babe, the scissored bamboo,
The cut bamboo
Where is it planted?
Where does it hang?

Bamboo is female in a number of love songs, such as the song "Yellow Bamboo." To the extent that Induan Hiling's bamboo carries female resonances, its singing and playing of the flute establishes it as a creative subject, not an object of courtship admiration. Induan Hiling's dominant metaphor, however, is not of bamboo as woman but of bamboo as hair; this is a common shamanic reference for a (gender-neutral) spiritual attribute of the body. To make the move to a *human* spirituality clear, Induan Hiling establishes the gender symmetry of her metaphor; as she explained to me, she simultaneously invokes a male subject, whose hair is "touching the shoulders," and a female subject, whose hair is "touching the waist." She transforms a reference to women into a reference to spiritual experience that holds equally for men and women. Her vision of a human spirituality unbiased by gender is strengthened through the other metaphors she draws into the portrait: she compares the bamboo to ritual streamers that are intricately "scissored" (actually, cut with a knife into designs) and finally "cut" (tied up) to close the performance; the bamboo is also, as references earlier in the song make clearer, the shamanic route itself, the pathway of spiritual expression. In this way Induan Hiling removes female resonances from the context of an asymmetrical male-female contrast, and places them among spiritual references as features of a human spirituality that does not depend on gender difference.

The dualism of love songs is not entirely lost in this transformation, however. Induan Hiling's vegetation enters into a different opposition—with mountains and rocks rather than birds and tree-cutters. She explained mountains and rocks as representing an internal inspirational knowledge, the as yet unarticulated wisdom of origins. In contrast, her vegetation represents the ritual apparatus used in shamanic ceremony and the well-worn ritual practices within which the shaman's chants emerge. Rocks and mountains contrast with vegetation as inspiration contrasts with tradition. Both elements, she implies, are needed for ritual efficacy: indeed, inspiration is articulated through tradition.

This complementarity is a motif repeated in much of her work. She sings of a fig tree on a mountain, which, as she explained, also refers to the hair growing on our heads:

> On the summit of a mountain
> There's a wild fig tree
> A hanging fig tree
> A swaying fig tree
> Hanging where
> Swinging there
> Our wild fig tree.

Elsewhere, she repeats the vegetation-mountain opposition in singing about bamboos on rocks, or, using an image borrowed from "city people," of flowers on a table. This is *not* a gendered opposition. Transcending the gendered imagery of the love song with non-gendered sacred text is essential to Induan Hiling's ability to cast her work as shamanism. Yet, her use of the two element opposition as motif has its roots in the love song.

The Dream Pictures

Induan Hiling draws the same opposition into her dream pictures. Pictures are not a common form of Meratus creative expression; besides the scribblings of a few schoolchildren, almost no one writes or draws. Her dream-inspired drawing and "writing" transform and revise familiar themes in a new medium of spiritual expression. The complementarity of rocks and plants, as text and ritual apparatus or inspiration and tradition, is also key to the pictures' message.

The drawing in Figure 5.2 shows a tree standing next to a rock. Induan Hiling explained that the tree is at the same time a ritual decoration complementing the rocks' written text, the scribbled lines that depict the internal knowledge of the shaman to be expressed in the chant. Although she herself could not read the message, she assured me that the scribbled lines in the rocks are "writing." (The English words on the side of the page do not represent "writing" in the same sense; I will come back to them.) She features this kind of

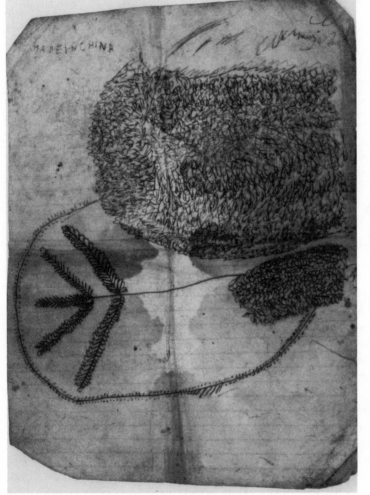

Figure 5.6. Flying over mountains, rocks, grass, and trees.

Figure 5.3. The shaman's book.

dream-dictated "writing" in a number of her drawings; in Figure 5.3, she has filled the page with it. She told me how painstakingly she had drawn the writing of Figure 5.3. Although unreadable, this dream writing is a carefully written text.

Figure 5.2 presents the opposition between tree and rock, or tradition and inspiration, as symmetrical: each element occupies one side of the page. Other drawings show further dimensions of her vision of the complementarity between these opposed spiritual elements. In Figure 5.4, she has drawn a spiritual mountain as seen from above. Crisscrossing over the mountain like vines are the ritual decorations known as "walkways of the gods"; these represent the paths of articulated ritual expression. Her "writing" fills one open quarter of the mountain; although visible only in this quarter, this is the inspirational text that energizes the whole mountain. In this drawing, the vinelike "walkways of the gods" are ritual paths that provide the superficial expression of the inspired text of the mountain.

Figure 5.5 shifts focus entirely to the intricate flowering of ritual

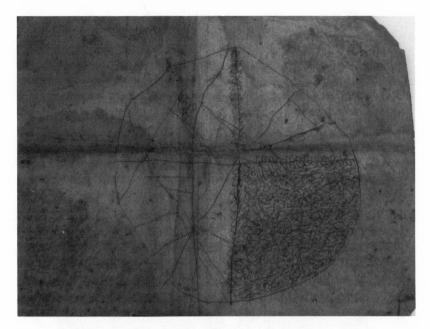

Figure 5.4. The mountain of spiritual encounter and the walkways of the gods.

form. This drawing represents ritual decorations; Induan Hiling has shown them here as delicate and plantlike. Each lobe is a "leaf"; each leaf is beautified and empowered by marks that can be interpreted equally as ornamentation or text.[10] She incorporates the text into the ritual apparatus. Although each drawing combines elements of text and ritual in different ways, the importance of a complementarity between inspiration and traditional form is reiterated in each. Even Figure 5.3, in which she has filled the page with inspirational message, reminds us of the importance of ritualized form precisely because it lacks any.

Induan Hiling's explanation of shamanism as inspiration externalized and articulated through traditional form is both an innovative and perceptive interpretation. Conventional shamanic apprenticeship encourages a reading of the chants that stresses the endless elaboration of complexity and diversity rather than oppositions. Mountains and vegetation are common symbolic elements in shamans' chants, but nowhere else did I see the two elements so clearly identified as complementary pairs, with such stably resonating reference to the pos-

Figure 5.5. The ritual set-up.

sibilities of spiritual expression itself. Induan Hiling's interpretation of the tradition successfully clarifies a number of key elements. Her oppositions speak to the necessity for both shamanic chants and ritual decorations in a performance. They also recall the complementarity of dreams and apprenticeship in learning, as well as the use of linked images of primal knowledge and carefully learned tradition within the chants themselves. Yet, her interpretation is also a challenging one, pointing to the possibilities of simplificiation and codification of that which, shamans say, could never be simplified or codified.

Induan Hiling's engagement with the dominant tradition of Meratus shamanism results in a perceptive interpretative framework. As a woman shaman, she has needed to forge original paths to achieve legitimacy. These paths have led her not only to innovative revisions, but also to imaginative and insightful views on Meratus shamanism.

[116]

The Conditions of Creative Production

Induan Hiling means her drawings as more than a critical appraisal: they are encapsulations of performance, a substitute for performance. The drawings—particularly the more complex ones—are themselves rituals. Indeed, the contrast between picture or script as ritual and the more conventional male-dominated ritual performance suggests a new dimension of Induan Hiling's contribution: her work makes evident the gendered grounds of Meratus ritual representation.

The complex drawing reproduced in Figure 5.6 presents a complete ritual performance, a curing ritual. Here Induan Hiling has drawn not only the mountain-vegetation opposition described above but also the shaman who brings together tradition and inspiration. On each side of the drawing are rocks; the triangles that dominate the landscape are mountains. On the rocks and mountains grow vegetation; at the peak of the darkest mountain is a wild fig tree, with its fruits; a wild palm grows to its immediate left; near that mountain's summit are herbs and grasses, including the plant that appears to have drifted off the top. But she has also drawn the dreamer herself in the form of an airplane (on the left of the picture). The airplane is the dreamer who energizes and experiences the dream landscape. Meratus generally interpret airplanes as the vehicles of spiritual travel. Here the representation of spiritual travel empowers the drawing as a shamanic ritual. Induan Hiling's sister, who was suffering from leprosy, kept this picture as an aspect of her cure. The drawing is not meant as a reminder of a shamanic performance; it is itself a curing ritual.

The picture incorporates several key elements of more conventional performances, particularly its addition of the spiritual travel of the shaman. There are, however, clearly significant differences between this picture and a conventional performance. Most important, perhaps, the picture involves no dramatic action. The picture flattens the performance, abolishing performance time.

Performance time is not just duration; it is the capture of attention. A successful ritual establishes the centrality of the shaman within the attention of the audience. Indeed, as the performances last all night, the listeners often sleep, but if they did nothing but sleep, the ritual would be less effective. And the listeners might just sleep—despite the beauty of the dance, the decorations, and the poetry—except for unpredictable elements in the performance and the possibility of various kinds of dramatic upsets or excess: the ritual preparations may

[117]

[118]

be badly done—the spirit will be angry; perhaps the shaman will be overwhelmed within his chant and fall into a faint, and it may be difficult to revive him. Unlike the decorations and the chants, these elements are never described as necessary to ritual—in fact, they involve messing up rather than following the rules—but they are key elements of performance time.

Dramatic upsets and excesses are also the performance elements most clearly associated with male experience and male political advantage. Outside of the context of shamanism, men more often than women use the threats and surprises of impressive speeches and angry outbursts to position themselves focally within social gatherings. When shamans improvise with their knowledge and ferocity, they call upon these dramatic talents to sustain the drawing power of the performance. This is not so much a matter of gender rules as of men's ability to go beyond the rules—and thus establish them (Tsing 1990).

One male shaman commented that women tend not to become shamans because they do not want to stay up through all-night performances. He was ignoring the fact that pinjulang do stay up all night to accompany the shaman. But there is a difference in the wakefulness of the shaman and the wakefulness of his woman accompanist: the attention of the former draws attention; the latter is awake merely for herself and for the shaman. The ability to wake up the audience, at least sporadically, is a crucial skill of the shaman.

Sometimes women can seize the dramatic center. The possessed women with whom Induan Hiling began her spiritual career manipulated audience attention with their wild dancing and bursts of spirit-inspired song. Without the women's dramatic excesses Induan Hiling might not have had a platform from which to rise. Yet most of the possessed women were willing to lend credence to shamans' views of them as patients rather than healers by representing themselves as inarticulate victims of spiritual power. As long as they were seen as patients, their dramatic performance did not threaten the men's preeminence. (Some of the women, close kin of male shamans, were motivated to support rather than challenge the men's authority.) Furthermore, the most ritually knowledgeable women, the pinjulang, avoided possession, thus reinforcing the idea that women could be knowledgeable (and shy) or dramatic (and inarticulate), but not both knowledgeable and dramatic. Without gender-appropriate ways of bringing together dramatic self-presentation and claims to traditional

[119]

knowledge, women have difficulty breaking into the mainstream of male-dominated spiritual expression.

Induan Hiling's work succeeds by sidestepping performance requirements that advantage men; thus, even in its omissions, it exposes gender asymmetries in the conditions of spiritual expression. In this regard, we also see some of the advantages for her of the love song format over the chant. If she feels more comfortable calling her chants "love songs," it is perhaps because the performance requirements of the two forms differ significantly—rather than because she would not know how to put together a conventional chant. Whereas shamans must convene a formal ritual event to perform chants, love songs are sung while minding children, lying around the house resting, and socializing with friends. Although both forms use an improvisational style that responds to context and audience, as well as the intentions of the singer, the kinds of audience attention shamanic chants and love songs seek are different: love songs tease, flatter, soothe, and flirt, thus drawing attention to the subtle attractions of daily interaction; shamanic chants alternately amaze, wheedle, praise, pontificate, or startle, but all in an attempt to convene a spiritual community around the performance of the shaman. Induan Hiling's innovation has been to use informal daily contacts, the audience of love songs, as a community to support spiritual leadership. Since public ritual performance privileges male expressive leadership, she ingeniously avoids it.

Her pictures even more clearly bypass performance requirements: they do away with performance entirely in favor of the codification of spiritual knowledge and· authority. This codification has a number of significant features.

First, her drawings, unlike shaman's performances, are easily reproducible. Induan Hiling was happy to allow me to copy the drawings; in two cases, she requested my copy and gave me the original, because my copy was on cleaner paper and seemed likely to last longer.[11]

Second, her drawings work toward an impersonal visual authority, rather than the contextually grounded authority of shamanic dialog. Shamans may claim to chant time-honored traditional poetry that cannot be altered, but in fact, every performance changes with the purpose of the ceremony and the particular moods and motivations of both shaman and audience; the drawings, in contrast, cannot change their shape as they are called into different contexts of healing (although, of course, interpretations may change).

Finally, Induan Hiling's drawings claim the authority of script. "Writing" gives her message the permanence of an artifact and disengages it from performance politics and its time. Her indecipherable writing collapses time in other ways as well: it brings the power of mysterious origins to bear on the spiritual meanings of the present.

In all these aspects of codification, writing becomes a woman's project—through which male privilege can be countered, evaded, and exposed. In avoiding the shaman's task of drawing an audience through unpredictability and drama, the "writings" show these performance elements as gender-asymmetrical conditions of expression. Her writing encodes a form of resistance to male performance privilege.

Writing the Horse of Gaps

Induan Hiling's difficulty breaking into the male-dominated domain of ritual performance has encouraged her development of new forms of ritual—spiritual songs with the melodies of love songs and pictures and texts that invoke the authority of codification rather than performance. Her empowering spirit familiar, "the horse of gaps," is her ability to weave her creativity in and out of the empty spaces of male-dominated modes of expression.

The feminist literary analysis that alerts us to the significance of such empty spaces draws particularly from French feminists (e.g., Marks and Courtivron 1980). French feminist literary critics have argued that because writing (in Western culture) is a male project, female writing finds itself in the gaps and the margins rather than along the lines that codify male dominance. This work does not differentiate writing from other modes of expression; the argument is that all signification is male-dominated, and writing is merely the most powerful example. In contrast, my analysis of Induan Hiling's "writing" points to distinctions between modes of expression as each promotes gender-linked possibilities for creativity and empowerment within particular cultural contexts. She uses "writing" in the Meratus context to undercut male-biased performance requirements.

Her "writing," however, does not tempt me to construct a theory of an essential "female" expression—even one tailored for the Meratus context—like the pre-Oedipal *écriture feminine* of Cixous (1980). Instead, it points me away from an analysis limited to gender to attend to the ways that the gender-specific features of any cultural project

[121]

are determined within a particular class and ethnic situation. Indeed, Induan Hiling's dream writing draws from a source of authority that, though not extensively exploited by male Meratus shamans, is ultimately male-dominated. Her writing invokes the authority of the written word as used by the government officials and Muslim traders and settlers who increasingly draw the parameters of Meratus possibilities.

Here we can return to the disturbing "Made in China" on the margin of Figure 5.2. No one besides me in the Meratus Mountains could read that phrase; I imagine Induan Hiling copied it off of an item bought at market, perhaps a tin plate. Yet she knew it was foreign writing—the powerful foreign writing, in any language, with any message, that motivated her commitment to the codification of Meratus tradition. Her dream of textualization grew within the challenge of competing foreign scripts. Indeed, just as dramatic excesses in performance reveal something of the conditions of shamanic expression, Induan Hiling's own marginal notes reveal something of the conditions of representation for her own project.

The very unreadability of her own written text—and note that she *could* have formed letters—follows from its opposition to the foreign letters, also unreadable, but in a different sense. Meratus tell a story of a time when God handed out the Holy Books: the Meratus ancestor ate his; thus, he ensured both internal inspiration and its essentially unarticulated script. (Similarly, perhaps the undomesticated fertility of Induan Hiling's plant-form, ritual decorations reaffirms that Meratus tradition, while constrained, is yet, by other standards, wild.) Gender assumes a secondary role as the project is guided by Induan Hiling's status as a Meratus Dayak, challenging and challenged by powerful literate foreigners on every side. In Figure 5.6, their words even have a central position, generating the text that replaces performance.

Induan Hiling explained the word in Figure 5.6 ("Astarama") as the name she had been given in the dream that generated this picture. She pronounced the word as "Irama," and her teenage son cued me to Rhoma Irama. Haji Rhoma Irama was a popular music star in Indonesia at the time, and his posters were prominently displayed in homes and stores in the market towns surrounding the Meratus Mountains.[12] In invoking Rhoma Irama, Induan Hiling portrays herself as combining the inspiration of a shaman and a rock star. The charismatic image of Rhoma Irama helps explain her use of *love songs* as shamanic text. Moreover, Rhoma Irama's name alerts us to Induan Hiling's stakes in a new, "modern" cultural identity for Meratus Dayaks. She creates a Meratus spirituality that she hopes can match that of the more powerful national Indonesian culture.

In making claims for her dream-inspired writing as spiritual expression, Induan Hiling leans on the prestige of literate outsiders with Holy Books and written traditions. Why have Meratus men not been drawn to "literate" codification? A comparison to another ethnic situation seems suggestive.

The use of writing as an ethnic marker, and its links to gender division for the Tamang of Nepal, has been nicely described by Kathryn March (1983). For the Tamang, men and women have complementary and parallel ethnic "codifications": men write and women weave. Although the two media are opposed in metaphors that contrast male and female points of view, both women's weaving and men's writing express Tamang ethnic and religious solidarity and their distinctiveness from outsiders.

In contrast, Meratus male leaders in Induan Hiling's mountain area shy away from pressing the distinctiveness of Meratus ethnicity; they emphasize their similarities to, and thus connections with foreign power to augment their leadership positions within the local community. The performances of both shamans and political leaders reproduce models of outside authority as Meratus understand these models. Male leaders generally do not pose the Meratus community *against* outside models, because this would undercut their leadership skills. Thus, in this area there have been few male attempts to codify Meratus "difference."

Women, on the other hand, have fewer opportunities for contact and communication with the powerful outsiders, such as market traders, government bureaucrats, and army men, with whom the men forge ties. This has disadvantaged women in relation to community performance and leadership. Yet as ethnic tensions have increased with the loss of Meratus lands to neighboring Muslims and with the emerging threat of state resettlement to crowded border areas, a number of women have played key roles in reformulating Meratus ideas about culture, and particularly shamanism, to pose an alternative to powerful outside models of "civilization" and "religion." Induan Hiling's early mentor, Uma Adang, is one outstanding example; indeed, Uma Adang influenced Induan Hiling to turn her work in this direction. The last two verses of the song of Induan Hiling's that I have been discussing are a self-conscious attempt to copy Uma Adang's message about the importance of codified local custom and religion under an imagined state protection (Tsing 1987). This section of the song begins with the following lines:

> Adu hai, let's sing
> Swept by the wind, and
> Riding the horse of gaps, singing,
> Counting custom and tradition
> in 41 paragraphs.

Here Induan Hiling's "horse of gaps" takes her beyond male strategies to the formulation of a more codified and distinctive ethnic identity for Meratus. Her "writing" also makes its own modest contribution to this emerging discourse, where gender challenges and ethnic challenges meet.

Induan Hiling's work inserts itself within a tradition in which men predominate as star actors and speakers. In its need to revise, sidestep, and transform that tradition, her work exposes some of the tradition's dependence on male privilege. It provides a critical interpretation of shamanic tradition in two senses: it provides an innovative reading of convention, and its inversions, revisions, and even omissions create through their imaginative refusals of this convention. In retreating from ordinary Meratus standards of performance and leadership, Induan Hiling challenges these standards and contributes to an emerging Meratus conversation on gender, creativity, and power.

Appendix: One of Induan Hiling's Songs

All song fragments discussed in the essay are from this song. My commentary appears in the right-hand column.

Adu hai,   *Clearheaded in spiritual*
Riding the horse of gaps.   *flight,*
Swept by the wind,
Riding the horse of gaps, friend.

Finished in a day—   *the shaman forges*
Forging spurs, babe,   *a spiritual route*
Finished in a day.
The horse of distances.

[124]

What shall be used, babe?
Forging spurs
Finished in a day.

Used to circle and contain, babe—   *and a message*
That striped cup   *that protects*
the gilded one, babe   *and contains*
That striped cup   *the community.*
The cup that is composed
to circle and contain.

Swept by the wind . . .

The child of a cobra, babe   *Going farther*
soaring to the sun.   *in flight,*
If it has scales   *the route is*
They cross across each other.   *mapped out*
The scales they point, babe,   *before and*
Where do they point, friend?   *behind.*
They point to its tail,
They point to its head,
Those scales, babe.

Let's plant bamboo.   *A spiritual path*
I'll plant some.   *is laid out*
A clump of bamboo,   *as bamboo grows:*
A stick of bamboo,
It may have hollow stems,
It may have nodes,
It may have a growing bud.

Those stems, babe,   *some paths go*
Isn't it so?   *farther than*
Half of them are tall,   *others.*
Half of them are small,
Half of them are high,
The growing buds, babe.

Adu, it's we ourselves,   *But all are*
Our own mountain, babe.   *ultimately*
The mountain called Jungku   *based on*
With two shoulders,   *knowledge of*
Hanging there   *the self,*
Swinging where
On our own mountain.

[125]

Anna Lowenhaupt Tsing

On the summit of the mountain   *as hair grows*
There's a wild fig tree,   *from our heads.*
A hanging fig tree,
A swaying fig tree,
Hanging where
Swaying there
Our wild fig tree.

Where does it sway?
Where does it hang?
Yes, it's you and I, babe.

There is a planting:
A cut bamboo.
A bamboo that plays the flute
A bamboo that sings.
We cut it off
Touching the shoulders,
The scissored bamboo
Touching the waist.
Babe, the scissored bamboo,
The cut bamboo,
Where is it planted?
Where does it hang?

Adu hai, let's sing,   *The songs*
Swept by the wind, and   *of shamans*
Riding the horse of gaps, singing,   *recount*
Counting custom and tradition   *local custom,*
in 41 paragraphs.   *as protected*
The constitution of custom   *by the state,*
The law of tradition
The prohibitions of the Basic
   Constitution.
We'll stand on the center of the five
   National Principles
To face our music in the world.

Adu hai,   *and by the*
At the moment   *legitimacy of origins.*
When God stood up,   *For as law and custom*
And first took care of custom: *were created*
The constitution of custom   *by God,*
The constitution of law.   *so too,*
At the moment   *human breath*
When God the One   *("divided into two"*

[126]

(I mean, not that God,
not that God—)
Stood up in the wind
It was divided into two
It was named
—Even water was not yet named,
Water was still one—
Du dat
Jat sat
Dat jur
Dat say
dat
Sut tup.

by the nostrils)
and consciousness
(that "named")
were forged
within the
ultimately
indecipherable
mystery of
original
knowledge.

Notes

1. The following review articles were particularly useful in introducing me to the nuances of 1980s work in feminist literary criticism: Sternhell 1982; Crosby 1984; Kolodny 1980. Another useful introduction to feminist criticism is Moi 1985, which only became available to me after this essay was essentially completed. Moi's analysis separates Anglo-American and French tendencies in feminist literary theory and criticizes Anglo-Americans particularly for their author-centered humanistic vision in which women's writing automatically reflects the "female" experiences of the author. My essay replicates some of these Anglo-American assumptions, but I would argue that they have at least some usefulness for contemporary cultural anthropology. The "texts" of cultures rather than their authors have been the objects of anthropological analysis. The male-centered unity of anthropological texts can be disrupted by a focus on "authors" that allows us to look at how the heterogeneous interests of ordinary people influence the continuing formation of "culture."

2. The Meratus have also been called "Bukit," but they consider this a derogatory term. "Dayak" refers to the non-Muslim indigenous people of Borneo.

3. The importance of Meratus performance standards in privileging men as political actors is discussed in Tsing 1990, which can be read as a companion piece to this essay.

4. Uma Adang's movement is discussed in detail in Tsing 1987. She "adopted" both Induan Hiling and myself, as well as numerous other fans, as siblings.

5. Conventions differ among the various shamanic styles associated with different Meratus regions. In Induan Hiling's area, women played the part of pinjulang in the most popular styles; in other styles, men tended to be pinjulang (also known as *patati*) as well as shamans.

6. Although in some Meratus shamanic styles women play the drums, in Induan Hiling's local area only men are drummers.

7. The women had divergent positions: some seemed more comfortable with the illness attribution than others. Two were young; in refusing to speak about their experience, they brought their behavior in line with that of children, who, according to local belief, are not uncommonly kidnapped by *dewa* spirits but remain mute about

their spiritual encounter after their return. Several were close kin of *dewa* shamans, and their possession behavior—whether they called it illness or inspiration—seemed closely related to their other attempts to further these men's careers within the community. But a few of the most articulate women told me with considerable self-assurance that they, like shamans, were receiving spiritual teachings.

8. Central mountain Meratus live in dispersed households and small social clusters, which affiliate to form "neighborhoods" of five to thirty families. Neighborhoods are political and religious communities; however, individual families and social clusters have considerable autonomy and are always free to join a different neighborhood or keep their affairs to themselves. Meratus community dynamics are discussed in Tsing 1984.

9. Among the Ma'anyan Dayaks of Padju Epat in Central Kalimantan, female shamans conventionally use rattling anklets (Alfred Hudson, personal communication). I do not know if Induan Hiling was aware of the Ma'anyan tradition.

10. A number of pieces of the ritual decorations for a shamanic festival are painted with plantlike designs. Decorated boards used in ritual stands are called *papan tulis* ("writing boards"). Induan Hiling draws upon this identification of decoration and writing in this drawing. Such an identification of decorated boards with "writing" is also found in the ritual practice of Central Kalimantan Ma'anyan (Hudson 1966). In other parts of Borneo, "writing boards" of rather different sorts are used to remind shamans of the stages of their chants (Harrison 1965). One source of Induan Hiling's ideas about writing is probably these common connections among decoration, "writing," and shamanic knowledge. Other sources involve her interpretation of the power of Arabic and Western scripts.

11. The issue of reproducibility is also relevant to love songs: love songs can be copied more easily than shamanic chants, for they are not so shrouded in secrecy and pass easily from one singer to another. Furthermore, Induan Hiling was aware of the mechanical reproducibility of recorded pop music, to which Meratus love songs are sometimes compared. (A number of young men have tape recorders on which they play tapes of the popular love songs called *orkes malayu*.) The last section of my essay suggests how Induan Hiling mixed her identification with local shamans with an emulation of national pop music heros.

12. Rhoma Irama himself is a master of combining genres and transforming symbols. One of his current posters showed him as a pious pilgrim in Arab dress, before an Islamic prayer rug, with a woman kneeling at his feet and his electric guitar in his hand. Another showed him with a bloody headrag—and his guitar—manning revolutionary barricades.

REFERENCES

Ardener, Edwin, 1975. "Belief and the Problem of Women." In Shirley Ardener, ed., *Perceiving Women*. New York: Wiley. Pp. 1–17.
Bell, Diane. 1983. *Daughters of the Dreaming*. North Sydney: Allen and Unwin.
Bernikow, Louise. 1974. *The World Split Open: Four Centuries of Women Poets in England and America, 1552–1950*. New York: Vintage.
Bruner, Edward, and Phyllis Gorfain. 1984. "Dialogic Narration and the Paradoxes of Masada." In Edward Bruner, ed., *Text, Play, and Story: The Construction*

and Reconstruction of Self and Society. 1983 Proceedings of the American Ethnological Society. Washington, D.C. Pp. 56–79.

Cixous, Hélène. 1980. "The Laugh of the Medusa." In Elaine Marks and Isabelle de Courtivron, eds., *New French Feminisms.* Amherst: University of Massachusetts Press. Pp. 245–64.

Crosby, Elizabeth. 1984. "Stranger than Truth: Feminist Literary Criticism and Speculations on Women." *Dalhousie Review* 64, 2: 247–59.

Freeman, J. Derek. 1968. "Thunder, Blood, and the Nicknaming of God's Creatures." *The Psychoanalytic Quarterly* 37, 3: 353–99.

Gilbert, Sandra, and Susan Gubar. 1979. *The Madwoman in the Attic.* New Haven: Yale University Press.

Gluckman, Max. 1963. "Rituals of Rebellion in South-East Africa." In M. Gluckman, *Order and Rebellion in Tribal Africa.* London: Cohen and West. Pp. 110–36.

Harrison, Tom. 1965. "Borneo Writing." *Bijdragen tot de taal-, land-, en volkenkunde* 121, 1: 1–57.

Herdt, Gilbert. 1981. *Guardians of the Flutes.* New York: McGraw-Hill.

Hudson, Alfred. 1966. "Death Ceremonies of the Padju Epat Ma'anyan Dayaks." In Tom Harrison, ed., *Borneo Writing and Related Matters.* Sarawak Museum Journal, Special Monograph no. 1, 13 (27). Pp. 341–416.

Kamuf, Peggy. 1982. *Fictions of Feminine Desire.* Lincoln: University of Nebraska Press.

Kapferer, Bruce. 1983. *A Celebration of Demons.* Bloomington: Indiana University Press.

Kessler, Clive. 1977. "Conflict and Sovereignity in Kelantanese Malay Spirit Sceances," In Vincent Crapanzano and Vivian Garrison, eds., *Case Studies in Spirit Possession.* New York: Wiley. Pp. 295–331.

Kolodny, Annette. 1980. "Dancing through the Minefield: Some Observations on the Theory and Politics of a Feminist Literary Criticism." *Feminist Studies* 6, 1: 1–25.

Lewis, I. M. 1971. *Ecstatic Religion.* Harmondsworth, England: Penguin.

March, Kathryn. 1983. "Weaving, Writing, and Gender." *Man* n.s. 18, 4: 729–44.

Marks, Elaine, and Isabelle de Courtivron, eds. 1980. *New French Feminisms: An Anthology.* Amherst: University of Massachusetts Press.

Moers, Ellen. 1976. *Literary Women.* Garden City, N.Y.: Doubleday.

Moi, Toril. 1985. *Sexual/Textual Politics: Feminist Literary Theory.* London: Methuen.

Showalter, Elaine. 1977. *A Literature of Their Own.* Princeton: Princeton University Press.

Sternhell, Carol. 1982. "A Whole New Poetics Beginning Here: Theories of Feminist Literary Criticism." Ph.D. diss., Stanford University.

Tsing, Anna. 1984. "Politics and Culture in the Meratus Mountains." Ph.D. diss., Stanford University.

———. 1987. "A Rhetoric of Centers in a Religion of the Periphery." In Rita Kipp and Susan Rodgers, eds., *Indonesian Religions in Transition.* Tucson: University of Arizona Press. Pp. 187–210.

——. 1990. "Gender and Performance in Meratus Dispute Settlement." In Jane Atkinson and Shelly Errington, eds., *Power and Difference: Gender in Island Southeast Asia.* Stanford. Stanford: University Press. Pp. 95–125.

Weiner, Annette. 1976. *Women of Value, Men of Renown.* Austin: University of Texas Press.

PART II

The Creation of Ethnography from Experience

[6]

The Absence of Others, the Presence of Texts

Don Handelman

In Memory of Henry Moses Rupert (c. 1885–1973)

A few years ago a friend passed on to me photocopies of a small corpus of fieldnotes on Washo shamanism that were collected during the early 1920s by Grace Dangberg.[1] Grace Dangberg, a pioneer of Washo ethnology, will be remembered for her published translations of Washo myths and tales. Of special interest to me were the notes that described the beliefs and attitudes of a man with whom I had spoken at some length during the summer of 1964. Henry Moses Rupert was a gifted person, a healer, and a fine teacher of the solvents of reality. Tucked among Dangberg's fieldnotes were two unpublished fragments that read very much like separate beginnings of accounts of her experiences of Henry Rupert. Both postdated 1967, the year in which I had first published a biographical article about him.

These fragments, one in particular, led me to think off and on about three varieties of the absence of the Other and their influences on ethnography and writing. The first of these absences is that of the voice of the native Other in ethnographic texts. Much discussed today, it is of some relevance to why the second variety of absence became important to me in relation to Henry Rupert. This second is the native at home, with his or her memories of absent anthropologists, who themselves are absent from their own texts that are based (or based in part) on information the native supplied. The ethnographer absent from his or her own text refers to objectivist modes of reporting. The third variety of absence is that of our own voices (our oral or informally written professional discourses) from one another's texts. This is so commonplace and common-sensical that it is quite ignored. Yet, this third variety of absence should push us to question our own cultural assumptions about the discipline of anthropology, not so much as an intellectual and aesthetic endeavor, but as an enterprise of individual careers that are identified with the ownership of the authorship of knowledge. This necessarily is a hierarchical pattern that obviates any significant place for dialogue within the text and is exemplified in the very logic of construction, of the packaging, of the ethnographic text.

The first variety of absence has pride of place today in discussions on the construction of ethnography. It has made more explicit, and rendered problematic, the status, the authority, and the authenticity of the native as Other, the object as subject, and the space that is made in texts for his or her voice, for the other's authorship of self, in counterpoint to ours of him or her. The absence of the native Other is redressed in degree through constructions that are called interpretive (Little 1980), dialogical (Tedlock 1979; Dwyer 1982), and polyphonic (Clifford 1983).

The second variety of absence is buried in particular contexts of field experience, and it rarely surfaces within ethnographic texts (but cf. Pandey 1972). This variety relates to the native as interpreter of ethnographers and as mediator of their imaginary discourse. It seems to be restricted to situations in which the native becomes the authoritative reporter on the contacts with ethnographers who had spoken with him or her in the past, for an ethnographer who is present but who cannot find the voices of these others in their own texts. The native and the ethnographer are then in a dialogue that is somewhat akin to discussions about a native Other who is absent. But here the Other at issue is the ethnographer, absent from his or her own text.

The third variety of absence is a shadowy complement of the first, although its absent Other seems much closer to home than the one who dwells and thinks elsewhere. The absence of this Other is cloaked by the treatment of him or her as "another," one more like you and me, one of the same kind. This sort of absence is structured rigidly by the logical strictures of book, monograph, and article. It is hedged in by conventions of writing, by mutual respect (and at times by fear), and by the very idea of "career" that many of us hold and that includes the "copyrights" to knowledge upon which the personal enterprise depends.

Though the voice of this third absent Other is muted and circumscribed in ethnographic writing, it influences no less than the native Other the ways in which the text is put together. I am referring, of course, to how we affect one another's writings, to how we do not insert one another's voices into the texts we construct, and to the structure of conventions of the "ownership" of knowledge that virtually demands our absence from one another's works. Certainly, we are active voices to one another, often in dialogue: yet, the narrow spaces we make for one another, indeed that we are permitted to make, bear a strong resemblance to those made for the natives in classical ethnography. Our capacities for usufruct speedily threaten the rights of others to the ownership of knowledge, and may quickly deteriorate into dark cries about stolen "ideas" and murmured mutterings about plagiarism, not to mention claims made to informants, ethnic groupings, whole communities, and even, in my experience, to entire cities with tens of thousands of inhabitants. So here the Other at issue is the ethnographer who is absent from the texts of others, who themselves are dominated by the privatized career and by the hierarchical logic of the structuring of the scholarly text.

Hermeneutic, dialogic, and polyphonic approaches to ethnographic construction broaden and deepen our uncertainty about, and thus our empathy with, that Other who lives out there, on our horizons. We still like to see ourselves standing alone, nearing that Other on the frontiers of comprehension, between worlds. Or so it seems. For this romantic image, as it appears explicitly or implicitly in innumerable ethnographies, effectively blocks from view the substrata of hinterland and home. Our conceit in deconstructing the myth of classical ethnographic authority (in James Clifford's phrasing) has enabled us to hold to the fiction that our relationships with one another are less relevant to how texts are constructed, and to the hegemonies over knowledge and expertise that such texts proclaim. There are excellent institutional and instrumental reasons for this state of affairs, but this does not make it any less so. If we cannot radically inlay the voices of other ethnographers in our own texts, and I question the likelihood of this, then I doubt the success of doing the same for the voice of the native Other.[2] For, structurally, each is a logical extension of the other. Therefore, their estrangement, which we continue to foster,

[135]

enables us to hide from ourselves the relevance of those premises about the ownership of the text upon which our careers, in large measure, depend.

Let me begin with how I came to recognize that there was an Other out there, with my trained naiveté, and with how Mr. Rupert and I came to talk to each other.

Who's Out There? The Voice of the Other

Before I met him, Henry Rupert had had contacts with (to my knowledge) six other ethnographers. To some he confided in detail about his beliefs and powers. Others he kept more at arm's length. Before approaching Mr. Rupert I was told that, for a period, he had made himself unavailable to ethnographers. Why was not clear. But, I was informed, he might be having a change of mind. Through the generosity of his eldest son and his daughter-in-law I was able to live close by, to try to engage him on what I had defined as the topic of healing.

I came to that place in the desert of Nevada with two significant typifications, "shaman" and "culture," which were part of assorted baggage acquired as a student.[3] "The shaman," I understood from my readings and from discussions with peers and professors, was a cultural role or persona whose incumbents did society's work of healing illness, fending off witches, and reducing anxiety, individual and collective, in certain kinds of cultures. This cultural role, I had learned, was one of many that an individual played, switching back-and-forth according to the dictates of value, norm, and situation. So Rupert, I thought, would be sometimes a shaman, and at other times would put this role aside in order to perform those other roles of his repertoire. I also thought that the objective typification, of SHAMAN, was what his information would signify. Once his information had filled this slot, the typification then would signify him, the person, made over in its image. These roles were part of tradition, and tradition part of CULTURE, in this instance Washo culture. Therefore, one step further along, the typification would signify something about Washo culture that, in turn, would signify a place within itself for the typification of WASHO SHA-MAN. In my text-to-come the typifications, my constructions and those of my discipline, would have pride of place. Rupert was a means to these ends.

[136]

We met almost daily, usually in the afternoon, seated on rickety chairs under a tree, shaded from the sun's blaze. From him I collected word lists, trait lists, information on aboriginal seasonal rounds, on myth and game, on hunting and fishing, and so forth. Now and then I would ask about power, healing, spirits, dreams, and the character of the afterlife. Aside from some information that he insisted was held by many Washo (as it was), he denied any special knowledge or ability. "I'm just a common man," he would reiterate, pursing his lips, "I don't know anything about these things." These intermittent interchanges continued for days.

One evening he stopped by my tent and asked whether I ever had let my imagination run loose. Tense with anticipation, I replied that I had. He told of the time, when a young man, he had gone fishing in a creek in the hills. He started for home just before sundown. Walking along the trail in the dim light of the forest he saw something white by a clump of trees, blocking his route. It moved. He stood still. It stood still. He moved, and it moved. He stopped. It stopped. He was terrified. Perhaps it was an animal waiting to pounce . . . or something else. He yelled loudly, and tears poured down his face. He broke out in a very heavy sweat. No one heard his cries of fear. Tentatively, he moved once more . . . and so did that white thing down the trail. After some time he screwed up his courage and dashed toward it. And . . . (I was so eager to hear) . . . and, it was an old undershirt, flapping fitfully in the uncertain breeze. Still, he added, he did wonder at the coincidence of motion and stillness, his and that of the undershirt. Dry chuckles popped from his lips; and, disappointed at what I had hoped would be a breakthrough, I joined in rather weakly.

During these days I met the first of those absent ethnographers. Henry said he was unhappy with the accuracy of some of the materials published about him in an article. I offered to correct these errors. He did not respond. Later I was given to understand, very indirectly, that this was why he had reported his own demise to interested ethnographers; this had been duly recorded in a footnote to a scholarly publication.[4] Yet I had been informed that he was on the verge of making himself available once more. Why this was so puzzled me greatly; but as yet I had not had any substantive hint that this information was accurate.

After some two weeks of these frequent talks, I gave up. I thought of our conversations as cat-and-mouse routines, and I had come not to doubt which of these was my part. I no longer had any expectations of learning from him anything about shamanism or healing. Mulling over the possibilities, I poked around in my rucksack of student-acquired knowledge. Over there, in the corner, under kinship terminology and resting on national character, there was a useful typification: the LIFE HISTORY. Yes, I told myself, I would try to get a life history from Mr. Rupert, that old so-and-so. At least there would be something down on paper about him.

The following day I broached this, and explained what I thought a life history entailed. He would tell me about his childhood, his kin, the jobs he had held, the places he had been, the people he had known, his children. From this we would get a sense of how his life was interwoven with that of his people, and with the recent history of the area. There was no mention of healing nor of power.

During the time I knew him, I saw him agitated twice. This was the first. He exclaimed again that he was just a common man; there was nothing special about him. I retorted that he was special, but did not elaborate. He gave me the Washo term for "healer," which indeed was common knowledge, and added that he had tried "that stuff" a few times, mainly through the use of massage. He gave an example that ended with the statement: "That's suggestion; that's mind power."[5] But, he reiterated, he knew nothing more than these simple things.

We drifted into an unusually lengthy silence. It was a hot and quiet afternoon, dusty with the whiff of a breeze. Looking at him I saw a wizened, still, small, and impassive man. His strong hands rested motionless on his jean-clad thighs, his work boots planted firmly in the dirt. There was no encouragement on that countenance. He had told me that once his mind was made up he never changed it. As time passed, I sensed we were in a sort of null zone of uncertainty and decision, and asked myself whether we ever would get down to the hard facts of the life history. At one point he looked into my face and quietly said, "Stop dreaming."[6] Once more he sank into silence. After many minutes, perhaps twenty or twenty-five, he spoke without any preamble: "My life has always been concerned with psychology. I was never a happy-go-lucky man like other Indians. I was always something of a recluse. I always tried to follow the laws of nature. . . ."

I was astounded. This moment was the severest shock I have experienced as an anthropologist, until then and since. I was jolted out of my academic typifications, out of the conceit that I had any entitlement to a privileged vantage point on the lives of others, out of the idea that I had any authoritative imprimatur on the creation of knowledge, out of the Other as object.

In retrospect, I thought that I understood what had happened, although we never spoke of this.[7] In my perception of reality I had replaced the ethnographic category of shamanism with that of life history, believing that in doing so I would leave the former behind, in my reality and in his. In other words, I had been thinking that these textual typifications bore a simple relationship of correspondence to the lived-in and lived-through reality of that Other, out there. Of course, I had done quite the contrary, for I had not understood that in the perceptions, the beliefs and feelings, of this man there was no sphere of living, of being a sentient human being, that was divorced from what he was in essence—a man of power. This was his "culture" (a term I found to have less and less utility). In a roundabout way I inadvertently had forced the issue, but the decision was his.

And into what was I jolted? Into simple yet profound intuitions: that whatever I would say and do would affect his response, and vice-versa; that I could reach out to him only on his own terms, and, therefore, always would be, in a sense, on personal trial (or "walking on eggshells," as I put it then); that I had few rights and many obligations, of which I still was ignorant (and remained so, in large measure, to my cost); that, for the duration of that summer, my own sense of self would become dependent on that Other for sustenance, and, therefore, that he controlled me as none of my academic instructors ever had or would.[8]

This dependency was one reason why I so sorely missed the presence, in their own texts, of those other ethnographers who had talked with him in the past. I needed the perspectives of others like me, with some of my interests, to help me to learn, even if only by contrast, something more of whom I was talking to—how they had felt toward him, whether they had succumbed to the problems they had encountered. But the spirit of such concerns was absent from their writings. The other reason I felt their absence from their own texts was that, from time to time, he made them present; and then I realized acutely my ignorance of what their past presence there had signified.

Kilroy Was Here: The Absent Ethnographer

Henry's concern for detail was acute: in responding, describing, reminiscing, philosophizing. The very act of following correct procedures in living and in healing was pervaded with significance and power. Therefore, utterances about various activities had to be accurate. These were not, for him, representations of what he thought and did—the act of talking of them was akin to thinking of them, and so of carrying them through, in a sense, of bringing them into being. Especially, talking of his healing was of danger to him, or to his abilities, and he made this clear at the outset. He had a passion for secrecy in knowledge, knowledge in secrecy; yet, he said that he could teach all he knew to someone else in a brief period—if that person were the right one. But, he added, "People are not supposed to ask me questions about my work. One guy came to see me for help and asked me all kinds of questions—he put me backwards in my work." He remarked on another occasion, "What puts me backwards in my work is someone comes to me for help and asks me a lot of questions about what I can do." And about another inquisitive character, he said "He asked me questions like you are doing, and I told him, 'That which is and that which isn't.' He never understood that."

Ethnographers asked him questions about the paranatural, about healing, and he puzzled us with wit and irony that shut topics of discourse just as they opened. Or such was my experience. These qualities of interaction are brought out, for example, in the following brief couplets of talk from my first meetings with him.

> D.H.: I've heard that there are Washo who can control the weather [which he was reported to do]. Did you ever come across anything like that?
> H.R.: If there was, wouldn't it be raining now?

> D.H.: Your friend Ike Steel told me there were Washo, hunters, who could control animals, put them to sleep. Did you ever hear about such Washo?
> H.R.: Fool thing! If they could, would they go hungry most of the year?

> D.H.: I've been told here that the Spirit World is just like this one.
> H.R.: (chuckling): Well, if that's so it must be getting pretty crowded there now.

"He asked me questions like you are doing," said Henry. Over the weeks I learned that this seemed to be the primary role that absent ethnographers played in our conversations. He inserted them contextually, and they became his mouthpieces, responding to my queries. He appeared to introduce them—characters who together with me belonged to the same category—to let me see how I looked to him. They were hardly constant companions, for their appearances were intermittent. But they were present, sudden visitations of whom I knew next to nothing, whom I could not grasp to make sense of him, for they had concealed themselves in their texts and so they belonged wholly to him. One appeared, for example, in the midst of a knotty metaphysical tangle that had me confused and skeptical. Henry told of explaining a similar point decades before to an ethnographer. That person had retorted, perhaps offhandedly, perhaps as a challenge to further exegesis, with an abrupt, "I don't believe you." Henry did not conceal from me how much this remark had rankled; and I was warned, via this absent Other, about my attitude.[9]

For Henry Rupert knowledge was experience. When I pushed him to speculate on matters he had not known firsthand, an absent ethnographer might enter the shady space where we talked. So, for example, on the subject of peyote: Henry was a vehement anti-peyotist who insisted that the substance poisoned mind and body, and who cited the experiences of a sister to that effect. When I pressed him further, he responded: "I don't know what peyote is or what its like. That fella from Berkeley asked me about it. I told him I had no opinion. He said I must have some opinion. I asked him how could I have an opinion if I never tried it. After I told him all this stuff, he said it was all just psychology. That's what he said, but after fifty years I haven't figured it all out yet." He followed these remarks with a favorite aphorism of one of his spirit-helpers: "What pertaineth unto one, another knoweth not."

I particularly wanted to watch him heal, and asked about this. Another ethnographer appeared. Henry commented that about a decade before he had allowed an anthropologist to observe a session of healing. The treatment had no effect, for the condition of the patient remained the same. Worse still, Henry could not "see": he did not experience the visions of diagnosis and prognosis upon which his techniques of healing had depended at that time. Since then, he added, no uninvolved or casual observers were permitted; and he quoted an injunction of a spirit helper: "If people just come to you for curiosity, to see how you work, your powers won't work."

When an ethnographer did insert himself into his own text, I suddenly and startlingly saw how Henry Rupert appeared to someone else. I had another perspective, points of overlap and argument, and someone with whom to compare my own perceptions—a sense, however brief, of another who momentarily put off center the hegemony of the native presence. One man did this, and although our points of view differed radically, I was grateful for his presence. He wrote:

> This man, Henry Rupert . . . when questioned about the old days, was a fair informant, seldom offering more information than was asked for and clearly enjoying the business of making a white man work for every scrap of information. He was also given to dropping subtle hints and waiting with stolid indifference to see if I had been alert. He did not deny his shamanistic practices but was less than willing to discuss them in detail. "I don't really do nothing but help nature," he said. When I replied that only some people know how to help nature he was gratified and smiled. "Oh well, it all psychological anyway," he answered, confirming Lowie's description of him as a sophisticate. (Downs 1961: 369)

Where Henry Rupert dwelled I stumbled over memories of other ethnographers when I least expected their presence. It was not simply that they were there before me, and that they had affected or altered the "field" in some way. For they had become embedded in his province of meaning; and I believe that they, or we as a category, may have come to have some particular significance for him. But what I wish to stress here is that of these others, of their contacts with him, I had to learn from Henry Rupert in bits and pieces. To invert a conventional version of discourse among ethnographers, these people were his construction: he embued them with a certain significance, and he mediated any potential or imaginary discourse I might have with them. Just as he edited information about himself (and the evidence of this is clear), so he edited those others into and out of our conversations.

Their absence from their own texts, as engaged persons in relation to him as a person, gave him the uncontested power to dominate their presence in a context (that of fieldwork) that influenced any text I might produce, and that magnified my dependency on him. Therefore, he was the pivot of any discourse about himself, and they in large measure were his creations. And the more they absented themselves from their texts, the more this was so. I believe that this irony was not lost on him. His comments on the multiplicity, and at times, the duplicity, of reality referred specifically to his own perceptions and beliefs ("What I know is real for me, but it's not real for anybody else"; "You don't know what I am talking about, and the same is for anybody

[142]

who reads this thing you write"). But intersubjectivity, he seemed to be saying, is limited by the visions of those who are joined through it.

Their absence, and later my own, from the texts that were produced, the stance of an objectivist ethnography, made of him an object of attention, a member of various typifications ("Washo," "shaman," "remembrancer of the Old Days," and so forth), that invited an absence of comprehension of who and what he was. The ethnographer's interest was what he or she could tell about what Henry Rupert represented as a bearer of our construction of "culture." Henry's performance of self was of little interest, for this was reduced to a signifier of "culture," and then was subsumed in reifications of "culture," and signified in turn by these. So it is not surprising that these texts either missed, excluded, or downgraded that which I came to see as outstanding in him—that he was a most creative individual, one who radically changed his own epistemology of belief in ways that had practical and substantive effects on his healing (Handelman 1967a, 1967b).[10]

I came away from that relationship with an ingenuous question that was absent from all of our texts. Why, after all, did he talk to any of us? There were some hints. But with the years and the aid of seminars and publications, I turned him back into an object of inquiry, and so I did not see perhaps one of the most apparent of interpretations. Not until, that is, I came across that fragment of Grace Dangberg's writing to which I have alluded. This reads in part as follows:[11]

Across the table from me sat the man who had acted as interpreter for me over a period of several months during which we had reached a rapport that gave promise of making me the confidant of a Washoe Indian medicine man or shaman. In the months when I had done fieldwork with this tribe I never even hoped that there might come a time when I . . . would be privileged to hear one who was a practicing medicine man tell of his intimate experiences in the world of religion and magic. Henry's eyes were very bright. They were fastened on me with quiet intensity and amused tolerance. He was willing to talk and as I review this day in my memory I feel that like Kim's holy man he was seeking a disciple. His experiences were not the private property of a magician—they were manifestations of power—a power that pervades the universe. He wanted others to share these impressive mysteries with him—to understand them—to speak of them to all men.

This was in the early 1920s. I kept my notes speculating what I might do with them one day when Henry could not be hurt by my giving an account of what he had confided in me. In this attitude, I am sure I erred. Henry wanted me to "tell the news" as it were and here in my narrow understanding of the significance of his revelation I failed him. Of this I became aware when a young student published a paper on the last of the Washoe medecine men or shamans. This was Henry whose full name is Henry Moses Rupert.

Today I believe that Grace Dangberg's intuition was correct. He was looking for a successor. Conversing with him in 1964, enchanted perhaps by my dependency, perhaps by what I felt was his essence, I had had similar feelings. Little by little these had eroded and become less poignant, as I wrote of him and made of him a character who served my purpose. Bound by injunctions of humility and secrecy, he had to proceed with care and with caution in checking possible can-didates against the personal and ethical guidelines that his spirit help-ers had stipulated for the passing on of his knowledge (Handelman 1972). Ethnographers were not excluded as candidates. No person was. The practice of his own theory of healing was universal. Ironically, ethnographers may have been among those persons who showed the most consistent interest in learning of his thoughts and doings. Given the social conditions that prevailed there, at least until the later 1960s, this may well have been the case.

Today I like to think of him, reclusive and self-contained, patiently waiting at the edge of the desert for the right person, checking us off one by one as we intermittently passed through, intent on our own doings—an image of humor and irony. For he and we may well have had goals that overlapped: yet, by making of him the sort of typification to which I have alluded, we subverted the further acquisition of knowl-edge that was, after all, the point of our efforts. It will not surprise those of you who have read my previous accounts of Henry that he found a solution to the passing on of certain of his talents before he died—one that was as unorthodox as the life he lived.

Who's in Here? Our Absence from One Another's Texts

I first wrote parts of this section with tongue in cheek, as a parody of those of us who are infatuated with the reflexive genre of anthropolog-ical writing—sometimes to the point of making the individual ethnog-rapher the rationale for ethnography, while reducing natives to props for self-preoccupation, and social order to an extension of the ethnographer's psyche. Ethnography as cosmic creation or navel-gazing? Perhaps some gentle joshing . . . but this became irrelevant when readers took these arguments seriously. On second look, so do I.

The struggle over the voice of the native Other is in part one over the (often dialogical) contributions that these others have made to the construction of the text. But what of our own contributions to the textual constructions of one another? Surely we have similar obligations to these Others as we have to the native? All of us converse with, listen to, and read others of our kind. There is no doubt that we influence one another's thinking and writing. Few ideas, or their denial, spring pristine from our minds to the written page; and I would subject to the most minute scrutiny those who claim otherwise. If our concern is with influences on textual construction, then we should render an accounting of all Others who are imprisoned in the text, and the degrees of freedom permitted them. For they are all representations, and misrepresentations, of active voices, of authorships that are stilled and pacified by the formal logics of textual construction. However, to pursue the logic of the voice of the Other in our texts is quickly to breach and to expose the systematic constraints and occupational fictions that underwrite and sustain our endeavors, and, therefore, that need to be blocked from view in scholarly debate.

It is an error of our epistemology to continue to evaluate the making of a place for the voice of the Other in ethnographic texts as a problem primarily of reflexivity, aesthetics, science, or ethics. The problem of the voice of the Other is conditioned by more elementary cultural ideas of "career" and of proprietary rights to knowledge and expertise.[12] These ideas (and others that relate to academic production) are problems of the means of cultural production that underlie and inform the continuum of Other voices, from the native's to other ethnographers'. Should the voice of the Other seem more immanent in the ethnographer-native relationship than in that between ethnographers,[13] then this is a product of our conventions of presentation and not of the dialogic of interchange. The radical opening up of the text to the voice of the native Other has addressed the simpler end of the continuum, one that does not depend for its very coherence on institutional infrastructures, from universities to publishing companies.

The "career" of the ethnographer is necessarily an individualist construct. Whatever the factors that go into its making, the career is thought of as owned by the individual ethnographer. It represents to others what he or she is in a professional and occupational sense;

therefore, it is a reflection and an index of his or her ideas, stature, and recognition. "Discourses," writes Foucault (1979: 148), "are objects of appropriation." The cooptation of discourse is one of the signal assets of the career of the ethnographer and is often a source of knowledge, of expertise, and of the production of texts under his or her name. In turn, these texts are thought to reflect the ethnographer's knowledge and expertise. One of the major sources of knowledge and expertise is the mind and action of the Other—access is gained through the informants, subjects, confidants, with whom one talks and at whom one looks. The products of these discourses are the commodities of the ethnographer's career; in varying degrees, he or she claims proprietary rights over them for professional purposes. Informally the ethnographer may lay claim as well to the sources of such discourse. Without these commodities, identified with his or her name, the ethnographer would be largely anonymous, and so unable to pursue a career.[14]

To ask us to cease treating native voices in the texts as commodities would require adjustments in the work, mainly, of the individual ethnographer. But to pursue this logic of Other voices in the text, to ask that we stop treating one another as commodities would demand far-reaching changes in our discipline, and in the institutions whose resources and decisions shape our professional lives. These institutions often control the signifiers of our accomplishments, of publication and promotion, for example. They demand our professional individuation, our formal separation from one another, in order to make these accomplishments significant. Therefore, the voices in the text, ours and others, must be ordered hierarchically to leave little doubt as to whose creation this is.

To continue to divide relationships in the "field" from those at "home" is to encourage the survival of the false dichotomy between the aesthetics of text construction, on the one hand, and the political economy of careers on the other. And the decolonization of the voice of the native Other will proceed apace at the expense of our continued colonization of one another's voices.

Let me take this argument one step further by looking at the simple organization and packaging of the scholarly book or monograph. The emphasis on hierarchy in its structuring accords well with ideas of the proprietorship or copyright of knowledge, and of our subordination of one another's voices. The monograph—a signal accomplishment of the career—reflects and extends the domination of the individual ethnographer, perhaps even while proclaiming the need for the dialogic.

The structuring of the book (Barry Schwartz's *Vertical Classification* is metonymic with this argument) is quite in accord with Whitehead and Russell's Theory of Logical Types. The book is put together through principles of hierarchy, of encompassment, of lineal progression, and—of course—of vertical classification.

The overall space of the book is produced and usually is owned by a publisher. The publisher encompasses the book. The book encompasses whatever is within it. Most of its outside space, the borders that separate it from entities of the same and other classes of phenomena, is called the "cover." As befits boundaries, the cover is of a different weight, thickness, and constitution than the interior of the book. Part of the cover is occupied by the name of the book. It is a particular named entity. The name of the book also may have another name. In this instance the other name is subordinate to the principal name and is called a "subtitle" (viz. *Vertical Classification: A Study in Structuralism and the Sociology of Knowledge*). In such a case, the title usually is more abstract (or poetic) and the subtitle more specific (or factual).[15]

A named book has an author or an editor who usually is a specific person. Yet, note that although it is possible for a named book to exist without an author (viz., anonymous), it is much more difficult for an author to publish a book without a name. (Think of the paradoxes of classification thereby generated.) The author is responsible for the text contained within the covers of the book. The author encompasses the text. The text is subordinate to the author; the author is subordinate to the named entity of the book, in its independent, printed existence; the book is subordinate to the publisher.

The text proceeds according to a lineal logic: title page, table of contents, chapters numbered from I to n, pages numbered from 1 to n. Chapter I is an introduction of some sort that signifies its function of beginning and contextualizing. The final chapter is a conclusion of some sort that signifies its function of closing and contextualizing. If the book is thought to be well organized, each successive chapter will depend for its coherence and comprehensibility, to a degree, on the chapters that precede it.

In other words, the entire structuring of the book signifies and over-signifies encompassment, hierarchy, and subordination; the more gen-

[147]

eral and the more particular rarely are confounded. These texts are logical exercises in the suppression of paradoxicality that is produced by the confusion of levels of abstraction, by the erasure of borders.

Within this structure are located the conventions that are used by the author to insert the voices of other ethnographers: in the ritualized offering of Acknowledgments (where the thanks may be profuse, but where the author takes all responsibility); imprisoned within quotation marks (where for a few sentences our words can be used without our consent, and in relation to which we often complain of being quoted "out of context"); locked in parentheses as citations; and plunked into footnotes and appendices as annotations and addenda to the principal text. The use of different typefaces, indentations, and so forth all attest to our presence as deviant (and so, subordinate) to the norms of the text. At best these are subtexts—again in the language of hierarchy and domination. These conventions no more allow for the voice of an authentic, ethnographic Other than they do for that of the native.

We live and experience these constructions and conventions, and accept their necessity in order to get on with our work, to get this published, and to be accorded proper authorship for that. Perhaps this is why we are less reflective about the implications of this ordering of the text. We endlessly protest our concerns for the culture of the native Other. But such texts are artifacts of our own culture; and to these, on the whole, we remain blind. For I read of no cries of anguish over our colonization, as object, of one another's voices. But, reflective or not, I am stressing that the tyrannies of the text derive from a textual construction whose very logic of organization is that of domination and subordination—a machine for the appropriation of discourse that is compatible with our ideas of authorship and proprietorship of knowledge.

Short of a revolution, one that likely is technological as well as epistemological, and one whose parameters may require alternatives to writing, I cannot see doing away with the tyrannies of Logical Typing that are embedded in the finished product of the ethnographic text. In this regard, as stimulating as they may be, the dialogical and the polyphonic are but pretty streamers of aesthetic protest that reaffirm the authority of hierarchy and encompassment; but they also conceal our textual domination of one another within a fiction—that the center of our work lies "out there," and not also "in here" where we dwell, embedded ourselves in institutional and professional constraints.

On the other hand, I have expounded another fiction here, one that we live with quite comfortably: that the finished text is isomorphic with its construction, and that it does indeed embody what our endeavors are about. But, after all, we know that our finished texts have only a limited relationship to how they actually were put together.

Afterword—To the Editors

You asked whether I could bring Henry Rupert back in at the end of this essay, perhaps to relate how his insights helped me to realize the hegemony of textual conventions. I procrastinated for a long time, because I was struck by the utter reasonableness of the request. It suggested the following line of thinking: Henry, in large measure, awoke me to the significance of the Other as subject, although I used other terms at the time. In counterpoint to the absence of native Others in textual representation, I was led to think about ethnographers' absence from one another's texts. Therefore, should not Henry's insights, and their impact on me, be related to my own thoughts on our textual domination of one another?

The logical coherence of this chain of thought belies its seductive powers and indirectly illustrates my contentions about the tyrannies of the text—that is why I cannot accede to the request. Convention: an ethnographic text should be synthetic, demonstrating logical development and coherence, seamlessly building on itself toward some sense of climax, its loose ends safely knotted or tucked away. The conclusion, the climax, finally integrates the text, closes it off, reflects on this, and transcends it. This is the end of the text and the end of the story that makes the text a proper story. Above all, this structure is aesthetically pleasing. It reads right, feels right—a job completed, cast into the world to make its way. Good enough to be independent of its author.

And, in this instance, it also is sheer poetism, to which we accede conventionally all too often. Poetism? A theory or presentation whose only claim for consideration is that it is aesthetically pleasing. If Henry Rupert influenced the way I see a book as the hegemony of textual conventions, I am unaware of this. It would be aesthetically pleasing to the organization of this paper if I wrote that it were so. It is not. Henry belongs to the parts in which he appears, and not to the others.

But I am saddened. It is not what I intended at the outset. He was to be the focus throughout. I am saddened that I could write him so

[149]

easily out of the text when he no longer fit, or had served my purpose. So here there only are loose ends that dangle sensuously in my memory of him, uncommitted and uncommitable to paper. In the beginning I wanted to tell you, Listen, listen to how much this man means to me. Now I'm no longer sure if it is the man or the symbol.

Notes

1. In aboriginal times the Washo were a hunting and gathering people, small in number, who wintered in the valleys of the west-central Great Basin and who spent their summers in the Sierra Nevada mountains and on the eastern shores of Lake Tahoe. Overviews of reconstructions of aboriginal Washo culture are found in d'Azevedo 1963. The most comprehensive overview of Washo shamanism during the modern period is that of Siskin 1983.

2. And by this I mean inlaid in the text itself, so that its proprietorship becomes blurred, and not in a subtext, for instance an appendix (cf. Bruner and Gorfain 1984), or by way of comments as in the early *Current Anthropology*.

3. This was not my first fieldwork. I had passed half a year studying the adaptations of West Indian migrants to a large Canadian city.

4. "Since we made our last field trip to the Washo Indians in 1956–57, we have learned that this shaman has died" (Freed and Freed 1963: 39).

5. He already had told me of how he learned hypnotism from a mail-order book (Handelman 1967a); and I did not attribute any special significance to this statement.

6. The implications of this utterance are profound, given the significance of dream or vision to the novice healer, and, more generally, in communication with the par-anatural (Handelman 1967a, 1972). During those minutes I did not realize this.

7. A month later he stopped speaking, just as abruptly, about these subjects. He explained that a spirit helper had warned him of the adverse effects of our conversations on his healing. We talked of other matters, but, with a single exception, never returned to that of power.

8. When I moved on to different work, he remained for me very much a teacher, and this was how I remembered him (Handelman 1977: xiv).

9. Some years later I asked the ethnographer in question about this incident, but he remembered nothing of it.

10. Some twenty-five years ago I submitted a manuscript about Henry Rupert to *Ethnology*. It was entitled "Creativity in Culture Change." The bulk of the manuscript was constituted of lengthy quotations of Henry's words, from my fieldnotes, articulated by my own commentaries and interpretations. At the time I had never heard of questions of textual construction, nor, for that matter, of exegesis. I did feel that he could represent himself better (in relation to the subject of the paper) than I could do this for him. Nonetheless, I still am certain that the choice of problem and the mode of its presentation are largely the prerogatives of the ethnographer-author. The editor, G.P. Murdock (who was also my teacher at the time), rejected the title on the grounds that "creativity," with its implications for the creative individual, was not a suitable topic for ethnographic inquiry rooted in the study of culture. Moreover, he rejected the format of the paper because it was not scientific. Today, I think he was disturbed by the extent to which my informant had come to dominate the text.

11. Quoted with the permission of Grace Dangberg, from her unpublished field-notes. Personal communication, 10 January 1985.

12. The most comprehensive overview to date (Marcus and Cushman 1982) discusses, in various terms, the cultural (ethnographic) production of texts, but does not even mention the significance of their cultural (institutional, occupational) means of production. The distinction of "work in the field" and "work at home" continues to be sustained, such that the major intersection of these spheres is through the medium of the individual ethnographer. This mystification of the reality of work continues to pervade ethnography. Aspects of my critique in this essay are continued in Handelman 1994.

13. Smadar Lavie pointed this out to me.

14. Clearly, proprietorship over the authorship of textual production is not universal. Writing of Bengali jatra playwrights, Farber (Sequin and Farber 1978: 343) notes that "while they are paid to write plays and while they relinquish claims over them, [they] do not keep copies of their plays, do not expect to be cited when the play is either rewritten or sold for 'movie or performance' rights, do not remember the titles they attribute to their plays, and do not assert the right to control the deployment of their literary energies." Farber attributes these characteristics of authorship to Bengali conceptions that creative energy is part of cosmic energy that cannot be owned but merely possessed or shared.

15. As, for example, in these titles plucked from my bookshelves—*Day of Shining Red: An Essay on Understanding Ritual*, or *Reality in a Looking-Glass: Rationality through an Analysis of Traditional Folly*.

REFERENCES

Bruner, Edward M., and Phyllis Gorfain. 1984 "Dialogic Narration and the Paradoxes of Masada." In Edward M. Bruner, ed., *Text, Play, and Story: The Construction and Reconstruction of Self and Society*. Washington, D.C.: 1983 Proceedings of the American Ethnological Society. Pp. 56–79.

Clifford, James. 1983. "On Ethnographic Authority." *Representations* 1: 118–46.

d'Azevedo, Warren L., ed. 1963. *The Washo Indians of California and Nevada*. Salt Lake City: University of Utah Anthropological Papers, no. 67.

Downs, James F. 1961. "Washo Religion." *Anthropological Records* 16: 365–85.

Dwyer, Kevin. 1982. *Moroccan Dialogues: Anthropology in Question*. Baltimore: Johns Hopkins University Press.

Foucault, Michel. 1979. "What Is an Author?" In Josué V. Harari, ed., *Textual Strategies: Perspectives in Post-Structural Criticism*. Ithaca: Cornell University Press. Pp. 141–60.

Freed, Stanley A., and Ruth S. Freed. 1963. "The Persistence of Aboriginal Ceremonies among the Washo Indians." In Warren L. d'Azevedo, ed., *The Washo Indians of California and Nevada*. Salt Lake City: University of Utah Anthropological Papers, no. 67. Pp. 25–40.

Handelman, Don. 1967a. "The Development of a Washo Shaman." *Ethnology* 6: 444–64.

Don Handelman

——. 1967b. "Transcultural Shamanic Healing: a Washo Example." *Ethnos* 32: 149–66.

——. 1972. "Aspects of the Moral Compact of a Washo Shaman." *Anthropological Quarterly* 45: 84–101.

——. 1977. *Work and Play among the Aged: Interaction, Replication, and Emergence in a Jerusalem Setting.* Assen/Amsterdam: Van Gorcum.

——. 1994. "Critiques of Anthropology: Literary Turns, Slippery Bends." *Poetics Today,* forthcoming.

Little, Kenneth. 1980. "Explanation and Individual Lives: A Recognition of Life Writing in Anthropology." *Dialectical Anthropology* 5: 215–26.

Marcus, George E., and Dick Cushman. 1982. "Ethnographies as Texts." *Annual Review of Anthropology* 11: 25–69.

Pandey, Triloki Nath. 1972. "Anthropologists at Zuni." *Proceedings of the American Philosophical Society* 116: 321–37.

Seguin, Margaret, and Carole Farber. 1978. "Whose Who's": Possession and Ownership in Hindi and Bengali." In Richard Preston, ed., *Papers From the 4th Annual Congress* (CES). Ottawa: National Museum of Man Mercury Series. Pp. 337–44.

Siskin, Edgar E. 1983. *Washo Shamans and Peyotists: Religious Conflict in an American Indian Tribe.* Salt Lake City: University of Utah Press.

Tedlock, Dennis. 1979. "The Analogical Tradition and the Emergence of a Dialogical Anthropology." *Journal of Anthropological Research* 35: 387–400.

[7]

"The One Who Writes Us": Political Allegory and the Experience of Occupation among the Mzeina Bedouin

Smadar Lavie

> Allegory arises in periods of loss, periods in which a once powerful theological, political, or familial authority is threatened with effacement. Allegory arises then from the painful absence of that which it claims to recover, and, . . . as the paradox of an order built upon its own undoing cannot be restricted to this one discursive mode, indeed, . . . the longing for an origin whose loss is the necessary condition of that longing is the character not only of all discourse but of human existence itself.
>
> —Stephen Greenblatt,
> "Allegory and Representation"

I

On 24 September 1978, Anwar Sadat, Menachem Begin, and Jimmy Carter signed an almost final draft of a peace accord at the Camp David retreat that was to give the accord its name. At that moment, thousands

This essay is based on thirty months of fieldwork carried out between 1975 and 1979 in the South Sinai Peninsula, and three additional short trips made in August 1981, December 1985, and April 1987, sponsored by the Ford Foundation and by the Lowie

of miles away, in the very Sinai desert on which all the diplomatic
hullabaloo had been focused, I labored in 'Ein al-Akhaḍar,[1] a Mzeina
oasis. An Israeli anthropologist of half-Yemenite, half-Lithuanian heritage, I listened to the Arabic version of the news as it wafted in a
scratchy voice across the hot, lugubrious atmosphere of the *mag'ad
rejjāl* (men's club).[2] Two days later I was to be the victim of the local
fool, who sent me to a deserted well in the middle of nowhere. There
I spent a memorable night alone on an empty stomach. The previous
day's tragedy was compensated for the following day by a remarkable
stroke of good luck: here, in the middle of nowhere, I met a Mzeini
woman. In a display of typical Bedouin hospitality and generosity, she
shared with me what little food she had and took me to her encampment.

A month later, my pride still smarting, I related my humiliation to
several Mzeinis. I was surprised at myself in that, despite my embarrassment I mustered—without really trying to—the calm, distanced style that typifies Bedouin storytelling. Had my audience been
professional anthropologists, I no doubt would have delivered a dis-
quisition on "The Impact of Global Politics on the Tribal Structure of
the Mzeina." But as my story represents not so much distancing,
objective observations by a detached scholar, but deeply felt experiences shared with the Mzeinis, it is best told as an allegory. After all,
at those points where my identity and that of the Mzeinis meet and
converge, the global politics observed and analyzed by scientists become the local poetics experienced and lived by the participants.

The mundane dialogues of the Mzeinis reflected their inconsistent
and insecure living conditions. These were consequences of the occupation of the Sinai, a political football tossed back and forth between
Egypt and Israel.[3] When the Mzeinis pondered how they ought to
relate to the Israeli or Egyptian soldiers, the military governors, the
civil administrators, the assorted settlers, and the international tour-

Fund of the Anthropology Department, U.C. Berkeley. The issues presented are
discussed in greater detail in my book, *The Poetics of Military Occupation: Mzeina
Allegories of Bedouin Identity under Israeli and Egyptian Rule* (Berkeley: University
of California Press, 1990). I am also grateful to the MaBelle McLeod Lewis Fund and
the Hebrew Free Loan Association for their support during the writing stages. And
last but not least, I wish to express my heartfelt gratitude to the 5000 or so Mzeinis,
to whose tradition of hospitality I am deeply obliged.

ists, they were faced by the dilemma of adapting traditional hospitality to quite untraditional "visitors."

Karwat aḍ-ḍeif, or the code of hospitality, was a pillar of Bedouin tradition. Mzeinis viewed it as a sacred commitment on the part of each tribal member to the honor of his or her community and tribe, and to the honor of the Ṭawara, the tribal alliance to which the Mzeina belonged. Hospitality also embraced spheres beyond the tribe. Hospitality toward any member of the community of Muslim believers (*al-umma al-Islamiyya*), or to anyone in the whole world (*ahl al-dunya*) visiting the South Sinai, was to bring honor to the Mzeini displaying it. The duty of hospitality involved both the tribal structure and its many organizational modes. Any stranger who came to the Sinai was traditionally considered a guest and was expected to introduce him- or herself according to a rigid etiquette reflecting tribal and regional affiliation. If a guest was not known to the host from previous meetings, the guest was to introduce him- or herself by name and give a three- to five-generation genealogy of his or her *khamsa* (feud group), clan and phratry affiliations, and the tribe of which he or she was a member. Since among the Mzeina descent and territoriality did not exactly correspond, the guest also mentioned the name of the regional alliance to which he or she belonged. Then, before turning to talk of other matters, the host and guest gossiped about the overlapping areas of their kinship and friendship networks.

Many of the Bedouin dialogues on the nature of hospitality degenerated into bitter arguments where the participants' value of honor, derived from being Bedouin hosts, was confronted by the indeterminacy characterizing their life as voiceless pawns of their uninvited guests. Many of these arguments ended abruptly and inconclusively. But sometimes, the collision between the many voices of the present, and a monologic voice that recited the inheritance of a pre-colonial tribal past, fractured the taken-for-granted construction of everyday reality (Berger and Luckman 1967: 19–28). During these fragile interstitial moments, existential paradoxes emanating from the world geopolitical situation surfaced in Mzeinis' everyday discourse.

At such moments, any person of theatrical and rhetorical talent might speak up spontaneously, playfully allegorizing an exceptionally painful or humorous yet mundane experience into a story told in the Mzeina traditional, monological storytelling style. In so doing, the teller transcended both personal and communal experiences and incorporated them into the tribal tradition. I refer to these tellers as

[155]

playing out "allegorical types." These "types" are my anthropological constructs. But cultures also pay tribute to creative personae. I found that some of "my" personae constituted the central characters in traditional stories (*ḥikayāt*) and poems (*gaṣīd*) recited by many Mzeinis.

Once, during a liminal moment (Turner 1967: 93–111) when the tradition of hospitality was called into question, I found myself acting as an "allegorical type." Allegorizing my memorable night experience, I was able to bridge the gap between the Mzeina's tradition of hospitality and the inconsistencies of their current lives. As guest and yet as the most marginal tribesperson, as a Jew of both European and Arab descent, someone conjoining Self and Other in herself,[4] I spontaneously staged an allegory enabling my audience and myself to reconstruct the tradition of hospitality in both reality and structure. I was thus able to momentarily resolve the ambiguities associated with Mzeina hospitality and the paradoxes faced by Mzeina (and myself) in relating to Western culture and politics.

II

I will begin decoding the contradiction and mystery of being sent to the wilderness by a Fool, and of being saved the next day by a woman, both members of the same tribe, referring to portions of my field diary.[5] All references to "days before" refer to the number of days before my encounter with the oasis Fool.

i

26 September 1978, Bir al-Sarādga
Dear Diary,

I thought my war scars from the Sinai healed since I treated them with anthropological hopes for mutual understanding. To hell with it! Here I sit, in the middle of nowhere, and instead of writing my regular evening fieldnotes, I stupidly write "Dear Diary."

After almost three years of fieldwork, years when I imagined myself crossing the emotional wilderness of mutual distrust, years when I assumed that I, an Israeli anthropologist, had exposed the essence of my Self to that Bedouin Other, and years in which that Other, in exchange, seemed to absorb me into itself. After all, we are but trivial beings who disintegrate into small particles in the shadow of the Arab-Israeli conflict.

The dark sky awaits the late moonrise. Smadar, how did you ever get into this?

21 September 1978, Farānje

Five days before.

The Pilgrimage to Farānje [Mzeina's ancestral tomb]—. . . . The ambitious and vague hopes of Camp David have shrunken here to penetrating questions: about the temporary borderlines that will separate families during the gradual return of the Sinai from Israel to Egypt between 1979 and 1982; about how to obtain licenses to visit relatives on both sides of these borders; about the shrinking possibilities of migrant work with the Egyptians and Israelis; about speculations that further development projects will be imposed on the locals. . . .

22 September 1978, Farānje, still

Four days before.

Ashes of the pilgrimage. Bedouin cynicism about the real importance of the Sinai in future peace treaties. And their nice rhyme. "The Sinai mountains—good for naught. Can't be used, can't be bought." *Jebāl Sīna—la lehum 'aida wamafish minhum faida.*

. . . Noon prayer—Afterward I join the *galīd* (or the Symbolic Battle Coordinator of the tribe), his one-eyed brother, and the entourage made up of three ancient customary judges. We bump along for about a half an hour—five nobles resplendent in formal robes and one anthropologist in baggy jeans and T-shirt, six people in a dilapidated pickup going to 'Ein el-Akhaḍar. . . .[6]

. . . 'Ein al-Akhaḍar—The green spring. The whistling wind in the wide wadi. Rounded black hills of metamorphic rock flowing forth from the windswept plateaus of the peninsula's watersheds. A few small fruit orchards and date trees embrace the wadi wall. Often the fruit does not ripen because of the cold. A well, buckets, a sweep. The Mzeina call this oasis, which sits on the fringes of their territorial center, "our heart."

24 September 1978, 'Ein al-Akhaḍar

Two days before.

. . . It is said, rather cynically, that the customary residence of the Symbolic Battle Coordinator is here, in the heart of Mzeina. But alas,

[157]

nothing stirs in this heart but two young goatherds, some twenty goats, and a donkey burdened with six empty water jerrycans. Every other morning the girls emerge from the yellow dunes, wash their long hair near the well, fill up the jerrycans, and disappear again into the dunes in the direction of their summer encampment.

Like Mzeina elders everywhere, the Coordinator and his entourage spend most of their days and nights sitting or reclining in the mag'ad. But the mag'ad in 'Ein al-Akhaḍar is the only sign of community life in this forsaken tribal heart.

. . . A transistor radio barks out news in Modern Standard Arabic (and thus it is only partially understood by these nomads because they speak a dialect). Someone painstakingly scans the dial in an almost desperate search for the elusive stations. Our ears strain to discern meanings amidst the scratches, while our eyes focus on a square drawn in the sand. Finger-made crosshatchings transform the sand into a checker board. The Judge and the Coordinator while away their days in a sequence of slow and calculated *shīza* games [a crossbreed between "checkers" and "go"]. One player moves small pieces of dry, pale camel manure; the other player uses small pebbles of red granite. Some of the entourage bless the players with their unsolicited advice, while others advise the advisors, until one can no longer tell players from advisors, or advisors from advisors of advisors.

"Shgēṭef, could you pour more tea?" the Coordinator nonchalantly requests the local Fool.[7] The Fool enters the mag'ad and for the umpteenth time pours us yet more cups of hot sweet tea.

. . . "So what did the news say?" the Coordinator asks the man with his ear glued to the transistor, but doesn't wait for an answer. "I'll tell you," he says with a half-bemused, half-serious expression, "No one will solve the problems between Russia and America. Only the Chinese will ever figure a way out. And when the day comes that they conquer the Sinai, that will be the end of that."

It's a good pun—the Arabic for "Sinai" is *Sīna*, for "Chinese" is *Sīni*—and we laugh heartily. But the Fool, perhaps betraying his deep wisdom, stares at us with eyes wide open.

The Coordinator continues, "The Greeks were here and left behind the Monastery [Santa Katarina], the Turks were here and left behind the Castle [in Nuwēb'at Ṭarabīn], and the British drew up maps, and the Egyptians brought the Russian army (and a few oil wells), and the Israelis brought the Americans who made the mountains into movies, and tourists from France and Japan, and scuba divers from Sweden

[158]

and Australia, and—trust Allah to save you from the devil—we Mzeina are nothing but pawns in the hands of them all. We are like the pebbles and the droppings of the shiza."

Everyone but the Fool again roars with laughter. The Coordinator points to me with his long index finger, saying in a commanding voice, "Write it all down, The One Who Writes Us!" (*di illi tuktubna*—one of my two Mzeini nicknames).

26 September 1978, 'Ein al-Akhaḍar, still
. . . Noon—Enough, I am shiza-ed out. Between shiza moves the men exhaust most of the possible scenarios for the near and distant future of the Middle East. The Egyptian-Israeli peace treaty may loom large on the global horizon, but locally it has been torn to shreds.
. . . I recall a nearby well, Bir al-Sarādga, six kilometers down the wadi. Several families encamped there during winter. I wonder how Sadat's peace initiative echoes in the walls of this well. The negotiated temporary border will pass right through it.

I ask Shgēṭef (the Fool) if there are any camels grazing in the surrounding hills and if it might be possible to rent one, to load it with cameras, cassette recorder, a huge and clumsy backpack (just thirty kilograms altogether) and travel to Bir al-Sarādga. Shgēṭef raises one eyebrow, a Bedouin gesture indicating a dubious "why not?" I join him in the search for fresh camel footprints. We search in vain. He stares at me, pretending to be amazed, and says, "Ya Smadar, owner of big hips [*omn al-ja'āb*—my other nickname], a tough and skillful Israeli like you, who lives with us in this desert, can't even load yourself up and go down the wadi as far as Bir al-Sarādga? The Bedouin encamp right there, winter and summer."

26 September 1978, Bir al-Sarādga
Here, again, at tonight's page—
. . . And I carried myself and my heavy load down the wadi. When I saw the well from afar—I felt relieved. The place hadn't changed since winter. For a moment I thought I heard a dog bark in the distance, suggesting the existence of an encampment. But alas, arriving at the well I found only the leftovers from the previous winter encampment. I dropped my stuff near the well and started walking quickly, almost hysterically, in one direction after the other, hoping to find someone, anyone, before nightfall. Within the radius of a kilometer not a living thing was to be found. Around the well were

[159]

many fresh footprints of women and children, but still I dared not hope.

I am afraid. I had trusted Shgēṭef, a channel for the region's gossip. But while the tribe's resplendent leadership expressed their anger at the Camp David Accord verbally, the fool, as a Fool, acted out his anger by dispatching the most available Israeli to the middle of nowhere. Now I know what the Mzeina mean when they say, "The fool's mind is sharp as a sword."

As the day recedes into dusk, I gather some dry twigs and light a small fire. I have no food, but at least I have enough cigarettes and matches to get me through the night. OK, I will try to fall asleep. Tonight, even the habitual sadness of sunset does not move me.

Maybe I deserve it?

27 September 1978, Bir al-Sarādga

... A new day—During the night I jolt awake several times, shivering with fear, unable to decide whether to be angry at myself or at Shgēṭef. Finally I wake up at 7 a.m. and decide that, if no one arrives at the well by eight, I will leave my stuff, fill my three canteens, and continue down the wadi for twenty-five kilometers to the settlement where Wadi al-Akhaḍar meets Wadi Firān. It is inhabited the year around, and this *I* know without having to count on any clever fool.

I am starved, and the sun beats down on everything. My back hurts from yesterday, but I've got to go on. After a hurried walk down the wadi I suddenly see a Bedouin woman, two toddlers, and a donkey loaded with empty jerrycans. Are these the owners of the footprints I found yesterday near the well? My eyes fill with tears of relief. The woman notices me and veils herself. From afar we exchange the customary greeting sentences said between a guest and a host. Hoping that she does not notice, I wipe my tears away with my Mickey Mouse T-shirt. Bedouin are not supposed to cry.

ii

After a month I returned to Dahab, a community in the process of sedentarization on the shore of the ʿAqaba Gulf. There lived the family that offered me tribal protection as an adopted daughter (*ṭanība*[8]), after I decided to adopt Dahab as a base camp for anthropological migration. But rumors of the misdeeds of Shgēṭef-the-Fool, and of my rescue by the woman with her two toddlers, arrived in Dahab even before I did.

28 October 1978, Dahab

Wintry Dahab—The north wind has already swept away the scents of dinner and the last whispers of the *'asha* (after-dinner) prayer. The tales of the fearful Abu-Zāyed, accompanied by the sad sound of a *rabāba* (one-string fiddle), ooze out of the transistor radios whose antennas are trained towards Egypt, and pour into the night.

Flattened cartons and wooden boxes, supported by dry palm branches, are the materials out of which Ghānma and Mūsa's hut has been fashioned. In the inner yard Ghānma, Abu-Mūsa (Mūsa's old father), who makes his living from fishing, and Omm-Mūsa (Mūsa's mother) sit in a circle around the transistor radio. The scene is faintly illuminated by glowing embers. A tea kettle bubbles above red hot coals. Next to Ghānma sit Mabsūṭa and Rāshda—two neighbors whose husbands are now employed as unskilled, underpaid, but tenured workers at the Israeli army camp at Sharm al-Sheikh. 'Id and Salīm, their elbows resting on their woolen body wraps, recline near Abu-Mūsa. 'Id is a neighbor temporarily hired several times by the local Israeli ranger to clean up the heaps of trash left by tourists. Salīm is married to Omm-Mūsa's brother's daughter, and lives in the western peninsula, to be returned to Egypt next summer. He is about to go job hunting in the Israeli town of Eilat. Smadar, an Israeli anthropologist, huddles in the corner, trying to write down every detail.

When the legendary feats of Abu-Zāyed are completed, Salīm nonchalantly turns the radio dial in search for the evening news. We gallop between Cairo, Monte Carlo, Damascus, Jerusalem, Amman, the Voice of America, London, straining to catch elusive radio stations amidst serious Standard Arabic voices relating bits of news.[9]

Mabsūṭa (puzzled): The people in the radios—they always say the same things. But each station and every state says it in its own way. It's something I don't understand. Never.

Omm-Mūsa (with an air of indifference): Every one and his rabāba.

'Id (sarcastically): Ah-ha—what's the distance between Abu-Zāyed's rabāba and the rabāba of the news—*(laughs to himself and lowers the transistor's volume.)*

Ghānma (briskly, switching the radio off): Enough! I'm fed up with the news. All or one, they're the same! Tea?

Pause. Ghānma once again fills the empty tea cups handed to her. Some, attempting to chill the boiling tea, whistle air through their lips.

Abu-Mūsa: Ya Salīm, soon we will need a passport and some licenses in order to visit you and your family—and your family is our family. [Salīm is a member in Musa's lineage in addition to his marriage to Omm-Mūsa's brother's daughter.] What do you think (*a mischievous look in his eyes*), will the Egyptians photograph my bald head in color, or black and white?

He laughs and the rest join in.

Salīm (with a raised voice): Folks, this is not the time for jokes! When the Egyptians find out that I drive a Russian jeep [left behind in 1967] you will probably need to apply for a license to visit the jail.

Mabsūṭa: Drop it. A lot of time has passed since then. They've forgotten all about it.

Salīm (louder): I swear to God, they haven't forgotten. (*Slowly, emphasizing each word*): When they got Ras-Sadr back [in 1976, due to Kissinger's shuttle diplomacy] they fined everyone who drove Russian vehicles. Those who couldn't afford to pay went to jail. I heard it from those who came [from the Egyptian-controlled] Ras-Sadr area for visits to relatives through the Red Cross.

Omm-mūsa (awakening): Aii-wa! (yeah), this is the time for us to start thinking where to hide what we took from the Egyptians, and to start "collecting" things from the Jews. [The term "Jews" was often used to describe the generic anyone who was not Bedouin and who came to the Sinai during the Israeli occupation, including tourists from all over the world, and even Palestinians.]

'Id (to Salīm): I heard that somebody from your encampment has "taken" a Mercedes taxi from Eilat with the help of friends, took it apart, hid it in the wadis, and the Israeli police couldn't find a thing.

Abu-Mūsa (playing with the prayer beads between his fingers, mutters to himself): Ḥarām! (taboo!)

Salīm (chuckling): They said that some got arrested in Eilat, but were freed. Lack of evidence, they said.

Abu-Mūsa (to himself): Thank God! (*Thoughtful for a moment*) Still, it's *ḥarām!*

A silent pause.

Mabsuṭa: My husband says he doesn't know what to do—to leave his work and start "collecting," or wait till the Israelis are about to leave and get his severance pay—he worked for them since 1972.

Omm-Mūsa: If they'll give him his severance pay in dollars, let him wait. If in Israeli pounds, he should "collect" other things since the Israeli money is nothing but worthless paper, buying us nothing from the Egyptians. But if you ask me, I think he should both "collect" *and* take his severance pay. This time, it doesn't look like these Israelis will return again for several years.

Abu-Mūsa (stops playing with his prayer beads, firmly): Ya wife, the Bedouin don't work at and steal from the hand greeting them with peace, be it Egyptian, Israeli, or Greek. Our God is one, and all of us wish to live in honor and peace. Enough of this ugly talk! Israelis, Egyptians, and all the rest of them are now our guests in the Sinai, and our code of hospitality is well known and respected!

'Id: You mean, every *'id, ṭīṭ,* and *'afrīt* ["holiday," "twitter," and "demon"] who arrives here must be received as if he were a Bedouin? I will go bankrupt if I have to host those strangers!

Ghānma (very angry): Ya Abu-Mūsa, guests don't give you ID cards and licenses and tell you where to go and where not to! Guests don't employ you or give you severance pay! Guests don't prescribe you medications or take your blood samples to Tel Aviv! Guests don't govern and punish you! What sort of guests are you talking about?

We are all quiet for several hesitant moments.

Rāshda: And what about the huts in al-Billij? [Al-Billij was the fake Bedouin village built by Dahab entrepreneurs for the many tourists seeking a vacation in an "authentic" Bedouin atmosphere, while sunbathing in various degrees of nudity or diving in spectacular coral reefs.] We have four huts. Now we have there a couple from near Tel Aviv, a German couple, three girls from some *moshāv* [Israeli agricultural co-op], and a strange American guy with a long beard—yuukk!—who doesn't haggle with my son over the price, and doesn't lie naked on the beach. Always, when the tourists come, they buy clothes like ours. And my son, he prepares for them *far-ashīh* [flat bread] and tea. Sometimes some suckers give him some of their food, because they think he's hungry. Afterwards (*bemused, chuckling*) they also pay for what he prepares for them. And this sort, they want to be like us. Sometimes, when I see them from

[163]

afar, dressed in our men's robes, believe me, I am not sure who they are.

Omm-Mūsa (angrily): We also have to "take" from them: sleeping bags, watches, dollars. Half of the day, when not dressed in our clothes, they go around naked and screw each other in front of all.[10] Disgusting! *(She spits on the ground.)* These are no Bedouin!

ʿId (shouts): So tell me, you, Omm-Mūsa! Tell me, you *(pointing with his long index finger at each person sitting in the circle)*, and you, all of you! Who are the Bedouin and who are the guests?! Our kids— they run around in Eilat and Sharm al-Sheikh with pants and shirts, and not only during worktime. *(Lowering his voice)* Do you remember the film that they shot about the life of—what's his name— Brian, in the Castle of Nuwēbʿa? That *Inglīzi* [Englishman] wanted forty Bedouin who would work with him [as extras]. When they came, they dressed up for work [i.e., with pants], and *he* was wearing a caftan *and* a headdress. He yelled at them: "You, Bedouins, should come to work as *Bedouin*, because you have to be Bedouin in the film." *(Raising his voice)* See how? Soon will be the day when men start showing up with pants to the magʿad!

There is a short, though disquieting, silence.

Abu-Mūsa (shaking his head, to himself): And we, where shall we go? These days, even the tradition of hospitality is not with us any more. We don't know who is Bedouin and who is a guest. We don't know whether our guests respect us nor how we should respect them. And Honor has left us, disappeared. . . .

A long silence prevails. When honor is mentioned, silence always descends: honor is holy. The stormy wind, still beating the date trees, now brings us the sounds of a faraway cassette recorder.

The anthropologist finishes writing Abu-Mūsa's question and I tell her to try to immerse herself in the dim and distant sounds of the field night. Instead, she embarrassedly points to the fact that my fresh memories of that scary Bir al-Sarādga experience are now emerging from the silence.

When I finally arrived at Dahab after the Shgēṭef-the-Fool episode, Abu-Mūsa and several other elders insisted that I take Shgēṭef and his khamsa to the tribal customary court for having sent me off into the wilderness. Yet as an Israeli I felt I hardly had any right to stay with the Mzeina, let alone sue them.

But this evening Abu-Mūsa's penetrating question shakes me. I want to tell the people present that, despite the intrusions of the many foreign agencies into their daily life, ideas like tribal structure, social organization, and rituals of tradition remain alive and well. As a matter of fact, every day I fill my notebook with them.

"I swear to God, ya Abu-Mūsa," I burst out. "Among the Mzeina, a guest is still a guest, and hospitality *is* hospitality. If one has a khamsa or is offered protection [*ṭanīb*] by such a group, if that person or the ones who have offered protection have only, really, only one karat of dates [every date tree contains twenty-four karats, which are twenty-four parts of shared ownership], then it becomes as clear as the morning's sun when one is a guest and when one is a host." In this way I repeat to Abu-Mūsa and 'Id what they once told me about tribal membership and hospitality.

All eyes are focused on me. I feel the urge to continue, and tell the happy ending to my 'Ein al-Akhaḍar experience.

"You might have heard how Shgēṭef-the-Fool fooled me when I wanted to visit the people of Bir as-Sarādga," I ask rhetorically.

"A deed which should not be done among us," some murmur to themselves.

I take a long breath. As I start narrating, the anthropologist reminds me: Smadar, now narrate your personal experience in Bedouin storytelling style. Don't be emotional. It is not allowed!

"After I spent the night alone, I woke up the next morning and decided to go down to where Wadi al-Akhaḍar meets Wadi Firan. I knew that people were there. I walked for a bit down the wadi. Suddenly I saw a woman, two toddlers, and a donkey climbing towards the well. When the woman noticed me, she veiled herself, took her kids, left the donkey, and fled to the surrounding hills. I think she thought I was from some tourist group because of the way I dressed. Since my 'father' told me that one can never simultaneously have his Self and be an Other [*mā fī wāḥad illi yākhodh zamāno wazamān gheiro*—a Mzeini proverb], I wear long pants and a shirt. Yet I cover my head with a Bedouin white headdress [*'amāma*] because it helps against sun and dust."

"Yes, it helps," echoes Rāshda, smiling and winking.

"It helps indeed," Salīm follows with a serious voice (cf. Basso 1984).[11]

" 'Good morning, a morning of roses and jasmines to you, the mother of children,' I shouted to the woman while she was running away. 'God will bring good to your children,' I continued with a dry

[165]

throat. Suddenly, the sound of rolling pebbles stopped. The woman stopped running. She was trying to listen carefully.

" 'I am from the people of Dahab, under protection of Khnēibish, son of 'Auda, son of Sabah, from [the agnatic blood group of] Wlad Salīm, of the [clan] Ghseināt, from [the phratry named] Wlad 'Ali,' I said in the way you taught me to introduce myself."

"Exactly in the way we taught her to introduce herself," Ghānma repeats my words to the rest, whose attention moves from my corner to her spot near the bubbling tea kettle, and then immediately back to my corner.

" 'Are you the one people call "the one who writes us"?' Her color is like yours, and your hips, like hers,' the woman shouted, removing her veil so that I could hear her more clearly [and also to connote that I was no longer a stranger].

" 'Yes it's me. I "cut" down the wadi [Mzeina's vernacular] from 'Ein al-Akhaḍar,' I said. She returned to her donkey, who stood calmly at the wadi's center and brushed his tail back and forth, trying to shoo the flies from his back. And I approached her. The moment her children noticed my clothes, they started crying. We greeted each other, hugging the back of each other's neck and rapidly uttering, 'Salamāt, Salamāt, Salamāt,' kissing the air three times, swaying back and forth to the rhythm of the greetings. This is exactly how you taught me to greet women."

"And this is exactly how we taught her to greet us," echoes Mabsūṭa, swaying her head back and forth.

" 'Shut up, kids! This is a woman from the people of Dahab, on the coast. That's the way our people there learned from strangers how to dress, so don't be afraid,' she soothed her kids while winking at me.

"Then she said quite formally, 'I am Fṭaima, daughter of 'Abdallh, son of Maḥmūd, from the Rawāḥla [clan]. Our people encamp in Umm Ba'atheirān, near here.'

" 'You must be the sister of Fattūm, son of 'Abdallh, son of Maḥmūd. I met him with the rest of the Shadhādhna [the phratry to which the Rawāḥla clan belongs] last week, during the pilgrimage to Farānje,' I said, trying to find mutual friends and relatives [*nās wa'ēila*]."

"Friends and relatives," Abu-Mūsa mutters to himself while rolling his prayer beads between his right-hand fingers.

" 'Yeah, my brother told me that you even donated money for repairs to the shrine, like all the rest. Allah's blessing upon you.'

"Suddenly we established eye contact. Fṭaima held my arms and said, 'You, what's wrong with you?! Your eyes are red and yellow! Last night—where were you?' I told Fṭaima the events of that night.

"'No one believes Shgēṭef. Three wives have left him. The Fool is *a fool*,' she said angrily. Immediately she searched the pocket sewn to the bottom of her headdress [*wugā*] and took out a mash of sweet and large dates. 'Eat, my child,' she said. I ate the dates as if they were manna from heaven and said, 'God will bring peace to the mother of children.' She smiled, and we started walking toward the well while gossiping about who's doing what in Dahab, and in Umm Baʿatheirān and vicinity.

"Arriving back at the well, Fṭaima seated me and her kids in the shade and then went to gather dried twigs. She soon returned and started kneading dough, from which she baked *gurs bil-nār* [a type of bread served to guests]. She served it with hot, sweet tea."

"So Fṭaima served her little guest *gurs bil-nār* soaked in tea," adds Salīm.

"We spent a whole day near the well. Goatherds arrived. A man on his camel passed by. A sheikh and his family on their personal pilgrimage to the shrine of Hbūs, there to ask for health, joined our lunch. Fṭaima told my story to everyone. 'The fool can't tell who's a guest and who is an outsider,' they said."

"The Fool is *a fool*," some of the audience murmur to themselves.

"Just before dusk we slowly carried ourselves back to Umm Baʿatheirān. Fṭaima brought me to the magʿad. She introduced me and my Bedouin *aṣal* [descent line] to the men and told them my story. One went aside and took from a box a long and narrow rug, reserved for guests. He spread the rug and told me to sit on his right. And we found out that we had all joined in on the last pilgrimage to Farānje.

"'The duty of hospitality is with us tonight,' said Fṭaima's husband, who sat down to my left, between me and the other man. He took green coffee beans from one of the boxes and roasted them in a pan on the glowing embers. Then we heard the blessed sound of a pestle beating the mortar, and echoes answered from the surrounding hills. We started to drink cycles of bitter coffee followed by sweet tea, as hosts and guests do."

"As hosts and guests always *must* do," Abu-Mūsa slowly and firmly repeats the end of my sentence while the rest nod their heads in agreement.

"'Tonight is a night of meat,' Fṭaima's husband declared solemnly.

[167]

" 'I am not so important that you need to waste your *ḥalāl* in my honor.' "

While I'm telling this detail to my audience, the anthropologist notes that I used the Bedouin vernacular, where *ḥalal* refers to livestock. Interestingly, she muses, in classical Arabic, as well as in the Mzeina vernacular, *ḥalal* is what is permitted to Muslims, as opposed to *haram*, the taboos. I cut short her scholarly meditations, reminding her that I'm in the middle of telling a Bedouin story to a Bedouin audience.

" 'I swear to God, I have no hunger for meat!' I said firmly, as you taught me to say in such situations."

"As we taught her," echoes Omm-Mūsa.

"So Fṭaima's husband didn't press any more. After the *maghreb* prayer, Fṭaima's eldest son brought a tray packed with rice and those precious dried fish. We blessed, ate, blessed again and washed our hands. After dinner, the men prayed the *'asha*. Then, we talked about things, the situation, and the world."

"Things, situations, and the world," Salim repeats the end of my sentence. "*Ya rab* [oh, God], how she learned to talk like a Mzeini," he continues with astonishment.

"Then Fṭaima returned, her hands loaded with blankets, and asked if I wanted to be hosted as a woman [i.e., to sleep at the corner of her family tent], or as a man [i.e., to sleep alone in the mag'ad]. After a short argument, I convinced her that my sleeping bag was quite adequate, the same way you taught me to say things in such a situation, and I slept in the mag'ad—as you instructed me when I asked you what I should do when I am invited to stay in a woman's tent while her husband is home."

"Right!" Omm-Mūsa approves of my action.

"Aa-ha!" agree some of the rest.

"Three evenings I spent with the men, and wrote about summer migrations, and date tree ownerships, and conflicts, and trials, and the Israeli and Egyptian governments, and the Camp David agreement, and on war and on peace. Three days I spent with the women, and wrote about marriages, and divorces, and births, and illness, and amulets, and herds, and on the Camp David agreement, and on war and on peace.

"Afterward I rented a camel and joined riders who came from 'Ein al-Akhaḍar, and we went down to the orchards of Ṭarfat al-Gdeirain.

And here I told you about Mzeina's tradition of hospitality, and this is the end of my story, and this is your peace."

The anthropologist instructs me here to end with this common closure of stories or rhymed epics.

"And this is your peace," everyone responds in unison.

Once again Salīm turns on the transistor radio and hunts for late night news.

iii

During the following winter I related my 'Ein al-Akhaḍar story five more times to groups of Mzeinis. The context leading to it was always some unsolvable argument about the Mzeina tradition of hospitality. Among the "guests" who arrived in the Sinai that winter were high-ranking army officers of Egypt, Israel, the United States, and the United Nations various developers of large-scale international tourism making preliminary surveys for the Egyptian government, and thousands of tourists, who felt that this would be their last chance to catch a glimpse of the "real" wilderness of the South Sinai peninsula before it lost its pristine charm forever.

I spent that spring in Jerusalem, completing my B.A. and classifying piles of fieldnotes in preparation for graduate school in Berkeley. I puzzled over whether my story reconstructed the Mzeinis' image of themselves, or their image of me, or perhaps even of my professional image of myself. I was also unsure whether my role as an anthropologist included telling the people I studied stories about themselves.

In May 1979, I returned to the Sinai but felt embarrassed asking why Shgēṭef and Fṭaima had treated me in contradictory fashions, what the meanings behind their actions were, and what meanings my story had generated.

Ramaḍān in August 1979 was the last month of my fieldwork. Arriving at Dahab, I told myself that this was my last chance to decode the mystery of contradictions. Was I just another Israeli to the Mzeina? And if so, why was I assigned a fictive genealogy and adopted into the tribe?

During the long, hot days of the daytime fast, everyone but the children napped between the daily prayers. In the shade of date trees on the outskirts of the settlement, men lay on the beach. The women rested in the huts. During the short nights men gathered in their mag'ad while women gathered in one of the huts, each group spending its time eating slowly, reciting long traditional poems, or discussing human relations.

12 August 1979, Dahab, 11:00

Since I didn't wake up and thus missed the late night meal, I go down to the coastline to gather some sea snails which I'll boil for lunch. I notice Abu-Mūsa and 'Id stretching after post-morning-prayer naps. In preparation for the noon prayer they go down to the tidal zone and wash their arms, legs, and faces in the sea. I finish gathering sea snails and sit nearby, under the shade of a date tree. On this dry, hot day the three of us are captivated by the moist caress of the breeze as we wait for the muezzin's cry. I am reluctant to interrupt the flow of silence, but I have only three weeks left.

As if talking to myself I hesitantly say, "Ever since last summer, I have been perplexed as to why Shgēṭef-the-Fool sent me, with all my equipment, to the deserted Bir al-Sarādga."

A long moment passes till 'Id says, "You are an Israeli. Very soon, all sorts of Jews will go away from here, and then the Egyptians will come. Now we don't owe you anything any more. Not that we want the Egyptians over here, but your peace has left us no choice. Shgēṭef knows that like the rest of us."

More long moments pass, during which I count over and over again the sea snails in my lap.

"If so, why did Fṭaima respect me with all the tradition of hospitality?" I ask with less hesitation.

Abu-Mūsa shifts his back, negotiating a new leaning position on the date tree trunk and says, "Because you are one of us. You are the one who writes us. Write that we have a proverb that says: 'O, flee from the friend who abandons you, in his hands lie your family's graves. But breastfeed him who breastfeeds you—tell your children to serve him like slaves' [min 'adāk 'adī—'omrok ma-hu fi īdo; wa-min dadāk dadī—wakhalli wlādoc 'abīdo]. Now, we breastfeed you with our lives and with the stories about our lives, and your children are the notebooks you fill. That's why you're almost twenty-five and still unmarried. And the stories in your notebooks on our lives and our words serve us too, and one day they'll also serve our children."

At this moment I suddenly perceive the paradox and say, "Once you taught me that one can *never* simultaneously have one's Self and be an Other."

Abu-Mūsa and 'Id spontaneously rhyme their answer, "But the one who writes us has taken both selves."

And then we laugh.

22 August 1979, Dahab, 17:00

The last day of the Ramaḍān fast. Ghānma's hut. Ghānma, Omm-Mūsa, and I have just finished cooking the meal that will break the fast. We try to keep talking in order to forget our hunger and the creeping time. I sneak in a tough question. "By the way, why did Shgēṭef-the-Fool fool me last summer?"

"Don't worry," says Omm-Mūsa. "Next year he'll do the same thing to every Egyptian who sniffs around 'Ein al-Akhaḍar. He didn't know that you're also from here."

My feeling that the politically alert "Fool" knew exactly what he was doing is strengthened. I guess that that "memorable night" was part of the price I pay for being an Israeli who studies a Muslim Arab culture. I am very sad and silent for a while, but still—

"And Fṭaima, God bless her, does she think differently?" I continue. Ghānma laughs, "The women of Umm Ba'atheirān saw the tourists only a few times in their lives. For them, every one who knows how to say, 'I am a Bedouin,' is a Bedouin. Ah—the people of the highlands!" And she laughs contemptuously.

I take a deep breath and dare to ask it: "So, what do I mean to you?"

Omm-Mūsa answers decisively: "You are the one who writes us. Once we had a silly argument about what kind of Bedouin we are, and you had your notebook opened, and read us one of the stories about our roots."

"OK, but other Israelis also write about your lives," I argue.

Omm-Mūsa thinks for a moment and says, "True, but all those people do not physically stay *only* with us when they come to the Sinai. They live in the settlements of the Jews."

Ghānma continues and compliments me on how well I fish and graze and churn yogurt and climb on date trees and ride camels and play the goatherd-flute, and whatnot, after four years of living with the Mzeina. Why does she try to make me feel so good about myself now, when I am about to leave? She has always been so

[171]

honest with me. I stop listening attentively and become immersed in my own thoughts. I perk up when I hear her say:

"And your eyes are as dark as ours, and you don't become a roasted lobster after long days in the desert sun." Noticing my response, she pauses.

It's my turn to talk now, but I can only search for the words. At this silent moment we once again become aware of the smell of the taboo food and of the animal coiled in our souls, ready to pounce at the moment the muezzin cries for the last time, "Eat now, you who are fasting!"

"My roots are jumbled." Thankfully, in the shade one cannot easily tell that I am blushing. It never occurred to me that my split Israeli ethnic identity would be of any interest to the Bedouin— aside from the fact that the many Mzeinis who went to the Al-Aqsa mosque in Jerusalem for the Friday prayer visited the nearby house of my grandmother. She speaks a Yemenite dialect of Arabic, one very close to the Eastern Bedouin dialect,[12] and she felt she had to reciprocate the hospitality her granddaughter received in the South Sinai.

"One of my halves is from Yemen. In Israel we are called Arab Jews." I immediately stop without finishing what I had intended to say. Suddenly I connect my Israeli label with Mzeina vernacular. In the South Sinai dialect of Arabic only Bedouin are referred to as Arabs. The rest are labeled peasants or city dwellers, who are Egyptians, Syrians, Lebanese, or natives of other Middle Eastern countries. For them, an Arab Jew is a Bedouin Jew.

"Aii-wah! [yeah!]" The eyes of the two women light up. "We know you, ya Smadar," says Ghānma. "Only you and Mister Marri, the English Bedouin, lived with us," continues Omm-Mūsa. And the anthropologist immediately connects Mister Marri with G. F. Murray, the only one to actually live with the Mzeina for a couple of years during the 1920s, and with his travelogue, *Sons of Ishmael* (1935).[13] "You came here to update and correct his book . . . Both of you always told us how beautiful it is to climb to the top of mountains just for looking at the rest of the mountains. Besides, my great-uncle taught Mister Marri to fish, and my husband taught you to fish. Old people like me know how to connect the past with the present [*illi kān lilmakān*[14]]," says Omm-Mūsa, and I wonder whether we are still in the same story or if perhaps we have started narrating another one.

[172]

III

More historically, we can note that allegory seems regularly
to surface in critical or polemical atmospheres, when for
political or metaphysical reasons there is something that
cannot be said.

—Joel Fineman

The Mzeini reality of the perpetual occupation of their land generates an atmosphere of continuous crisis. The polyphony of many
Mzeini voices presented here means that one of the few avenues for
protest still open to tribal members, torn between economic and cultural survival (Lavie and Young 1984; Marx 1977, 1980), is transmuting
their experience into ongoing allegories rooted in tradition.[15] These
allegories have a dialectical nature (Benjamin 1985: 175): they sustain
the Mzeina's belief in the immortality of their collective tribal past,
and they demonstrate to the Mzeinis the extent to which they are
entrapped in the global fluctuations of the present.[16]

At that moment of "emergence" (McHugh 1968: 24–8) in Ghānma's
hut, I could link the tradition of hospitality to the here-and-now-in-
Sinai of the Camp David Accord in only one way: by stylizing the
month-old pain and frustration expressed in my field diary into an
emotionally detached story of *the present*. But, my story of the present
recalled to Omm-Mūsa a story of the "once upon a time" genre, the
story about Mister Marri.[17]

Unlike other literary forms, allegories can be conceived as cultural
narratives that contain within themselves a critique of that very narrative (cf. Frye 1967: 89–90; Quilligan 1979: 25–6);[18] they are thus the
"tropes of tropes," "representative of critical activity *per se*" (Fineman
1981: 27). Therefore, allegories voice simultaneously subjective and
objectified representations of the text and its many meanings. It can
be noted that the same ideas were unfolded, refolded and unfolded
again in my field diary, in the evening conversation at Ghānma's hut
followed by my distanced story, and in conversations with Abu-Mūsa,
'Id, Ghānma, and Omm-Mūsa eight months later. My "memorable
night experience" is reflected in my story, and my story reflects the

[173]

shared experience of Mzeina and myself—an experience transcending the temporal boundaries of my fieldwork. Such stories within stories about stories evoke a hall of mirrors. Mirrors, like allegories, attempt at capturing the inclusiveness of time spans and the completeness of spaces (Wimsatt, 1970: 215–21).

During my four years of fieldwork among the Mzeina, I recorded many mundane, after-prayer conversations that degenerated into loud and painful arguments. Some of these arguments were open-ended, abruptly discontinued, and never resolved. Others ended in a communal agreement accompanied by an elevated feeling of "communitas" (Turner, 1969: 96–7).

In my third year I noted in my field diary that the latter kind of debate reminded me of a sonata form. Like the first movement of a sonata, these conversations/debates consisted of a thematic exposition, a development phase exploring and exhausting the many variations of that theme, and a grandiose finale in which the original theme is recapitulated. The Mzeina's after-prayer arguments did not match the sonata's rules of vocality, however; the exposition of the argument's theme and its many explorations was multivocal, but a solo voice recapitulated the theme. Although the voice was single, it had the persuasive power to tie together the debate's loose ends, bringing the argument to a harmonious finale.

Tracing the sources of such powerful solos, I discovered a handful of people, including myself, who had the theatrical talent to play on the fact that, though Mzeina's tradition is marginal to everyday life circumstances, it nonetheless defines the identity of each tribesperson. Common to all of us was the fact that, like that "otherness" (allos) of allegories,[19] we were all capable of conjoining the Mzeini Self and the occupier's Other within ourselves. When any of us chose to rise up spontaneously and participate in the discussion, he or she changed the abrupt open-endedness of the argument by recapitulating its major theme.

I call these creative individuals "allegorical types." Gifted with the dramatic power to persuade, they summated the arguments by improvising on traditional tribal forms and poetically "adjusting" these forms to the lived experience of the present.[20]

I also recorded traditional stories and poems about most of these characters. One was "The Western yet Bedouinized Explorer," a category to which Mister Marri and I belong. The poems and stories made me realize that our lives as the allegorical types of the present

[174]

extend beyond the life span of us as individuals. Hence, one might argue that allegorical types are creative personae.

When individuals acted as allegorical types they improvised upon their own life experiences and recapitulated them as stylized stories.[21] In so doing, they communicated not only a message about themselves as particular types but also one about the historical context of Mzeina's general social structure and cultural action. But these creative personae were also ordinary persons. The question poses itself: what in the social context allowed these persons to move into and out of their allegorical selves?

In the midst of their ad hoc routines (Garfinkel 1967: 35–6), conversations of Mzeinis sometimes drifted from matters of daily life to the very essence of their being-in-the-world as members of a Bedouin tribe.[22] Reflecting about themselves in this reductionist fashion, Mzeinis' routine typifications of reality became discrete, contradictory, anomalous, and paradoxical (Grathoff 1970: 58–61). Imbued with liminal qualities, the paradoxes characteristic of ritual transformations surfaced into both the context and text of everyday dialogues—until the participants in the situation were struck by their powerlessness in defining their own situation (McHugh 1968: 42, 52).

At that moment a creative person sometimes rose up, became a persona, and acted as an allegorical type. By entering into an inconsistent social situation with an allegorized experience, he or she reconstructed the thematic meaning of the social context. In this way the person/persona was able to eliminate open-ended discontinuity and to transmute the paradoxes of the precarious reality the Mzeina take for granted into an allegory of temporary make-believe linked to the immortality of tradition (Handelman and Kapferer 1980; Handelman 1981, 1986).[23]

The allegorical type transformed all the participants in a mundane situation into partakers in the non-negotiable frame of ritual/play (Handelman 1977). The ritual/play was constructed according to the unambiguous messages of the person about him- or herself as a type. Hence, the social selves (Mead 1962: 140) of others became irrelevant during the type's performance. Nevertheless, as may be seen in my example, the selves of the audience were implicitly involved in the telling and interpreting of my allegory (G. Clifford 1974: 36; Quilligan 1979: 226). In retrospect, the allegory evidenced an identity that the participants sensed in themselves before the artistic intrusion of myself-the-type into their everyday life. Therefore, during the myself-

[175]

the-type performance, each phrase was acknowledged by "expletives signaling that the images created are not simply understood, but are enhancing the listener's appreciation of the story" (Basso 1984).

Northrop Frye has argued that allegory *is* interpretation, "an attaching of ideas to the structure of poetic imagery" (1967: 89–90). I would add that, in the Mzeina case, the interplay of allegorical images affected both poetics and politics—conjoining new experiences attached to the traditional structure of tribal poetics with global ideas affecting the old yet liminally unforgettable political structure of the tribe.[24] Mzeina's allegories were, therefore, "successful as allegory only to the extent that [they] could suggest the authenticity with which the two coordinating poles," the poetic and political, "bespeak each other" (Fineman 1981: 83). And the reservoir of authentic types who performed these allegories of current experience, living personae who at the same time are the main characters of traditional stories, helped the Mzeina to construct their identity as an "ideal type" (Weber 1949) of a Bedouin tribe.

Whenever I related my "memorable night" story to a Mzeini audience, I became that quirky tension dissolver, that Mzeina theatrical figure who appeared on the societal stage when Mzeinis asked themselves whether their tribe exists at all, and if so, at what level of organization. Narrating my personal experience, I-the-type bridged the geopolitical paradoxes of the present and the traditional forms and figures of the past. In this way I provided a set of specific answers to certain existential and organizational dilemmas arising from the unpredictability of everyday life in the Sinai.

But the allegorical type is an objectified analytical concept. Paradoxically,[25] by becoming one such concept myself, I have become my own anthropological construct. Is this yet another puzzle to solve in this double-reflexive text?

IV

Writing about the process of authorship in allegorical narration, Paul de Man has argued that "the moment when th[e] difference" between the persona of the author and the persona of the fictional narrator "is asserted is precisely the moment when the author does not return to the world. He asserts instead the ironic necessity of not becoming the dupe of his own irony and discovers that there is no way back from his fictional self to his actual self" (1969: 200). And interestingly, both de Man (ibid.) and Arthur Koestler (1964: 73) have viewed allegory and irony as the two poles of a similar genre.

I think it would be somewhat easier for someone who feels like an equal member of Western Culture to agree with de Man's assertion. Nonetheless, I feel that my allegorical Other (The One Who Writes Us) and my personal Self (consisting of both The Anthropologist and Smadar the woman) are fused. Searching for my identity, as the Bedouin do, I find that it is not at all an essence but entirely conjunctural, arising out of the circumstances of my being born into a certain family in Israel, and my choice of profession.

Part of my identity is that of a Western-trained professional anthropologist. Moreover, my father was a Northern European. From my mother I have my Arab culture, color, and temperament. In spite of the fact that ethnic identity is determined by the Israeli government according to the father's origin, and thus I appear as a European piece of data in bureaucratic statistics, it is my Arab half that counts socially. Since I am of dark complexion, Israelis always assume that I am a full Yemenite and treat me accordingly. Unlike my European descent, my Arab heritage qualifies me (at least in Israel) as a genuine, semicivilized Other. During my graduate studies, as I went back to classifying and analyzing my fieldnotes, I noticed that a theme of two exotic and voiceless Others emerged: my life experience in Israel was somehow mirrored in the life experience of the Mzeinis—and theirs in mine.

As a woman anthropologist, I was fully dependent on the Mzeina's hospitality once I reached the South Sinai. When the tradition of hospitality was called into question, despite my embarrassment I felt an urge to rise up and allegorize my Shgetef-the-Fool and Ftaima-and-her-two-toddlers experience. In spite of being a stranger dressed in baggy jeans and a Mickey Mouse T-shirt, I had been taught how to introduce myself to my hosts. Whenever I introduced myself to my Bedouin hosts, I momentarily became a living representation of their traditional tribal structure and organization. I was adopted by the tribe and was shown the path of Mister Marri. I was breastfed on stories about the life of the Mzeina, and now, by telling you my anthropological interpretations, I am enacting once again "the one who writes us."

Insofar as my Self is composed of two quite distinct identities, I am myself a composite of two Others. Each half of me is the Other of my other Self. I am able to be an Other both to European Israelis and to the Bedouin Mzeinis. In an ever more complicated relationship, I could spontaneously satisfy the Mzeinis' need to have someone play the part of an Other who, simultaneously, is not an Other. As neither identity may be reduced to the other, like those other quirky Mzeini tension dissolvers, I am in myself a metaphor of bifurcation, of unity in division, of a paradox without resolution. History and geography thus dictate the biography of an individual—and that of a tribe—in metaphor, the real poetics of politics.

Notes

1. The Arabic words in the following text are transliterated according to the Mzeina vernacular, not according to Modern Standard Arabic. Therefore, in the vernacular, the classical "q" becomes a "g," pronounced like the "g" in "good." In transliterating Mzeina vernacular, I have oriented myself more or less on the standards of the *International Journal of Middle East Studies*.

2. *Mag'ad rejjāl*, hereafter, simply mag'ad, is a space designated for Bedouin men and their guests. In a semipermanent settlement such as 'Ein al-Akhaḍar, it consists of a structure of one or two parallel stone walls, supported by wooden pillars and roofed by sheet metal. The mag'ad is at the spacious center of the settlement. In a temporary summer encampment, the mag'ad consists of a stretched sheet of woven goat hair, providing protection from sun and wind. It is located at the outskirts of the tent cluster, so that the men and their guests are set apart from the camp's hustle and bustle, and so that the privacy of the women and children is not invaded. In the middle of the mag'ad's designated space is a circle of stones marking the stove area in which there are some burning coals. In the corner are two to three storage boxes where coffee beans, tea, sugar and flour are stored, together with a pestle and a mortar, a roasting pan for the beans, a copper coffeepot, an aluminum teakettle, special cups for tea and coffee, and sometimes a round piece of sheet metal on which flat bread is baked. Long, narrow, handwoven rugs, the best of which is reserved for guests, are used for sitting or reclining in a circle around the embers.

3. In the last century the Sinai Bedouin have been governed by the Ottoman Turks, the British, the Egyptians, and the Israelis. During the last thirty-five years, the government of the South Sinai changed hands six times: from the 1940s until 1952, the Sinai was governed by the Egyptian King Farouq and patrolled by British army units. Between 1952 and 1956, it was under independent Egyptian control. In 1956, it was occupied by Israel, backed by France and Britain. Between 1956 and 1967, it was returned to the Egyptians, who were aided by the Soviets. Between 1967 and 1975, it was occupied again by Israel. Between 1975 and 1982, Israel withdrew from the Sinai in five stages in order to return it to Egypt once again.

4. I wish to thank Don Handelman for pointing out to me this crucial point.

5. I wrote my field diary in Hebrew. I also wrote my fieldnotes in Hebrew, but I recorded the voices of the Mzeinis in Arabic, using the Hebrew alphabet. Arabic and Hebrew letters are written as different graphic symbols but represent similar vowels and consonants. Since many Mzeinis owned cassette recorders and used them

[178]

to record their friends reciting poetry or rhymed epics, or songs and favorite radio programs, I noticed that many people felt uncomfortable when I asked permission to use a cassette recorder to record their daily dialogues. They suggested I write their mundane conversation in my notebook while sitting in some corner. It was much easier for me to write Arabic in Hebrew letters as I write Hebrew more quickly.

6. The reader familiar with purdah cultures, of which the Arab World is one example, may wonder why I, as a woman, appear here and throughout this essay in male and female contexts. Because the South Sinai Bedouin have long been accustomed to the influx of tourists, developers, soldiers, and other Westerners, both male and female, it was not difficult to develop strong nonsexual friendships with Mzeini men. Both Mzeini men and women poked fun at my facility in moving between the genders, saying, "Smadar has the body (*jism*) and soul (*nafs*) of a woman and the logical mind (*'agl*) of a man." They explained that I could churn yogurt and play the flute, as well as gallop on camels and talk foreign currency rates. My time in the field was divided equally between the daily and ritual spheres of men and women. Both employed me as a go-between in romantic trysts. This would suggest that, despite my "trans-gender mobility," I enjoyed the trust of both. In retrospect, the only person to suffer from these circumstances was myself. After four years of genderless identity, my four years in the field, it was a real struggle to regain a distinct sense of womanhood. Interestingly, Amal Rassam [Vinogradov] also mentions that the men "graciously put up with [her] female presence in their jama'as," or official gathering places (1974: v). This despite the fact that the tribe she studied did not live in the surreal context forced upon the Mzeina, on which I elaborate in subsequent pages.

7. Many communities of the Mzeina have a male character called the "fool," or *al-ahabal*. This person is allowed to violate many of the tribal codes of conduct; thus, he is able to serve as a legitimate device for criticism of both tribal ideology and everyday life (cf. Lavie 1984, 1990, 1991).

8. Tanīb (sing., masc.) or ṭanība (sing., fem.) is a person who does not belong to any lineage of the Mzeina, and who is given fictive kinship ties by a patrilineage of the tribe, so that he or she is protected by the Bedouin legal system.

9. The following conversation has been generously pruned. The names of the participants appearing in the following vignettes have been changed. The translation seeks a middle way between the claims of literalness and those of aesthetics.

10. This may sound rather fantastic to someone unfamiliar with some of the tourists who arrived in the Sinai during the Israeli occupation. As a matter of fact, more than a few hippie backpackers engaged in coitus in front of the shocked Bedouin, who later named it "Film Screening for Free," or *Cinema Balash*. The Bedouin organized one delegation after another, each of which pleaded with the peninsula's Israeli military governor to put up signs requesting the tourists to wear bathing suits. The military governor advised these pious Muslims to learn to enjoy the "show," and refused to take any further action. The Bedouin had to acquiesce, because hippie tourism was a major source of household income in Dahab and a much more attractive choice than cleaning toilets in Israeli hotels in Eilat. When a famous *Ha'aretz* (major Israeli newspaper) journalist became interested in the moral costs to the Mzeina of the extracurricular activities of the military governor, I was harassed for several months by the governor and his aides.

11. Such echo statements are the dialogical participation of the audience during monologic storytelling sessions. They usually appear at the end of each episode. This issue is further developed by Basso (1984), who terms the responder to a monologue a "What Sayer"; in this article she discusses that person's crucial role in the preservation of traditional knowledge in nonliterate cultures.

12. (See also note 1.) The consonant "q" is pronounced "g" in many Bedouin dialects and in the Yemenite dialect of Arabic my grandmother speaks.

13. See Murray 1935.

14. *Kān ya ma kān*, or *kan ya-makān*, is one of the sentences used to mark the opening of a story. It has a built-in ambiguity, literally meaning "it had or had not happened," contextually meaning "once upon a time, there was a place."

15. Indeed, literary critics view allegory as a story of the present that reflects the stories of some mythical or occult past (see de Man 1969, 1979, 1981, Fineman 1981, Fletcher 1964, Greenblatt 1981, Quilligan 1979, Todorov 1970, and Wimsatt 1970. Allegory thus "heals the gap between the present and a disappearing past, which without interpretation, would be otherwise irretrievable and foreclosed" (Fineman 1981: 29). Dialectically, allegory is capable of dancing between these pasts and presents by "renouncing the nostalgia and the desire to coincide," so that "it establishes its language in the void of this temporal difference" (de Man 1969: 191).

16. I thank Fredrik Huxley for pointing out this dialectical nature of Mzeina allegories.

17. I do not wish to be identified with my desert predecessor. One summer I checked out Murray's book from the Hebrew University Library and read to many Mzeinis (and members of other tribes), during the pilgrimage to the tomb of Sheikh Graii, the largest event of the tribal alliance, the parts discussing the South Sinai tribal alliance. They were amused and shocked by the fairy stories their fathers had told that young British explorer. During this pilgrimage, the three chief customary judges of the Mzeina officially appointed me to correct the "funny shame our parents brought on the writers of the Sinai." I was asked daily to read aloud my personal observations of the day, although reading interviews aloud was considered an invasion of the interviewed person's privacy; many details were added during those readings.

18. Despite my deep appreciation of Quilligan's comprehensive analysis of allegory, as a scholar of nonliterate cultures I cannot agree with her assessment that "unlike epics, which can be oral, allegories are always written" (1979: 25).

19. The word allegory is composed of *allos*, a Greek word meaning "other," and *agoreuein*, "to speak in the *agora*," to speak openly in the assembly or market. *Agoreuein* connotes public, open, declarative speech (Fletcher 1964: 2). Apparently, the paradox of Self talking openly about Self's Other is built into the concept of allegory.

20. Among the Mzeina members who may act as allegorical types are the Fool (see Lavie 1984), the Madwoman (Lavie 1983), the Sheikh (Lavie 1989), the Symbolic War Coordinator and the Judge (briefly described in this paper), the Anthropologist, and several others who are discussed in greater detail in my book (Lavie 1990).

21. Interestingly, discussing the enactment of allegories, Fletcher (1964: 5) argues that "it is the mark of allegory that its *dramatis personae* are abstract concepts; they have no separate existence or legend, such as the characters of myth enjoy; and as a rule they are created *ad hoc*, to suit a particular occasion. The occasion gone, the symbolism loses its meaning."

22. In these cultural circumstances, when the Mzeina seek the deep meaning of their being-in-the-world qua members of a Bedouin tribe, I feel that they reduce the cultural text to its essence both semiotically, à la Claude Lévi-Strauss (1967: 271) *and* phenomenologically, à la Edmund Husserl (1962: 48). In this context, a *noesis-noema* relation may be viewed as some kind of intersubjective signifier-signified relation.

23. In a pioneering article, Don Handelman and Bruce Kapferer (1980) discuss the emergence of symbolic types in ritual settings. Handelman (1981, 1986) further develops the concepts of symbolic typification and its relation to the performance of ritual

transformation. My analysis of allegorical typification departs from the concepts discussed in these articles.

24. Surprisingly, whenever I asked a Mzeini for the meaning of "tribe," the first explanation was something along the lines of the "fission and fusion" model developed by E. E. Evans-Pritchard (1940; cf. Lavie 1990).

25. The paradox I refer to is one of the "class of all classes which are not members of themselves," discussed by Russell and Whitehead in their mathematical theory of logical typification (1910).

REFERENCES

Basso, Ellen B. 1984. "Monological Understanding in Dialogic Discourse." Paper presented at the Annual Meeting of the American Anthropological Association. Denver, Colo.: November 16.

Benjamin, Walter. 1985. (1963). "Allegory and Trauerspiel." In W. Benjamin, *The Origin of German Tragic Drama.* Trans. J. Osborne. London: Verso. Pp. 159–235.

Berger, Peter L., and Thomas Luckman. 1967. *The Social Construction of Reality: A Treatise in the Sociology of Knowledge.* Garden City, N.Y.: Doubleday.

Clifford, Gay. 1974. *The Transformation of Allegory.* London: Routledge and Kegan Paul.

de Man, Paul. 1969. "The Rhetoric of Temporality." In C. C. Singleton, ed., *Interpretation: Theory and Practice.* Baltimore: John Hopkins University Press. Pp. 173–210.

———. 1979. *Allegories of Reading: Figural Language in Rousseau, Nitzsche, Rilke, and Proust.* New Haven, Conn.: Yale University Press.

———. 1981. "Pascal's Allegory of Persuasion." In Greenblatt, ed., 1981. Pp. 1–25.

Evans-Pritchard, E. E. 1940. *The Nuer.* Oxford: Oxford University Press.

Fineman, Joel. 1981. "The Structure of Allegorical Desire." In Greenblatt, ed., 1981. Pp. 26–60.

Fletcher, Angus. 1964. *Allegory: The Theory of a Symbolic Mode.* Ithaca: Cornell University Press.

Frye, Northrop. 1967. *Anatomy of Criticism: Four Essays.* New York: Atheneum.

Garfinkel, Harold. 1967. *Studies in Ethnomethodology.* Englewood Cliffs, N.J.: Prentice-Hall.

Grathoff, Richard. 1970. *The Structure of Social Inconsistencies: A Contribution to a Unified Theory of Play, Game, and Social Action.* The Hague: Martinus Nijhoff.

Greenblatt, Stephen J. ed. 1981. *Allegory and Representation.* Baltimore: Johns Hopkins University Press.

Handelman, Don. 1977. "Play and Ritual: Complementary Frames of Metacommunication." In A. J. Chapman and H. Foot, eds., *It's a Funny Thing, Humor.* Oxford: Pergamon Press. Pp. 185–92.

———. 1981. "The Ritual Clown: Attributes and Affinities." *Anthropos* 76 (1/2): 321–70.

———. 1986. "Charisma, Liminality, and Symbolic-Types." In E. Cohen, M. Lissak, and U. Almagor, eds., *Comparative Social Dynamics: Essays in Honor of S. N. Eisenstadt*. Boulder, Colo.: Westview Press. Pp. 346–59.

Handelman, Don, and Bruce Kapferer. 1980. "Symbolic Types, Mediation, and the Transformation of Ritual Context: Sinhalese Demons and Tewa Clowns." *Semiotica* 30 (1/2): 41–71.

Husserl, Edmund. 1962. *Ideas: General Introduction to Pure Phenomenology*. Trans. W. C. Boyce Gibson (first published in English in 1931). New York: Collier Books.

Koestler, Arthur. 1964. *The Act of Creation*. London: Macmillan.

Lavie, Smadar. 1983. "The Madwoman: Spontaneous Theatre and Social Inconsistencies among the Mzeina Bedouin of Sinai." Paper presented at the Annual Meeting of the American Ethnological Society. Baton Rouge.

———. 1984. "The Fool and the Hippies: Ritual/Play and Social Inconsistencies among the Mzeina Bedouin of the Sinai." In B. Sutton-Smith and D. Kelly-Byrne, eds. *The Masks of Play*. New York: Leisure Press. Pp. 63–70.

———. 1986. "The Poetics of Politics: An Allegory of Bedouin Identity." In M. J. Aronoff, ed., *Political Anthropology*, vol. 5: *The Frailty of Authority*. New Brunswick, N.J.: Transaction Books. Pp. 131–46.

———. 1989. "When Leadership Becomes Allegory: Mzeina Sheikhs and the Experience of Occupation." *Cultural Anthropology*. 4(2): 99-135.

———. 1990. *The Poetics of Military Occupation: Mzeina Allegories of Bedouin Identity under Egyptian &Israeli Rule*. Berkeley and Los Angeles: University of California Press.

———. 1991. "The Bedouin, the Beatniks, and the Redemptive Fool." *Quarterly Review of Film & Video*, special issue, "Discourse of the Other: Postcoloniality, Positionality, and Subjectivity," edited by H. Naficy & J. H. Gabriel, 13(1-3):23-43.

Lavie, Smadar, and William C. Young. 1984. "Bedouin in Limbo: Egyptian and Israeli Development Policies in the Southern Sinai." *Antipode* 16 (2): 33–44.

Lévi-Strauss, Claude. 1967. *Structural Anthropology*. Garden City, N.Y.: Anchor Books.

Marx, Emanuel. 1977. "Communal and Individual Pilgrimage: The Region of Saints' Tombs in the South Sinai." In R. P. Werbner, ed., *Regional Cults*. London: Academic Press. Pp. 29–51.

———. 1980. "Wage Labor and Tribal Economy of the Bedouin in South Sinai." In P. C. Salzman, ed., *When Nomads Settle*. New York: Praeger.

McHugh, Peter. 1968. *Defining the Situation: The Organization of Meaning in Social Interaction*. New York: Bobbs-Merrill.

Mead, George H. 1962. *Mind, Self, and Society*. Chicago: University of Chicago Press.

Murray, G. W. 1935. *Sons of Ishmael: A Study of the Egyptian Bedouin*. London: George Routledge and Sons.

Quilligan, Maureen. 1979. *The Language of Allegory: Defining the Genre*. Ithaca: Cornell University Press.

Rassam (Vinogradov), Amal. 1974. "The Ait Ndhir of Morocco: A Study of the Social Transformation of a Berber Tribe." *Anthropological Papers* no. 55. Museum of Anthropology, University of Michigan. Ann Arbor: University of Michigan Press.

Russell, Bertrand, and Alfred North. Whitehead. 1910. *Principia Mathematica.* Vol. 1. Cambridge: Cambridge University Press.

Todorov, Tzvetan. 1975. *The Fantastic: A Structural Approach to a Literary Genre.* Ithaca: Cornell University Press.

Turner, Victor. 1967. "Betwixt and Between: The Liminal Period in *Rites de Passage.*" In Victor Turner, *The Forest of Symbols: Aspects of Ndembu Ritual.* Ithaca: Cornell University Press.

———. 1969. *The Ritual Process: Structure and Anti-Structure.* Chicago: Aldine.

Weber, Max. 1949. *The Ideal Type and Generalized Analytical Theory.* In Talcott Parsons, ed., *The Structure of Social Action.* Glencoe, Ill.: Free Press. Pp. 601–10.

Wimsatt, James I. 1970. *Allegory and Mirror: Tradition and Structure in Middle English Literature.* New York: Pegasus.

[8]

The Return of the Mexican Ballad: Américo Paredes and His Anthropological Text as Persuasive Political Performances

José E. Limón

This essay's principal argument is that a particular anthropological text and its author, largely ignored in wider anthropological circles, have played a central influential role in the formation and development of a Mexican-American political culture in our time. I refer to Américo Paredes and his *With His Pistol in His Hand: A Border Ballad and Its Hero* (1958, 1971), a study of the Mexican ballad, or *corrido*, and its sociocultural context along the lower Texas-Mexico border. Although an important part of this book's significance stems from its superb scholarship and its anticipation of certain contemporary intellectual practices, in this analysis, I want to call attention to that influence which flows from the author's career and part I of his book as cultural rhetoric, as unified, contextually persuasive, textual performances. Paredes's life and his book, in their narrative organization and poetics, recall the aesthetic politics of their scholarly subject, the Mexican ballad of border conflict; through their artistic transformation of the ballad, they exert a compelling influence on a new generation.

It is not often that an anthropological study and the life of its author become persuasive, artistic, textual performances, if by the latter phrase we at least imply, following Jan Mukarovsky (1977), that a textuality partakes of what he calls "poetic designation," meaning the "every use of words occurring in a text with a predominant aesthetic function" (1977: 65) where this aesthetic function renders "the sign itself the center of attention" (1977: 68). However, Mukarovsky does not wish to be misconstrued on two important issues: one, such a designation and function apply not only to formal poetry or other figurative language; "this function participates, at least potentially, in every human act" (1977: 69), whether poem, ritual, conversation, or anthropology; and, two, that this focus on the sign "itself," while weakening the relationship to any immediate reality, "does not preclude a relation between the work and reality as a whole; on the contrary it is even beneficial to this relation" (1977: 71). He summarizes and concludes in a statement that is a charter for this essay. "The aesthetic function . . . is potentially present in every utterance. The specific character of poetic designation, therefore, rests solely in its more radical exposure of the tendency inherent in every act of designation. The weakening of the immediate relation of poetic designation to reality is counterbalanced by the fact that the poetic work as a global designation enters into relation with the *total* set of the existential experiences of the subject, be he the creative or the perceiving subject" (1977: 72–73).

We are only too aware of the poetic designation inherent in traditional literary practice in its various genres. However, other human acts, and indeed "every human act," are beginning to receive increasing attention in these terms, including those discourses, chiefly intellectual, that often inherently and strongly define themselves with a claim to *non*-poetic designation. The analysis and the self-conscious *practice* of poetic designation in ostensibly non-poetic intellectual discourse, while not yet mainstream, gains increasing prominence, a tendency that Clifford Geertz, one of its exemplary practitioners and theorists, calls "blurred genres" (1980). We also think of Hayden White in history (1973, 1978), Harold Bloom in literary criticism (1982), and in anthropology, with Geertz, others including Boon (1982), Marcus and Cushman (1982), Bruner (1986), and Clifford and Marcus (1986).

I will also argue that, as practice, Paredes's poetically designated anthropology anticipates this contemporary trend toward "blurred genres"; my own essay pretends to be an ethnically keyed, theoretical intervention in this new trend. Thus, in union with Paredes, I want to help allay James Clifford's concern that ethnic marginality may be a necessary constraint on textual experimentation or its theoretical analysis.[1]

Further, this essay proposes to be a modest effort to restore Mukarovsky's full formation, whose social intent is often repressed in

[185]

contemporary analysis.[2] There is, it seems to me, in such analysis, a too singular concern with the first half of his formulation, with the text as pure sign rendering it the "center of attention," and a relative lack of concern with the poetically designated text "as a global designation" which "enters into relation with the *total* set of the existential experiences of the subject, be he the creative or the perceiving subject." I want to take Paredes's poetically designated text and his career beyond their obvious reference to an immediate reality (the Mexican ballad and a community of ballad specialists) to its more global designation as a persuasive, political cultural text that, marshalling the influence of the ballad, addresses and helps to form a generation of poets, intellectuals and activists all engaged in a political movement. I propose then to focus on the poetics of *With His Pistol in His Hand* and its author, firmly taking into account, to paraphrase Mukarovsky only once again, a near totality of the social experiences of those political, creative, and perceiving subjects involved in the textualization of this author and his work.

The Appearance of *With His Pistol in His Hand*

Paredes's book is generally a continuation of a scholarly tradition of folk cultural studies on the Mexican-descent population of the U.S. Southwest. When published in 1958, it represented a sharp break with the interpretive politics of this tradition, which consisted either of a conservative formal textualism, as in the case of Aurelio M. Espinosa's work on New Mexico, or a liberal utopian romanticism, as in J. Frank Dobie's work on Mexican Texas (Limón n.d.). As I suggest in this section, Paredes offered a conflictual model of cultural process which took into account, at least implicitly, questions of class, domination, and cultural creation and resistance. In this respect his work was an early alternative in critical anticipation of a body of later, functionalist anthropological work on this population (Rosaldo 1985). However, as I began to suggest earlier, *With His Pistol in His Hand* is substantively a study of the Mexican border ballad or corrido as it appears and develops along the lower Texas-Mexico border, South Texas, since the Spanish settlement of the area in the mid-eighteenth century. More specifically, it is a study of the life, legend, and corpus of ballads generated by the activities of one individual, Gregorio Cortez. My interpretation of Paredes's book requires the reader's knowledge and understanding of these events: what follows is the known history of the incident as set out by Paredes.

Until 12 June 1901 Cortez was a rather ordinary Mexican-American in Texas, an agricultural laborer like so many others who, from his own perspective, was witnessing the intensification of a largely Anglo-American and capitalist domination of Texas, including the predominantly Mexican-American region of South Texas. This domination of the native and increasingly immigrant Mexican-descent population took the form of class and racial subordination, the latter evidenced in part in the rough and ready lynching "justice" often administered to Mexican-Americans accused of crimes (Limón 1986). Such was the fate that Cortez undoubtedly expected on 12 June in the moments after he killed Sheriff W. T. Morris in Karnes County in central Texas in an exchange of pistol fire which also left Cortez's brother, Romaldo, seriously wounded. In his last official act, Sheriff Morris, an ex-Texas Ranger, had come out to the farm where the Cortezes, migrants from the border, were sharecropping. The sheriff was looking for reported horse thieves. Because neither he nor his accompanying deputy spoke Spanish well, if at all, they mistakenly accused the Cortezes of the thievery, and the sheriff drew his gun. Probably thinking they were about to be gunned down in cold blood, Romaldo charged the sheriff, not knowing that his brother had a gun hidden behind his back. Morris shot Romaldo but in the next instant was himself cut down by Gregorio, even as the deputy ran for his life and help. With the sheriff lying dead before him, Cortez knew that he faced certain Texas justice. Entrusting his brother to his family, Gregorio began a long horseback ride of escape to South Texas and the Mexican border. Along the way he evaded numerous posses through skillful riding and help from local Mexican-Americans. He also killed a second sheriff. Eventually, Cortez learned that the authorities had incarcerated his wife and children and were carrying out reprisals against those who had helped him. He turned himself in to the authorities near Laredo, Texas, where Mexican-Americans still had some measure of political control. Nonetheless, he was returned to Karnes County where, under constant threat of lynching, he was tried and convicted. In one of those paradoxes characteristic of Texas, he was eventually pardoned by an Anglo governor.

By 1901 the Mexican-Americans of Texas had experienced a half century of domination. Cortez's encounter with this domination and his largely successful, adventurous ride to freedom stirred the folk

[187]

imagination of this community; its folk singers turned to a traditional musical form—the corrido—to speak to these events. As a song narrative the corrido had as its ancestral form the medieval Spanish *romance* such as those of *El Cid*. Then, as now, this form served communities well in recording important historical events and artistically rendering their perspectives on these events. Soon after, or perhaps even during, Cortez's ride, the folk singers began to compose and sing the ballad of Gregorio Cortez, as Paredes says, "in the *cantinas* and the country stores, in the ranches when men gather at night to talk in the cool dark, sitting in a circle, smoking and listening to the old songs and the tales of other days" (1971: 33). They sang this song in the traditional octosyllabic metre with rhyming quatrains of *a b c b* and in duets of two guitars. One of the better versions of the ballad which Paredes offers as a representative text follows:

El Corrido de Gregorio Cortez

In the county of El Carmen
A great misfortune befell;
The Major Sheriff is dead;
Who killed him no one can tell.

At two in the afternoon,
In half an hour or less,
They knew that the man who killed him
Had been Gregorio Cortez.

They let loose the bloodhound dogs;
They followed him from afar.
But trying to catch Cortez
Was like following a star.

All the rangers of the county
Were flying, they rode so hard;
What they wanted was to get
The thousand-dollar reward.

And in the county of Kiansis
They cornered him after all;
Though they were more than three hundred
He leaped out of their corral.

Then the Major Sheriff said,
As if he was going to cry,

"Cortez, hand over your weapons;
We want to take you alive."

Then said Gregorio Cortez,
And his voice was like a bell,
"You will never get my weapons
Till you put me in a cell."

Then said Gregorio Cortez,
With his pistol in his hand,
"Ah, so many mounted Rangers
Just to take one Mexican!"

Cortez's epic encounter was neither the first nor the last of such encounters with Anglo-Texan authority, nor was it the first or last to inspire corridos. Ten years before Cortez, Catarino Garza, journalist and guerrilla leader, had taken up organized arms against the Texas Rangers and inspired a balladry. Fourteen years after Cortez, new corridos could be heard along the border about *los sediciosos* (the seditionists), bands of Mexicans who, again, rose up in armed rebellion in 1915–1916 against Anglo-Texan authority. In reprisal the Texas Rangers carried out massive killings of combatants and civilians alike, a practice that even an eminent champion of the Rangers, historian Walter Prescott Webb, felt obliged to criticize as an "orgy of bloodshed" (1935: 263).

In an attenuated form, the tradition of conflict and corridos continues through the present, although by the 1930s the intense conflict and the epic corridos of the past had diminished (Peña 1982: Limón 1983). Nonetheless, the subordination of the Mexican-descent community continued even while new leadership elements emerged to speak on its behalf, albeit in an assimilationist rhetoric. It was in the waning moments of the epic corrido and amid this new assimilationist ideology that Américo Paredes came to maturity. I shall say more of his life later; for now, I note that he is Professor of English and Anthropology at the University of Texas at Austin.

When it appeared in 1958, *With His Pistol in His Hand* received its principal attention from the communities of folklorists and scholars of the West and certain elements of the Anglo lay public in Texas. It might have remained another circumscribed, scholarly book for specialists. However, in the 1960s the book found a sociopolitical context and a wider audience of socially-designated perceiving subjects that gave it a far more global meaning. The 1960s provided these when

[189]

the first significant groups of largely working-class Mexican-American youth attended colleges and universities in the Southwest, and joined with other youth in the political protest and cultural rebellion of the time. For Mexican-American youth, of course, there was a very particular focus on the continuing socioeconomic plight of their native community. This activity among this college youth became the Chicano movement which, in addition to its practical politics, also generated a great deal of intellectual and artistic work on the Mexican-American community (Gomez-Quiñones 1978; Ybarra-Frausto 1977). Published on the eve of this political, intellectual, and artistic florescence, Paredes's book proved to be not only a scholarly, anthropological folklore study but also a text written in such a poetically designated way that, almost as if by design, it became a powerful influence on a new generation of Chicano writers, intellectuals, and activists as they produced a new critical social discourse. The late Tomás Rivera, former chancellor of the University of California at Riverside and still the leading Chicano fiction writer, had this to say concerning his introduction to *With His Pistol in His Hand.* He writes of a time when he was a graduate student at a small state college in San Marcos, Texas between Austin and Karnes County.

> One day I was wandering through the library and I came across *With His Pistol in His Hand* by Américo Paredes and I was fascinated. I didn't even know Paredes existed though we were only thirty miles away . . . but there was no communication at all, because there wasn't a Movement or anything like that. I checked out that book. I was hungry to find something by a Chicano. . . . It fascinated me because, one, it proved it was possible for a Chicano to publish; two, it was about a Chicano, Gregorio Cortez and his deeds . . . and, the ballads too. I grew up with the *corridos* in Texas. That book indicated to me that it was possible to talk about a Chicano as a complete figure. . . . More importantly, *With His Pistol in His Hand* indicated to me a whole imaginative possibility for us to explore. Now that also was in 1958, and it was then I began to think, write, and reflect a hell of a lot more on those people I had known in 1945 to '55. (Bruce-Novoa 1980: 150)

Taking Rivera's statement as a representative text for the Chicano movement, I now want to examine the persuasive poetics of Paredes's book to suggest interpretively how it could become such influential cultural rhetoric.

Given the account of Gregorio Cortez Paredes has given us in *With His Pistol in His Hand,* it is not difficult to see a general and simple basis for the book's appeal to a new audience of young Chicanos. Seeing themselves in a renewed confrontation with the gringos, Chicano community activists would certainly find an inspiring model in the figure of Cortez, his pistol in hand, resisting Anglo authority. For Chicano critical scholars, Paredes's superb, counterhegemonic scholarship would also prove influential, particularly for a group that had precious few examples of such scholarship in its historical background. Finally, as Rivera demonstrates, Chicano creative writers certainly responded affirmatively to Paredes's fine, engaging depiction of Cortez.[3]

However, I submit that, in addition to its political, scholarly, and literary qualities, or better still, subsuming all of these, *With His Pistol in His Hand* and its author work as cultural rhetoric, as a total poetic global designation for the Chicano movement. We must understand this influence then beyond the artificial divisions of politics, letters, and scholarship. In their narrative composition, the author/text recall and transform the residual though still powerful social poetics of the Mexican ballad for social subjects who were still keenly aware of this native poetics. As Tomás Rivera attests: "I grew up with the corridos in Texas," and so did many of us. It is as if, through the possession of this traditional aesthetics, *With His Pistol in His Hand* and its author were composed as a transformed "ballad," and we, the participants in the Chicano movement, were able to read them as such. Drawing on this shared aesthetic, Paredes and his text may have played an important part in producing the form and character of the Chicano movement as a total cultural enactment. It was a movement that could and did respond to the corrido directly in its "naive" form[4] but one that also needed and found a mediated and transformed corrido that would both evoke the traditional aesthetic yet respond to a new socioeducational reality. As a "model of" the past, this new corrido also offered a "model for" producing a political movement in our time (Geertz 1973).

My analysis will focus on those major elements in the book that, since its publication, have contributed to its rhetorical influence as another ballad of Gregorio Cortez.

The Return of the Mexican Ballad: The Author's Text

Paredes's book opens with an unusual dedication, one that is an important part of the public text. His dedication in free verse "to the

memory of my father / who rode a raid or two with / Catarino Garza"
continues:

> and to all those old men
> who sat around on summer nights
> in the days when there was
> a chaparral, smoking their
> cornhusk cigarettes and talking
> in low, gentle voices about
> violent things;
> while I listened.   (1971: 6)

This poetic text at the beginning of the book is important because it
establishes the author's relationship to his father and to an older generation and their folklore (a point to be pursued later); it also establishes
the writer's special authority to recall and transform the past which,
on those summer nights, would have included the singing of corridos.
In his use of free English language meter and verse and in his evocation
of his youth, the author is also establishing his authority to speak to
the present generation increasingly educated in a modernist and postmodernist climate.

A brief introduction is next, as if the author is anxious to move us
quickly to the main text; its precise economy, however, alerts us to
the traditional model that will inform this text. The author uses his
introduction to set up his rhetorical strategy in three ways. First,
Paredes tells us: "This book began as the study of a ballad; it developed
into the story of a ballad hero. Thus it became two books in one. It
is an account of the life of a man, of the way that songs and legends
grew up about his name, and of the people who produced the songs,
the legends, and the man. It is also the story of a ballad, 'El Corrido
de Gregorio Cortez,' of its development out of actual events, and of
the folk traditions from which it sprang" (1971: 3). This statement of
textual division permits Paredes to present technical, formal scholarship and analysis of the Mexican ballad in a separate, second section,
with the strategic rhetorical effect of making available to the reader,
should he or she need it, the defining material for understanding this
genre. At the same time, by bracketing this more technical, "scholarly"
data in a separate and second section, he does not impede the narrative
flow of part I for those who may already possess a good deal of the
necessary and perhaps native knowledge concerning the corrido form.
(For others, the result is an engaging, informative good story.)

Second, as if to alert us explicitly to the style of his text even as he provides useful information, Paredes also provides a brief and general definition of the corrido: "*Corrido*, the Mexicans call their narrative folk songs, especially those of epic themes, taking the name from *correr*, which means 'to run' or 'to flow', for the *corrido* tells a story simply and swiftly, without embellishments" (1971: 3). I suggest that this is precisely what we will recognize when we begin the main text, a story told "simply and swiftly, without embellishments."

Finally, however, it will not be a simple story about just any balladry or for that matter, any Mexican balladry; it will be a story about the balladry of borders and conflict, particularly the border and conflict between those of Anglo and Mexican descent in the United States. With this third rhetorical move, Paredes locates his Chicano readers and appeals to their general experiential sense of this conflict in the same way that a traditional ballad singer along the border might say, as part of his brief introduction, "I'm going to sing a corrido about the americanos," and everyone would understand the social relation he was evoking as the context for his song.

Having just told us that this will be a book about corridos, Paredes next presents us with a partial version of one printed on a single page without commentary (1971: 6). We might say that, on one level, it is there as a useful example of what he will soon be discussing. In my interpretive terms, however, it also has the rhetorical effect of re-minding Chicano readers of the style of our traditional folk form and of its sound for those who can read the musical notation that Paredes also provides (not included on p. 6). Moving to the next page, we have the model of the corrido fresh in our consciousness, a visible reminder of the tradition that Paredes is about to transform for our use.

To proceed further in understanding this transformation, we must move momentarily to part II of the book; here, we obtain a fuller definition of the corrido that we can use as context for the corrido-like quality of part I and for a comparison of the two corridos, that of tradition and that of scholarly prose. According to Paredes, a "scenic structure . . . is typical of the Border heroic *corrido*. The setting in motion of the action in a few swift lines, the introduction of the hero speaking out his boast in the second scene, after his first exploit, thus giving the whole narrative a middle-of-things feeling, the tendency to tell the story not in a long continuous and detailed narrative but in a series of shifting scenes and by means of action and dialogue—all these are stylistic devices typical of the Border *corrido*." And, in such ballads, Paredes continues, "a couple of stanzas get the story going and then the hero appears shouting out his boast or his defiance. From that moment on, the story moves swiftly to its conclusion, with point of view shifting rapidly from the hero to his adversaries and back again, and from one position in space to another if the action covers a great deal of ground" (1971: 187).

To this we might add the following, with which Paredes would not disagree. The corrido of border conflict is embedded in a history of social conflict, and therefore, as a text, it continually signifies and refers to the confrontation of larger social forces defined by ethnicity and class.

Armed with this extended definition of the border corrido, we can now closely examine part I of *With His Pistol in His Hand* and its author's biography as they incorporate and transform this traditional poetics into a compelling rhetoric for our time. As a textual transformation of tradition, we should, of course, not expect *With His Pistol in His Hand* to be a ballad. Rather, as a text, it reveals the stylistic influence of its folk subject, drawing upon its simple power and transforming it for an audience. This audience draws upon its knowledge of this traditional poetics yet needs it transformed to speak to a new social and intellectual political climate.

The first chapter of part I called "The Country," like the first stanzas of a corrido, establishes the setting and scene of the action in a relatively "few swift lines." "Country" here, however, means more than the geographic locale of the story; it encompasses a careful delineation of the opposing social forces—Anglo and Mexican—which a traditional corrido singer could far more easily have assumed to be part of his audience's everyday, intense, social experience. They would have immediately understood the full signification of stanza I of "The Ballad of Gregorio Cortez," where a sheriff has died, and stanza II, where the killer is identified as Cortez, although the particular details of the incident and its aftermath await the rest of the ballad narrative. In our time we require a few more words to delineate a social structure that, while somewhat obscured and mystified, still retains its force today. For as Paredes began to "sing" his corrido to his new audience, he did so within an ongoing social structure that produced segregated barber shops around the University of Texas at Austin in the early 1960s and sanctioned the use of Texas Rangers to break up Mexican farm worker strikes in the Lower Rio Grande Valley. And yet, as I've suggested, like the corrido singer, Paredes is careful not to use too many words lest he lose his audience and distort the clarity of the situation. In only twenty-six simply and elegantly written pages, we who still appreciate corrido-like simplicity are told the essentials of what we need to know to grasp the full social significance of the Cortez incident which is to follow. However, our relative lack of intense social experience—our generation was never lynched—and, paradoxically, our higher education create our need for the longer opening "stanza" of chapter I.

As Paredes has noted, the traditional corrido usually introduces the hero in the next few stanzas in legendary proportions. "But trying to catch Cortez / Was like following a star," which are maintained as the ballad narrative unfolds: Cortez directly addresses and taunts the pursuing Texas Rangers; three hundred surround him at a single moment, yet he escapes. These are the fictive elements permitted to the composer in the exercise of his poetic license. They draw on a larger store of legend with its own independent oral existence, which, present in the community's consciousness, enhances their appreciation of the sparse, sung ballad.

Following the ballad pattern, Paredes introduces us to the legendary Cortez in chapter II called "The Legend," our second "stanza." Amplifying what the ballad suggests, the legend tells us that Cortez was a quiet, polite, good man: a fine horseman, a knowledgeable farmer, and a superb shot with rifle and pistol. He was living a quiet life along the predominantly Mexican border country when his brother, who "was just like the young men of today, loud mouthed and discontented," persuaded him to leave the border country and to "move away from the river and go up above, where there was much money to be made" (1971: 36). This chapter then recapitulates the legendary proportions of the shooting incident in Karnes County and the dramatic flight southward told in the ballad narrative.

As in chapter I, Paredes takes a few more lines in his "ballad" to accomplish for his audience what a traditional singer in 1901 could assume about his, namely, that the legend of Cortez was in the people's consciousness, and that they would bring it to bear in their appreciation of his sung ballad. Paredes's audience requires a direct, elaborated, albeit economical prose version of the legend; this is his historically necessary way to "sing" his ballad.

Like much folklore, however, the corrido is not simply a narrative of totally mythic fictions. It is an historical account that, within a mythos and an ideological perspective, permits its audience to discover a remarkable range of social reality. Whatever the fictive dimensions of this particular ballad, its audience learns that, in fact, Cortez had killed a sheriff in a place called Karnes County, and afterward claimed his right to do so in defense of his life and that of his brother. They also learn certain true details of the southward flight, of which the most general and important is that Cortez did outride and outshoot the vaunted Texas Rangers who, in fact, "captured" him only when he turned himself in after learning about the reprisals taken against his family and community.

Within his textual narrative constraints, it would have been next to impossible for Paredes to narrate legend alternating with historical fact: he does the next best thing, staying close to the corrido narrative conventions. He separates out the historical facts of the case based on primary research in chapter III, called "The Man." Here we learn, interestingly enough, how remarkably close the legendary aspects of the ballad are to the emergent historical narrative as Paredes discovers and constructs it. In presenting his historical reconstruction, Paredes is also attentive to another corrido convention: telling the story "with point of view shifting rapidly from the hero to his adversaries and back again" (1971: 187). Unlike the Anglo historical reconstructions extant in 1958 and still not much improved, Paredes's ballad narrative actually tells a great deal about the Anglo point of view and, like the corrido brings it to life, a favor rarely returned except in the dubious form of stereotypes. What we discover to some extent in the original corrido and to a larger extent in Paredes's "corrido" is that Anglos are people; they show fear, doubt, anxiety, anger, fairness, meanness, pettiness, and generosity, although frankly, at that historical moment, where Mexicans are concerned, the negatives predominate. Using two chapters then, Paredes reproduces, in his more elaborated version with economical and simple words, the legendary and factual historical narration—the substance of the ballad—and brings it to a conclusion.

But if the ballad and Paredes's transformations of it come to a structural close with chapter III, we would seem to be left with a superfluous final chapter IV in part I called "The Hero's Progress." In this closing chapter Paredes simply reviews the fact and fancy, the variants and versions of the Cortez legend and balladry and demonstrates their intertwined relationship. This chapter, clearly intended as a summary, bears no narrative structural relationship to the preceding three chap-

ters. Yet, from my analytical perspective, it has the interesting rhetorical effect of reading like a conversation, albeit in English prose.

In this final chapter Paredes offers, in his own restrained prose, a
summary of the conversations that men might have after a corrido
performance as they evaluate the corrido, its hero, its circumstances
and try to get at the truth. As a postnarrative review, Paredes's final
chapter resembles this kind of polyphonic conversation and as such
is as integral a part of his total performance as it would be for a
traditional corrido sung to an audience. Hence, I would argue even
the seeming "review" character of chapter IV recalls a corrido
performance.

I have suggested that *With His Pistol in His Hand* constitutes a
transforming narrative response to the aesthetic influence of its scholarly subject, the border Mexican ballad. I would now like to amplify
this argument by suggesting that to this balladlike anthropological
performance, we can add its author's biography. As a social text, it,
too, responds and seems shaped by the influence of the border ballad.

The Return of the Mexican Ballad: The Author as Text

When Chicano movement people gather and the conversation turns
to the subject of Américo Paredes, one can often detect the gradual
emergence of what I shall call an unsung proto-ballad–legend of Américo Paredes. Such conversations—a kind of Chicano movement oral
tradition—seem to construct the known life and career of this man
into a folklore narrative, combining ballad and legend. Like all narratives, this narrative varies from group to group and performance to
performance. Certain motifs are sometimes stated, sometimes implied, but an overall narrative structure does emerge, one which recalls
the thematic structure of the traditional ballad and legend.

As with the traditional ballad, these conversations first establish a
time and place setting, and imply a social context for the appearance
of the hero and the central narrative action. This initial narrative
sometimes starts with a key incident of confrontation between the
hero and the Anglo authorities (Gregorio Cortez and the Sheriff). An
Anglo teacher tells the young Paredes that college is not for boys "like
him"; has he considered attending vocational school? Or, an assimilationist, middle-class, Mexican-American publisher in San Antonio

[197]

refuses to publish Paredes's early, stridently ethnic, nationalist poems. Or, perhaps most dramatic of all, the University of Texas Press in the late 1950s refuses to publish *With His Pistol in His Hand* unless Paredes deletes all critical references to Walter Prescott Webb, J. Frank Dobie, and the Texas Rangers. Paredes refuses to do so, threatens to publish the book elsewhere, and the University of Texas Press finally relents. When the book does appear, a former Texas Ranger actually tries to get Paredes's address from the press so that he can "shoot the sonafabitch who wrote that book."

This conversational proto-narrative may then fill out the author's background and key aspects of his career in a way that is almost entirely factual and yet has the aura of legend. Our hero was born in the auspicious year of 1915 during the height of the Texas Ranger killings in South Texas. He is said to be a good and simple man, as was said of Cortez, but from the beginning he is a bit extraordinary. As a young man in South Texas, he is something of the bohemian, exceptionally attractive to women and highly respected by men; a well-known popular singer on radio programs, a prize-winning poet and a journalist; a man who could and did defend his family's honor. The narrative continues. The hero is said to be highly gifted intellectually, restless and curious about life beyond South Texas. Like Cortez, Paredes leaves the border country and eventually winds up in central Texas near Karnes County at the University of Texas at Austin, after spending a few years as a correspondent in Japan and China after World War II. "Did you know that Don Américo covered the Chinese Revolution?"

When he does arrive at the University of Texas to study English and creative writing—his central career goal—it is not before another confrontation with those who dominate. This time it is the U.S. government, which initially refuses a visa to his wife, who is a Japanese national. For a moment Paredes thinks of living in Mexico. But the obstacle is overcome, and his advanced college education begins; he has had one year of community college work. Already in his mid-thirties, he has children; by overloading his course schedule, he completes his B.A. with highest honors in two years, an M.A. in one, and the Ph.D. in two more years in which he teaches several sections of freshman English to support his family. During this period he also publishes a few scholarly articles and writes a prize-winning novel. He also completes a dissertation on the balladry and life of Gregorio Cortez (later *With His Pistol in His Hand*), and after teaching one year in El Paso, he is invited to rejoin the Department of English at Texas as a faculty member.

As a faculty member during the period 1958–66, Paredes engages in intellectual politics, continually attacking the dominant society's disparaging view of Mexican-Americans by demonstrating the latter's active historical presence through careful, creative scholarship such as that of *With His Pistol in His Hand*. He also tries to promote social activism among the university's Mexican-American students, but an assimilationist perspective is still too prevalent among them, and they do not respond to his efforts. Like Cortez, Paredes finds himself engaging the opposition largely alone, although he does find a Romaldo-like brother in Professor George I. Sanchez, a progressive figure in his own right (Garcia 1989: 252–72).

Cortez arouses the consciousness of his community by riding and shooting his way toward them and receiving their help. Paredes's native ideological and cultural community actually begins to come to him in the mid-1960s as the Chicano student movement starts to develop in Texas and in other southwestern universities. The hero and his community struggle in mutual support around issues such as the farm workers, Mexican-American studies, and increased political representation. With this social activism, the dissemination of his book, and visits to other campuses, the hero's legend continues to develop to the present in the conversational form that I have sketched. Though neither a ballad nor a legend in any formal narrative sense, this conversation partakes of both and gives us a sense of a ballad and a legendary hero in formation.

The Return of the Mexican Ballad and the Chicano Movement

One of the most active participants in and a better observer of the Chicano movement has noted the tendency of this movement to draw on historical models. "The entire Chicano leadership pattern, in fact, closely resembled the pattern of the Mexican Revolution, where revolutionary juntas and local leaders emerged. These leaders took care of their home bases and were supported by their own followers . . . all adhered to this basic pattern, inspiring intense loyalty among their followers" (Acuña 1981: 360).

We can expand this perceptive formulation by considering other

[199]

historical models and the Chicano movement as a social narrative—
to see the movement as an unfolding social enactment that followed
the model of the most potent Mexican narrative—the corrido—as it
had learned it in mediated form from the widely popular Américo
Paredes and his ostensibly anthropological text. Taking this author–
text as one of several possible important cultural models, I want to
generally trace its influence on the Chicano social narrative.

We may begin by noting that, like our legendary heroes Cortez and
Paredes, these Chicano students were also from the border, if not
literally from the U.S.-Mexico border, then certainly from the borders
and margins of U.S. society. Although by no means from the most
deprived sectors of U.S. society, they largely represented a wage-
labor, working-class segment, particularly those from the literal border
or even close to it—West San Antonio, Albuquerque, Phoenix, East
Los Angeles, areas that reflected persistent socioeconomic marginal-
ization. At a critical moment these students also experienced Cortez's
journey. According to folk legend and to a considerable degree in
historical fact, Cortez and his family had been drawn away from the
border by the work made available as a result of the capitalist economic
transformation of Texas. Similarly, as a result of new federal civil rights
and educational aid policies beginning in the late 1950s, Chicano students found themselves attracted to the new socioeducational "north."
For Texas students, as with Cortez and Paredes, such movement for
opportunity was perfectly congruent with geography as they left the
southern border area to come north to the University of Texas at
Austin. (At the University of California at Los Angeles, the movement
was east-west.)

This movement "north" brought many of these students into conflict
with other aspects of the culture there. For while U.S. society presented new opportunities, it had not done so for the masses of Mexican-
American society; the most telling evidence of this clear shortfall
was (and is) the continuing plight of border society, and particularly
the plight of the farm workers. Further, from the point of view of the
students, who despite their own change in culture were still, in the
words of the poet Juan Gomez-Quiñones, "just Mexican enough"
(1973: 73), the colleges and universities receiving them were themselves sociointellectual embodiments of the same sociocultural power
that dominated their parents and had lynched their grandparents. Not
Sheriff Morris of Karnes County, but U.S. society, as these students

[200]

experienced it, was still a dominating force as it had been for Américo Paredes when he tried to publish his book.

For the students, the most direct confrontation came through the labor struggles of the largely Mexican-American farm workers in the mid-1960s in the Southwest. In Texas, the ballad narratives of the past took on special pertinence when farm workers from the border made a pilgrimage to Austin in 1966, only to be denied a hearing for their grievances by then governor John Connally, certainly as representative a symbol of Anglo-Texan class and cultural power as any symbolic anthropologist could have hoped for. To this denial Connally added injury, and stepped right alongside the models of history by sending the Texas Rangers to break up, with violence, farm worker strikes along the border; parallel confrontations occurred in California.

The student sector of the farm worker movement actively participated, and found its own beginning in these farm labor struggles; in Texas students had confrontations with the Rangers along the border. For, like Cortez, these students returned to the border not to escape but to engage; in so doing, like Cortez, they reestablished their links to their native community. (In Texas this meant literally following the general path that Cortez took as he rode south, except this time the path was taken in car caravans.) This initial participation and linkage with the home community soon widened as students lent their support to other issues in the society, particularly the serious deficiencies of public schooling. Soon Chicano college students throughout the Southwest were organizing strikes in the public schools to protest substandard educational conditions and, in so doing, enlisting public school youth in the movement (Foley et al. 1977). From the wider struggles in the larger community, the students also returned to the universities to bring them to account for their own denial of Mexican-American society, particularly for the failure of higher education to draw more Mexican-Americans into its ranks and to devote more intellectual attention to Mexican-American society and culture.

As in the ballad, legendary heroes to lead the struggle appeared early in the Chicano social narrative. Given the centrality of the farm labor movement, it is not too surprising that Cesar Chavez should be among the foremost of these—a "simple, good man"—but there were others as well, not always simple or good, whose rhetorical powers and personal charisma quickly lent them near legendary status. Rodolfo "Corky" Gonzales of Colorado, Reis Lopez Tijerina in New Mexico, and José Angel Gutierrez in Texas were surely among these (Hammerback, Jensen, and Gutierrez 1985). And, of course, in the political world of intellect and letters there was Américo Paredes, whose personal "ballad" developed dialectically with this movement and whose written "ballad" *With His Pistol in His Hand* was, starting in the early 1960s, an influence upon it; countless Mexican-American students read it.

Paredes has suggested that the ballad of border conflict and its hero, such as Gregorio Cortez, epitomize "the ideal type of hero of the Rio Grande people, the man who defends his right with his pistol in his hand, and who either escapes at the end or goes down before superior odds—in a sense a victor even in defeat" (1971: 124). Something like this might be said—and it is only one perspective—of the Chicano movement in 1966–75. While it did "shoot" an institutional "Ranger" or two, its achievements were limited though real; farm labor legislation was passed; more Mexican-American political figures were elected; Mexican-American studies departments were established. Nonetheless, for many Chicanos various versions of a new social order did not come to pass, leading them to judge the movement a failure, though with some compensations of "a victor even in defeat." Even as I write—and my words are perhaps a contribution—discussion and debate are taking place after the performance of our "ballad" (the movement) with its narrative of conflict between a community with its legendary heroes and a dominant social order denying this community. Like others after a performance of a traditional sung ballad, we, too, are asking and debating. "What was the meaning of this ballad?" "How good was it?" "Shall we sing another one?"

I have offered for interpretive consideration the interrelated propositions that Américo Paredes's public career and his major anthropological text, *With His Pistol in His Hand*, formally and thematically mediate the influence of the Mexican border ballad and, in turn, become themselves cultural texts that help to shape the character and development of the Chicano movement. By no means were these the only influential cultural models. As Acuña has suggested, the social drama and heroes of the Mexican Revolution were also important, as were the mythic practices of the pre-Conquest peoples of Mexico and the drama of the Conquest itself. I am suggesting that closer to these students' home culture is another cultural model—the corrido available to them as part of their folk tradition and represented to them by Paredes's life and his corrido-like, politically and intellectually elaborated, simple and well-told story, both well known and appropriate to the students' liminal moment. Paredes's textuality had this particular mission: at this moment, it may be appropriate to assign it another for which it may also be an important text.

The Return of the Mexican Ballad and the "Experimental Moment in the Human Sciences": "A Last Word"

The purpose of Paredes's last chapter, called simply "A Last Word," is simultaneously to reaffirm the local character of the Mexican border ballad and to demonstrate its clear comparative relationship to world balladry. Of particular importance here is the close parallel that Paredes draws with Scottish balladry and political resistance to English domination. I submit that this chapter also had a rhetorical and instructive effect on its Chicano readership: always to attend finely to the character of the local experience of resistance while locating it as part of a larger pattern in the interest of generalizing and linking struggles. To this end, and in the interest of enhancing its hitherto localized reading, I shall offer my own parallel "last word" on Paredes's textuality by locating it among three broader issues that constitute part of what George E. Marcus and Michael M. J. Fischer, in their subtitle, have called "an experimental moment in the human sciences" (1986).

I alluded above to the first of these, although for my purposes I approach it from a somewhat different perspective than does Marcus in an independent statement (1986). He correctly complains that ethnographers, in describing their various societies and cultures, have not "portrayed the role of these worlds in the sort of events and processes that make history, so to speak. . . . The world of larger systems and events has thus often been seen as externally impinging on and bounding little worlds but not as integral to them" (1986: 166). While Paredes's text is least satisfactory here—for example, we wish to know more about the particular character of the capitalist development that was transforming Gregorio Cortez's world—nonetheless, in his account of a folk world not in a pure state, but responding dialectically to imposed change through the creative process of corrido and legend, Paredes, writing in the mid-1950s anticipates somewhat a new trend toward this desirable sort of ethnography. From another perspective, his consistent effort to locate this local folk resistance in relationship to other world efforts foreshadows a new desire to move beyond the bounds of localized ethnography.

The two remaining issues locate Paredes's text in perhaps sharper anticipation of this experimental moment not only in the human sciences but in literary criticism as well (if the distinction is even warranted). I refer to the personal role of the anthropologist, really the intellectual, in the production of his discourse and, to return to the place where I started, to the poetics of such discourse and its relationship to ethnic marginality.

Here we should recall Clifford's concern that ethnic intellectuals may be more constrained about textual experimentation in the production of their discourse; it is, he suggests, considerations of tenure and promotion and other forms of institutional acceptability that are constraining. Nonetheless, he is, "uneasy with a general notion that privileged discourse indulges in esthetic or epistemological subtleties, whereas marginal discourse 'tells it like it is.' The reverse is too often the case" (1986: 21). He is quite right; the reverse is often the case, and I have tried to suggest as much in the case of Américo Paredes in terms of both his writing and his career. I want to specify this relationship a bit more.

As his own example of the reverse case, Clifford points us to the ethnic works that Fischer discusses in an excellent essay on the ways that ethnic autobiographical writing can enhance experimental writing in anthropology. Fischer argues that such autobiographical writing offers to ethnographers models of desirable writing practices: "intertextuality, inter-reference, and the interlinguistic modalities of postmodernist knowledge," creative techniques that can "contribute to a reinvigorated ethnographic literature, one that can again fulfill the anthropological promise of cultural criticism" (1986: 202).

By intertextuality Fischer refers in part to the tendency in some ethnic autobiography to shape the present text as an often transforming repetition of "behavior patterns previously established toward some prior significant other," often a father figure (204). This is the psychoanalytical concept of the transference, "the return of the repressed in new forms" (206), which results in the generation of the ethnic text as the "conquest of an anxiety . . . that cannot be articulated in rational language but can only be acted out" (204). In a different version of this essay, I argue that *With His Pistol in His Hand*, as a kind of ethnic autobiography, textually reenacts this sort of relationship between Paredes as a younger writer and the ballad world of his father, whom he clearly acknowledges as an influence in the dedication (noted earlier) only to transform him in the figure of Cortez (Limón 1992: 61–80). As Fischer also notes, such relationships are the subject of Harold Bloom's work on the poetics of influence (1973, 1975).

Interreference and the interlinguistic modalities of postmodernist knowledge are, for Fischer, expressed in ethnic autobiography through its creative use of, among other techniques, "multiple voices and perspectives, the highlighting of humorous inversions and dialectical juxtaposition of identities/traditions/cultures, and the critique of hegemonic discourses" (1986: 202). I submit that Paredes's text—both the "ballad" he has written and the "ballad" about him—are exemplary in this regard. I have already noted the multiple voices and perspectives that enter into the construction of a corrido and the way Paredes's texts are also constructed in this polyphonic way. In *With His Pistol in His Hand* this polyphony also involves the clear dialectical juxtaposition of "identities/traditions/cultures," the more obvious one of Anglo vs. Mexicans and the varying identities within the Mexican-descent community itself. A few examples. In chapter II, "The Legend," a fictional traditional figure, recalling the singing of "El Corrido de Gregorio Cortez," says, "That was good singing, and a good song; give the man a drink. Not like these *pachucos* nowadays, mumbling damn-foolishness into a microphone; it is not done that way. Men should sing with their heads thrown back, with their mouths wide open and their eyes shut. Fill your lungs, so they can hear you at the pasture's end" (1971: 34). And we discover that our mythic hero also has varying identities, including some not so mythic, which speak to gender differences and which Paredes handles with a kind of humorous inversion. For when Cortez is finally captured and brought to jail, *several* women show up to claim him as theirs even as his poor wife waits in the jail.

Humor, irony, and inversion, however, best serve Paredes in attacking hegemonic, Anglo, racist discourses about Mexicans in Texas; here too he borrows from the corrido tradition which often makes fun of Anglos. Paredes quotes the dominant Anglo historical authority on the subject of Mexicans. "Without disparagement," says Webb, "there is a cruel streak in the Mexican nature" (1935: 14). Webb attributes this partly to the heritage of the Spanish Inquisition and partly to Mexican Indian "blood," which, however, "when compared with that of the Plains Indian, was as ditch water" (1931: 125–26). Nevertheless, despite his "cruel streak," the Mexican is an inferior warrior; "the

[205]

whine of the leaden slugs stirred in him as irresistible impulse to travel with rather than against the music" (1935: 14). To all this, Paredes wryly comments: "Professor Webb does not mean to be disparaging. One wonders what his opinion might have been when he was in a less scholarly mood and not looking at the Mexican from the objective point of view of the historian" (1971: 17). Later, in his discussion of the shooting between Cortez and Sheriff Morris, Paredes ironically appropriates and juxtaposes Webb's observations in a new context. After Morris is shot, his deputy runs, according to Paredes, preferring to "travel with rather than against the music" made by "the whine of leaden slugs" (1971: 63).

Multiple voices, inversions, humor and irony, and the dialectical juxtaposition of "identities/traditions/cultures": these are for Fischer substantial elements of the creative imagination found in ethnic autobiography which can be of service to the writing of a new kind of ethnography. I suggest that, at least in some incipient anticipatory way, Paredes's book involves just such practices, as well as a larger juxtaposition, a blurring of genres between ethnic autobiography, historical ethnography and, as I have been particularly concerned to argue, between folk poetic forms and, to borrow a subtitle, "the poetics and politics of ethnography" (Clifford and Marcus 1986).

We need to consider as well another level of the juxtapositions of identities and traditions in the production of discourse. As I come to the end of my own discourse, I am becoming even more convinced, to return to Clifford, that when it comes to ethnicity, and experimental and ultimately subversive writing, the reverse *is* more often the case. From the margins of ethnicity, we may be able to obtain a more reflexive, innovative and critical discourse. We should not, however, be in an insular fortress—ethnicity peering in fear and suspicion at the "out there"—but work rather more as a guerrilla ethnicity, creatively and dialectically at the margins of various discourses. By the same reasoning, this approach need not be confined to the "traditional" ethnic groups, although I suspect that, under present conditions, they will be a more likely source. While certainly not a "trend," there seems to be increasing interest among nontraditional "ethnics" to locate in their respective heritages some resources for the development of new discourses: Harold Bloom returns anxiously to his Jewish Gnostic influences and analyzes the Jewish present (Bloom 1982); Frank Lentricchia recommends that "the intellectual of working class background, or more broadly of a background outside the social, racial, ethnic, economic, gender-biased, and homophobic mainstream . . . re-trieve his outsider's experience" and "bring it to bear in critical dia-logue with the traditional confirmation he has been given" (1983: 8), referring, by way of example, to his own southern Italian origins. One also thinks of Raymond Williams's engaging discussions of his creative relationship to his working-class Welsh background (1979: 21–38).

If this kind of creative ethnic juxtapositioning in one's career is also an emergent part of the experimental moment in contemporary dis-course, then here too we find Américo Paredes anticipating and pro-viding an early model, doing so not as a propagandist for simple ethnicity nor as a community "activist" but as a literary intellectual, a *specific* literary intellectual, as Lentricchia would say after Foucault: "one whose radical work of transformation, whose fight against repres-sion is carried on at the specific institutional site where he finds himself and on the terms of his own expertise, on the terms inherent to his own functioning as an intellectual" (Lentricchia 1983: 6). In the 1950s Américo Paredes was, and he continued to be, this kind of intellectual, drawing creatively on his own cultural background and bringing it to bear in critical dialogue with his traditional intellectual training. His writings and career represent a transformation of his political/poetic past—the corrido—in the service of a radical work of transformation in the present for the Mexican-descent community and as a possible anticipatory model for the emergence of a new critical discourse among intellectuals at large.

For the immediate future, it is for his poetic politics with persuasive reference to the Mexican-descent community in the United States, particularly its activist intellectuals, that Américo Paredes will be best known. This is a considerable achievement in the context of the re-stricted and transient nature of much contemporary intellectual work. Like his Texas-born and raised contemporary and fellow "outsider" C. Wright Mills, Paredes used and continues to use "the wit of the satirist, the passions of the partisan, the imaginative attention to detail of the novelist" in a fight against repression (Miller 1986: 83). Like Mills, Paredes too, is "a poet of political possibilities" (Miller 1986: 83). With one singular book and career, Paredes also might be de-scribed, though in the present tense, in something of the terms that Miller uses for C. Wright Mills: "Dramatizing his political vision in 'sociological poems' that he aimed at the widest possible readership, [he] reached a mass audience and—perhaps more importantly—in-spired a handful of young activists. Through these students, who re-

José E. Limón

vered his images and took his ideas to heart, he fostered a rebirth of democratic idealism . . . he left a legacy of vivid intellectual style, frequently brilliant social analysis, a beguiling icon of democracy and a seductive new rhetoric of vernacular radicalism" (Miller 1986: 101). For this and more, we are grateful to Américo Paredes.

Notes

1. "It may be generally true," says Clifford, "that groups long excluded from positions of institutional power, like women or people of color, have less concrete freedom to indulge in textual experimentations. To write in an unorthodox way, Paul Rabinow suggests in this volume (Rabinow 1986), one must first have tenure. In specific contexts a preoccupation with self-reflexivity and style may be an index of privileged estheticism. For if one does not have to worry about the exclusion or true representation of one's experience, one is freer to undermine ways of telling, to focus on form over content" (Clifford 1986: 21).
2. This divorce of the sign from society as part of the "postmodern" and the "poststructural" has been the subject of critiques from various perspectives on the left (Anderson 1984; Jameson 1984; Lentricchia 1980; Rabinow 1986; Said 1982).
3. See Saldivar 1990: 26–46.
4. Indeed, this Chicano movement produced corridos of its own (Limón 1983).

REFERENCES

Acuña, Rodolfo. 1981. *Occupied America: A History of Chicanos.* New York: Harper and Row.
Anderson, Perry. 1984. *In the Tracks of Historical Materialism.* Chicago: University of Chicago Press.
Bloom, Harold. 1973. *The Anxiety of Influence: A Theory of Poetry.* New York: Oxford University Press.
——. 1975. *A Map of Misreading.* New York: Oxford University Press.
——. 1982. *Agon: Towards a Theory of Revisionism.* New York: Oxford University Press.
Boon, James. 1982. *Other Tribes, Other Scribes.* New York: Cambridge University Press.
Bruce-Novoa, Juan D. 1980. *Chicano Authors: Inquiry by Interview.* Austin: University of Texas Press.
——. 1982. *Chicano Poetry: A Response to Chaos.* Austin: University of Texas Press.
Bruner, Edward M. 1986. "Ethnography as Narrative." In Victor W. Turner and Edward M. Bruner, eds., *The Anthropology of Experience.* Urbana: University of Illinois Press.

Clifford, James. 1986. "Introduction: Partial Truths." In Clifford and E. Marcus, eds., 1986. Pp. 1–26.

Clifford, James, and George E. Marcus, eds. 1986. *Writing Culture: The Poetics and Politics of Ethnography*. Berkeley and Los Angeles: University of California Press.

Fischer, Michael M. J. 1986. "Ethnicity and the Post-Modern Arts of Memory." In Clifford and Marcus, eds., 1986. Pp. 194–233.

Foley, Douglas, et al. 1977. "From Peons to Politicos: Ethnic Relations in a South Texas Town." Austin: Center for Mexican American Studies Monograph. University of Texas.

Garcia, Mario. 1989. *Mexican Americans: Leadership, Ideology, and Identity*. New Haven: Yale University Press.

Geertz, Clifford. 1980. "Blurred Genres: The Refiguration of Social Thought." *The American Scholar* 29: 165–79.

Gomez-Quiñones, Juan. 1973. "Song." In *5th and Grande Vista (Poems, 1960–1973)*. New York: Editorial Mensage. P. 73.

———. 1978. *Mexican Students por la Raza: The Chicano Student Movement in Southern California, 1967–1977*. Santa Barbara, Calif.: Editorial La Causa.

Hammerback, John C., Richard J. Jensen, and José Angel Gutierrez. 1985. *A War of Words: Chicano Protest in the 1960s and 1970s*. Westport, Conn.: Greenwood Press.

Jameson, Fredric. 1984. Foreword. Jean-François Lyotard. *The Postmodern Condition: A Report on Knowledge*. Minneapolis: University of Minnesota Press.

Lentricchia, Frank. 1980. *After the New Criticism*. Chicago: University of Chicago Press.

———. 1983. *Criticism and Social Change*. Chicago: University of Chicago Press.

Limón, José E. 1983. "The Rise, Fall, and 'Revival' of the Mexican-American Ballad: A Review Essay." *Studies in Latin American Popular Culture* 2: 202–07.

———. 1986. "Barbarians, Christians, Jews: Three Narrative Scenes in the Sociolinguistic Legacy of the Mexicans of Texas." Paper presented at the annual meeting of the Texas State Historical Association, Austin, Texas.

———. 1992. *Mexican Ballads, Chicano Poems: History and Influence in Mexican American Social Poetry*. Berkeley: University of California Press.

———. n.d. "Mexicans in the Southwest: The Tropics of Folkloristic Discourse." Unpublished manuscript.

Marcus, George E. 1986. "Contemporary Problems of Ethnography in the Modern World System." In Clifford and Marcus, eds., 1986. Pp. 165–93.

Marcus, George E., and Dick Cushman. 1982. "Ethnographies as Texts." *Annual Review of Anthropology* 11: 25–69.

Marcus, George E., and Michael M. J. Fischer. 1986. *Anthropology as Cultural Critique: An Experimental Moment in the Human Sciences*. Chicago: University of Chicago Press.

Miller, James. 1986. "C. Wright Mills Reconsidered." *Salmagundi*, nos. 70–71: 82–101.

Mukarovsky, Jan. 1977. *The Word and Verbal Art*. New Haven: Yale University Press.

Paredes, Américo. 1971 [1958]. *With His Pistol in His Hand: A Border Ballad and Its Hero.* Austin: University of Texas Press.

Peña, Manuel H. 1982. "Folksong and Social Change: Two Corridos as Interpretive Sources." *Aztlan* 13: 13–42.

Rabinow, Paul. 1986 "Representations Are Social Facts: Modernity and Post-Modernity in Anthropology." In Clifford and Marcus, eds., 1986. Pp. 234–61.

Rosaldo, Renato. 1985. "Chicano Studies." *Annual Review of Anthropology* 14.

Said, Edward W. 1982. "Opponents, Audiences, Constituencies, and Community." *Critical Inquiry* 9: 1–26.

Saldivar, Ramon. 1990. *Chicano Narrative: The Dialectics of Difference.* Madison: University of Wisconsin Press.

Webb, Walter Prescott. 1931. *The Great Plains.* Boston: Ginn.

——. 1935. *The Texas Rangers.* Cambridge: Houghton Mifflin.

White, Hayden. 1973. *Metahistory.* Baltimore: Johns Hopkins University Press.

——. 1978. *Tropics of Discourse.* Baltimore: Johns Hopkins University Press.

Williams, Raymond. 1979. *Politics and Letters: Interviews with New Left Review.* London: New Left Review Books.

Ybarra-Frausto, Tomás. 1977. "The Chicano Movement and the Emergence of a Chicano Poetic Consciousness." *The New Scholar* 6: 81–110.

[9]

Pilgrimage to Meron: Inner and Outer Peregrinations

Barbara Myerhoff

Introductory Note

Barbara Myerhoff left instructions before she died that her notes on Lag B'Omer should be used to form a paper for *Creativity/Anthropology*. This piece still has the character of a series of notes, and has been only lightly edited because it was desirable to preserve her inimitable style. I shall therefore summarize her argument to help the reader, and end with some words of comment.

Barbara Myerhoff shows Lag B'Omer, the period between Passover and the harvest festival of Shavuot, to be a time of "fasting, continence, reflection, and sorrow." She unfolds the complexities of Jewish blood and grain symbolism that demonstrate this point. The pilgrimage to the shrine of Shimon Bar Yoḥai, a saint and scholar, at Mount Meron during Lag B'Omer, particularly the receiving of the Torah on the mountaintop of Meron—a kind of Sinai—is the experience of "revelation" at the end of a time of hardship. Barbara Myerhoff likens the whole process to (a) a rite of passage with a liminal phase; (b) the hero's passage, in which the hero ventures into the underworld to encounter his buried self as Dragon, emerging with a newborn soul; and (c) the shaman's journey, in which the shaman goes through death to rebirth, receiving the capacity for flight, a mobile soul. Historical paradigms of this process, in particular the hardships of the Jews under

[211]

the Romans after the fall of Jerusalem in 70 A.D., at which time Bar
Yohai took refuge in a cave, are also external features of a deeper
process in the soul. Her thesis is amply borne out by the prevalence
of dreaming among pilgrims to the shrine, as she puts it, "the dropping
into the unconscious that precedes understanding and that generates,
through dreams, what is not-yet-born." Thus, historical processes are
but a part of the long-worked-out religious process whose domain
spreads from the mundane down beneath the psyche of the psychol-
ogists into the deepest levels of the soul.

Barbara Myerhoff reminds us that Jewish Orthodox teaching insists
that religious action is not metaphorical at all, but the thing itself. For
instance, the seder *is* the Jews' last meal before the exodus from Egypt.
This understanding colors her dream and the cryptic ending of her
notes, an ending that also displays much of her typical humor. A
picture rises to the mind's eye of anthropologists in great yeshiva-like
halls struggling with abacuses in the hopes of cracking the Rosetta
Stone–like code of the Pentateuch—according to legend, deliberately
hidden there by Moses in the form of the *gematria*, the mystic number
values of the Hebrew alphabet, a language Moses employed to impart
the wisdom of the Kabbalah. This sort of research would then seem
to be all that mattered—just to crack the code. At a certain point we
can even see that this is right. At other times Barbara Myerhoff's
dream appears to be nonsense. Carlos Casteñeda's writings have the
same effect.

Barbara Myerhoff's piece is many things: it constitutes a challenge
for the reader to unravel hidden truths; it is a typical Myerhoff tour
de force of symbolic analysis as is her book *Peyote Hunt;* it is a game;
and very seriously, it is a study of what kind of world this creative
persona, Shimon Bar Yohai, touches upon, and the process of his
drawing others, the Moroccan dreamers, into it.

I am proud to be associated with what is possibly Barbara Myerhoff's
last anthropological publication.

EDITH TURNER

The ability of an ancestor or saint to give significance to an ordinary
life through conscious modeling is occasionally deepened to a more
profound influence when an individual is invaded by a forebear or
"creative persona" through dreams that provide a powerful, direct

experience wherein one may fuse with the life of such a one. Dreams of this kind occur during the liminal period of Lag B'Omer, during pilgrimages to the tomb of the second-century Jewish saint and scholar, Shimon Bar Yohai, at Mount Meron, Israel. Pilgrimage is then at once an inner and outer journey, the geographic, collective peregrination running parallel to the voyage down into the unconscious, where the traveler has a sacred encounter between saint and self. This lower voyage provides a personal, unconscious, psychic, and subjective dimension for the cultural occasion of pilgrimage so that history and biography blend, and a private life partakes of a larger, collective tale—each enlarging and reinforcing one another.

Furthermore, a connection runs between the feasts of Passover, Lag B'Omer, and Shavuot that adds a vertical/horizontal dimension to the here/there, near/far topographic model of pilgrimage, stressing the relations between liminal passage through an underworld into the ascent, the rise to the mountaintop, the receiving of the Torah, and the redemption. Looked at this way, the pilgrimage corresponds to rites of passage, the shamanic journey, and the hero quest in mythology. These new dimensions become clearer when one realizes the importance of dreaming in Meron, and that the pilgrims consider the time between Passover and the ascent to the mountain at Lag B'Omer to be a time when Jews are asleep, and dreaming. Lag B'Omer (which means the thirty-third day in the counting of the *omer*, the first sheaf) is a period of purification with signs of life suspended, a time of fasting, continence, reflection, and sorrow; it continues until the harvest. Then comes the revelation: the saint Bar Yohai leaves his cave. No longer do grain and blood need to be kept so severely apart as at Passover; the *chometz* (leaven) is reabsorbed and readmitted into the home. The patterns appear to be parallel. Analogs of the same process call for further research, notably the distinctions between: herder (producing blood) and agriculturalist (producing grain); the suspended life in the Passover period, and harvest and the Torah celebration; the purification and separation of grain and blood, and not only grain and blood, but barley and wheat; normality as distinct from special times—*rejoined* as the Torah is received on the mountaintop at the height of the pilgrimage and The People is brought into being.

Now how can all this be made real and immediate to each person? How can it be the experience of each? How can the social, external pilgrimage be made into an occasion for self-awareness? For the dropping into the unconscious that precedes understanding and generates

[213]

what is not-yet-born? Through dreams. These are the mediums for transmuting the public into the private, for using collective symbols to speak to the deepest levels of being. "The Zohar teaches that on Sinai a voice is heard that divides itself into six hundred thousand personal meanings appropriate to each soul there present." This is truly a dream, coming from within. The dream is the "letter we have written to ourselves from some previous reincarnation" (Zalman Schachter Shalomi), or the voice of God, or the message from unconscious to conscious. "The prophet Nathan scolds David the king who has just been told the allegory of his life, saying 'Thou art the man!' (2 Sam. 12:7). The story is not about someone else" (Kushner 1981: 21). The one in the dream is always oneself, coming from within, experienced as without. All the psychologies teach: the dream is always about oneself.

"It is said that the teachings of the kabbalah . . . were first entrusted by God himself to a special group of angels in Paradise. After Man had been expelled from the garden, some of the angels communicated the lessons to Adam, thinking to help him back to felicity thereby. From Adam the teaching passed to Noah, and from Noah to Abraham. Abraham let some of it slip from him while in Egypt and that is why sublime wisdom can now be found in a reduced form in the myths and philosophies of the gentiles. Moses first studied it with the priests of Egypt but the tradition was refreshed in him by the special instructions of the angels" (Campbell 1956: 268).

Paradoxically, I was called to Israel after Passover in 1983 by the myths and philosophies of the gentiles, by Victor and Edith Turner whose studies of pilgrimages throughout the world—Ireland, Japan, and even Disneyland—led them at last to Israel. Victor Turner had the capacity to take in the beliefs of others, mingle them with his profound devotion to the essential issues of religion everywhere, temper, refine, and distill the original "minute particulars" until they were measured and raised to a higher, more general level, and then to return them to those who gave them, enlarged and purified. In 1981, I had left with the Turners for a pilgrimage in Japan. It is important to name the thing I was seeking. Is it too facile to say my "self"? Shall I say my "spiritual self," or my "emerging self"? What I have remembered is that Edie and I squeezed ourselves, her bigger form and my smaller one, through a hole in the earth under a tree, wriggling mud-covered out of the tunnel into the light, not knowing our new names or state, and vaguely smiling at each other. We were profoundly copilgrims, as we had been the morning before, sharing the sacred saki at dawn in a shrine atop a mountain of stairs, at the hands of a priest who danced us through a communion more with each other than any gods. Perhaps, then, pilgrimage is for those who cannot leap through their own minds to God, but experience it laterally, as *agape,* and trust their fellows to carry part of the burden of possibility. Or perhaps it is *only* about connection in the end. Connection of any kind, to the Above or to the Side, to parents or to siblings, will do. Yet there is a loftiness in pilgrimage, a vulnerability so acute that it is beyond fellowship. I know the most important thing I brought back from Japan was in that moment.

Lag B'Omer falls between Passover and Shavuot. My 1983 Passover shortly before I made the pilgrimage to Meron, Israel, with the Turners was spent as a pilgrim in Fairfax, Los Angeles. I attended seven varied kinds of seders, ranging from secular to gay feminist to an ultraorthodox one with the Naftali Estulins of Chabad. I hired my son, Matthew, then twelve, as my field assistant to help me keep track of all that cannot be written down, and to draw him into my concerns.

At the Estulins' Passover, we are instructed to be very careful with the *shmure matza,* "guarded" matza that has been watched to see that nothing crept into it of chometz. Chometz looms as a very large part of Passover, more than I had ever imagined. The neighborhood has deposited its foods containing chometz at the Chabad storefront shul/ bookstore, which has symbolically bought it so that all remaining homes are officially clean; chometz is locked away or sealed in cupboards. (So too all of Israel is "bought" by non-Jews wherever it may have come in contact with chometz for this period—Vimala Jayanti, personal communication). The separation issue looms and grows. Whole congregations, too busy to kosher their homes completely, depart literally for the desert (Palm Springs), where in luxury hotels they live through this period. Riv-Ellen Prell-Foldes writes me despairing, exhausted letters about the difficulty of integrating her schedule as a professor in a secular world with the requirements of the holiday: she is spent but has done what is required. The Estulins not only clean cupboards; they wash the ceilings, empty out the pockets of the clothes in the closet, change the sockets of electrical outlets. It is mad, obsessive, fierce. New clothes are bought. Thousands of dollars are laid out for this very expensive matzot. I see perhaps for the first time how Orthodox Judaism rivals the Mexican Indians' religion in terms of consuming money, attention, time, requiring one to be altogether inside this world of religion, and so making dim the competing secular spheres. It levels, absorbs, transforms. In my childhood seders, as even now in most places, people only *spoke* of the things that in the Estulin household are performed at Passover.

As Matthew and I enter, we step through a doorway into an absolutely new world. The Estulins really recline at the Passover table, they do not merely say they recline; even Shlime, the two-year-old, precariously and mischievously hangs out over the edge of her high chair. Reb Naftali eats a matzot sandwich, holding the pieces in both hands as he leans, closing his eyes rapturously, as I have seen the Indians eat peyote. This is how mere matzot becomes what it is supposed to be. Perhaps the real religious lessons are only learned through others who already know, in whose very beings it is the genuine reality, and only when we see them actually in Paradise can we understand the absence of metaphor in all religious experience.

This is iconic, pointing at nothing else but the essential experience itself. Here is something to explore in the anthropology of experience. Again, only ritual can actually give us experience as our own. Only performance, never merely discursive symbols, makes us the embodiments of the stories we tell. A rabbi instructed me about experiential time. In Judaism (in all religions, I believe), time does not extend before and after, running over us or through us from beginning to end. There are no anniversaries, no previous events celebrated again. All is new and for the first time. Time enwraps us, or rather we circle around it as in a Copernican universe or as a typefont ball strikes letters out on the page; each hit is fresh, though the characters repeat. This sense is even beyond Richard Schechner's restoration of (imaginary) behavior (1985: 35–116). It is the first storage, experienced, not commemorated.

In Judaism, there are in particular three such events: Sinai, where we all really were there to receive the Torah, all six hundred thousand (as in the poem of the Yiddish poet Jacob Gladzstein): "Our whole imagined people received the Torah at Sinai. In Auschwitz we gave it back." We *are* those who received the Torah at Sinai, as we are one with the ancestors on Passover; there is no "as if." Through performance we become them. (So too, with the Huichol pilgrims in Paradise, Wirikuta, where it is not a matter of acting, only of being, not imagining but experiencing.) The two other such events in Judaism are Passover and Rosh Hashana. We are all there when the world is created, new, each new year. These days are not anniversaries. Here

religion is like poetry, making new, scouring off the rust of inatten-
tiveness and habit to take us into the experience ourselves. Kabir, a
fifteenth-century Indian mystic, said, "Unless you have lived through
something it is not true." Lawrence Kushner said, "And God spoke
to each one at Sinai so as not to frighten them—in the voice of their
parents" (1981: 59). All genuine learning is the self's disclosure to
itself. The voice issues with such clarity that the ones who learn refuse
to believe it is their own. At Sinai everyone is a student. According
to our myth, all hear the voice of the Teacher. But not only is it a
clear, publicly audible, external voice, it is also a voice that is the
sound of our own breathing, a very precious alert silence. This then
is the revelation, that what is without is also within: the primary human
yearning for this unification is that toward which all religion and science move.

There at the Estulins, we eat *maror*, bitter herbs, that are so strong
we really weep. "More, more, eat up!" Reb Naftali shouts lustily at
Matthew. "If you eat this, it is your suffering for a whole year. Your
mother will not be able to scold you again, until next Passover!"
Silently, I agree. If Matthew can pull this off, I may vow never to
scold him again, any year. We are admonished not to let our matzot
crumble as we eat it, not even to let the crumbs fall to the tablecloth
where they may be in contact with wine; the moisture leads to fermentation. Nor do we eat anything that grows now, not lentils or
sprouts. I begin to see this holiday as forbidding growth, fermentation,
and that the proscription means life and regeneration.

There are very deep oppositions abiding here. They concern the
conflict between the slaying of the lamb, the near-slaying of the first-
born, and the use of blood to signify simultaneously life and death
associated with animals and the natural. These seem to be kept rigidly
separate from the growing of plants, the fermentation from seeds, of
grain, the domesticated bloodless life of sedentary farmers. There are
many oppositions always, some practical, some symbolic, between the
ways of life of herders and planters. They compete for land, but more
important, depend on absolutely differing life rhythms; the planters
live by controlling nature; the herders must live alongside it, not
entirely differentiated from its connection to their own blood, their
own lives. As with hunters, the life of the herd is continuous with
one's own line, and it is only among such people that sacrifice of an
animal is really substitutable for human life. Was not Israel in a state
of transition here, not unlike the Huichol Indians' transition from

hunting to agriculture (Myerhoff 1974: 57–58)? And was not the lamb the master's god? The spring lamb, the paschal offering, was an Egyptian god to be slain by the slaves, as an indication of the coming of their rebellion and flight to freedom. It is the blood of this lamb that was smeared onto the doorposts of the house, as a sign not to God (who already knew) but to the slaves, to set themselves most dramatically apart from their masters' way of life and from their bondage, and, of course, to identify blood as a symbol of their unity and identity as a people.

Now if we step back and look at the greater and lesser pilgrimage cycle, that without and that within the self, what do we see? If there is pilgrimage without, there is also an inner geography imposed on the landscape and performed by actual movement. If the inner pilgrimage is a journey of self-completion, and if it is always the same, in the form of a rite of passage (classically a three-part movement), that is, in/out/in-with-a-difference; old/in-between/new; social/psychological-reflexive/return-to-social; and so on, then it can be seen that the pilgrimage also conforms to the shape of the Great Hero passage, as delineated by Campbell (1956: 36–37). The hero sets forth from the everyday world to descend into the underworld and encounter the buried self as Dragon; he brings something back from the struggle, crosses the threshold of earth in order to ascend to the upper world of flight, to freedom, and above all to the achievement of consciousness, in short, self-awareness; he then returns to the mundane world but with a newborn soul acquired in the process. The shaman's journey corresponds to this: first, being called; then the death/rebirth through dismembering and being reassembled; finally, the ever-abiding capacity for flight and the ability to move freely through under- and upperworlds: the acquisition of a mobile soul.

Now if the shape of these—the inner pilgrimage, the hero's passage, and the shaman's journey—are seen as one, certain phases must regularly reiterate: the period in the underworld, or liminal phase, must precede revelation (consciousness), which usually occurs at the top of a sacred mountain, or some such image of height and flight. Returning to the Passover-to-Shavuot period, we can look for some corresponding phase, characterized by being in the desert or in the underworld, to precede the receiving of the Torah at Sinai on Shavuot. All through Lag B'Omer intimations of this occurred. It is not enough that Simeon Bar Kochba and his sons hid from the Romans in caves for twelve years—a story associated with Shimon Bar Yohai's refuge in his own cave. It is not enough that the Jews wandered during this time in the desert, genuine liminals. It seems there is something even beyond this social and psychological level of liminality, deep in the underworld where the genuinely new occurs, something to correspond to the unconscious, to the place/time of exploration, encountering nameless chaos, that leads to regeneration, social and personal.

Various shamanic symbols find their place in this phase. One is fire: the use of fire to separate Paradise from this world; the fire of the Angel Gabriel and his sword; the fire of the Huichols in Wirikuta which marks exactly the point where the sacred touches the secular. "At the center of the fire they carve a small shallow depression out of the earth. This is spoken of by the Huichol pilgrims as 'the cavity of the world.' It is a doorway to the center, and Ancient Ones come and go through it" (Myerhoff 1974: 106). The Huichols' fire is also the fire of creation, utility, and transformation, at once hearth, Clearer-of-the-Fields, and Grandfather-of-the-People. The Judaic fire when lit brings in the Sabbath and cannot be extinguished until the invisible sacred world of Paradise departs after the Sabbath-closing rites of *Havdalah* (separation). Separation again is effected through fire, and so forth. It is to fire, the beacon fire on the roof of Bar Yohai's tomb, that the hair of the small boys is consigned after the initiation rite of haircutting is performed, separating them from the community of angels, making them into real mortals.

Moreover, the symbolism of the underground is everywhere: Lag B'Omer is in a period of mourning, of purification, between Passover and Shavuot, the moment of lifting of grief when new clothes may be bought, hair cut, weddings arranged, and life affirmed. It is a time when no harvest is permitted, with the exception of the offering of wheat (barley was offered at the Temple on Passover). All is suspended until the first fruit ceremonies of Shavuot. "The counting of the Omer period is prescribed in Leviticus . . . which enjoins the bringing of a sheaf (omer) of the harvest to the Temple priest the day after Passover, and keeping count seven full weeks thereafter. On the fiftieth day, an offering of grain from the new harvest is to be brought to the Temple. These seven weeks between Passover, which marked the ripening of the barley harvest, and Shavuot, which was the feast of the wheat harvest and of the first fruits, were crucial to the agricultural economy of ancient Israel. The counting of Omer served as an expression of Israel's faith in God's ensuring a fruitful year" (Vainstein 1953: 130–32). So Lag B'Omer is the brief respite, bracketed by the two harvests,

[219]

keeping the Israelites from full life; it also means preserving the not-yet-ripened crops from a too-early harvest. Again, as with the Huichols on their pilgrimage, all is in suspension between the holy days that mark the end of the pilgrimage cycle and the first fruits ceremonies. Much growth is still in the earth, under the ground, to be protected and preserved until harvested and commemorated with offerings and sacrifices. What could the connection have been in the time of the Temple between the sacrifice of the paschal lamb of Passover and the Omer? "What is underground must be preserved." What substitution may have occurred for this? Could such a substitution underlie why the sacrifice and the sheaves are kept apart?

"When the Holy one brought us back to Zion, we were like ones in a dream" (Psalm 126:1).

Here is the answer: the Jews are dreaming while they are awaiting the Torah. Here is all the underworld one needs: here is the falling into the darkness where a soul is achieved, clarified and made public, made into the inner *and* outer on Sinai. It is through the dreaming that the rite of passage becomes collective pilgrimage, that the microcosm and macrocosm finally merge.

Evidence of dreaming accumulates, from my own experience and that of others, including Yoram Bilu's scholarly work on the dreaming at Meron in which he describes how the Moroccan Jewish women pilgrims see the figure of Bar Yohai in their dreams, in a very personal form. He demands, even against the wishes of their husbands, that they journey to the shrine; he anticipates their future, gives names for their children, teaches them about the continuing of life and death by allowing them to deal with their missing or slain soldier-sons and -daughters, announces the impending conceptions of other children, creates their connection to the actual land by announcing (in the logically inconceivable yet universally sensible logic of the psyche) that the Moroccans' ancestor saints are buried here in this new land of Israel—making the rupture of immigration the dream and illusion, the *connection* the reality.

We see them dreaming in the shrine: the old women, curled up on the white benches surrounding the tomb, their bodies heaps of colored cloth, not really here at all; the much more corporeal rotund men in *jalabiyas* (long outer garments), slippers awry, prayerbooks splayed on their bellies, lost to us, gone to their soul's destination. That night, Victor Turner, sleeping at the field school around the slope of Meron, has a dream. He says: "I was walking up the hill toward Meron, when

I was met by a young *yeshiva bocher* [student] in sidelocks, *shtreimel* [traditional fur hat of the Hasidim], caftan, and beard. In his hand he carried something green, possibly myrtle, the kind they bring to the Western Wall on the Sabbath. The Hasid was standing in such a way as to protect me from the crowd. We spoke. I was holding a book. Before, we were going in opposite directions. I turned, and we went up the hill together into the light of the dawn. We were exchanging wisdom; there was some expression of surprise, something that hadn't been seen before. The Hasid was carrying on my studies, I could hand over to him. I felt I was watching my own youth walk away with both relief and regret."

And we the scholars, on the scholars' holiday, talk of these and other matters through the Sabbath. I learn this: that Shimon Bar Yohai's teachings were supposed to have been drawn from the *chokma nistara*, or hidden wisdom of Moses, finally incorporated cryptically in the first four books of the Pentateuch, from which it can be extracted by a proper understanding and manipulation of the mystical number values of the Hebrew alphabet. The lore and techniques for rediscovering and utilizing it constitute the Kabbalah.

As we ponder, it slowly occurs to me that we are surrounded by spring flowers and paradoxically housed in bunkers, a life/death contrast that is literal. And then I remember a dream I had and recorded before I came, a dream that prefigured all this, before I had ever seen a picture of Bar Yohai. The dream occurred some time after Passover when I was immersed in questions about how to do religious studies, how to approach absolute belief with a relativistic perspective. I was learning nothing new, Reb Naftali had told me, since all was already recorded in the Torah. This seemed the very opposite of the "everything is new, never reexperienced" character of sacred time. How could it be both at once?

Here is my dream: I am in a small white square concrete box (later identified as a bunker) on a bunk bed, with several middle-aged, white-haired women (variations of myself?), a jazz musician friend, and a *sofer* scribe (holy scribe who writes out the Torah) with a long, square, white beard. He is poring intently over his work, utterly absorbed and silent through the dream. Atop his book is an abacus. The jazz musician invites the women to speak in turn about deeply personal things. All begin to talk at once, and into the din I try to articulate a great understanding I have achieved. No one listens in the dream, but I awaken with the understanding intact and realize that it is a lesson to myself about my questions concerning the proper attitude with which to do a study of the anthropology of religion. Here is the teaching:

If one does religious study in a proper and religious manner, this is well done. But there will be no new information, since all that is religious is already known, eternal and immutable.

If one does a religious study with a nonreligious attitude, this is improper and will not give a valuable interpretation; there is no hope of an understanding.

If one does a nonreligious study with a religious attitude, one is a fool. There is only dogma, no new information.

If one does a nonreligious study with a nonreligious attitude, one is a bore and boring. This is mere secular trivia, for engineers, not anthropologists.

How is one to learn, then?

Perhaps the clue is in the abacus, not a computer nor an adding machine, but an ancient and very precise instrument, never mechanical—the device here for probing beneath the words into their iconic value, the gematria: the mystery that underlies the talk.

REFERENCES

Campbell, Joseph. 1956. *The Hero with a Thousand Faces*. Cleveland: Meridian.
Kushner, Lawrence. 1981. *The River of Light*. San Francisco: Harper and Row.
Myerhoff, Barbara. 1974. *Peyote Hunt: The Sacred Journey of the Huichol Indians*. Ithaca: Cornell University Press.
Schechner, Richard. 1985. *Between Theatre and Anthropology*. Philadelphia: University of Pennsylvania Press.
Turner, Victor. 1969. *The Ritual Process*. Chicago: Aldine.
Turner, Victor, and Edith Turner. 1978. *Image and Pilgrimage in Christian Culture: Anthropological Perspectives*. New York: Columbia University Press.
Vainstein, Yaacov. 1953. *The Cycle of the Jewish Year: A Study of the Festivals and a Selection from the Liturgy*. Jerusalem: Department for Torah Education and Culture in the Diaspora, World Zionist Organization.

PART III

Collective Creativity

[10]

Bar Yohai, Mystic: The Creative Persona and His Pilgrimage

Edith Turner

The existence of a creative persona may involve a root metaphor embodied in a string of other individuals living in eras prior or subsequent to the persona in question. Rabbi Shimon Bar Yohai—as Moroccan Jews call him—was a second-century saint revered by the Sephardim and Hasids. The root metaphor he represents is *zohar*, meaning splendor or enlightenment. Popular belief attributes to Rabbi Shimon Bar Yohai the authorship of *The Zohar*, the renowned Kabbalistic text of Jewish mysticism. Bar Yohai, identified with *The Zohar*, stands at the head of a series of ancient Hebrew personages touched by the divine, starting with Enoch in the Bible (who became the angel Metatron) and continuing to Abraham and others down the ages, eventually focusing in the nodal point of Bar Yohai. In the other direction, forward in history from Bar Yohai, extends an equal string of personages up to the present, including great Hasids such as the Lubavitcher Rebbe of New York and many others, as well as the crowds of Israeli-Moroccan Jews who visit Bar Yohai's shrine at Meron in Israel on pilgrimage. The transformation of Bar Yohai into a legendary figure, the role of his visionary thought in Jewish ritual, and his present-day interaction with his devotees in dreams and their subsequent transformation show him to be an "allegorical type." Certain

This essay is dedicated to the memory of Barbara Myerhoff.

[225]

persons in a society take on, often willy-nilly, an allegorical role, and become a type that speaks to the society or to the outside world on behalf of that society: in other words, an agent of reflexivity, a particular kind of performer. Smadar Lavie (1986: 143–44), who first proposed the concept of the allegorical type, wrote, "They appear in solo performances on the societal stage in phases of transition, when [the society asks itself] whether it exists, and on what level of organization it does so. The types bridge the geopolitical paradoxes of the present and traditional forms and figures of the past. In this manner they provide sets of specific answers to existential . . . dilemmas which arise in the course of everyday life. . . . By entering into the inconsistent social situation with an allegorical experience, he or she reconstructs the thematic meaning of the social context. In this manner the person/persona is able to eliminate open-ended discontinuity and to transmute the paradoxes of . . . precarious reality into an allegory . . . linked to the immortality of tradition"[1] (p. 143; see also Handelman 1981; Handelman and Bruce Kapferer 1980).

In his role as creative persona slowly maturing through history, the figure of Bar Yohai has become in effect an allegorical type, but he is also known on the pilgrimage simply as "the zaddik." A zaddik, defined as a righteous or saintly person, is commonly but not invariably a great scholar of the scriptures. Rabbi Shimon Bar Yohai was a scholar par excellence, and, according to tradition, a saint of great power. A tradition of zaddiks penning or studying visionary texts exists in Judaism and also to a certain extent in Islam. In the West the thaumaturgical power of sanctity is linked in believers' minds with prayer and self-sacrifice, hardly ever with biblical scholarship. Not so with the scholarly zaddiks, saints whose tombs often became the source of healing miracles. Thus, during the great folk pilgrimage of Bar Yohai, when Victor Turner and I arrived at Meron in 1983 to conduct research with fourteen scholars in anthropology, folklore, psychology, and history,[2] we were able to celebrate a "scholar's holiday" (a term that Barbara Myerhoff delighted to use) for ourselves at the shrine of the saintly scholar.

Little is known about Bar Yohai's life. According to historical records, he was famous as a scholar and a patriot who opposed the Romans' occupation of Israel. He lived for twelve years in a cave, hidden from the Roman forces sent out to destroy him (Shokeid 1974: 75). Bar Yohai seems to have been content to occupy himself with studying the scriptures and, according to an unsubstantiated but strong tradition, with writing the sublime book—a scripture in itself—*The Zohar, the Book of Light*. Be that as it may, Bar Yohai was known to have retreated from the violence of political power, from what was truly an "inconsistent social situation," that is, the era after the fall of Jerusalem. The liminality of his situation in the cave was well-nigh total. He was a scholar in an age of military power, in refuge on the northern frontier of Galilee, in the mountains halfway up from the earth, a member of the mystical tradition of Judaism and not the legal tradition; and his sanctity resulted in miracles, outside of the natural. (The pilgrimages to his shrine in later ages also showed strong liminal features.)

Bar Yohai not only received inspiration himself but was taken over by his society and was shaped, by means of legendary accretions, into a source of meaning for it, a mirror for it. He therefore possessed more than charisma, a characteristic of certain well-attested historical personages; he held strong allegorical and affective value for almost two millennia.

The zaddik's life, his reputed authorship of *The Zohar* with its particular message to the Diaspora about the "ingathering of the scattered sparks of God's light," and the history of his cultus in the ages long after his death, tell the following story. First the rabbi himself receives inspiration; in later ages he is taken over by his society, especially through the agency of Moses de Leon in the Middle Ages, whose *Zohar* is the only version we have; then the ideas in it, fertile with the call to an ingathering of the sparks, reach the Diaspora; there is an immediate response to *The Zohar* among Jews scattered over the world, which, later still, culminates in the return of the Jews to Israel. For many Jews Bar Yohai is the greatest of the scholars: it cannot be denied that the pilgrimage to his shrine is the largest in Israel, leaving devotion to the tomb of Moses far behind.

In my discussion below, I trace the antecedents and the continuation of his legend; mark his place in the story, including his own root paradigms and the ones he or Moses de Leon created; show his effects on Judaism in different stages of history; and demonstrate an actual chain of personas, each link resonating with the same creative theme.

For believers, the human root paradigm from which Bar Yohai and *The Zohar, the Book of Light* grows is "the visionary man." (Other translations of *Zohar* are "mystical perception," or "enlightened state of being.") Bar Yohai's roots extend far back in time. He undoubtedly shared the interest that scholars of his era showed in their past, for whom "the first chapter of Ezekiel, the vision of God's throne-chariot (the 'Merkabah') was among the favorite subjects of discussion and interpretation, which it was apparently considered inadvisable to make public" (Scholem 1961: 42). Ezekiel himself saw his vision at the bitter time of the Babylonian captivity, 590 B.C.E. Before Ezekiel, never forgotten, was the figure of Elijah, who was taken up to heaven in a chariot. And before Elijah, Moses saw God in the burning bush, a major symbol of divine light. (Many believers say Bar Yohai is the reembodiment of Moses.) Before Moses there was Abraham, who according to the Kabbalah represented the stage of love balanced with rigor—two branches, one on each side of the world tree or *sephirot*, the mystic diagram of the Kabbalah. And way before, in a kind of glowing mythical age of angels and heavenly wisdom, Enoch lived with God and was "translated" at his life's end; that is, he never saw death but was transformed into the angel Metatron, ablaze with fiery torches. All this was recorded by the Merkabah mystics, the mystics of the chariot—the chariot being the vehicle of religious experience.

Bar Yohai, other mystics such as the Rabbi Akiba ben Joseph, and scholars such as the second Hillel were said to have inhabited the general region of Sefat and Meron. Like many authors of books in the Bible, they are said to have ascribed what they wrote to previous sages. They did so in awe of the numinous subject matter. And they hid the texts carefully. There is dispute about the accuracy of the legends of their doings. It is probable that some extraordinary book of mysticism *was* written, but owing to the secrecy, no book, no hard facts can be found. The tradition of the location of Bar Yohai's tomb at Meron is also in dispute—though certainly not among pilgrims; they are sure. "Hiddenness" enters the story continually and is the despair of the textual scholar, but it may be our meat and drink.

What followed in later centuries makes the desperate secrecy of the Jews understandable. To read what the Crusaders did in Jerusalem in 1099 makes one's blood run cold. These long-frustrated and self-righteous men, at their final successful capture of Jerusalem, strode through the city "red to the armpits" on one of the worst slaughter rampages of history, where 100,000 Jews died. Many remaining Jews fled to Spain, where in the course of time a golden age of scholarship unfolded. Kabbalism itself started to develop, making connections later with a revived Merkabah teaching. Again the writers ascribed what they had written to previous sages, and again they hid their work from all but the initiated.

Some time between 1280 and 1286 a great event manifested itself. The scholar Moses de Leon was somehow or other vouchsafed the text of *The Zohar,* "Bar Yohai's own book," and he wrote it down. A fascinating conflict has raged about this event. Had there really been an actual book, *The Zohar?* Did Moses de Leon get hold of it to make his copy? Did he merely absorb the tradition from the Kabbalistic movement of the time? This latter must have been the case, say textual analysts, since Kabbalism, implicit in the theme of the book, did not exist in Bar Yohai's time. Did he simply sit at his desk and make it all up, as his wife seemed to believe? Or was the book produced by automatic writing as his friends in later ages say?

Dante purported to write down a dream; we have it in the three books of *The Divine Comedy,* a great deal of which has a dream quality, but maybe not all. The same applies to John Bunyan's *Pilgrim's Progress;* William Blake's prophetic books also emanate a shamanistic quality. From what level does this material come? When dealing with mystics it is hard to know *who* wrote their works, an "angel" from a different realm or previous age, or they themselves. Furthermore, the cosmology implicit in this kind of poetic production is a dynamic, hidden doctrine, a matter of the intuitive flash, "illuminating and disappearing as sunbeams play on the surface of the water," as Moses de Leon himself described *The Zohar* (*The Zohar* 1:41b). On a mundane level, Kabbalism derived from the ancient texts of the time when Bar Yohai was the greatest saint, suggesting some kind of connection. Certainly all believed the book to be authored by Bar Yohai.

Spain was no permanent resting place for the Jews. The Inquisition began its cruel work, resulting in the expulsion of the Jews, many of whom migrated to Morocco and other parts of North Africa; others left for western Europe and various Mediterranean cities. These Sephardim (Spanish Jews) brought the Bar Yohai devotion with them. (The most important Jewish shrine in Morocco in recent times was the Moroccan "tomb" of Rabbi Shimon Bar Yohai, visited before the 1950s by 15,000 annually.) Of *The Zohar* itself there is little mention until the sixteenth century, when Isaac Luria, a German-born young man living in Cairo, met a man with a holy book that turned out to be *The Zohar.* Luria acquired it, and his life changed. He spread its fame everywhere, finally leading a new group of mystics to northern Galilee where he reestablished the community of Sefat. He became a saint; his title, *Ari,* meant "the lion." Many said he was the reembodiment of Bar Yohai himself, just as Bar Yohai was the reembodiment of Moses.

Now that *The Zohar* was found, it was printed (1558–60) and disseminated with astonishing rapidity all over the Diaspora. It was eagerly read and incorporated into much of Jewish thinking and ritual. In the Carpathian mountains, the *Ba'al Shem Tov* ("The Master of the Good Name"), the founder of Hasidism, on reading *The Zohar* said:

> With the light created by God during the six days of Creation
> Adam could see from one end of the world to the other.
> God hid the light away for the righteous in the hereafter.
> Where did he hide it?
> In the Torah.
> So when I open *The Book of Zohar*, I see the whole world.
> [Epigraph in 1983 edition of Moses de Leon, p. 2]

Hasidic tales relate that during the Ba'al Shem's nighttime studies this saintly scholar radiated a holy light (Levin 1932: 42–43). *The Zohar* grew in fame through the devotion of the followers of the Ba'al Shem Tov and that of the Hasids who lived all over northern Europe, where they faced much anti-Semitism. The Hasids and the Sephardim have been the book's greatest adherents, the Hasids being the principal scholars, and the Sephardim the divines, the chanters of the holy verses as a kind of ritual.

Centuries passed before the beginning of the *aliya* (the going-up), the return to Israel, the ingathering of the sparks. B'nai Brak, the Hasid "city of Holiness," was settled in Tel Aviv in 1924. During the Holocaust, scholar-mystics in Europe faced the unspeakable in persecution. But the tradition survived. After World War II the Hasids arrived in Israel and developed their communities; in B'nai Brak today *The Zohar* lives once again, still in private, to be sure, for only male elders are considered fit to read the sublime script. In 1955 Moroccan Jews, expelled by the Moroccan government in retaliation for the dispossession of Palestinian Arabs, were ingathered into Israel. The scene was set for a great revival of the cultus of Bar Yohai.

Viewing the history of this culture we see a curious pattern. It consists of much "looking back," in fact, writing books and ascribing one's words to the ancients—pseudepigraphy, Scholem calls it—a pattern that runs through both the Old and the New Testaments. I express the process by arrows in Figure 10.1. This process is important to the

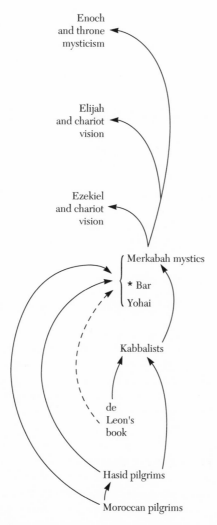

Figure 10.1. Looking backward: the links between pilgrims, mystics, and Bar Yohai.

formation of a creative persona and to his or her further development as an allegorical type. In this case, the Merkabah mystics, of whom Bar Yohai was clearly the principal, treasured in their secret lore— "looked back to"—Ezekiel's chariot vision, Elijah and his chariot story, and Enoch, the angel Metatron. The Kabbalists later treasured the Merkabah mystics, deriving their visions from them. They too "looked back"; Moses de Leon in Spain used Kabbalism in writing *The Zohar*

[231]

and ascribed authorship of his book to Bar Yohai, who lived much further back in time than the Kabbalists. The Hasids grew up on *The Zohar;* they too venerated Bar Yohai as its author. In the present age the Moroccan Jews, originally from Spain and now in Israel, look to the Hasids as their reference group, albeit with ambivalent feelings, and visit Bar Yohai's tomb in the hundreds of thousands for healing and enlightenment. Time's direction moves forward, but the present is busy creating the past.

Thus, Bar Yohai has been popularly sacralized as the hinge of all Jewish mysticism—constituting a strange story of performance and reperformance down the ages, but not a surprising one when the theme is mysticism. There may be vital cultures based on the most shadowy of protohistories. The pilgrimage is a kind of "restored behavior," Richard Schechner's term for

> living behavior independent of the causal systems that brought them into existence; they have a life of their own. The original motivation of the behavior may be lost, ignored, or contradicted. How the strip of behavior was made, found, developed, may be unknown or covered over, elaborated, distorted by time. Originating as a process, it is used to make a new process—a performance. The strips of behavior are "material." Restored behavior offers to both individuals and groups the chance to rebecome what they once were or to rebecome what they never were. Restored behavior is "out there" symbolic, reflexive . . . and may be created from a distant place or an actual past. [Schechner 1983: 164, 166]

Schechner's diagram (1983: 167) may be adapted for the Bar Yohai pilgrimage and *The Zohar;* in Figure 10.2 I illustrate how the "non-event" (in Schechner's terms) of Bar Yohai's authorship (one impossible to verify) is responsible for the pilgrimage to Bar Yohai. The event, the authoring by Moses de Leon, results in the restored event when the book is read. These two, non-event and event, are joined when a worthy pilgrim, that is, a mature male Hasid, studies it.

The Doctrine

I turn now to the actual Kabbalah (much of it deriving from Isaac Luria), since the devotion to Bar Yohai is basically related to its teaching. Here the Kabbalistic creation myth, which differs from that of

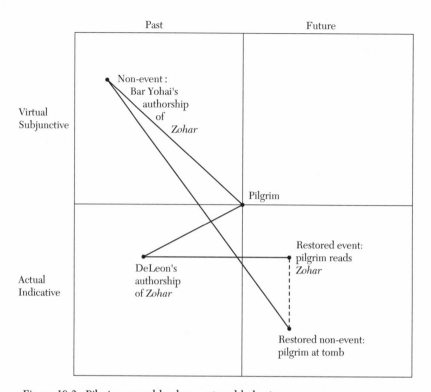

Figure 10.2. Pilgrimage and book as restored behavior.

traditional Judaism, is most relevant. To describe it, I use the words of Gershom Scholem (1961; see also Victor Turner's comments on this passage, 1985b):

> The Midrash refers to God as having concentrated His Shekhinah, His divine presence, in the holy of holies, at the place of the cherubim, as though His whole power were concentrated and contracted in a single point. Here we have the origin of the term *Tsimtsum* [concentration], while the thing itself is the precise opposite of this idea: to the Kabbalist *Tsimtsum* does not mean the concentration of God *at* a point, but his retreat *away* from a point.
>
> What does this mean? It means that the existence of the universe is made possible by a process of shrinkage in God. How can there be a world if God is everywhere? If God is "all in all," how can there be things which are not God? How can God create the world out of nothing if there is no nothing? This is the question. The solution became of the

[233]

highest importance in the history of later Kabbalistic thought. God was compelled to make room for the world by abandoning a region within Himself, a kind of mystical primordial space from which he withdrew in order to return to it in the act of creation and revelation. The first act of *En-Sof*, the Infinite Being, is therefore not a step outside but a step inside, a movement of recoil, of falling back upon oneself, of withdrawing into oneself. Instead of emanation we have the opposite, contraction.

The first act of all is not an act of revelation but one of limitation. Only in the second act does God send out a ray of His light and begin his revelation, or rather his unfolding as God the Creator, in the primordial space of His own creation. More than that, every new act of emanation and manifestation is preceded by one of concentration and retraction. In other words, the cosmic process becomes two-fold. Every strain involves a double strain, that is, the light which streams back into God and that which flows out from Him, and but for this perpetual tension, this ever repeated effort with which God holds Himself back, nothing in this world would exist. There is fascinating power and profundity in this doctrine. [260–61]

There are two other important ideas in later Kabbalism. They are the doctrine of "the Breaking of the Vessels," and that of *Tikkun*, which means mending or restitution of a defect. The divine light which flowed into primordial space unfolded in various stages. It came to pass within a realm of existence called the *Pleroma*, or the "fullness" of divine light. The first being which emanated from the light was Adam Kadmon, the "primordial man." Adam Kadmon is the first configuration of the divine light which flows from the essence of *En-Sof* into the primeval space of the contraction. The lights of the Sefiroth, spheres of manifestation, burst from his eyes. It was necessary that these isolated lights should be caught and preserved in special vessels. But the light broke forth all at once and its impact broke and shattered the vessels. [265–66]

Thus there is no sphere of existence that is not full of holy sparks which are mixed up with the broken vessels and need to be separated from them and lifted up . . . the process of *Tikkun*, restoration. [280, 283]

The doctrine itself demonstrates in a curious way the actual long-term history of the root paradigm of Bar Yohai and the mystic tradition. We can mark the links of the root paradigm that produced not only Bar Yohai but his later redactors and the final efflorescence of the pilgrimage. One can follow the double strain of contraction and light as expressed in Judaic religious protohistory and in later action deriving from that protohistory. The double strain appears as a series of contractions alternating with experiences of light:

Contraction:	the creation, including Adam Kadmon
Light:	light from Adam Kadmon's eyes
Contraction:	breaking of the vessels, scattering of the sparks
Light:	the angel Metatron with his fiery torches
Contraction:	slavery in Egypt (among many other episodes)
Light:	Moses' burning bush
Contraction:	the Babylonian captivity
Light:	Ezekiel's chariot vision
Contraction:	the Roman conquest
Light:	the experience and teaching of Bar Yohai and the Merkabah mystics
Contraction:	the hiding of the mystic books during the Diaspora
Light:	*The Zohar, The Book of Light*
Contraction:	the Spanish Inquisition; hiding of sacred books
Light:	the spread of *The Zohar* into the Diaspora; its effect on the Ba'al Shem Tov
Contraction:	anti-Semitism and the Holocaust
Light:	the aliya, ingathering of the sparks, to Israel; the pilgrimage to Bar Yohai's tomb

Victor Turner likened the empty point in the Kabbalah doctrine to the liminal phase in a rite of passage (1985b: 210). The implications are that in the process of the generation of creativity in any culture these empty points do exist, and are times that have to be filled, as a vacuum has to be filled. They are the times of "negative capability," as John Keats called them. In the process outlined above we see a prolonged oscillation throughout history between these two poles or "strains."

The light and its origin in the *Shekhinah*, the Divine Presence, are symbolized in one of Judaism's most emotional songs, the hymn greeting the Sabbath Queen, the female figure of the *Shekhinah* returning from her exile. It was composed by one of the later Kabbalists, Solomon Alkabez (Scholem 1965: 141), and begins, "Go, my beloved, to meet the bride / Let us receive the face of the Sabbath."

"On the Sabbath the light of the upper world burst[s] into the profane world" (Scholem 1965: 139) and is welcomed by the ceremony of Kabbolos Shabbos, when the congregation "turns westward on the Sabbath eve and bows to the approaching Bride." Scholem continues,

"It is recorded that Luria, standing on a hill near Sfat, beheld in a vision the throngs of Sabbath-souls coming with the Sabbath-Bride. A strange twilight atmosphere made possible an almost complete identification of the *Shekhinah*, not only with the Queen of the Sabbath, but also with every Jewish housewife who celebrates the Sabbath. This is what gave this ritual its enormous popularity" (Scholem 1965: 140–41). The symbolism of the lights (oil or candle flame) ritually lit by the mistress of the house on the Sabbath Eve is related to the same doctrine of light, the *Zohar*. The Kabbalah shows its influence all through Jewish life.

The ingathering of the sparks is an act that God is unable to accomplish alone. It is humanity's task, part of the oscillating process of contraction and expansion. From this primal charter derives much of the sense of task and mission that is the dynamic behind the Jewish religion, behind the growth of the mystical tradition, behind the survival of the Jews under later persecutions; it has been a great incentive for Zionism, the return of the Diaspora to its homeland. The promise "next year in Jerusalem" derives from the same source. One could compare the power of this primal charter with that of the Irish legend set in the fifth century A.D., which recounts how St. Patrick climbed Croagh Patrick Mountain and there maintained such a fierce asceticism that God himself was frightened and sent Gabriel to buy him off. Before St. Patrick would come down from the mountain he exacted four promises from God, one of which was that Ireland should be a united country. It is this legend that is behind the acts of the IRA in Belfast today.

Let us return to Bar Yohai sitting in his cave, contemplating, we suppose, the vision of God's throne and chariot. As noted, many of his devotees regard him as the reembodiment of Moses, and in the sixteenth century, Isaac Luria, the Ari and source of the later Kabbalah, was in his turn regarded as the reembodiment of Bar Yohai. Moshe Shokeid, describing his own participation with Moroccans in the pilgrimage of 1966, hinted that when a certain "old man of learning" came to his fire and asked to warm himself, Shokeid's Moroccan friend associated their visitor with the supernatural (Shokeid 1974: 82–83). The assumption was that it was Bar Yohai. On a visit to the tomb in 1980, I encountered an old Hasid in circumstances that suggested he was more than he appeared. The tradition is shot through with such connections, and they show how the creative persona seems to overstep time. Other noted examples of legends of the reembodiment or revisitation of a creative persona are King Arthur, "the once and future king," who, legend says, will return one day to lead the British; Sir Francis Drake, in a poem by Henry Newbolt, *Drake's Drum;* Bonnie Prince Charlie, for the Scots; Emilio Zapata for the Mexicans, said to come again to the villages of Morelos whenever peasants are oppressed; John F. Kennedy; Caitanya of India, who, during the Portuguese and Mogul invasions, was believed to be the avatar of Krishna; Jesus, believed by his followers to be the son or embodiment of God who will come again; and many more. What do they have in common? Boldness; living at a liminal time, in an era of discontinuity; charisma and the quality of the allegorical type; that is, each in his time represents and is identified with his suffering society, and is intensified by the retroactive shaping of that society. It is as if such personages were vouchsafed a repeated life: one life bursts its natural span and spreads into other lives, eventually flooding their successive environments with supernatural power.

The characteristics of a major creative persona begin to emerge. First, the identity of such a one may not be limited to his or her life span; it oversteps time and is thought to be reembodied later. Second, the era of the creative persona's life, the "heroic time," as Victor Turner called the date of an epic event (1985a: 98–103), is at some turning point in history, a time of discontinuity when the society is in the throes of change. Usually a maturation period intervenes, lasting until another liminal age when the society has again been shaken and is in need of answers to its dilemmas. At this time the resources of the past are tapped by gifted individuals, and the great teachings or events of the past may be written down. This is "narrative time" in Victor Turner's terminology. In the case of Bar Yohai the task was taken up by Moses de Leon in *The Zohar*. "Documentary time" occurs later, as when Isaac Luria and his band of scholars worked with large parts of *The Zohar* in redactions and recensions of the doctrine. Such an era includes the critical attacks of the historian Heinrich Graetz (1975) and the careful textual analysis of Gershom Scholem. And it includes the fundamentalist viewpoint of the earlier and later Hasidic scholars (who probably understood this school of mysticism best), producing new variants such as Martin Buber, Marc Chagall, Isaac Bashevis Singer, and influencing many others, such as Jacob Boehme, William Blake, and Patrick White (*The Riders in the Chariot*).

Thus, there are complicated connections between creative personas

[237]

and liminality. The creative personas are dressed by society in allegorical robes; their new power supports their followers in future ages in their dark hours, and resupplies them with their sacra, the holy doctrines. Changes in the use of the doctrine also occur in liminal pockets. One may cite other examples. *The Kebra Negast*, the ancient text of Ethiopia, gives power to the Rastafarian movement and to reggae music in Jamaica today; the tale of the martyrdom of Hussein and its reenactment in Muharram is vitally important in contemporary Iranian politics; the biblical tale of Exodus was used in the U.S. civil rights movement as well as in the modern aliya to Israel.

The third characteristic of the creative persona is that of the "constellated individual." In psychology "constellation" refers to a group of related thoughts or feelings clustered around one central idea. A neo-Jungian psychologist, Anthony Stevens, made daring statements about the concept at the 1984 conference "Neurobiology, the Social Sciences, and Religion" sponsored by the Institute for Religion in an Age of Science. Stevens reminded us that in Jung's psychology of individuation the healer's aim is to produce a full "Self," that is, a creative persona. Jung shows the Self as an individual in a social setting, sharing an unblocked collective unconscious and consciousness with all humanity. It is a mystic's concept. Stevens equated this Self with "Anthropos," the gigantic figure of the Human, none other than Adam Kadmon, the Primal Man of the Kabbalists. But Stevens went further and identified this concept with "Gaia," meaning not only all humanity but the whole earth as one organism. The struggle toward this all-inclusive soul can be recognized in some of the creative personas in the essays in this book. At the conference Stevens described how "the Anthropos may come out as constellated by an individual human being. Later this may fall away and appear in another" (Stevens, personal communication). Put a different way, it is the collective archetypal "sense-of-itself" of a broad group, or even of the whole of humanity, emerging as a configuration in the personality of some highly conscious individual. Bar Yohai has been taken up by Sephardic and Hasidic Jewry as such a figure, transformed from a simple scholar to the epitome of Judaism, holy, luminous; *The Zohar*, the book of light and healing, in his hands (as he is pictured in the handouts at the tomb). Both the tomb of the saint and his book are reckoned to have healing power. And the book is undoubtedly the greatest spiritual book of the Jews after the Talmud.

The Pilgrimage: Background

The pilgrimage to Meron demonstrates how deep may be the effect of an allegorical type on future generations.[3] The old tomb of Bar Yohai in northern Galilee (never quite neglected, it seems) began to increase in popularity with the arrival of the Sephardic immigrants after 1955. Meron was a liminal shrine for a liminal people on a liminal occasion, celebrating the mystic, liminal branch of Judaism.

Each year the number of pilgrims at the yearly festival increases. The national bus company has taken over transportation, and police put up barriers to control the crowds. Every year a market appears by the main road, and a tent city materializes around the tomb. Inside the first and second courtyards of the tomb, barriers divide the space into two equal parts: one giving access for the ten thousand Hasids to the main hospice (including a private passage leading to the back of the tomb), and the other funneling over 200,000 Sephardim into the main tomb room. The central rabbinate in Jerusalem, representing law-minded, orthodox, and non-Hasidic Judaism, continually issues warnings on television and radio that men and women should not touch one another in the crowd, and that no menstruating women should approach the shrine. They also announce: "This is not a suitable event. Do not attend. There is bad slaughtering at Meron" (Haim Hazan and Judith Goldberg, personal communication). The rabbinate also forbids any hint of saints' worship, with minimal success.[4]

Neither Hasids nor Sephardim at the pilgrimage are politically sophisticated. To the Hasids on pilgrimage little is of any moment save the vision of God, while the Sephardim are far from being politically organized.[5] This is a popular celebration, with a long history that shimmers through the events at various points.

A Pilgrimage Narration

In the following transcript I am my own informant, and give what this informant "dictated" to my notebook the day after the pilgrimage. My informant, a Catholic, had her own feelings, opinions, and biased religious attitudes.

I remember Lag B'Omer with great fondness—even the dust, heat, thirst—thirst that was quenched at the welcome steel faucets. So what is Meron? A turnoff near the northern border of Israel, where the territory ends among wild mountains and forests, dominated by the father of mountains, white-haired Hermon himself. Out on those foothills, lodged on the spurs overlooking Galilee, stand the holy villages of the mystics. From the heights of old, those bearded men, Bar Yohai, Rabbi Akiba, Rabbi Hillel, and later, the Ari, Moses Cordovero, Hayim Vital, and Solomon Alkabez stared upon the mists, forever drawing forward in their minds the threads of the even more ancient writings—the legends of angelic Enoch, Abraham's act, the Song of Songs, Ezekiel.

The greatest of the searchers, Shimon Bar Yohai, a little after Christ, began to write—so the folk tell us—the great mystic book of the *Zohar*. No, this is untrue, say modern scholars, Moses de Leon wrote it a thousand years later. But where did de Leon, a relatively insignificant man, get the ideas? Bar Yohai wrote in his own tradition shortly before the regularizers of Christianity began to get busy building institutions and creating structural rules. This mystic, however, kept the faith so that later Christian mystics, the Rhinelanders, Boehme, and Blake, could light their tapers from his testament (or was it his?) of light. And just as in India when a holy man dies and the simple people feel his touch of mystic communion, perhaps more after his death than before, so the legends about Bar Yohai started, legends of healings, favors, even resurrections at his tomb.

It is said that the common people don't know anything about Bar Yohai's doctrine, they haven't been allowed to learn it, they don't care to, the shrine is merely a center for folk medicine or magic. There's no explaining why the folk hit on a certain saint. But how did this shrine hold the attention of many of the Jewish people from way back, all through the reign of the Dark Ages in the rest of Europe? Here at Meron the devotion must have been assisted by the coming and going of the ancient Jewish mystic sages between Sefat and Babylonia. The tomb then withstood Islam, how we do not know—while Palestine itself continued the decline begun by the Romans. But again thinkers and mystics returned to these northern rain-obscured heights in the sixteenth century, having brought back from Spain—where the "cabals" had gathered—the sacred *Zohar*. They were treasuring, under the old human law of anamnesis, what might one day save the human race.

And now under the burning ripe sky, we crowd up and up, walking with our fellow humans, stopping like them at some sideshow or gambling game, or Begin's election booth, plastered with signs saying, "Vote for the Freedom Party." Then comes a group of non-Hasidic ultra-orthodox on the left side of the road, displaying long black-thonged arm bands, *tefillin*, which they urge men to come forward and be bound with; then a loving couple walking entwined. Just opposite is an encampment, one of hundreds that have been set up by the path. A cheerful young Sephardi woman and her family are out by the wire fence with a young live sheep, which the small boy is petting. Our anthropologists passing by twit them about the pity of killing it. Sure enough, next day the family is proudly displaying its carcass that they've skinned and strung up for the passerby to admire. The family is going to invite the public in to share the meat.

Now, while Vic rests his arthritis for a moment in a folding chair, up through the crowd pushes a group of young people led by a singing woman and a young man with a drum. They clap and dance in a wide line, then pass on jovially. Now we proceed upward past an old Sephardi in a white jalabiya gown, selling blessings, and a couple of rascally beggars on the right, sitting comfortably on the ground with tin cans for money beside them. And at last we see in the crowd a group of young men in skull caps and ordinary clothes, toiling upward and singing. One of them bears in his arms a large object flowing with veils, topped with two crowned knobs. It is the Torah in Her silver case; they are bringing Her up to Her ark in the shrine. Men stop on seeing the group and come forward to kiss the Torah with great emotion, weeping. The Moroccans, now that they are here, need not fear oppression, their beloved and main unifier is with them like a sacrament.

A party of Hasids scissor past through the crowd, touching no one. They wear beards and sidelocks, black coats and black wide-brimmed hats. They stride purposefully, minds elsewhere, with hands turned back, the skin of their faces pale and pure. The crowd parts to give them room. We press upward, now passing an incense seller on the left who displays on the ground incense grains heaped in different colors, with medicines too, perhaps from the ancient Kabbalistic tomes—so far from sorcery really, this joyous crowd with its love of the zaddik, who was not just a law-rabbi, but a visionary. And the thrill is here in the crowd in the deep sun. The zaddik's holy picture is in everyone's hands. He is depicted bearing the scroll of *The Zohar*, and even I can read the title in the very holy Hebrew script. The germ of thrill, still small in us because we know so little, grows as we get pressed through the shrine doors and deposited finally at the rail of the little stone container of his body—nearly two millennia old.

Women are all around me; Rachel, a student, is by my side translating. Everyone feels excited—the women are on the point of dancing Moroccan style. One woman turns out to be weeping; she tells us she is barren, and if only the zaddik would send her a son she would name the child Shimon. Another, laughing, says, "I'm menstruating. Do you think they'll throw me out?" I answer via Rachel, "I don't mind, myself. I think you're lucky to be of childbearing age." One of them has many children, and we congratulate each other. We all proceed to throw candles into the tomb area—only I find I have thrown in the Easter candle I keep in my purse. Ah, well. There is a high drift of candles already accumulating in the tomb area. It would be impossible to light them here—the shrine would roast—but they pile up in white waxen innocence, saying love, flame, prayer. They will be used for bonfires on the roof.

The faces to my left are faces gone, gone into prayer and light and faith, round with the knowledge, "We are here," and with "Hear my prayer, Zaddik; if you grant that my child gets well I will come every year." I pray for my daughter, Irene, who is pregnant. I pray for the down-bearing power to be given to her older womb; how can we tell whether the instincts will be strong after thirty-five years? Her body needs to be fully used, with no Caesarean.[6] Give her this grace, Zaddik, blessed are the givers.

Leaving the shrine I look for good camera stances, leaping about clumsily, never tired, pushing on, greeting strange women, hearing Brooklyn accents at one point—it is a Lubavitcher wife who has made the trip specially with her husband. We chat and get on a treat. I venture farther up the hill to the Sephardi market, where they sell holy oils for the fire, candles, fezes, and the like. I'm taken aback at a high black stall like a wall—it consists of tier upon tier of huge black volumes of *The Zohar*, on sale to the public. (*The Zohar*, like the tomb, will heal the sick and bring prosperity.) Three times I've asked passersby, "Do you read *The Zohar?*" And three times they've answered, "It's only for advanced scholars." But will this state of things continue with the books so easily available?

As Rachel and I pass the arches at the back of the shrine, we're offered paper plates of couscous by a man seated on the ground by the back entrance. The couscous is very welcome; in fact it's delicious. We offer him some arrack we have brought, which he accepts. A terrible noise breaks out from the barred compartments in the public hospice farther on. Two Moroccan woman are fighting over a sleeping place in it; they screech like dragon-sized petulant peacocks in a wild crescendo of barbwire sound. Alarmed relatives gather and try to separate them; one contestant pulls the other's bedding away and throws it out, the other grabs it back, battering bodily against her foe. Will it subside? We pass on like Dante and Virgil, with bowed heads.

Then to the long avenues of tents where I found peace and comfort everywhere, some of the tents with portable television sets, some with electric generators costing $4,000, stoves, water pails, huge vacuum flasks of chilled drinks, carpets on the tent floors, wall hangings consisting of romantic velvet paintings, national flags everywhere, pictures of Bar Yohai, photographs of Navon, David Levi, Arik, Herzl, and Begin, political leaders and founders of Israel. And here the children play with wide eyes, as happy as if they were on the beach. The big fig tree by the caves, which exudes sap like mother's milk, is covered with tags of cloth. (Crapanzano 1973:80 describes the same among the Berbers). "Give us babies," is what the tags say. The grand instinct goes on. It'll stop with a jerk when the economic crash arrives and hurts the people—as history has shown before. But for now! This is what their presence tells us: "There's glory. We have the strength of numbers, the voting power, it's our country and we could make Israel into a more blissful Morocco, as long as we have jobs, schools, and a synagogue. Our religion's favored, there's no anti-Semitism; we all turn to Bar Yohai. But we don't rejoice in our sons being far away and in danger. No." I saw the awe and stillness in their eyes when they spoke of their sons in the army. These people weren't saber-rattling, they were, as I would put it, "keeping their fingers crossed."

Inside one reception tent, the table was exquisitely laid with lace and a silver tea service. The lady of the tent house leaned over and poured out tea for us. Her husband is a sanitary engineer in Tel Aviv; they're originally from Morocco. They complained to us about the Hasids. "We're gentiles to them, yet we keep the Sabbath like they do. Although they all wear black and get called 'the blacks,' they're 'whites,' and they treat us like blacks." A little old woman said, "They poured garbage on top of us from up there" (pointing to the Hasid yeshiva building). "They don't think we're human." "And the Hasids are mean," said the tent lady. "They charge us a lot for blessings." "That's a shame," I said.

In one tent a young Moroccan family had meat to offer and we stopped by. They complained about the Hasids like the others, but when a party of Hasids passed behind the tent they were happy enough to comply with our suggestion to ask them in for a chat. We wanted to talk about *The Zohar* but the Hasids refused, saying they were too young. But they entertained us all by telling Hasidic tales of Bar Yohai in his early days.

The Hasids said, "How do you Moroccans enjoy yourselves, living for a week outside? Never mind, we all have a Jewish heart." The Sephardim said, "You Hasids are the true believers, not like us. Look how you pray, dancing in a ring. We're only interested in food."

As Barbara Myerhoff, Vic, and I drew near one tent we found that the family had collected a Yemenite, a Spaniard, a German, an Algerian, and were now delighted to add an American, a Scotsman, and an Englishwoman. The father put on his white jalabiya robe and fez, and his wife danced to the tape recorder, swaying like a temptress in her long brocade gown. I danced, too—I was reminded of the African belly dance. This wasn't the world of sin and resistance to temptation. The wife was dancing for her guests with her husband's approval, simply enjoying herself. Barbara talked to the Spaniard in his own language.

Night had fallen and the moon was full: it was now time for the people to light the bonfires on the flat roof. There would be two barrels, each with a fire, one on the Sephardi side of the roof and one on the Hasids' (the separation of these groups remained strict throughout, save for that one meeting when we heard the Hasidic tales). The light of the fires *was* the "Splendor," the light of the *Zohar* itself.

We ascended the stairs and penetrated through the crowd to the Hasids' barrel. This turned out to be a wide-rimmed, upright concrete cylinder, about twice the size of an oil drum, set on a wide concrete dish to catch burning debris. It looked phallic somehow. It was surrounded by a group of Hasids who were mounting it up with fuel, candles mainly, and papers on which were written the name of the devotee, his or her mother's name (proving that he or she was a Jew), a request, and a prayer. The crowd of Hasids gradually thickened around the barrel, many wearing *shtreimel*, fur hats, some with vodka bottles protruding from their pockets. Singing began and circling dances, like a great pot slowly boiling. They were all touching one another in ecstasy. A tiny rebbe with an ancient white splayed beard approached, which he was only enabled to do by dint of the elbow work of stalwart young Hasids who fought outward against their com-

[244]

rades to allow their elder to pass. Was he going to light the fire? A flash in the darkness—and a great shout as the first flames shot up, and grew, and grew. They fed it candles and emptied into it bottles of holy oil, then laid on an entire *capote* garment, folded—sacrificed on this altar. I saw arms silhouetted against the flame, pouring oil.[7] The roof was one mass of black coats, hats, and pale faces; voices shouted "Bar Yohoi!" in harsh song—all the men moving and moving in a chain embrace until they were in trance. The dawn at the end of night would be the Shekhinah, the glory of God. As for me, I was perched up on the dome itself, while Vic and the others were shoved farther and farther away across the crowd until they reached the edge of the roof where there was a wire fence. Here Henry Abramovitch took up Vic's folding chair and fended off the crowd with it. Earlier Vic had been found resting his arthritis in that chair by the front entrance of the shrine, chatting to beggar women and, so he said, putting out his own hand with theirs every now and then, saying "*Tsadaka,* alms. Pity the poor anthropologist."

We managed to make our way down from the roof to gather at the cafe. Barbara and I told the others how nobody had stopped us climbing on the dome; the boys up there with their black clothes, fresh blooming faces, skull caps, and long ringlets, made way for us. "Though we took their places, they let us," said Barbara. "The communitas paradigm reigned." At the cafe we eagerly devoured lamb in pocket bread, the meat hardly cooked and still warm from the slaughtering, helped down with lots of hot sauce along with beer to quench our thirst. We rested, listening to the eastern music.

The obverse of the sublime on the roof was the official slaughter yard, situated some way beyond the shrine. Here a man in a white shirt, black pants, and skullcap gutted a sheep and skinned it. Another sheep lay on the ground with its throat cut but not yet butchered. A couple of rabbis stood by to perform the koshering, along with a couple of workmen. Half a dozen of the ordinary public hung around. The floor was concrete with long drains, where feces and blood were being washed down with hoses. High rails were slung with carcasses, all stamped "RABBI KOSHERED." Three cows lay nearby, sleeping.

We left the spot, determined to finish for the night. But far down toward the parking lot, one single tent was still in action. Around a tall fire sat a group of hippies, one with a cowboy hat; they were drumming and singing, so that we could not resist their invitation to join in. Barbara started making friends, and after a bit she turned to us and said, "You go on to bed, I'm staying up all night." The anthropologist in her was hooked.

The Haircutting

Here in the context of the Bar Yohai pilgrimage, three-year-old Hasid children were to be initiated by the cutting of their hair. Up to this time they had been "angels," now they would belong to the earthly world.

Up and down the rails dividing the courtyard of the shrine the Hasid wives pressed and craned toward their husbands and children on the sacred side—never shouting, but showing in their faces the strong will, the mild yet frightening persistence I had seen before. They wore the mandatory wigs, headscarves, long-sleeved dresses, stockings, and shoes of ultra-orthodox women. Their faces were not really with us; they were watching the scene beyond, where their children moved above the crowd of black coats and hats, perched on their fathers' shoulders. The innocent overblown pink little faces—overblown with tears in one case—were girlish faces, crowned with beautiful long hair tied on each side with pretty spangled bands, leaving the front hair curly and free. They clung affectionately to their fathers as they faced this way and that, borne in the dance to the sound of music. I was impressed at first how well the fathers were looking after their little daughters. Where were the sons, though? They were supposed to be so important. Then I noticed that every one of the "girls" was wearing pants, as well as an embroidered skull cap. These were the sons.

Someone put up a pair of scissors by a child's head and snip, the tress on one side was gone, leaving the curls in front to develop as side locks. The hair was taken away to be added to the furnace on the roof, destined for the angelic light. The boy was whirled on in the dance, displaying one side cut. When next I saw him, the cutting was completed, and his father had placed on his head his own huge shtreimel, under which the child labored, comforted only by a pacifier stuck in his mouth. He was now a real male, no longer just like his sister and belonging to the mother's world. Now that the traditional time of mourning, between Passover and Shavuot, was in abeyance, his hair could be ritually cut and he could celebrate his new membership of the holy Hasids while at the shrine of light. A collective celebration often triggers off individual ones.

[246]

Now the boy would be ready for the Torah. His father would gradually teach him the holy letters, and the long specialization would
begin, a training such as is hardly to be found on this globe. He would
advance to the stage of Bar Mitzvah, when the wise boy, like the boy
Christ in the Temple, would admonish us all, reading from the Great
Scroll. He would proceed to long years of studying, sharpening and
deepening the brain-weapon, then on to princehood in the courts of
his Rebbe father, pointed out as a future rebbe, his clothes perfect.
He would celebrate the festivals in collective groups, dancing in the
synagogue, waiting in chastity. His marriage would be ordained by
the rebbe: the bridegroom now trapped into the polluting if pleasur-
able task of fathering sons, and the wife keeping the home pure and
kosher. And thus to the stage of fatherhood himself, involved with his
son's bris (circumcision)—the son as a toddler wheeled about by the
father in a pushchair among his other great progeny, all dressed in
holy clothes. And the father, growing to middle age, in some business,
handling papers with practiced efficiency, slapping them here, slapping them there, neatly pocketing pen and glasses. The yet older,
knowing father in his huge shtreimel and huge beard at his son's
wedding, teasing him, using solemn, witty words with hidden meanings, slipping sly smiles, making big gestures, continuing for seven
evenings after the wedding at the feast at the end of each day of prayer.
Or perhaps he would follow the more solemn route, the holier, that
of the rebbe—consulted privately by husbands bearing little cloths
from their wives to prove clearness from blood. The endless exegesis
of the Book, the growing holiness, surrounded by reverent juniors,
his beard now white, shoulders bent, the marvelous visage long and
wrinkled, the ancient book under his arm. He has endured a life of
study. Will not his prayers eventually prevail against God's wild and
unwise creation, prayers in a life of perfection greater than anything
God could have invented? Maybe the rebbe doesn't know what's good
for us all, certainly we don't. But the man is a searcher.

So I press to the rail watching the slow swirl, the cram of "blacks"
in front of me, and behind, the constant pushing drift of Sephardim
into the shrine of the tomb.

What was not part of my own observations was an altercation on
the roof later in the night of the bonfire, toward sunrise. Yoram Bilu
reported that a large group of neo-Kabbalists, whose title is "Those
Who Return to God in Repentance," went up to the roof to "bring in

the Light." This was a young group from the city, unrelated to the traditional Hasid world community, mainly concerned during the last decade with reading and explaining *The Zohar*. They had women with them on the roof in an outer circle. Their rabbi was reading from *The Zohar* and interpreting it to the group. The Hasids began to that the neo-Kabbalists were too young and should not read *The Zohar* until they were over forty, and that women were wrongly hearing it, too. An argument began; the Hasids reportedly became violent and started a fisticuff fight. In an instant the police were on the spot and put a cordon between the two groups. Peace was restored by expelling the neo-Kabbalists.

Here the contradiction between the dominant symbol of Kabbalism, light, and its traditional milieu, secrecy, was brought out into the open. *The Zohar* should be, as in the Western hymn, "in light inaccessible hid from our eyes." Victor Turner, who held intensive one-to-one conversations with several Kabbalists[8] during our stay in Israel, said, "The fire on the roof, the full moon, the dawn, and *The Zohar*, all are symbols of light, the Splendor, and mean the Shekhinah, the presence of God. If these are made too cognitive, it is a bad thing." So the Moroccan women themselves in the tomb room throwing unlighted candles symbolize the hidden nature of the Splendor, supplying by an indirect act, not an interpretation, what is needed to create the fire which can be seen for miles around. As we have seen, the Jewish housewife herself becomes the Shekhinah on the Sabbath, in the eyes of Kabbalists. (It is to be noted here that the Hasids' argument is not merely a matter of antifeminist prejudice.)

As for the full moon, of which we were very conscious during the pilgrimage, it too has a strong association with the Shekhinah. The Shekhinah, a bride and a queen, is often in exile. The lessening of the moon is a symbol of the Shekhinah's exile. The Shekhinah herself is the "holy moon." In redemption the moon would be restored to its original state (Scholem 1965: 151–52).

Thus, the light symbolism ought to come into consciousness by a back way, not through exegesis given openly at the shrine but through kinetic knowledge (probably via the limbic system of the brain into right-hemisphere consciousness, the nonexegetic but metaphoric one—to use the terms of modern neurobiology). The symbolism of the ingathering of the sparks was indeed shown at Meron. The pilgrimage looked at as a whole was the means whereby Hasids and

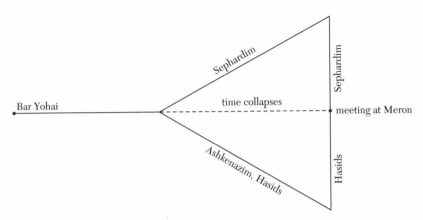

Figure 10.3. The ingathering of the sparks.

Sephardim met in propinquity, certainly closer than on any other occasion in conflict-ridden Israel. Their origins were so diverse, from northeastern Europe to Morocco on the southeastern end of the Mediterranean, that this was an extraordinary event. Figure 10.3 expresses it schematically.

So Bar Yohai and his book, *The Zohar*, have survived the obstacles of history into our own turbulent age. He points beyond us to the still hidden world of mystical enlightenment. He was a person who made himself into a "Self" (in Jungian terms) as a scholar of unusual gifts and one who went through the process of being created as a constellated individual by his own society as well as later ones. His virtue as a creative persona caused him to accrete to himself the allegories and root paradigms (in Victor Turner's sense) of former days; later ages built legend and allegory upon him. He cannot now be known for what he actually was in his day; his life is a "non-event," a life inextricable now from what later ages have done to it. Thus, to encompass the creative persona, we have had to follow his larger persona into the diachronic dimension, to examine the way liminal historical events have intensified the impetus and power of his persona. We have had to mark the response of society to its own creation, and to observe, if only partly, both the consciousness and the unconscious of that society (Myerhoff, this volume; Abramovitch and Bilu n.d.).

Why does society produce these rare individuals who pass through the nets of the statisticians, and have such fundamental effects on humankind for thousands of years? Such figures intrigue me greatly, and I am speculating that there may be a natural, providential supply of them produced by society just as the body produces antitoxins and endorphins to ensure survival and creativity. Furthermore, what "Bar Yohai" is effecting seems to be something we have not properly analyzed yet—it exists whether we understand it or not; there is anamnesis involved. We shall not know, until future events show us, how important such figures are.

Notes

1. There is a difference between the symbolic type (Handelman 1981) and the allegorical type (Lavie 1986). The symbolic type more often appears in actual rites of passage, in which it frequently enters as a clown figure; it is not a historic personage. Someone enacts the role. Both types mediate among the inconsistencies of the transitional social situation, but the symbolic type brings about the necessary changes without apparently effective or moral action. It acts like a catalyst. The allegorical type is more intrinsically concerned in his or her role, growing into it, as it were; the role is also shaped with meaning by society. He or she gives leadership, whether by the ability to hold up to society a picture of itself as it is or as it was in some previous golden age, or to point beyond all to a mystic, unifying vision.

2. These were Henry Abramovitch, Batsheva (a Hebrew University anthropology student), Yoram Bilu, Yoram Bilu's assistant, Yair Boni, Shifra Epstein, Harvey Goldberg, Richard Hecht, Barbara Myerhoff, Norit Ramon, Rachel Rosen, Norman Stillman, Yedida Stillman, and Shalva Weil. I gratefully acknowledge their valuable assistance and information.

3. In order to understand the modern context and root this essay on spirituality in reality, it is necessary to show a little of the political and community structure of Israel after immigration and war. In 1955, after the Moroccan government expelled the Jews in what has been called the Moroccan "holocaust," the labor government of Israel invited the refugees to Israel. Burdened with an austerity budget and a severe housing shortage, the government was hard put to resettle the vast numbers of immigrants. The existing, small *kibbutzim* and *moshav* farms were progressing well, run by internally democratic groups of educated Ashkenazim from Europe. But few were either able or willing to invite large numbers of Moroccans to share their lives. So the labor government set about building "development" towns on unoccupied land and on newly occupied and possessed territory in the northern and southern peripheries, often consisting of barren hills and desert. Some Moroccans were settled near Jerusalem. In 1983 I saw various settlements in southern Israel sited in strategic positions like fortresses along hilltops, far from sources of employment. There was a dead atmosphere in many of them, for unemployment was rife and many were on welfare. Owing to their negative feelings about the secularist labor party who, one might suppose, would favor this new working class, and because of their own political background, the Moroccans and other North Africans generally espoused the cause of the Likud, Begin's conservative party. Eventually, some found blue-collar jobs in Tel Aviv and elsewhere

and began to grow prosperous, enriching Israel's popular culture with their festivals, music, dancing, sense of enjoyment of life, and their value set on hospitality.

4. The central rabbinate, the most powerful branch of Judaism, derived its teaching from the Torah, the biblical books of the law, rather than the Kabbalah. It sought to control the Sephardim's religion, but many of the Sephardim shrugged off the directives. The festival of Bar Yohai was the high spot of the year for the Sephardim, much as the carnival and Umbanda are focuses for black Brazilians in Rio de Janeiro—also a large population without much political development but a high sense of ritual and festival.

5. The account that follows gives examples of bad feeling expressed by Sephardic pilgrims, particularly complaints against the Hasids. Obviously the Sephardic accommodation at the pilgrimage center was not catered for like that of the Hasids, who were Northern Europeans. The Sephardim are labeled "primitive" by the law-minded orthodox, who stay home at pilgrimage time, considering the rite of candle-throwing to be pagan. In Israel the sophisticated are often in the labor party, a somewhat secular group that largely disapproves of the Meron pilgrimage and complains of the Moroccans' political backwardness. This is not the place to draw conclusions about Israeli politics, merely to show "the predicament of homecoming" for the Moroccans, as Deshen and Shokeid (1974) termed their condition in their study of the North African Jews in Israel.

6. Oddly enough little Rose was born prematurely, just when we returned from Israel. Bar Yohai was overdoing it a little.

7. At the 1984 pilgrimage to Meron the following year the fire spilled over the rim of the barrel and set the roof itself ablaze, causing considerable damage.

8. Mordechai Rotenberg, Eliezar Goldman, Moshe Idel, and Professor Halamish.

REFERENCES

Abramovitch, Henry. n.d. "Sacred Shrines and Holy Chance: Two Pilgrimages in Northern Israel." Typescript written for the Sackler School of Medicine, University of Tel Aviv.

Abramovitch, Henry, and Yoram Bilu. n.d. "Dreams of the Pilgrimage: In Search of the Saint." Typescript written for the Sackler School of Medicine, University of Tel Aviv.

Crapanzano, Vincent. 1973. *The Hamadsha*. Berkeley: University of California Press.

Deshen, Schlomo, and Moshe Shokeid. 1974. *The Predicament of Homecoming: Cultural and Social Life of North African Immigrants in Israel*. Ithaca: Cornell University Press.

Graetz, Heinrich. 1975. *The Structure of Jewish History*. Trans., ed., and introd. by Isman Schorsch. New York: Jewish Theological Seminary.

Handelman, Don. 1981. "The Ritual Clown: Attributes and Affinities." *Anthropos* 76, 1/2: 321–70.

Handelman, Don, and Bruce Kapferer. 1980. "Symbolic Types, Mediation, and the Transformation of Ritual Context: Sinhalese Demons and Tewa Clowns." *Semiotica* 30, 1/2: 41–71.

Lavie, Smadar. 1986. "The Poetics of Politics: An Allegory of Bedouin Identity."

In Myron J. Aronoff, ed., *Political Anthropology*, vol. 5, *The Frailty of Authority*. New Brunswick, N.J.: Transaction Books. Pp. 131–46.

Levin, Meyer. 1975 [1932]. *Classic Hasidic Tales*. New York: Penguin Books.

Moses de Leon. 1983 [1280–86]. *Zohar: The Book of Enlightenment*. Trans. with introd. by Daniel Chanan Matt. New York: Paulist Press.

Schechner, Richard. 1983. *Performative Circumstances from the Avant Garde to Ramlila*. Calcutta: Seagull Books.

——. 1985. *Between Theatre and Anthropology*. Philadelphia: University of Pennsylvania Press.

Scholem, Gershom. 1961. *Major Trends in Jewish Mysticism*. New York: Schocken.

——. 1963. Introduction to *Zohar, The Book of Splendor: Basic Readings from the Kabbalah*. New York: Schocken.

——. 1965. *On the Kabbalah and Its Symbolism*. London: Kegan Paul.

Shokeid, Moshe. 1974. "An Anthropological Perspective on Ascetic Behavior and Change." In Deshen and Shokeid 1974.

Stevens, Anthony. 1982. *Archetype: A Natural History of the Self*. New York: Morrow.

Turner, Victor. 1985a. *On the Edge of the Bush: Anthropology as Experience*. Tucson: University of Arizona Press.

——. 1985b. "Liminality, Kabbalah, and the Media." *Religion* 15: 205–17.

[11]

Ilongot Visiting:
Social Grace and the
Rhythms of Everyday Life

Renato Rosaldo

Why do rituals never begin on time? In casual conversation an anthropologist colleague half-seriously, half-jokingly elevated this fieldwork anxiety into a pressing theoretical issue. Ethnography's major puzzle, she said, is to understand how natives can figure out when their own rituals are about to begin.

When anthropologists speak informally about the pleasures and hardships of fieldwork, they often reflect on the liberation and bafflement of abandoning clock-time for quite different tempos of life. In some versions the people are habitually late. In others, they have a different sense of time. In yet others, they have no sense of time at all. Yet, for all the work on the cultural construction of time, little has been written on the tempo of everyday life in other cultures. Evidently, a paramount reality of other people's daily lives has eluded the ethnographer's grasp.

Ethnographers' sentiments probably echo feelings learned closer to home. The English labor historian E. P. Thompson has described the sense of "time-discipline" that appears so natural in Anglo-American society as the outcome of a protracted historical struggle. Thompson succinctly states his argument as follows: "In all these ways—by the division of labour; the supervision of labour; fines; bells and clocks; money incentives; preaching and schoolings; the suppression of fairs and sports—new labour habits were formed, and a new time-discipline was imposed" (1967: 90). Those in our society who fail to conform with the painfully imposed "time-discipline" are commonly described as living by C.P.T., Indian Time, or Mexican Time. To make my own position clear, I should hasten to say that my having known Mexican Time from the inside has not kept me from having experienced the ethnographer's dilemma of being just plain perplexed about when ceremonial events in other cultures were about to begin.

The tempo of social being I shall attempt to characterize in this essay usually has been described by its absences, or more precisely, by contrast with its supposed opposite. "We" have "time-discipline," and "they" have, well, something else (or, as we say these days, Otherness). The former quality of time can be described in relation to cultural artifacts, such as clocks, calendars, appointment books, and the like. More significantly, it can be understood in connection with capitalists' desire to discipline and synchronize the labor force, rationalizing production and maximizing profits, but probably not enhancing the quality of life. Certainly this is the drift of the persuasive analyses put forth by E. P. Thompson, and before him, Max Weber.

Max Weber made the very qualities he studied, discipline and rationalization, appear strange by contrasting them with what he called traditionalism. He illustrated his argument with a hypothetical case in which the employer, who pays piece-rates, tries to speed up the labor process by increasing the rates. The employer's move produces a clash between work discipline and traditionalism, which Weber explains in the following terms:

> But a peculiar difficulty has been met with surprising frequency: raising the piece-rates has often had the result that not more but less has been accomplished in the same time, because the worker reacted to the increase not by increasing but by decreasing the amount of his work. A man, for instance, who at the rate of 1 mark per acre mowed 2½ acres per day and earned 2½ marks, when the rate was raised to 1.25 marks per acre mowed, not 3 acres, as he might easily have done, thus earning 3.75 marks, but only 2 acres, so that he could still earn the 2½ marks to which he was accustomed. The opportunity of earning more was less attractive than that of working less. He did not ask: how much can I earn in a day if I do as much work as possible? but: how much must I work in order to earn the wage, 2½ marks, which I earned before and which takes care of my traditional needs? This is an example of what is here meant by traditionalism. A man does not "by nature" wish to earn more and more money, but simply to live as he is accustomed to live

and to earn as much as is necessary for that purpose. [Weber 1958: 59–60]

Weber argues that, although "we" assume that people will earn as much as possible in a day, in fact, such behavior is historically and culturally peculiar, and requires further investigation. In making capitalism appear strange, and hence demand explanation, he follows the technique of negative characterization, and makes traditionalism a residual category, more a matter of human nature than an appropriate subject for social analysis. In analytical terms, traditionalism occupies an empty space.

Although ethnographers have made their project the comprehension of traditionalisms, they have not escaped the problem of characterizing the tempo of social life in "traditional" societies more through absences than in positive terms. The anthropological linguist Susan Philips, for example, has called attention to the quality of time I should like to explore. In a fine paper called "Warm Springs 'Indian Time,' " Philips correctly criticizes ethnographic writings for reducing time to segmentation and sequencing. Her analytical goal is to broaden the range of temporal phenomena under study. Her point of departure is that Indian Time appears primarily when non-Indians attend or participate in Indian events: "They [non-Indians] try to learn from Indians at what time the event will begin. Often the person questioned will say he doesn't know, but if pressed, he may give a specific time—e.g., 8 P.M. or 'some time after 9.' The non-Indians will arrive at that time, only to find that 'nothing is happening' yet, and no one seems to know when something will happen. They may wait anywhere from twenty minutes to several hours before the event 'begins' " (Philips 1974: 94). Philips's analysis of Indian Time concentrates on a series of social factors that produce variability and indeterminacy in the timing of ceremonial events. Her factors include: whether individuals commit themselves to participate, the degree of interdependence among actors, the number of participants needed for an event to take place, and whether the number of repetitions of particular actions is preset or open-ended. Indian Time thus reaches its maximum with: absence of commitment to participate, high interdependence among actors, an indeterminate number of actors needed, and open-ended repetitions of particular actions.

By identifying the sources of indeterminacy Philips has gone partway along the path I wish to follow. My analysis begins where hers leaves

Renato Rosaldo

off. Instead of concluding with the identification of sources of indeterminacy, I shall start by suggesting that they constitute a social space
within which creativity can flourish. In my view optionality, variability,
and unpredictability produce positive qualities of social being rather
than negative zones of analytically empty randomness. Far from being
devoid of positive content (presumably because of not being rule-
governed), indeterminacy enables a culturally valued quality of human
relations where one can follow impulses, change directions, and co-
ordinate with other people. In other words, social unpredictability has
its distinctive tempo, and it permits people to develop timing, coordination, and a knack for responding to contingencies. These qualities constitute social grace, which in turn enables an attentive and
gifted person to enjoy and be effective in the interpersonal politics of
everyday life.

I shall argue that, among the Ilongots of northern Luzon, Philippines, zones of indeterminacy, particularly in social visits, promote a
human capacity for improvisation in response to the unexpected, and
this very capacity can be celebrated as a cultural value. For the moment, however, let me follow Ilongot decorum, as this essay in its
presentation imitates its subject matter, by approaching the topic of
visiting gradually. As a first step, the Ilongots and their notion of
visiting require more extended introduction.

The Ilongots are a group of some 3,500 hunter-horticulturalists who
reside in an upland region some ninety miles north of Manila in Luzon,
Philippines. They cultivate rice, root crops, and vegetables in rain-
fed gardens, and they fish and hunt wild pigs and deer. Local groups
comprise roughly forty to sixty persons who reside in four to eight
dispersed households. Postmarital residence is uxorilocal, kinship is
cognatic, and putative descent defines predominantly territorial ag-
gregates called *bertan*. Head-hunting has long been central in defining
the group's cultural identity.

Ilongot Visiting

Visiting defines and displays the qualities of Ilongot social relations
even more centrally than the kinship system. My field journal is simply
laced with the arrivals and departures that make up the fabric of
everyday life. During some six months of 1969, for example, I recorded

[256]

the number of people who slept overnight in the home where Michelle Rosaldo and I resided. In that period our household of fourteen permanent members had a low of six and a high of thirty-six people sleeping overnight. The totals for a representative sequence of days ran as follows: 14, 17, 8, 25, 16. In addition to their brute frequency, visits are a staple of ordinary conversation. They are frequently talked about, both as noteworthy events in themselves and because they bring guests who provide news about other people and places. Here the key term is *beita*, referring at once to a kind of speech, small talk (as opposed, for example, to oratory or storytelling), and to its content: a noteworthy item or news.

Visits, or at any rate the practices Ilongots call *ba-at*, occur between households of different local groups, rather than within a single local group. People, of course, do drop by to chat or borrow things from other homes within their own local group, but that is not called *ba-at*. People can visit simply to visit, or to trade, or to borrow, or to court, or to plan a raid; they can be invited to lend their labor for housebuilding, pollarding, planting, or harvesting; they can come to support family members afflicted by serious illness; they can arrive to participate in meetings about bridewealth or local conflicts. Visits can, of course, have multiple purposes, carried out simultaneously, in sequence, or both. A visit can also begin as one thing and turn into something quite different. The casual visitor, for example, can be enlisted to hunt, or the young man who came to help pollard can initiate a courtship, or be obliged to stay on during an uncle's illness.

Marked by open-endedness, visiting often serves as a metonym for social life. In describing their past lives, for example, Ilongots speak of walking on paths that meander, like the courses of streams they follow, in ways that cannot be foreseen. In depicting residential moves, they talk about a coordinated unfolding among agents at once autonomous and accountable to one another. Ilongot visiting, in such contexts, comprises a concrete exemplar of forms of social life marked by mutually adjusted action and an openness to uncertain futures. Visits are improvised, made up as people go along; and social grace, a culturally valued quality of human intelligence, consists of one's responsiveness to whims, desires, and contingencies, whether these emanate from one's own heart or from those of one's partners in action.

[257]

Typifications of Arrival Scenes

When asked to describe a visit from beginning to end, Ilongots started with the host's account of the guest's arrival, rather than with the latter's departure from home. Ilongots say that when a visitor approaches the house hosts and guests alike neither speak nor make any other noise. Silence is the only form of greeting.

Tukbaw said, "If you talk, the others will think you're talking about them. The host [pan-abung, house owner] should speak first. That person can say a number of things, like, 'Are you people from there well?' If we just talk abruptly, people take it badly."

Tukbaw's sister-in-law Sawad said that visitors do not speak first because they wait "for their sweat to sink in, for their heart [rinawa] to stretch in happiness [ruyuk]. The host then asks, 'Are you people from there well?' " Visitors speak first only if there is urgent news, like the incipient arrival of soldiers or enemy Ilongot raiders. Otherwise, Sawad elaborated, the visitor "simply waits to be fed."

Talikaw said, "We hush up the kids because they are too noisy for our visitors." When visitors arrive, he said, "We give them betel quids. We go to pound rice because they are hungry. When they finish eating we ask for their news [beita]. We ask, 'Are you people from there well?' "

A cognitive anthropologist could readily rewrite Ilongot typifications of arrival scenes in the form of culturally appropriate expectations. These expectations have comprised the evidentiary basis of cultural description for ethnoscientists, such as Charles Frake (author of the pertinent classic essays "How to Ask for a Drink in Subanun" and "How to Enter a Yakan House") who has depicted his project as follows:

> This conception of a cultural description implies that an ethnography should be a theory of cultural behavior in a particular society, the adequacy of which is to be evaluated by the ability of a stranger to the culture (who may be the ethnographer) to use the ethnography's statements as instructions for appropriately anticipating the scenes of the society. I say "appropriately anticipate" rather than "predict" because a failure of an ethnographic statement to predict correctly does not necessarily imply descriptive inadequacy as long as the members of the described society are as surprised by the failure as is the ethnographer. The test of descriptive adequacy must always refer to informants' interpretations of events, not simply to the occurrence of events. [1980a: 145]

[258]

Cultural typifications thus are understood as distillations of past experience that allow natives and ethnographers to anticipate (but not predict) what will happen during future arrival scenes. Viewed in this manner, Ilongot arrival scenes could be segmented into the following phases: (1) the proper greeting of silence; (2) the hosts give their guests betel quids and food; and (3) the hosts ask the guests for their news, saying, "Are you people from there well?" Such typifications better enable ethnographers and natives alike to understand how variations in the actual enactment of these scenes can be interpreted (in relation to a standard code) as perfunctory, clumsy, angry, formal, proper, or graceful (Frake 1980b: 214). Yet the inclination of cognitive anthropology has been to delineate the code and ignore the actual performances, whether perfunctory or graceful.

I shall return to these arrival scenes with a view to exploring the insight yielded by moving from the code of cultural expectations to the social qualities at play in actual practices. The analysis of typifications, I shall argue, is but a point of departure, and by itself says little about the qualities of social relations displayed and created in the context of arrivals. For the time being, however, let us move one step at a time and continue to mimic the meandering path of visitors.

How I Registered Arrivals

My field journals are filled with reports on (and accounts of discussions about) the comings and goings of visitors and the news brought by them. Visits were intricately woven into the fabric of daily life. Indeed *ba-at* soon became a distinct ethnographic category entered on four-by-six cards. A typical early entry runs as follows: "Lapur stayed with his brother-in-law. He spent three nights."

When I wrote my entries on visits it did not occur to me that I was following a conventional form often found in smalltown newspapers. *The Listowel Banner* from western Ontario, Canada, for example, carries a regular Personals section with about thirty weekly entries on such transitions as deaths, births, weddings, illnesses, and visits. The vast majority of these entries, however, concern visits. The following are representative examples of such entries (all from the September 26, 1984, issue, p. 16):

—Mrs. Goldie Thompson and Mrs. Cathy Cahill of Toronto spent a few days with Mr. and Mrs. George Greer of Holland Centre.

[259]

—Mr. and Mrs. Lang Vogan, RR 2, Wroxeter, have returned home following a nine-day holiday trip to Cape Cod. The local couple travelled by bus, crossing into the United States at Niagara Falls. Mr. Vogan notes that it was raining as they left Listowel and raining as they returned, but the sun shone every day while they were away on their trip. They also found the leaves were in vivid colors as they made the return journey.

—Recent visitors with Mrs. Margaret Hawksbee included Mr. and Mrs. Adam Hackett of Vancouver, B.C., Miss Lillian Hackett of Mitchell, Canon and Mrs. C. F. Heathcote of Burlington, and Mr. and Mrs. Harvey Bride of Don Mills.

My entries and *The Listowel Banner*'s resemble one another in being cultural forms that register visits as bits of news. Not unlike Ilongot typifications, these news items are more often marked by arrivals than departures. Mr. and Mrs. Lane Vogan, for example, become newsworthy, not as they depart, but after they return from their sunny vacation in Cape Cod.

The Web of Visits

When entries on "visits" were juxtaposed in a string, however, they began to tell a different story. Compiled over a period of days, visits (both actual arrivals and news brought from elsewhere) revealed the fluid intricacies of changing plans. Such shifts of trajectory involved complex judgements about myriad contingencies and unfolding patterns of coordination among individuals.

Coordination among autonomous individuals requires a particularly high degree of flexibility and responsiveness because of cultural notions that make it difficult to predict another's conduct. Ilongots can try to persuade their fellow humans to do as they wish, but they cannot simply tell them what to do. Culturally speaking, they simply do not know what is inside another's heart (*rinawa*) unless that person speaks and reveals it. Michelle Rosaldo paraphrased Ilongot talk on the matter as follows: "We cannot see the hearts of others; we hear words spoken by strangers but fear that these come only from the surface, not from the inner motions of their hearts" (1980: 43). She elaborates in this manner: "Ilongots speak of 'hearts,' then, not to explain behavior by reference to character, motives, or a well-imaged personality, but to indicate those aspects of the self that can be alienated—or engaged—

in social interaction. Through talk of hearts, Ilongots characterize the relation between the self and its situation, in terms of whether hearts are closed or open, light or heavy, itching or at ease. What matters in such talk is not 'psychology' as we understand it, but the 'passions' generated in a self that can always be in conflict with its environment" (1980: 43). Individual actions, rather than forming larger patterns that reveal or emanate from more global entities resembling our notion of character, are shaped by the play of relatively discrete passions.

Once, for example, Insan visited another group to swear a peace-keeping oath by salt (sanctioned by the notion that, like salt in water, violators will dissolve in death); a young man in their party deliberately did not hold the salt because he had treachery in his heart. Years later Insan told me that he had had no inkling of the young man's designs because "when we left that time, he [the young man] did not tell us what was in his heart." Insan surmised that the young man's heart must have said (to himself): "I'm surveying the way I'm going to walk when I go on a head-hunting raid against these Butag people." Insan did not learn what was in his companion's heart until it was too late. When Insan's paternal grandfather later died of a gunshot wound, the seeming accident was attributed to the violated oath (R. Rosaldo 1980: 66–79).

In order to illustrate the meandering pattern of coordination in Ilongot visiting I have summarized and pieced together the following relevant entries from my four-by-six cards of 1974:

—Nov. 3: Two young boys arrived at night from Pengegyaben. Their host Tepeg immediately (without a period of silence) asked, "Is something wrong? Is somebody sick?" Tepeg explained that he blurted his questions because the young boys' nocturnal arrival appeared to mean that something was wrong. His eldest son, Keran, was in Pengegyaben at the time.

—Nov. 4: A visitor arrived and told his first cousin Dilap that his wife's return from Keradengan would be delayed because their children were ill. The two cousins said they would hunt together, and then go on to meet the wife and ailing children.

—Nov. 4: Kangat sneezed (a bad omen) as he was about to go and carry home his brother-in-law (who was incapacitated from snakebite). He did not go that day.

—Nov. 5: News arrived that a green viper bit Tepeg's son, Keran, as he started on the trail home.

—Nov. 9: The two cousins set off to hunt, but Dilap returned without

Renato Rosaldo

seeing his wife and ailing children because his house-mates and neighbors had gone to distant evangelical services, leaving nobody else home to feed the pigs.

—Nov. 12: Dilap's wife and children arrived, along with others, including Keran. The boy's mother had worried because news had come that her son was going to arrive two days sooner than he did.

My field journal conveys the mood surrounding the group's arrival: "Then, close to dusk, people got all excited; the people from Pengegyaben are here; they saw them walking by Asibenglan—we've been eager for their arrival. They came across the river looking all dressed up and pretty, Ilongot fashion. Keran was walking with a cane [because of his snakebite]; his uncle was across the river, drinking, and would come; his cousin wasn't clear on when we were going to Pengegyaben." A young woman who arrived with the group said she would stay one day and then guide me and Shelly to Pengegyaben, near her place. People in our household asked the young woman to stay overnight and help in the garden.

—Nov. 14: The young woman spent the night at a house downstream, but she still did not return home because it was raining too hard today.
—Nov. 15: We walked to Pengegyaben with the young woman.

Strung together, the entries tell about how plans changed in coordination with other people. Ever flexible and shifting, the visitors have developed a fluid responsiveness to the contingencies of everyday life. By their very nature, of course, contingencies cannot be listed as a finite complete set because as yet unlisted items will always come up as life goes on. In the two-week period reviewed above the contingencies included: sickness, snakebite, rain, gardening, hunting, evangelical services, pig-feeding, and sneezing.

Comparable forms of responsiveness have been vividly depicted for Athabascan hunters. Hugh Brody has described how their decision making takes account of multiple factors in this manner:

To make a good, wise, sensible hunting choice is to accept the interconnection of all possible factors, and avoids the mistake of seeking rationally to focus on any one consideration that is held as primary. What is more, the decision is taken in the doing; there is no step or pause between theory and practice. As a consequence, the decision—like the action from which it is inseparable—is always alterable (and

[262]

therefore may not properly even be termed a decision). The hunter moves in a chosen direction; but, highly sensitive to so many shifting considerations, he is always ready to change his direction. [1982: 37]

Not unlike Ilongots, these hunters make synoptic judgments informed by sensitivity, responsiveness, and flexibility. Planning, schedules, and time-discipline indeed are at odds with such an open-ended quality of action.

Ilongot visiting shares this quality of open-endedness. Open-endedness has positive content in that it enables a social capacity to improvise and respond creatively to life's contingencies. It is precisely this capacity, social grace and a sense of timing, that Ilongots so esteem as a cultural value (R. Rosaldo 1986).

A Man Who Could Not Sleep

Lest it appear that social grace never fails Ilongots, the case of Kama from Butag is especially pertinent. Kama was from a distant group that had just celebrated an initial covenant, to make amends for past beheadings, with the Kakidugen people. Much to everybody's surprise, Kama appeared as a visitor in our house very shortly after the preliminary settlement.

He arrived, looking fresh, bold in his carriage, and dressed in his finest garb. As Ilongots usually do on formal visits, he had stopped near the house at a stream, where he rested, washed, groomed, and put on his body adornment. My companions admired both his elegant dress and his remarkable courage. His arrival proceeded thus: "In the early afternoon of February 17, Kama and his companion entered the house in silence and sat down. Without a word Tukbaw prepared a betel quid and, as he placed it in my hand, whispered that I should enhance the formality of the occasion. Following my 'brother's' wishes, I walked in measured steps across the room and, with my left arm bent horizontally before me, I squatted and, moving in slow motion, handed Kama the quid with my right hand" (R. Rosaldo 1980: 103–4). The silence and slow decorum marked an occasion of high formality. The hosts and guests told stories of settlers and began to discuss the return covenant through the afternoon and on into the evening.

After Kama left the next morning, his hosts began to talk in awed tones about their visitor. They spoke of his bodily elegance, how he

[263]

carried himself and his fine adornment. His decorations had cowrie shells, thin brass wire, white horsehair, boars' fangs, and a tall black feather; they adorned his waist, calves, upper arm, and head. He stood erect and moved in a deliberate manner.

Kama's visit had surprised Tukbaw, who admired the man's boldness. Tubkaw said he would never dare visit after celebrating only the initial and not yet the return covenant. Disa, an older woman in the household, chuckled because she had slept near Kama. He was not, she said, as fearless as he appeared. He had not slept during the night because he feared that his hosts would kill and behead him if he did so.

It would never do to leave the impression that Ilongots, by their own standards, never stumble as they manage their social relations. Even Kama, one of the more graceful among them, made Disa and her companions chuckle. At the same time, Kama's vigilance was a condition of his exceptional performance. Had he not been watchful (*taikut*), he would not have dared do as he did. Valued and cultivated qualities still are, at times, ambiguously realized in everyday life.

An Afflicted Man

Let me return for a moment to Brody's analysis of the Athabascan hunters. He characterizes the ways that hunting decisions (probably not the right word for such an ever-changing fluid process) unfold in this manner:

> Although the mode is still one of wait and see, at the end of the day, at the close of much slow and gentle talk about this and that, a strong feeling has arisen about the morning: we shall go to Bluestone, maybe as far as the cross. We shall look for trout as well as moose. A number of individuals agree that they will go. But come morning, nothing is ready. No one has made any practical, formal plans. As often as not— indeed, more often than not—something quite new has drifted into conversations, other predictions have been tentatively reached, a new consensus appears to be forming. As it often seems, everyone has changed his mind. [1982: 36]

Perhaps a meander best describes the trajectory of such action. If the meander describes a pattern, it fails to characterize how human actors are purposive and take account of multiple human and natural factors.

[264]

The ways people chart their courses involve complex judgments and intricate forms of human responsiveness and cooperation.

In a case in point, Tagu, a man long afflicted with tuberculosis, became acutely ill. A group of Ilongots and I hastened to see him, as I noted in my field journal:

> About 10:00 A.M. I went with Bayaw and Lakay to see Tagu. While I was there he got really, really sick: he was talking about whom he would give his things to; he said he was dying; he said he had no bad feelings about anybody there [in other words, after death his spirit would not return to afflict the living]. Lots and lots of people came. His brothers were in tears. They sent for another brother and sister because they were afraid he would die. Shelly came by and gave him a shot with shaking, trembling hands. It seemed to make him a little better. I was moved by the concern, the way they cared for him.

People told me that an Ifugao shaman who resided nearby was coming to perform a curing ritual. They spoke, at least to my ears, as if the ritual were going to start that day or the next.

It was not, however, until eleven days later that a young man came to tell me that the Ifugao shaman, in response to our request, had said that we could take notes but no pictures. Three days later, a full two weeks after I thought the shaman was on his way, the ceremony seemed close to beginning; I wrote the following in my field journal:

> About 5:15 P.M. people began to arrive for the ceremony. . . . The expectation was that the ceremony would take place here, but then it turned out otherwise. . . . Shortly after we ate, Ingal arrived and said the shaman was doing a ceremony downstream, so we had best go to sleep because he wouldn't be here until late. . . . We chatted a while and, very uncomfortable with the early hour, we went to bed about 7:30 P.M.—as we were going to sleep the house was a virtual hospital, with a skeletal Tagu, his brother with rheumatism, lots of people with colds. As we went to sleep, then, we felt pretty depressed: low, itchy, uncomfortable with the early hour, sad at the pervasive sense of illness. At 1:00 A.M. we were awakened. People arrived from downstream. The shaman had awakened them as he passed by; Tagu's brother had come by here to say that the shaman just passed by one house and went to another across the stream [where he would hold the ceremony]—the idea is that you treat a person at the place where he got sick.

My clock-bound frustration simply permeates the journal entry. Besides noting the time repeatedly, I feel discomfort with going to bed

[265]

earlier than usual and depression brought on by the creeping, to me befuddling, pace of things.

The Ilongots themselves, of course, were mildly puzzled because the Ifugao practices were not fully known and because a shaman's performance, as part of its charisma, cultivates uncertainty and ambiguity. But the sense of frustration was much more mine than theirs.

The gradual unfolding, the multiple messages, the piece by piece revelation of when and where the ceremony would happen, gave the key participants an opportunity to prepare themselves for the shaman's intervention in a life-threatening crisis. Tagu did appear close to death. The shaman was expensive. The social support mobilized was extensive. The dangerous, afflicting spirit of Tagu's dead brother was invoked and felt to be present during the ceremony. In retrospect, it is little wonder that the event gathered itself together in bits and pieces, moving now forward, now backward. People needed time to collect themselves, both literally in one house, and by becoming oriented to a critical event where the stakes were high and the prognosis was uncertain.

A Brother-in-Law's Arrival

The anthropological literature could lead one to infer that the distinctive tempo of Ilongot visiting ends when the formal ritual begins. From this perspective it would seem that local versions of Indian Time fall by the wayside as formal procedures regulate the tempo of programmed ritual time (cf. R. Rosaldo 1985). In order to contest this widespread anthropological view, it is worth returning to an actual arrival scene marking the formal opening of a visit.

Recall that indigenous typifications made such arrivals appear formal, with a normal sequence of (1) silence, (2) betel quids and food, and (3) a request for news ("Are you people from there well?"). Contrast the typifications with the following actual arrival scene (recorded by Michelle Rosaldo) that took place when a group of visitors reached our household at about 4:30 P.M.

After about five minutes of relative silence, Bayaw, the male host, who was still lying down, said, "Give them a betel quid. I have no piper leaf." (Such commands, both here and in what follows, are called *tuydek*. They have been extensively studied in M. Rosaldo 1982.)

[266]

The host's nephew began to prepare a quid, and then told a young male visitor, "Your areca nut now."

Tepeg, another male visitor, told Sawad, his sister and the female hostess, "Give me my pouch; give me the stuff for making a betel quid."

Sawad, in turn, told a child, "Give it to him, Lemmik."

A young male visitor told the host's nephew, "That tobacco of yours now."

The host's nephew told his aunt Sawad, "Give me your tobacco, aunt."

Two more minutes went by and Sawad told a young girl, "Ulling, go and fetch some water."

Then two people begin to talk.

The visitor Tepeg cursed in the general direction of his sister Sawad, the hostess.

As soon as Tepeg cursed, about ten minutes after the visitors' arrival, Sawad began to prepare a meal.

Although cultural typifications can make such arrivals appear routinized, they emerge in practice as a flow of tugs and pulls, requests and counter-requests, where tempo and grace are of the essence. Among other things, the casually reclining host was telling his brother-in-law not to stand on formality, indicating closeness verging on disrespect. The brother-in-law was making claims on his sister the hostess by being blunt and eventually cursing because he'd not been given a visitor's due: a betel quid and a meal.

This arrival scene's interpersonal content was manifest in such matters as timing and the directness or obliqueness of requests. Rather than being an end point for analysis, the formal sequence—silence, betel quid and meal, and request for news—served more as a background for understanding actual practices. The precise tempo and mode of unfolding reveal, both as reflection and ongoing negotiation, the quality of social relations among participants.

Conclusion

Writing about Algerian peasants, French sociologist Pierre Bourdieu has described the tempo and the politics of so-called reciprocity in terms so apt as to serve as a conclusion to this paper:

[267]

When the unfolding of the action is heavily ritualized, as in the dialectic of offence and vengeance, there is still room for strategies which consist of playing on the time, or rather the *tempo*, of the action, by delaying revenge so as to prolong the threat of revenge. And this is true, *a fortiori*, of all the less strictly regulated occasions which offer unlimited scope for strategies exploiting the possibilities offered by manipulation of the tempo of the action—holding back or putting off, maintaining suspense or expectation, or on the other hand, hurrying, hustling, surprising, and stealing a march, not to mention the art of ostentatiously giving time ("devoting one's time to someone") or withholding it ("no time to spare"). [Bourdieu 1977: 7]

Where Bourdieu and I, or most probably Algerian peasants and Philippine hunter-horticulturalists, diverge is in our descriptive aesthetics. His paradigm of challenge and response suggests the aesthetic of the marital arts. The Ilongots and I in following them would choose instead to emphasize social grace, the tempo and rhythms that shape the dance of life. My project has been to open the question of the differing aesthetics that shape the tempo of everyday life where clock-time is not the paramount reality.

REFERENCES

Bourdieu, Pierre. 1977. *Outline of a Theory of Practice*. Cambridge: Cambridge University Press.
Brody, Hugh. 1982. *Maps and Dreams*. New York: Pantheon.
Frake, Charles O. 1980a. "A Structural Description of Subanun 'Religious Behavior.'" In Frake, *Language and Cultural Description*. Stanford: Stanford University Press. Pp. 144–65.
———. 1980b. "How to Enter a Yakan House." In Frake, *Language and Cultural Description*. Stanford: Stanford University Press. Pp. 214–32.
———. 1980c. "How to Ask for a Drink in Subanun." In Frake, *Language and Cultural Description*. Stanford: Stanford University Press. Pp. 166-73.
Philips, Susan. 1974. "Warm Springs 'Indian Time': How the Regulation of Participation Affects the Progression of Events." In Richard Bauman and Joel Sherzer, eds., *Explorations in the Ethnography of Speaking*. Cambridge: Cambridge University Press. Pp. 92–109.
Rosaldo, Michelle. 1980. *Knowledge and Passion: Ilongot Notions of Self and Social Life*. Cambridge: Cambridge University Press.
———. 1982. "The Things We Do with Words: Ilongot Speech Acts and Speech Act Theory in Philosophy." *Language and Society* 2: 203–7.

Rosaldo, Renato. 1980. *Ilongot Headhunting, 1883–1974: A Study in Society and History*. Stanford: Stanford University Press.

———. 1985. "While Making Other Plans." *Southern California Law Review* 58, 1: 19–28.

———. 1986. "Ilongot Hunting as Story and Experience." In Victor Turner and Edward Bruner, eds., *The Anthropology of Experience*. Urbana: University of Illinois Press. Pp. 97–138.

Thompson, E. P. 1967. "Time, Work-Discipline, and Industrial Capitalism." *Past and Present* 38: 56–97.

Weber, Max. 1958 [1904–5]. *The Protestant Ethic and the Spirit of Capitalism*. New York: Charles Scribner's Sons.

[12]

Performance and the Cultural Construction of Reality: A New Guinea Example

Edward L. Schieffelin

It is not an uncommon experience for an ethnographer toward the end of the second year of fieldwork to realize suddenly that some issue or activity, long since thought to be thoroughly understood and laid to rest in his or her fieldnotes, had an unsuspected dimension that required its significance to be entirely reexamined. For me, the realization arrived while I was writing my fieldnotes the morning after attending a late-night spirit séance in a Kaluli longhouse. I had attended many of these performances before. The moment in question was not an unusual one for this kind of thing: the medium—or rather the voice of the spirit—had come up without identifying itself and simply begun to sing. Singing at first alone, the tiny voice was eventually answered by a chorus of the men gathered around, filling the

This chapter first appeared in *American Ethnologist* 12:4, November 1985, and is reprinted by permission of the American Anthropological Association. Many people have contributed to the richness of this paper. I would like especially to thank Steven Feld, Sherry Ortner, Martha MacIntyre, Debra Battaglia, Bruce Knauft, Roy Wagner, Lee Schlesinger, Bill Murphy, and DeVerne Smith for many useful comments and criticisms. My research was undertaken in Papua New Guinea in 1966–68 and 1975–77 with grants from the National Institutes of Mental Health and the National Science Foundation. Assistance in administering these grants was provided by the Institute for the Study of Human Issues, and the Research Institute for the Study of Man. Their help is gratefully acknowledged here.

darkness around the medium with resonance and human presence. The song was a Gisaro song (Schieffelin 1976; Feld 1982) and, as is usual for this genre, concerned brooks and gardens, house sites and sago places in the nearby tropical forest. The places named began to trace out a route or track (*tok*) from the distant longhouse of Kokonesi to the community of Nagibeden where the séance was being held. As the places named seemed to move closer and closer, describing fishing sites and stands of arrow-making cane, cries of "alas!" and whistles of sympathy and dismay escaped from listeners in the darkness; suddenly, with loud wails of grief, a man beside me began to weep. The significance of the song and the people's reactions to it were all familiar to me. The spirit was that of a small boy of the Nagibeden community who had died while visiting Kokonesi longhouse the year before. The path traced out by the song was the track followed by his relatives as they brought his body back to Nagibeden for the funeral. The man weeping in anguish beside me was the boy's own father.

As I was writing about this in my fieldnotes, I was aware that my explanation of what was happening was correct as far as it went, but I realized that this was no professionally detached description that I was writing down: in order to convey and account for the deeply moving and compelling quality of the performance, the rapt engagement of the audience, and my own enthrallment with what was happening, what I was writing was not so much a description of the events as an attempt to evoke the experience.

It was not just that the places named in the song outlined a path that recalled a tragic event still very painful to those who were involved—it was also the way the names engendered suspense as the path, at first unknown, gradually began to become clear; it was the pain engendered as the places named and hence, in imagination, the body of the child, drew nearer and nearer. It was not what the spirit said that distressed the father so much as the presence of his voice in the darkness. These things could not be conveyed simply by recounting them in a straightforward descriptive manner; the events had to be interpreted by understanding how they evoked the audience's feelings (and my own), if they were to make adequate sense at all. The issue here is a larger one than simply providing an accurate ethnographic account of the significance of a dramatic cultural performance. It involves the more intriguing question of the relation between the nondiscursive (dramaturgical and rhetorical) levels of ritual performances and their meaning.

[271]

Most anthropological studies of ritual in recent years have addressed the problem of what rituals mean and how they work by focusing on the symbolic meanings embodied in the structure and content of ritual symbols themselves, viewing ritual acts and statements as a kind of coded communication, a cultural text. The analysis of the ritual then tends to take the form of a textual analysis, and the main weight of the analysis rests on the demonstration of the permutations and transformations in the symbolic materials themselves. Often it seems as if the participants are thought to undergo ritual transformations automatically upon being exposed to the symbolic meanings of the ritual as they unfold (cf. Kapferer 1979); thus, understanding how ritual symbols are effective is simply a matter of understanding the logic of thought that underlies them.

Many anthropologists have been aware of the limitations of this emphasis on the logico-meaningful, discursive aspects of ritual meaning. They have called attention to the nondiscursive aspects of ritual, emphasizing that rituals gain their effectiveness by being performed. It is through participation in ritual singing and dancing, or through viewing dramatic presentations of sacra, emblems and masks, or through being subjected to painful ordeals that participants come to see symbolic representations as having a force of their own. Vivid ethnographic accounts of exotic rituals make this intuitively apparent. However, the means by which the *performance* accomplishes this, beyond providing dramatic or emphatic presentation of ritual symbols and provoking strong emotional arousal, is rarely examined. The problem is not to recognize the importance of nondiscursive elements for the efficacy of ritual but to understand exactly how they work.

In this essay, I explore the problem and develop the idea that rituals and their symbols are effective less because they communicate meanings (though that is also important) than because in performances, meanings are reinnovated in social interaction. The participants are engaged with the symbols in the mutual creation of a performance reality, rather than informed by them as knowers. To examine this process we return to the Kaluli séance.

The Kaluli Setting

The Kaluli people live in about twenty longhouse communities scattered throughout the tropical forest on the Great Papuan Plateau just north of Mount Bosavi in the Southern Highlands Province of Papua New Guinea. Kaluli believe the world has a visible aspect, which is the context of everyday life, and an invisible side (largely coextensive with the everyday, but hidden from it), which is the abode of the spirits and the dead. The inhabitants of each side "show through" to some extent into the world of the other. Spirits appear to human beings as certain kinds of birds and animals (Schieffelin 1976; Feld 1982), and every human person has an invisible aspect that appears to the spirits as a wild pig or a cassowary.

Among the population of twelve hundred or so Kaluli people in the early 1970s, there were about fifteen spirit mediums. A medium is a man who has married a spirit woman in a dream or vision experience, often associated with a severe illness. Thereafter, he is capable of leaving his body in séance and traveling in the invisible spirit side of reality. At the same time, spirit people from the invisible may enter his body and converse with the audience gathered around.

Kaluli call séances for a variety of reasons including general entertainment, but, most commonly, they ask a medium to journey to the invisible in order to cure illness or to find lost pigs. One of the principal causes of illness from the Kaluli point of view is an invisible attack on the victim's body by a witch (*sei*). A sei is a living man or woman who has an evil aspect in the heart. This evil thing creeps out of the sei's body while he or she is asleep, and, assuming the form of its host in the invisible, attacks the invisible aspect of the victim's body, dismembering it and carrying off the pieces to hide for later consumption. The victim comes down with a severe illness whose symptoms correspond to the parts of his body which have been been (invisibly) injured. Thus, a person whose legs have been cut off cannot walk; a person whose head has been removed is delirious, a person whose heart has been cut out dies. It is the job of the medium and his spirit helpers to seek through the invisible and locate the patient's missing (invisible) body parts and stick them back on his or her body.

The Séance Performance

When someone becomes ill, his or her relatives will often seek out a medium (*a:s tih'nan kalu*, lit., goes down to the spirits man) and ask him to go into the invisible to see what is the matter. A séance always takes place at night and has a characteristic form. The

[273]

medium lies on his back on a sleeping platform in the men's section of the longhouse, and the men and youths of the community gather about him seated on the floor. These men are called the *kegel*, which has the meaning more of "chorus" than of "audience." They form the core of those who actively participate in responding to the performance. The women, mainly onlookers, lean over the nearby partitions of the women's section or sit on the floor at some distance behind the men.

When all is ready, the fires of the longhouse are banked to provide almost complete darkness. After a while, there is a long hissing breath from the medium indicating his soul is leaving his body. That is followed by gasping sounds and bird calls (Kaluli believe spirits take the forms of birds) as the first spirit comes up and softly begins to sing. The song, invariably about the hills and streams near where the spirit lives, is nostalgic and moving. The *kegel*, chorusing the spirit, are drawn into the same mood. When the song ends, the spirit identifies itself, and the people ask him to go and take a look at the sick person and see what is the matter. The spirit child then departs and searches the spirit realm to see if the patient's body from the invisible side has been injured (invisibly) by a sei. If it has, the spirit child must locate the dismembered portions of the body which the sei has hidden and stick them back on the body again. If he is successful in this, the patient will recover.

In the meantime, while the medium and his spirit child are off on their (invisible) errands of healing, other spirit people come up through the medium's body to sing and provide the people at the séance a chance to talk with their dead, or with other invisible personalities of the locality, and to enjoy themselves. Séances often become quite engrossing performances. The mood ranges from deeply affecting as people weep while talking with their dead, to fearsome and thrilling as fierce and belligerent spirits come up with growling voices, smacking lips and thumping and banging on the sleeping platform. Or the séance may be hilariously salacious as when an unmarried spirit woman and the young men of the longhouse lewdly tease and provoke each other. In this context spirit people of the locality become well-known and even beloved personalities, and Kaluli develop a closer general relationship between themselves and the invisible side of their world.

All during the performance the kegel sitting around the medium maintain an active participation by chorusing the singing, asking questions and engaging in conversation with the spirits—and in commenting and speculating among themselves about the meaning and quality of the performance itself. Often this discussion is led by one or two self-appointed shills who, while not in collusion with the medium, are familiar with his style and know how to anticipate what he is likely to do next. They often give a running commentary and interpretation of the performance as it goes along.

During the course of the night, the medium's spirit child continues his attempts to help the patient. I have examined this healing process in the séance through a meaning-centered analysis (Schieffelin 1976, 1977). I argued that, in everyday life, Kaluli tend to interpret and deal with many different kinds of situations as though they were situations of opposition or confrontation that could be solved by reciprocity. Illness is assimilated to this model. That is, illness is interpreted (in séance) in terms of the opposition between the patient and the sei who has stolen part of his body. The opposition is mediated and resolved in a reciprocity-like transaction performed by the medium's spirit child when he finds and returns the missing parts of the patient's body that have been dismembered by the sei. The basic thrust of the argument, following Lévi-Strauss (1967), was that by assimilating the patient's suffering to a metaphoric version of a widely significant cultural scenario of resolution, the séance provided a means to make sense of, and to order and resolve, his problematic bodily experience. Subsequent research in Bosavi has shown that this cannot be what happens, at least not in the way outlined by most meaning-centered arguments of this sort. I will return to this point later on. In any case, the séance usually continues well into the middle of the night until all of the various spirit tasks have been successfully (or unsuccessfully) accomplished. Then the medium returns to his body and sits up.

This brief overview outlines the basic events in a Kaluli curing séance. Understanding what is happening here, however, is more than a matter of showing that the séance provides a logically and symbolically plausible resolution for a problematic situation. It is also necessary to show why Kaluli people accept what they see in the séance as a convincing, even compelling, reality. This is not so much a question of what Kaluli believe is happening as it is of how what they believe is brought to life and galvanizes social reality.

Edward L. Schieffelin

Playing the Urgency of the Social Situation

The compelling quality of the séance begins long before the performance itself begins, in the depth of the social concern out of which
it arises. Although people sometimes request a séance just for the
amusement of talking to the spirits, they call most of them to deal
with some problematic circumstance. The people who gather about
the medium in the longhouse are not only excited about the prospect
of the performance; they are worried or angry and hope to obtain some
answers. This anxiety and expectancy charges the atmosphere with a
certain tension before the séance begins, and it is this tension that
the séance must pick up and deal with, develop or resolve if it is to
make a difference—and in the process become real. Some mediums
have a keen sense of this preliminary urgency and play on it to create
the proper opening mood. Walia of Anasi, one well-known medium,
was a master at building the tension of community worry and expectation to an agonizing pitch. When asked to go out to the spirits, he
would be diffident, complaining that he did not feel well, or that the
kids in the longhouse were too noisy and would disrupt the séance.
The people who wanted the séance would plead with him, offer him
food, promise to monitor the children, and clear off their sleeping
platforms for him to lie on. Walia would continue to grump reluctantly
and threaten to leave right up to the point where he lay down for the
séance, by which time audience tension was highly keyed and people
were anxious to begin the performance.

The Séance Setting

When the medium lies down on one of the sleeping platforms to
begin the séance, there is an atmosphere of hushed excitement. The
kegel and other onlookers settle themselves in the darkness to await
the arrival of the first spirit. Although this situation is reminiscent of
a Western theater audience quieting down before the curtain rises,
the resemblance is superficial. The cultural assumptions that shape
the internal structure of the performance space for the séance are very
different from those which inform a proscenium stage. As a result, the
implications for the relationships between the audience, actor, and
characters are also very different. The stage in a proscenium theater
defines a special space to house an imaginative reality, which excludes

[276]

the audience, but is kept in place by their suspension of disbelief: that is, the audience may accept for the performance that they are in the presence of the court of Richard II, but not that they are part of it. Indeed, they cannot be part of it for the performance to retain its integrity. A member of the audience who mounts the stage because he believes what he sees there is real finds himself among actors, not kings, disrupts the imaginative space, and spoils the show.

For the Kaluli séance, the situation is reversed. In the seance the imaginative space of the proscenium stage is exchanged for the liminal realm of the medium's trance; the actor (that is, the medium) is excluded from the performance (since his soul has left his body), and the characters (the spirits) then enter reality. This is accomplished by a double transfer across the line between the visible and invisible sides. The medium ascends to the invisible while the spirits descend to the human plane. Thus theater becomes reality: where spirits who are birds converse with men in human voices. It also means that the interactions with the characters (spirits) have real consequences. The thrill of fear at the appearance of a fierce and belligerent spirit is not vicarious. If the spirit becomes angry and causes the medium's body to thrash about on the sleeping platform, the audience may flee the longhouse.

As the séance commences, however, the performance space—where "the characters enter reality"—is not simply taken for granted. It must be continually re-created during the course of the performance. This means that the medium must commit the audience to the task of participating in its construction, and this is accomplished in large part through the spirit's songs.

The Spirit Songs

The spirits come up one by one, and each sings a song that is chorused by the audience. Each song may be followed immediately by another song, or by a period of conversation between the spirit and the audience.

Although mediums[1] do not speak about the artistic skills required to perform a good séance (indeed they would deny they were even present), it is evident to an observer that certain requirements have to be fulfilled if the structure of the séance is to be sustained and the performance made to work. One of the most important is to control

[277]

the focus of everyone's attention and to maintain the right unity of mood throughout the performance. The medium accomplishes this mainly through adept management of the songs. Most of the power and energy of the séance come not from conversations with the spirits but from the songs. It is through the people's participation in chorusing the songs that their divided attention is brought together and focused, and it is through the content of the songs that the mood of pathos and nostalgia appropriate to speaking with the spirits can be evoked and intensified. A successful trance medium has to have the ability to compose, during performance, in trance, as many as thirty new songs, each one with a different set of underlying implications. For our purposes, it will be enough to summarize one or two points to provide understanding of how they can be used as powerful rhetorical devices.

Superficially, the songs seem simple enough. They refer to various named places—hills, streams, garden spots, old longhouse sites, and the like in the local forest region. Often the places are named in such a way that they mark out a definite path (*tok*) through the local forest region, naming landmarks and singing the calls of birds as though one were passing through there. The localities named are familiar to many members of the audience and have a special poignancy for those who have spent parts of their lives there and for whom they represent the contexts of social relationships and events of times past, activities shared with beloved friends and others now dead or gone away. The poignancy is enhanced as the song frames its passage through the various localities in poetic images evoking nostalgia, longing and loneliness.

In the séance the spirit frequently sings about the places he has lived in that represent his relationship with people in the audience. A spirit of the dead may sing of the localities it shared with members of the community when alive, or, as in the case cited at the beginning of this essay, trace a path associated with the events of his or her death. Spirits of the locality (who have never been alive) may sing of the areas in which they live, or of places along the path they took coming to the séance. If the spirit was off on an errand of healing, it may sing of the places it has traveled in carrying it out.

Thus, the places sung by the spirits are loaded with implications and messages for the listeners. A given locality may mean different things to different individuals according to their experience and social relationships there—or they may imply several different things to the same person. The ambiguities of who (which spirit) is actually singing,

[278]

which locality or what events the song refers to are only slowly sorted out as the song proceeds, and the track it unravels becomes clear. The people present at the séance eagerly try to figure all this out as they participate in the chorus, or simply listen. As the song continues, one can hear exclamations of "There's Dogon hill! that must be my mother's brother, old so-and-so. He used to garden there." "No, no, he also sang the Galinti pool; it's somebody further downstream." Tension mounts while the people search their minds to figure out the riddle of the singer until the song ends and the spirit announces itself. If the song has built up the right mood, the spirit's living relatives break down at this point and weep. Alternatively, if the spirit that comes up is a local place spirit, not one of the dead, there will be exclamations of welcome. Often people do not know whether they will be weeping until the very last minute.

In a still deeper strategy of the same kind, the song may not contain any place names at all; it may simply mention trees and river pools and sago stands as though they were passed on a track without any indication of where they actually might be (Feld 1982: 152). Those present are led to search their memories for an area that would match, and the tension and speculation mount until the mention of one or two place names near the end of the songs suddenly precipitates recognition of the locality, and, at the same time usually, the identity of the spirit—followed perhaps by a flood of weeping. These mystifications and ambiguities within the song tantalize members of the audience and force them to turn reflectively inward by invoking the places that they know and love.

This focusing of attention in nostalgia and pathos is further intensified and given momentum by the strategies of performance by which the medium puts a series of songs across. To some degree these strategies seem to be a matter of personal style. Two contrasting examples will illustrate this point.

Aiba of Kokonesi was a socially dynamic man of considerable presence. Intense and somewhat intrusive, he had a disconcerting habit of suddenly being present when least expected.[2] He had an extraordinary knowledge of the forest geography over most of the Kaluli region; nearly every village knew him. In my experience he was an opportunistic, persistent, and manipulative individual in everyday life.

In séance, Aiba projected his spirit songs in a strongly focused and carefully constructed manner. His songs were less stylized and textually and musically more diverse than those of other mediums. He

[279]

seemed to create a personal rhythm aimed at centering the séance participants' attention on him and what he was doing, drawing them onto his ground of performance where he could control them and make them, in effect, dance to his tune. Once those at the séance were hooked, they were driven by his energy. His carefully pointed songs were frequently deeply affecting and often moved some people to tears. However, because the energy of his performance derived mainly from himself, there was a tendency for its intensity to collapse between songs unless the level of tension was sustained by someone weeping.

By contrast, another medium, Walia of Anasi, was a rather marginal character. Scruffy, wheedling, and unreliable, he was a responder to rather than an initiator of any significant social action. Yet he was an incredible trance performer. Walia, in séance, did not focus people's attention on himself; he seemed more oriented to orchestrating group synchrony. His songs, particularly at the beginning of a séance, tended to be highly stylized and predictable (Feld, personal communication), using the same or similar melodic patterns and similar poetic images and song forms over and over again. Walia was finely attuned to his audience's response and the predictable regularity of his songs seemed aimed at getting his chorus to sing together well, to synchronize themselves to the same rhythm. Once they were unified, he did not manipulate them; he acted more as an orchestrator and catalyst to group process. It usually took Walia a longer time than Aiba to build the right momentum, but once he did, it tended to sweep up the greater part of those present and carry them forward with an enormous force that maintained momentum through spirit conversations to the next song.

The songs, then, provide several dimensions to the performance. The singing of them, with the kegel chorusing the spirit, provides unity of purpose, concentration, and rhythm to those present at the séance, building a compelling musical momentum that supplies the sense of energy and forward motion to the performance. The singing of lands and waters presents the listeners with an intriguing but ambiguous message which they strive to interpret. Amid mounting suspense and expectancy, they try to figure out whom they are singing with. Finally, when the song is completed, they are so steeped in nostalgia for their lands and longing for their dead that they are in the right mood of emotional expectancy to converse with the spirits.

The Spirits

The spirits are the central characters in the séance and provide both its edifying and its entertaining aspects. As the audience engages in conversation with them, they become living personalities. At the same time, the work of the séance gets done. In the darkness, the presence of a spirit is marked by a change in the medium's voice quality. Generally speaking, spirit voices sound rather pinched and smaller than the medium's normal voice and speak in a somewhat higher register. Some mediums used the same spirit voice for most of the spirit manifestations, but the best, or at least the most dramatic performers had a different voice quality for every different spirit.

Experienced mediums could present a cast of twenty or more spirit characters, in addition to the spirits of the dead. Some of the spirits of a medium's locality had long-term traditional relationships with the local community, had appeared through a series of mediums over a period of years, and were well known or even beloved by those present in the audience. (I was able to trace the history of the relationship between one such spirit and a nearby community over eighty years, back to the turn of the last century (Schieffelin 1977)). Other spirits appeared only through a particular medium and might not make appearances through other mediums after his death. As with the dead, these place spirits were associated with particular localities, and séance fans could often guess by the songs which one was coming up. The Kaluli distinguish four types of spirit that can appear through a medium. Spirits of the dead generally precipitate a great deal of weeping if their relatives are present. Conversation with them generally concerns such things as where the spirit is now residing, and what has happened in the way of family news since his or her death. In former times there was frequently some discussion to determine the identity of the witch responsible for the death.

Most of the spirits who come up on a medium, however, are place spirits, spirits associated with a locality. These spirits often have distinctive personalities and reputations among séance-goers for their different indiosyncrasies and abilities. One of Walia's favorite spirit personalities (which he had inherited from his mother's brother, who was also a medium) was a spirit named Kidel, who lived at a place called Bolekini. Kidel had a deep, friendly voice and was known to be fond of tobacco. He would frequently ask someone to pass a smoking tube in his (the medium's) direction during the seance. When he came up upon Walia, he projected the character of a tough, far-traveled person, and was relied upon to predict when the government patrols would visit the area. An older spirit, he would sometimes talk about how his children were growing or comment on recent changes in the spirit world.

Another favorite, particularly with the bachelors, was a young unmarried woman named Daluami. She was rather forward and provocative and spoke with a coy, falsetto voice; her conversations with the young bachelors of the community quickly became lewd and ribald repartee, accompanied by howls of laughter throughout the longhouse.[3]

These spirits of the ground are usually the ones to perform the most dramatic séance tricks. For example, in one famous performance, a spirit invited the people attending to light the medium briefly so they could see him. When they did so, they saw a hornbill's beak (from the spirit's bird manifestation) sticking out of the medium's mouth. Another spirit asked to borrow a shell necklace in order to dance in a Gisaro ceremony in the spirit world. A necklace was placed on the medium's chest and disappeared. Sometime later, at another séance, the spirit returned the necklace stained with the fragrant vegetable resins used to annoint a ceremonial dancer.

A third type of spirit is called a Newelesu. Characterized as a weedy little man with an oversized head and an enormous penis, he lives in the top of small *wani* palms (a decidedly inferior dwelling compared to the gigantic buttressed trees normally inhabited by spirits). A Newelesu is a clownish, trickster-like figure, always horny and mischievous. He comes up on a medium with a squeaky voice and a shrill, high-pitched laugh and usually demands to be given a woman. Hilarious conversation follows. The Newelesu is known to be a witch on the spirit side, responsible for the demise of animals occasionally found dead and decaying in the forest. Men in the audience frequently ask him to "ripen" a wild pig or cassowary so that it will fall prey to their traps or hunting arrows. Newelesu has an angry streak in him and sometimes sends the medium back to his body, terminating the séance if he is teased by the people too much.

Finally, there are fierce spirits known as *kalu hungo:*, or "dangerous, forbidden men." These spirits are known to be rough and short-tempered. They usually appear in séance smacking their lips hungrily or uttering battle cries and speaking in deep spooky voices. Kalu hungo: are known to strike people down if they get angry, and it is they who tend to frighten the audience out of the longhouse. Conversations with kalu hungo: are generally excessively polite and conciliatory, and Kaluli appeared to enjoy the thrill of danger that these spirits provided.

In the course of a séance (and depending on the medium), a wide range of different spirit characters would come up. Some would only reveal their names before departing. Others would stay to converse, argue with or tease the people at the séance for a considerable time. It is the conversations with the spirits, especially given their lively variety that break the flow and accumulated intensity of the songs and give Kaluli séances their episodic character. From time to time during the night, the medium's spirit child returns to report on his progress on helping the patient on whose behalf the séance was called. But apart from this, there is usually little apparent continuity between one spirit conversation and another. Sometimes, however, a medium will link the succession of spirit conversations with an underlying dramaturgical strategy that sets up the audience and then pulls a switch on it, leaving everyone surprised and disconcerted. In one séance, for example, Daluame, the provocative, unmarried female spirit, came up and engaged the young men of the community in an extended racy repartee. There was much hilarity, and an atmosphere of randy excitement developed. After she departed, another female came up, but this one was of demure and timid character. The young men of the audience were still full of ribaldry from their conversation with Daluame and teased the second spirit mercilessly until she departed in flustered embarrassment. The performance then turned the tables on them: a cooing, high-pitched voice came up, heralding the appearance of a third woman. As the young men prepared to launch into further lascivious provocations, the spirit made several remarks so outrageously salacious that the bachelors, despite their raucous mood, were taken aback. In the bewildered silence that followed, a shrill gale of familiar silly giggles revealed that the spirit was not a woman but a Newelesu, trickster.

These conversations with the spirits in the darkness of the longhouse create a lively scene. The wails of grieving relatives, the matching of wits in outrageous repartee, the thrill of danger from fierce kalu hungo: are all deeply engrossing and enjoyable interactions quite apart from the particular purposes for which the séance was called. If at times these conversations strike an outsider as having the quality of play, it is not like the play of make-believe; it is like the play of joking relations, of playing with fire: playing in an arena of forces that can have dangerous consequences.

If people's attention begins to falter during the spirit conversations, new songs will reestablish the mood, rebuild momentum and intensity, and maintain continuity.

The "Audience"

The kegel gathered immediately around the medium forms the principal core of the séance participation. They do the chorusing of the spirit songs and generate most of the joking and banter. Other, usually older, men sit as spectators at the periphery of this group or in other parts of the men's section, talking among themselves, occasionally joining the singing, but always alert to what is going on. Women too mainly observe, but make their presence felt through comments and exclamations at the performance or occasionally prompting a question to the spirits.

It should be obvious by now that the people gathered to attend the séance are an integral part of the performance, and that the term "audience," with its implication of passive attention, is probably not the right word for this group. I have used it, sparingly, to refer to both active participants (kegel) and more passive onlookers. The reality of the spirit world as it is embodied in the séance is not the result of the performance of the medium alone; it is created in the *interaction* between the people present and the spirits. If the people are unresponsive, or unwilling to participate, the energy drains away, and the séance collapses and comes to an end.

While the medium depends on the people's response to keep the performance going, he is also subject to their judgment. Members of séance audiences are sophisticated. Séance performances form a genre, and most of those present have seen other séances before and know how to evaluate them. People not only sing along and converse with the spirits; they also make comments aloud among themselves about the spirits' character and style, comparing the way they seemed in other performances or how they appeared with another medium. Thus, information about performance adequacy and character roles is made available during the performance itself where it may be considered by others present or act as feedback to the medium, if he can hear them while in trance. During the performance people may make exclamations of praise or approval for a particularly well-done song or enjoyable conversation. They have also been known to denounce the séance or walk out on it in disgust if they believe that the spirits do not know what they are talking about or that they are being tricked. The audience thus becomes the arbiter of the authenticity of the spirit séance, and at least as much as the medium, the guardian of the rigor of its tradition.

The Ostensible Work of the Séance

Dialogic Modes of Constructing Reality

It is in the midst of deep audience engagement that the work of the séance gets done. The question is: what does it actually accomplish and how? From the Kaluli point of view the two most important tasks of séances are the curing of illness and the recovery of runaway pigs. Nevertheless, the actual proportion of séance performance time devoted to such matters varies a great deal, sometimes being a rather insignificant and perfunctory part of the performance, and sometimes being lengthy and dramatic. In regard to curing, I have already discussed the symbolic process in the séance curing scenario where the illness is construed as a loss (on the invisible plane) and is then resolved through a symbolic analogue of social reciprocity carried out invisibly by the medium and the spirits. (See also Schieffelin 1976: chap. 5.) It seems reasonable to argue, following the outlines of Lévi-Strauss (1967), that the powerful symbolic process embodied in the curing scenario, delivered to a deeply engaged audience, might actually have the effect of transforming the experience of the patient. However, unless we postulate the operation of paranormal effects, this cannot be the case because usually the patient is not present at the séance. In addition, Kaluli believe that patients must be asleep for the medium to have proper access to them from the invisible side. This means that despite the powerful symbolic scenario embodied in the curing process, it cannot affect the patient in any normally understood way. Nevertheless, Kaluli laymen and mediums alike insist that the reputation of a medium rests on the success of his cures.

In the séance context, if the power of the curing sequence cannot affect the illness process of the patient, it can perhaps shape the expectations of the patient's community about the outcome. That is, during the performance, the medium may form an assessment (even just a guess) about the patient's condition and gear the level of success of his invisible curing efforts to correspond with his notion of the most probable outcome; if he does not think the patient will recover, he will have difficulty in locating the dismembered legs taken by the sei or performing other acts of curing. In this way he will be preparing the people of the community for what to expect—making a prediction in the guise of an attempt to cure. Be this as it may—and the evidence is not very clear on the matter—the curing scenario can be seen as a very important part of another aspect of the séance, namely, that aspect dealing with witchcraft (to which we shall return). Some of what the medium is doing in the cure will be clarified by turning to a more minor matter: the finding of runaway pigs.

In listening to mediums (or rather, spirits) discuss lost pigs with the audience, an observer notices that they show great subtlety in negotiating information to construct an appropriate response. During one séance I observed, the medium's spirit child was sent to locate a missing pig described as a female with cropped ears and a white patch on the chest. Later returning to the séance, the spirit declared: "I saw the pig but I do not know the name of the ground." He went on to describe a place where a small brook ran into a larger creek with a particular kind of sago palm nearby. I recorded the discussion in my fieldnotes:

"There is also a *Wolu* (river) banana garden nearby," he said. The (audience) said: "No, it is the Gulu (river) you are talking about" (The particular type of sago at the confluence of two waters was the clincher here for recognizing the area since there was a stand of that kind of sago at the confluence of the Gulu and Gudep streams.) The audience then figured out among themselves that the banana garden referred to was probably the one at Mosogosaso. The spirit then described a old fish-dam diversion ditch and an abandoned garden. The audience agreed in discussion that this described the general area around the mouth of the Gudep stream. One man prematurely identified the area as a place called Gwabidano which is nearby, but was overruled by others in favor of the Gudep again when the spirit mentioned a pandanus garden which they identified as belonging to one of themselves. By now even the writer could recognize the area from the description. That was where the pig was supposed to be. Only one man remained skeptical. He believed the spirit must have the wrong pig, because he thought the

[286]

one they were looking for should have been at another place closer to the Wolu river.

On the following day when the pig owner visited the place designated by the spirit, he did in fact find a female pig with cropped ears and a white patch on its chest. But it was the wrong pig. This pig was a little one; the one he was looking for was much larger. He returned to the longhouse disgruntled.

In the séance, the spirit's information comes across as markedly ambiguous. There are dozens of places in the tropical forest that would fit his initial description. However, by "not knowing the name" of the ground, he avoided pinpointing a specific location.[4] This allowed the people present to figure out the location by drawing implicitly on their knowledge of local lands and the behavior of pigs. The area the people actually considered was restricted to a region on the Gudeb stream not too far from the lost pig's normal range. Thus, they took issue almost at once with the spirit's suggestion that the pig was somewhere near the Wolu river. From then on, the various details suggested by the spirit were sufficient for the audience to piece together a picture and reach a consensus about where the pig was located. When the location of the pig was finally determined, the séance participants doubtless felt that they had received it on spiritual authority; to a Western observer, it appeared that they had constructed most of it themselves.

This event in which the spirit communicates the whereabouts of a lost pig epitomizes the process of the social construction of reality in the séance. The spirit imparts information at once clear and ambiguous (a definite place described, but the location not named), and the audience attempts to figure out where it is. The effect is reminiscent of the speculative mental search people employ with each new song to figure out which spirit is singing. The deciphering of the spirit's message is a cooperative construction of reality in the guise of a search and clarification of hidden meaning; that is, as the people search for clarification of the spirit's message, they create the meaning they discover.

Dramaturgical Means of Constructing Reality

Not all of the séance reality derives from the dialogic interaction between the séance-goers and the spirits. Directly dramaturgical elements incorporated in or utilized by the performance shape the significance of the dialogue and serve as major means by which séance and everyday realities overflow and spill into each other. This is particularly clear in the way the séance articulates the dark side of Kaluli life, witchcraft and death. Witches (seis) are a frequent topic of séance conversation. At times when there is sickness in the area, discussion of seis, their habits and whereabouts may dominate conversations in séance. Fear and dismay over their activities are aroused through lengthy and often harrowing discussions between the audience and the spirits concerning efforts to locate the (invisible) dismembered pieces of the victim's sei-torn body. At such times, the ambiance of anger and anxiety coupled with a jumpy alertness to small noises of the night can generate a spooky awareness of evil presence that may prickle the scalp of even an observer.

In the middle of one such séance I attended, while the participants were deeply involved in chorusing the song, there was a peculiar noise outside the longhouse. The spirit voice suddenly fell silent, and the chorus was left stranded at the edge of response. In the ensuing moments of consternation in the darkness of the longhouse, everyone was poised to listen. The strange noise and the sudden disappearance of the spirit voice meant a sei was creeping just outside. There could hardly be a more jarring interruption of the performance than this. Through the abrupt silence, the thrill of fear, and the sudden alertness of the audience, the presence of the invisible sei-creature was rendered virtually palpable. Its presence was realized not by anything that was said but through the dramatic moment it evoked. Although the context was set up and interpreted through cultural assumptions and symbolic understandings, it took an act of performance to precipitate the sei sensually into reality. The drama did not end there: the medium was paralyzed, his soul blocked from returning from the spirit world by the presence of the sei. It took twenty minutes of concerned activity, including prayers to Jesus by Christian converts and the efforts of another medium who called down the mouth of his stricken colleague to his own helpers in the spirit world, before the spirit path was cleared of the sei's presence and the seance could continue.

In this kind of highly charged context, discussions of seis take on a dismaying immediacy. The spirits, again, rarely give the names of the seis they see, but they provide (as for the songs and the pigs) enough information for the members of the audience to construct their own conclusions. Once they have constructed them, they are committed to them. In traditional times, if the sei was responsible for someone's death, the result might have been a retaliatory murder.

The reality of seis, marked by the interruption of the séance (or, at other times, by mysterious whistles in the night forest) provides the context in which the instrumental activities of sticking (invisible) dismembered limbs back on bodies appear as urgent, meaningful, and effective behavior. It makes sense because the séance does not simply discuss seis, it presents them concretely as real. In this sense theatre becomes reality: the characters are not on the stage, they are out in the world.

Séance Performance and the Construction of
Cosmological Context

While séances construct realities on the ground, they also articulate everyday realities with cosmological ones from above. Séances are, of course, understood by Kaluli in terms of cultural beliefs and assumptions about the nature of the world and the relationship between spirits and human beings. It is customary in anthropological analysis to approach the understanding of cultural performances by grasping them within such a context of the larger system of belief; that was our strategy in outlining Kaluli spirit beliefs at the beginning of this paper. However, a case could also be made for pursuing the matter the other way around. Kaluli spirit beliefs do not form a thoroughgoing and consistent system. Systematic inquiry reveals that beyond a basic set of common understandings (such as outlined at the beginning of the discussion of séance), there is a great deal of variation in the amount that people know about the invisible realm, and many lacunae and inconsistencies in the content of this knowledge. The piecemeal and miscellaneous nature of individuals' knowledge of the invisible reflects to some extent the piecemeal and miscellaneous nature of the contexts in which they acquire it. There is little formal instruction in the lore. What one learns is picked up informally in everyday context from casual remarks and conversations, from accounts told by knowledgeable people about spirit or witchcraft-related events, from the atmosphere of alertness to peculiar sounds of the forest, and from attending and discussing seances. Kaluli laymen are generally not aware of the variation and inconsistency in their knowledge of the invisible. When it is pointed out, they are as puzzled by it as the ethnographer; usually they suggest that he go and talk with a medium. Mediums are the final authorities on the invisible, not because they are in possession of greater traditional knowledge, but because they have been to the spirit side and seen it for themselves.

Medium's accounts of the invisible are visually detailed and systematic, lending credence to their claim to having actually been there during trance. However, while a common set of cultural themes seems to underly their accounts, the various mediums' versions of the invisible differ from each other considerably (as well as from the laymen's). Mediums, however, do not discuss their trance experiences much among themselves and are largely unaware of the degree to which they differ. Moreover, their differences do not effect the way they perform their séances and are rarely significant in the details of performance content. The inconsistencies of the system rarely surface and, thus, do not pose difficulties for the Kaluli, only for the ethnographer.

One interesting consequence of this situation is the difficulty it poses for conventional ways of talking about a "belief system." A common approach would be to look for common themes and cultural assumptions that underlie the variant accounts, but to give an account of this system by reducing it to its common denominators would clearly distort it. Instead, the best way to preserve its ethnographic integrity is to look at it in terms of the way that it is socially constructed: that is, as a system which consists in the continuing interaction between what people already know of spirits from oral tradition, everyday conversation, and remembered (or reported) past séances, and whatever new experience comes up in the present séance performance. What people know serves as a general background and constraint on what they will accept in a séance performance, but the performance is the presence of the spirits themselves and provides continuing information to the audience on the state of their relations with them. This material, which may contain innovative information, is then reassimilated by the people present to their stock of knowledge. It may be communicated to others who did not attend that particular séance, held as information for future use, or conveniently forgotten. Mediums themselves sometimes contribute further by describing to others in their longhouse some of the things they have seen in their trance journeys that did not emerge in séance. In this way, knowledge of the spirit world is kept, within certain general limits, continually in flux, being constantly generated and renewed and irregularly distributed throughout the

[290]

social field—where it forms part of the context for understanding new séance performances and spirit-related events. Heterogeneity is automatically part of the system no less than its underlying shared cultural assumptions. In this sense, it is more the performance of séances that accounts for the nature and content of Kaluli belief than the other way around. The accumulated knowledge of the spirit word clearly takes second place to the presence of the spirits themselves in performance, and the spirit world, like the identities of the singers of the songs, or the locations of lost pigs, seems at once familiar and just out of reach.

It is when Kaluli reach out to the spirits in séance that they becomes most clearly aware of the larger, cosmological scheme of things that the spirits represent. It is in the séance that they are most likely to experience the direct articulation of that order in their own life space. This articulation is, of course, implicit in the conversations with the spirits and the participation in chorusing the songs. But to take a more explicit example, it is in séance conversations that people enter into relationships with the spirits that individualize, consolidate and legitimize their relationship to the land. One informant told me the story of a taboo area near his longhouse where no one was permitted to hunt or fish. Years before, he explained, a fierce kalu hungo: spirit had come up in a séance and declared that he was the owner of the area: "Don't cut the trees or the arrow cane there," he had told them, "or I will cut off your clan." Commenting on the story, my informant remarked: "He made the arrow cane like our soul." This meant, in one sense, simply: "We die if we cut it." But on another level what looks simply like a lethal threat is regarded by the Kaluli as more like a covenant. The taboo is a sort of mutual agreement between the community and the spirit and, rather than distancing the two, it brings the people into closer and more familiar touch with the forces that animate their locality.

Conclusion

While symbolic analyses would tend to look at the Kaluli séance as a text or structure of meanings, I have tried to move beyond this to see it as an emergent social construction. The reality evoked in the performance does not emerge directly from its following a coherent ritual structure (though it does follow one) but rather, within that,

[291]

from the process of dialogic interaction between the medium and the participants. What renders the performance compelling is not primarily the meanings embodied in symbolic materials themselves (the spirit characters and their pronouncements) but the *way* the symbolic material emerges within the interaction. Starting with the people's anxiety and expectation over problems in everyday life, the séance develops its force by weaving over and around these concerns its own theatrically generated tensions and ambiguities. The songs tease and provoke the listeners, drawing them into the interaction. The séance makes sense not so much by providing information as by getting the audience into motion, bearing down on curiosity and nostalgia to force out dramatic and emotional as much as cognitive significance. It entices, arouses, and intrigues so that the participant constantly strives to get a hold of something that always seems just out of his grasp. The performance is gripping not because of the vivid display of symbolic materials but because the symbolic material is incomplete. Reality and conviction reside not in the spirit's message but in the tension produced when something important he says seems clear, while, in fact, it is still ambiguous. It is this experience of inconclusiveness and imbalance that gives the people little choice but to make their own moves of creative imagination if they are to make sense of the performance and arrive at a meaningful account of what is happening. In so doing, however, they complete the construction of its reality.

In this way, Kaluli people contact the fundamental symbolic understandings of their culture and arrive at solutions to their problems, not in a cognitive or intellectual way so much as in a participant one, whose cognitive shape is not necessarily very well worked out for a given individual, but which is assumed to make sense because the realities it represents are so vivid. Once this (séance) reality is constructed, it may spill over into everyday life so that it not only reflects Kaluli cultural situations, but also defines, constructs and realizes them. In the end, the performance, in effect, becomes life, no less than life is reflected in the performance; the vehicle for constructing social reality and personal conviction appears to be just as much drama as rational thought.

It is evident that it is impossible to separate the dramatic aspects of ritual symbols from their meanings if we want to know their significance or why they are compelling in the emerging performance. This is not just a matter of presentation: many things are cognitively accepted in performance precisely because they are dramatic, impressive, or mysterious rather than because their rational significance is understood, provided, of course, it does not stray too far outside the limits of cultural common sense. The presence and reality of the sei was made palpable by the jarring interruption of the seance, but the interruption itself would have had no meaning if it were not for the existence, for the Kaluli, of the sei.

It is the socially emergent dimension of performance, constructed through the interaction of the performers and participants but not reducible to them, that constitutes the reality in which the actual work of the séance gets done. This emergent dimension stands beyond the text or structure of the performance itself (while at the same time embodying it), so that the séance confronts the participants as an event in which they are involved and which can have consequences for them and their particular situation. This being so, the work of a performance, what it does and how it does it, can never be discovered only by examining the text, or the script, or the symbolic meanings embodied in the ritual alone. It must be sought further in the emerging relation between the performer and other participants (and the participants among themselves) while the performance is in progress.

It is because ritual in performance is a reality apart from its participants that the participants may not all experience the same significance or efficacy from it. Indeed, unless there is some kind of exegetical supervision of both performance and interpretation by guardians of orthodoxy, the performance is bound to mean different things to different people. In the absence of any exegetical canon one might even argue there was no single "correct" or "right" meaning for a ritual at all—or at least not a specific one. In this sense the performance can be seen as an arena in which each participant creates, together with the central performers and other participants, the meaning that the ritual has for him or her. The structure of the ritual, together with its conventionally understood exegesis and intent, will circumscribe the range of that participant's experience within it, but rarely fully determine it, for the participant contributes his own construction to the ritual events. The performance receives its validation socially from the participants when they acknowledge that they have shared in its action and intensity and agree about some aspects of its meaning, whatever else each person may think about it. It follows that the meaning of ritual performances is only partly resident in the symbols and symbolic structures of which they are constructed. In significant part (and particularly in events like the Kaluli séance), the meanings of the symbols and of the rite itself are created during the performance, evoked in the participants' imagination in the negotiation between the principal performers and the participants.

This being the case, rituals (certainly Kaluli séances) do not exist in a vacuum of structural scripts and frames. Insofar as they are performed, they have historicity. However much a genre, a conventional, structured, symbolic enactment with a limited range of meanings, the séance is also an event which the participants help construct and to which they contribute that part of the ambiance, action, and final significance that it evokes from them.

Notes

1. The Kaluli mediums that I knew did not exhibit any unusual or outstanding characteristics as individuals in ordinary life. Quite the contrary. The six mediums that I worked with represented a wide range of personal styles, degrees of extension of social connections, and general social influence. They ranged from one man of considerable influence, who was widely traveled in the region, through less widely connected individuals of more average standing and limited range, to two socially marginal men.

2. This habit was disconcerting to the Kaluli as well as to the ethnographer and may have been part of the reason that in addition to being respected as a medium, he was also feared as a sei.

3. It is worth remarking that this kind of raucous, lascivious joking and teasing between the young men and spirit women practically never went on between men and women in real life, and certainly never in public. Kaluli would be too embarrassed or afraid to do such a thing. The social repercussions (should relatives of the woman find out) would be serious, since such activity would imply the young man was taking marital/sexual liberties with the woman that were her family's alone to dispose of; hence, he would be acting as if he were "stealing" her (*afa di*). Because marriage/ sexual activity with a spirit woman is impossible in an everyday context, such sexual joking is harmless fun. It never leads to a spirit marriage that results in a man becoming a medium.

4. I should mention that the medium in this performance was not from the longhouse where the performance was being held and was not himself very familiar with the local grounds.

REFERENCES

Feld, Steven. 1982. *Sound and Sentiment: Birds, Weeping Poetics, and Song in Kaluli Expression*. Philadelphia: University of Pennsylvania Press.

[294]

Kapferer, Bruce. 1979a. "Introduction: Ritual Process and the Transformation of Context." *Social Analysis* 1, 1: 3–19.

——. 1979b. "Entertaining Demons: Comedy, Interaction, and Meaning in a Sinhalese Healing Ritual." *Social Analysis* 1, 1:108–52.

Lévi-Strauss, Claude. 1967. "The Effectiveness of Symbols." In Lévi-Strauss, *Structural Anthropology*. New York: Anchor Books, Doubleday.

Schieffelin, Edward. 1976. *The Sorrow of the Lonely and the Burning of the Dancers*. New York: St. Martins Press.

——. 1977. "The Unseen Influence: Tranced Mediums as Historical Innovators." *Journal de la Société des Oceanistes* 33, 56–57: 169–78.

——. 1980. "Reciprocity and the Construction of Reality on the Papuan Plateau." *Man* 15, 3: 150–56.

[13]

Ritual, Violence, and Creativity

Richard Schechner

I

Whatever the future of ritual, its past is pedigreed. Ethologists observe animals performing rituals. Ethologically speaking, in ritual ordinary behavior is condensed, exaggerated, repeated, made into rhythms or pulses (often faster or slower than usual) or frozen into poses. In animals, ritual behavior is accompanied by the development and display of conspicuous body parts, dramatic changes in color, or both—the moose's horns, the peacock's tail, the red rump of a baboon in estrus, the brilliant colors of any number of fish species.

But when ethologists use the word "ritual" to describe certain kinds of animal behavior, are they actually detecting analogies and homologies between animal behavior and human rituals, or are they begging the question?

Is human ritual like animal ritual because the evolution of the body, brain, and genetic codes includes the evolution of behavior? Or is the supposed link between animal and human ritual an example of anthropomorphism? It is not easy to answer this question.

In both animals and humans, rituals arise around disruptive, tur-

An earlier version of this essay appeared as "The Future of Ritual," *Journal of Ritual Studies* 1, 1: 5–33.

bulent, and strongly ambivalent interactions where faulty communication can lead to violent even fatal encounters. These interactions usually concern sexuality/mating, hierarchy, and territory (an interdependent triad). Ritual both forestalls "real events" and increases the clarity of signaling. Thus animals and humans get through these difficult transactions/interactions—"passages," if you will—with a minimum of harm. But human rituals do much more than get people through. They act out tradition as well as create new meaning, they mediate tensions between continuity and change, they integrate individuals into social systems, they offer time out from—or distinctly focus—daily activities. And, of course, they are often celebratory.

Ritual action is very close to theater. There, too, behavior is rearranged, condensed, exaggerated, and made rhythmic, while colorful costumes, masks, and face and body painting enhance the displays; there, too, difficult passages are acted through; there, too, the action is symbolic, a "standing for" or "in place of." What is replaced (displaced, redirected, transformed) is violence. The violence of ritual is simultaneously present and absent, displayed and denied, as when the vanquished wolf suddenly offers his throat to his opponent, thus guaranteeing not the savage slitting of his jugular but the immediate appeasement of his rival's rage; or when one person is sacrificed on behalf of, or instead of, others. Or even when symbols of symbols are manipulated, as when the priest raises the Eucharistic bread and wine, flesh and blood, offering communicants a chance to participate in Christ's sacrificial, redemptive *sparagmos.*

Violence, sexuality, and theater converge in the two main Western traditions, the Greek and the Hebraic-Christian. These traditions combine Middle Eastern, northern European, and Eurasian elements— fertility rites, sun worship, and shamanism. Even a cursory study of Christian iconography and painting as it developed through the Middle Ages reveals the orgasmic, not to say orgiastic, elements of martyrdom. This display of violence against the body is not limited to bygone epochs. Violence against the body and things is a strong theme in contemporary performance art. Chris Burden specialized in assaulting his own body, going so far as to have himself shot; Stelarc exhibits his body suspended by hooks and cords; Ralph Ortiz practices a "destruction art" where furniture is hacked to pieces. The violence of punk rock and other forms of popular music is well known. American football, boxing, and especially professional wrestling celebrate a highly theatricalized violence. Special automobile shows called "demolition

[297]

derbies" feature high-speed car crashes and "monster trucks" whose specialty is crushing other vehicles beneath their giant wheels. With the exception of wrestling, these events—as distinct from the extraordinarily graphic scenes of violence shown in the movies (often in slow motion in order to emphasize the spectacularity of the violence)—are not simulated. Any close look at these violent displays cannot but disclose their essentially erotic content.

But what about non-Western arts and rituals? Everywhere initiation rites are violent and sexual. Initiations—which are a form of participatory theater—are rife with circumcisions, subincisions, vomitings, beatings, and other bloodily violent acts. These initiatory ordeals are not any "gentler" when viewed from within the cultures that practice them. Nor is this violence linked to sexuality characteristic only of male initiation. As more information about women gathered by women becomes available, it is increasingly clear that the initiation of girls too—in its own ways—is sexual and frequently violent. Nor are the healing arts of shamans placid exercises of homeopathy. They are more likely to be full-fledged perilous journeys and magical combats climaxing in a direct plunge into the guts of the sick person from which the shaman extracts the disease (or its symbol). Often enough the sickness thus removed is displayed for all to see. These invasions— dare I say "penetrations"?—of the body are considered necessary and healing. So, sometimes, are animal and even human sacrifices.

Why go on? Displaying if not celebrating violence of a sexual kind is a chief intercultural characteristic of theater and ritual. Such performances suggest that *all* violence is sexual and experienced as dangerous, crying for some means of control. Feminists argue that this association of sex and violence is phallocentric; that female sexuality, when untainted by male values, is nonviolent or at least less violent. That may be true. But at the present moment, and for as far back in history as scholars can reliably look, nothing seems capable of eliminating violent impulses and actions. Amplified to worldwide dimensions by technology, violence is being flung outwards as (phallological) state policy: wars, nuclear and conventional arms, defense departments, terrorism and counterterrorism. But that has not kept violence from also being enacted within the molecules of social existence—child abuse, murder within the family, street crime, alcohol and drug addiction—or from being re-released in floods of popular entertainments ranging from sports to pop music to horror films to such videocasettes as *Faces of Death*, a best-selling item "made up of scene after graphic scene of actual human and animal killings . . . [showing] everything from the electric chair to the slaughterhouse" (Associated Press). Sales of *Faces of Death* are described as "phenomenal."

The fascination with violence is neither a contemporary nor uniquely Western jag. Take for example the classic Sanskrit epics, *Ramayana* and *Mahabharata,* episodes from which are enacted throughout southern Asia. The *Ramayana* pivots around the disequilibrating lust of Ravana, the ten-headed demon king of Lanka who kidnaps and attempts to seduce/rape Sita, the wife of Vishnu incarnate, Rama. The *Mahabharata* turns on the lust and greed of the Kaurava family as they cheat their Pandava cousins of their kingdom and wealth even as the Kauravas try to strip and rape the Pandavas' joint-wife, Draupadi. The story goes through many episodes of adventure, exile, disguise, and return. There are literally hundreds of side-tales absorbed into the *Mahabharata.* But ultimately the narrative is resolved at the great battle of Kurukshetra where cousins slaughter cousins, students annihilate gurus. One of the climactic scenes of the epic, performed so powerfully in kathakali, is Bhima's revenge against Dusassana, the chief humiliator of Draupadi. With his great war club Bhima crushes Dusassana's thighs, then he rips open Dusassana's stomach, drinking his blood and eating his intestines. Finally, as he had sworn to do, Bhima washes Draupadi's hair in Dusassana's bloody guts. Only after this ultimate revenge is Dusassana permitted to die.

Japanese noh drama is more restrained visually speaking, but many of the plays tell stories of murder, suicide, adultery, vengeance, and sacrifice; the characters include mad women and uneasy ghosts seeking a rest they never find.

In Africa south of the Sahara, among the Banyang of Cameroon as elsewhere, the belief in witchcraft and bush spirits is very strong. "Recovery from the fevers and other disorders which the witches bring from their secret 'place' is only possible after the person owning the wicked animal familiar [a male owl, a python, or a wild pig] has confessed, either as an open statement before the people as witness, in daylight, or by confession plus ritual purification by a cultic society" (Thompson 1974: 209–10).

In the Basinjom rites, dances lead to a direct confrontation with these witches. Facing the accused, Basinjom raises his special "knife of vision" over his head, as he "specified certain selfish acts, breaches of cooperative contracts, lapses of generosity" (214).

He called their names. He asked "have you done this?" They answered, "Yes." They apologized and said that they did not know that their powers had been so destructive. They begged forgiveness. They offered material amends and these were accepted. They were purified by Basinjom, who said, "from today I do not want to see any further trouble from your house." A goat was sacrificed. The women swore not to do such evil a second time. They were purified by Basinjom and forgiven. The case was closed. [214–15]

Thompson emphasizes that what he saw was a drama: "The accused women were conscious actresses in a public drama meant to inculcate deep decorum, meant to warn the world of the dangers of polluting social landscapes by dark and hidden thoughts. The ritual humiliation was, in a sense, more performance than trauma, an artistically phrased combat between real or imaginary sources of evil (the witches) and metaphoric opposition to this action (Basinjom)" (216).

Thompson understands, as few have, the connections between performance, ritual, meaning, and what he calls "intimate things, divinatory insights, thoughts, dreams." It is a link Freud forged at the turn of the century.

II

What of all this violence? It is not part of "real life," no matter how violent ordinary experience might be. Even *Faces of Death* is one step away from actuality, as was rebroadcasting again and again in 1986 the explosion of the space shuttle *Challenger* or, twenty-three years earlier, the assassination of John F. Kennedy—as if seeing the horrific image enough times would ease the pain. The first-time or "original" violence of real life is anything but redemptive. People need to "make something out" of it, if at first only by repetition. Rebroadcasting, sheer repetition, is a low-level ritualizing, an attempt to absorb and transform violence. When official violence approaches the absolute, as at Auschwitz-Birkenau, memorials and museums are marked off to which school children are bussed. But the children I watched at Auschwitz in May 1985 were more interested in the displays of T-shirts imprinted with Michael Jackson's face for sale at the Auschwitz tourist kiosk than in any confrontation with Polish-Jewish-German history.

Perhaps this is as it should be: the ritual of going-to-Auschwitz-as-part-of-school erases the pain of seeing what was/is there. But I, part of no group, walking alone the mile or so from Auschwitz to Birkenau, standing among the wild grasses growing over the rail line terminating between the wrecked but recognizable twin gas chambers–crematoria, watching the bees work the spring flowers while a couple of Polish boys on bikes rolled down the rail path, stopping to talk, then casually turning around and pedaling out again—I felt the stunning void and heard only the wind in my ears.

III

Until very recently, when work on animal cognition began to be taken seriously, it was assumed that animals have no Oedipal choices to make: they act, they do not mull. Their minds entertain neither skepticism, irony, nor subjunctive negativity ("Ought I do that?" "What will happen if I don't do that?"). Animals suffer no wedges driven between impulse and act. Perhaps a splinter of subjunctivity is present in the so-called speaking animals: chimpanzees, gorillas, dolphins. But even if there were some gorilla Oedipus, he would be a far cry from the character in Sophocles' play. Animal ritual deals with crises on a nonideational basis, through action not rumination.

Human ritual as well might be said to short-circuit thinking, providing at-hand solutions to difficult problems. Most people (being neither Oedipus nor Hamlet) deal with crisis through ritual action, not thought. Individual and collective anxieties are relieved by performances, whose qualities of repetition, rhythmicity, exaggeration, condensation, simplification, and spectacle stimulate the brain into releasing opiumlike endorphins directly into the bloodstream, yielding ritual's second benefit: a direct experience of pleasure. Marx may have been correct, biochemically speaking, to link religion and opium. To say that ritual short-circuits thought means that ritual provides ready-made answers to what thinking works through. But ritual is also creative because, as Victor Turner showed, the ritual process is an opening up of a time/space of antistructural playfulness. And whereas in animals the noncognitive is dominant, in humans there is always a struggle between the cognitive and the noncognitive; they may be hard-wired for subjunctivity, reflexivity, and negativity. Ritual performances are like animal ritual; the ritual process generating those

[301]

performances is more open, unfinished, "liminoid" (Turner 1982; Schechner 1985).

Many human rituals integrate music, dance, and theater. The display of masks and costumes; the processions, circumambulations, singing, dancing, storytelling, food-sharing, fire-burning, incensing, drumming, and bell-ringing; the body-heat, press, and active participation of the crowd create an overwhelming synaesthetic environment and experience for the audience, tribe, or congregation. At the same time, rituals embody cognitive systems of values that instruct and mobilize participants. These embodied values are rhythmic and cognitive, spatial and conceptual, sensuous and ideological. In neurological terms, ritual excites both the right and left hemispheres of the cerebral cortex: it is truly total theater. People are more than susceptible to rituals of all kinds—religious, political, sportive, aesthetic; they manifest a need demanding the kind of satisfaction only rituals can provide.

But why violence? This is a particularly appropriate question for a person like me to ask, because dramatic narratives and theatrical actions are so often, and in so many diverse cultures, explicitly violent. At the start of the Western "great tradition," we have Clytemnestra's murder of Agamemnon, the dismemberment of Pentheus by his mother, Agave, and Oedipus, who stabs to jelly and then rips out his own eyeballs. Later we have the slaughter that concludes *Hamlet*, the blinding of Gloucester in *King Lear*, and the multiple atrocities that characterize the Jacobean drama. Nor is the modern repertory exempt, full as it is of murders, suicides, torture, and "psychological violence," as even a cursory reading of Henrik Ibsen, August Strindberg, Bertold Brecht, Luigi Pirandello, Jean Genet, Eugene O'Neill, and Sam Shepard shows. Farce, of course, has always been poised at the edge of chaotic violence: think of the forty victims of rape-murder in Eugene Ionesco's *The Lesson*. I have referred to but a very few of the countless examples of the violence endemic to Western theater.

René Girard in his *Violence and the Sacred* explains that real, actual violence always threatens the social life of a group. "Inevitably the moment comes when violence can only be countered by more violence. Whether we fail or succeed in our effort to subdue it, the real victor is always violence itself. The mimetic attributes of violence are extraordinary—sometimes direct and positive, at other times indirect and negative. The more men strive to curb their violent impulses, the more these impulses seem to prosper" (1977:31). Girard links violence and sexuality:

> Like violence, sexual desire tends to fasten upon surrogate objects if the object to which it was originally attracted remains inaccessible; it willingly accepts substitutes. And again, like violence, repressed sexual desire accumulates energy that sooner or later bursts forth, causing tremendous havoc. It is also worth noting that the shift from violence to sexuality and from sexuality to violence is easily effected, even by the most "normal" of individuals, totally lacking in perversion. Thwarted sexuality leads naturally to violence, just as lovers' quarrels often end in an amorous embrace. [35]

Girard believes (and I agree) that ritual sublimates violence: "The function of ritual is to 'purify' violence; that is to 'trick' violence into spending itself on victims whose death will provoke no reprisals" (36). All this sounds very much like theater—especially a theater whose function is cathartic, or at least a theater that "redirects" violent and erotic energies. Cathartic or not, theater always manufactures substitutes, specializing in multiplying alternatives. Is it accidental that so many of these alternatives combine the violent with the erotic?

The "sacrificial crisis," as Girard sees it, is the dissolution of distinctions within a society—from the erasure of the reciprocal rights/responsibilities of parents to/from their children, to the elision of all hierarchy. Incest and regicide are radical attacks on differentiation. Girard, a dyed-in-the-wool advocate of caste, says: "Wherever differences are lacking, violence threatens" (57). The enactment of ritual death—whether the victim is actually or theatrically killed—restores distinctions by emphasizing the difference between the victim and the rest of society. "The surrogate victim plays the same role on the collective level as the objects the shamans claim to extract from their patients play on the individual level—objects that are then identified as the cause of the illness" (83).

In theater the substitutions are more complex than in shamanism. In theater the actor is a substitute for a surrogate. The actor who plays Oedipus or Lear or Willie Loman is not that "character" who itself is not a "real person." There may be no "real person" at all behind the scenes, but only the play of embodied representations:

[victim] $\longrightarrow$ character $\longrightarrow$ actor::audience $\longleftarrow$ society

At the place where the actor meets the audience, that is, in the theater building, the society faces the sacrificial victim twice-removed. The audience itself is once-removed from the society of which it is a part. Individuals "leave" society and "go to" the theater, where they then play the role of society, responding more as a group than as individuals. The actor represents the character which means that the actor's performance is a representation of a representation.

In ritual performances one layer of a representation is stripped away: there is neither character nor audience. In ritual the encounter is:

$$[\text{victim}] \longrightarrow \text{actor::society}$$

The priest performing the Eucharist "stands for" or "elevates" Christ while the congregants are Christianity itself. The actor::audience interface is looser, more given to playfulness, change, and individual creativity than the actor::society interface. In some ritual performances the victim faces society directly, and an actual sacrifice takes place:

$$\text{victim::society}$$

This is not usually the sacrifice of a life. It may be a cutting, or scarring, or burning, or the exchange of rings, the giving of a thread, an immersion, or some other painless but irrevocable act. In such cases the victim is not a victim but a person, or persons, to be celebrated. Still, one might ask, is there a shadow of a sacrificial victim behind even the most celebratory ritual actions? And is not the ambition of theater to present convincingly an analogy of such sacrifices?

There are ways other than Girard's to explain the apparently universal association of violence, sexuality, ritual, and theater. In *Totem and Taboo* Sigmund Freud proposed an analogy between the thought of animists, neurotics, children, and artists.

It is easy to perceive the motives which lead men to practice magic: they are human wishes. All we need to suppose is that primitive man had an immense belief in the power of his wishes. [1962: 83]

Children are in an analogous psychical situation. . . . They satisfy their wishes in an hallucinatory manner, that is, they create a satisfying situation by means of centrifugal excitation of their sense organs. An adult primitive man has an alternative motor impulse, the will, which is later destined to alter the whole face of the earth in order to satisfy his wishes. This motor impulse is at first employed to give a representation of the satisfying situation in such a way that it becomes possible to experience the satisfaction by means of what might be described as motor hallucinations. This kind of representation of a satisfied wish is quite comparable to children's play, which succeeds their earlier purely sensory technique of satisfaction. [83–84]

This "omnipotence of thoughts," as Freud called it, makes a world where "things become less important than ideas of things" [85]. Neurotics also live in this "world apart" where "they are only affected by what is thought with intensity and pictured with emotion, whereas agreement with external reality is a matter of no importance" [86]. Freud notes that neurotics undergoing psychoanalysis are "unable to believe that thoughts are free and will constantly be afraid of expressing evil wishes, as though their expression would lead inevitably to their fulfillment." In this way, neurotics reveal their "resemblance to the savages who believe they can alter the external world by mere thinking" [87].

Freud, a cultural evolutionist, argues for a progression from an animist view of the world to a religious view to a scientific view.

At the animistic stage men ascribe omnipotence to themselves. At the religious stage they transfer it to the gods but do not seriously abandon it themselves, for they reserve the power of influencing the gods in a variety of ways according to their wishes. The scientific view of the universe no longer affords any room for human omnipotence; men have acknowledged their smallness and submitted resignedly to death and to the other necessities of nature. None the less some of the primitive belief in omnipotence still survives in men's faith in the power of the human mind, taking account, as it does of the laws of reality. [88]

Each successive stage credits "external reality" with more autonomy. Too bad that Freud did not know that even as he was proposing his evolutionary scheme, Niels Bohr and Werner Heisenberg were developing their ideas of indeterminacy—a theory that categorically denies to "external reality" its independent existence while also denying to the human mind all claims of omnipotence.

Freud notes one mode of "civilized thought" that remains unreconstructed.

In only a single field of our civilization has the omnipotence of thoughts been retained, and that is in the field of art. Only in art does it still happen that a man who is consumed by desires performs something

[305]

resembling the accomplishment of those desires and that what he does in play produces emotional effects—thanks to artistic illusion—just as though it were something real. People speak with justice of the "magic of art" and compare artists to magicians. But the comparison is perhaps more significant than it claims to be. There can be no doubt that art did not begin as art for art's sake. It worked originally in the service of impulses which are for the most part extinct today. And among them we may suspect the presence of many magical purposes. [90]

Extinct impulses? If we look at Freud's ideas through a contemporary lens, we must throw out the notion that some humans are more "primitive"—or "aboriginal"—than others. Biologically and culturally speaking, all Homo sapiens have been on earth the same amount of time. Although, as Freud believed, the child might be the parent to the adult, the so-called primitive is not the child to the so-called civilized. Nor is the neurotic an unreconstructed child/primtive/artist—or vice versa. What we have is a diversity of cultures, none of which is closer to the beginning of human history than any other; and a set of human actions whose similarities with each other are discomforting to those who wish to place cognitive thinking only at the crown of human achievement.

Each culture embodies its own system of organizing experience. Crediting Freud with extraordinary insight, how can his ideas be restated to suit today's view of things? Perhaps we should say that certain systems are more porous in relation to the unconscious than other systems. But the ways in which this porosity is encouraged or repressed, guarded, regulated, and used differ vastly, not only from culture to culture but within every culture. Children, crazies, and "technicians of the sacred" each encounter and filter differently what Anton Ehrenzweig, following Freud, calls "primary process" (1970). Children are porous to the unconscious because they have not yet learned how to repress material streaming into consciousness; their egos are in the process of formation. Neurotics are by definition people whose defenses are weak or wrongly positioned; but behavior that might be "neurotic" in one culture, or one setting within a given culture, might prove very effective in other contexts. Extremely neurotic people have been not only great artists but royalty, presidents, tycoons, and war chiefs. Shamans, artists, and others who perform the "omnipotence of thoughts" seek out teachers and techniques to help them master the powerful impulses streaming into consciousness.

[306]

Account after account tells the story: a future shaman is "called" but resists the call. But she or he cannot control the experiences "coming" in the form of dreams, visions, uncontrollable impulses, and sickness. After a period of doubt and often terror, the neophyte submits, finds someone to teach her or him the tricks of the trade. Becoming an artist, even in the West, is not unlike learning to be a shaman; the techniques and ambivalent social status of artist and shaman approximate each other. In modern Western cultures, it might be said that the impulses from which art is made out of the experiences of the artist (the shaman's "call," the artist's "raw material") originate in difficult confrontations between daily life and the unconscious. In many cultures such impulses are said to originate with gods, ancestors, demons, ghosts, and so forth. I believe these impulses represent material streaming into consciousness from what Ehrenzweig calls primary process. The impulses manifest themselves in dreams, visions, obsessive thoughts, trance possession, speaking in tongues, and half-hidden, feared yet irresistible, violent, and erotic wishes. Sometimes these impulses and their manifestations make the recipient feel ecstatic, happy beyond the power of description, and sometimes the recipient is terrified.

Ehrenzweig's theories fit nicely those of Girard. Girard believes that lack of differentiation brings about the "sacrificial crisis" which is remedied by the mimetic violence of ritual. Ehrenzweig celebrates what he calls the child's "global vision," which "remains undifferentiated as to its component details. This gives the younger child artist the freedom to distort color and shapes in the most imaginative and, to us, unrealistic manner. But to him—owing to his global, unanalytic view—his work is realistic" (1970: 22).

Ehrenzweig sounds like Girard when he says that "the truly unconscious and potentially disruptive quality of undifferentiation" threatens to introduce "the catastrophic chaos which we are wont to associate with the primary process" [37–38]. But that which terrifies the neurotic, the artist seeks to play out publicly. Or, as is frequently the case, the artist-neurotic (or shaman-neurotic) is compelled to explore the very process that terrifies her or him. It is fashionable today to say that artists are healthy while neurotics are sick—that ten years of art are worth a psychoanalytic cure (Jean Paul Sartre on Jean Genet). Perhaps. But from an operational perspective, art and neurosis are closely linked because both behaviors are generated by a porous and shifting boundary between the unconscious and the conscious. And

[307]

what art manipulates on an individual basis, ritual does collectively. Ritual gives violence its place at the table of human needs. As Franz Kafka noted: "Leopards break into the temple and drink to the dregs what is in the sacrificial pitchers; this is repeated over and over again; finally it can be calculated in advance, and it becomes part of the ceremony" (1954: 40).

IV

Human beings need to perform rituals. Where is this need located? Eugene d'Aquili, Charles D. Laughlin, Jr., and John McManus place it in the brain (1979). As Turner put it in one of his last writings: "What is the role of the brain as an organ for the information in the production of mental, verbal, or organic behavior? . . . If ritualization, as discussed by Huxley, Lorenz, and other ethologists, has a biogenetic foundation, while meaning has a neocortical learned base, does this mean that creative processes, those which generate new cultural knowledge, might result from a coadaptation perhaps in the ritual process itself, of genetic and cultural information?" (1983: 225, 228). Or as d'Aquili, Laughlin, and McManus say: "Human ceremonial ritual is not a simple institution unique to man but rather a nexus of variables shared by other species. . . . One may trace the evolutionary progression of ritual behavior from the emergence of formalization through the coordination of formalized communicative behavior and sequences of ritual behavior to the conceptualization of such sequences and the assignment of symbols to them by man" (1979: 36–37).

D'Aquili, Laughlin, and McManus propose what they call a "cognitive imperative." A human being "automatically, almost reflexly, confronts an unknown stimulus by the question 'What is it?' Affective responses such as fear, happiness, or sadness and motor responses are clearly secondary to the immediate cognitive response" (168). If their thesis is true, then humans work from the top down, from the present to the past (evolutionarily speaking). Furthermore, narrativity—the need to construct a plausible story—is not only hard-wired into the brain but dominant. This contradicts what I discussed earlier: the way ritual short-circuits thought.

The resolution to the contradiction is to suppose that ritualizing— the performance of ritual—is not a simple, one-step, one-way operation. It appears to me, from conducting workshops full of intense performative experiences (Schechner 1973, 1988), that rhythmic activities—especially if movement and sound-making are carefully coordinated and maintained for long periods of time—invariably lead to feelings of "identical opposites": wholeness/"astral projection," omnipotence/vulnerability, tranquility/readiness for the most demanding physical action. In other words, the narrative-cognitive stimulus works from the cerebral cortex down, while the movement-sonic stimulus works from the lower brain up. Or to say it another way, the performance of ritual is both narrative (cognitive) and affective; these working together comprise the experience of ritualizing. And if d'Aquili, Laughlin, and McManus are right, the affective states aroused by ritual are necessarily nested within a narrative frame. But from within—as a person performing a ritual—the narrative frame dissolves as the ritual action continues.

Barbara Lex, another of d'Aquili's associates, proposes that trance, and other supremely affective states of flow,[1] result from the extreme stimulation of both the ergotropic and trophotropic systems of the brain.

> Exposure to manifold, intense, repetitive, emotion-evoking stimuli ensures uniformity of behavior in ritual participants. . . . Rituals properly executed promote a feeling of well-being and relief, not only because the driving techniques employed in rituals are designed to sensitize or "tune" the nervous system and thereby lessen inhibition of the [neocortex's] right hemisphere and permit temporary right-hemisphere dominance, as well as mixed trophotropic-ergotropic excitation, to achieve synchronization of cortical rhythms, in both hemispheres and evoke a trophotropic rebound. [Lex 1979: 120, 144–45].

People seek experiences that provide a "rebound" or "spillover," simultaneously exciting both left and right hemispheres of the forebrain (Fischer 1971; Turner 1983; Schechner 1988).

These ethological and neurological theories answer some questions, but what they do not explain, because they cannot, are the creative and playful aspects of ritual. Nor do they address the problem of violence. Ritual's creative and antistructural qualities fascinated Turner (1969, 1982, 1983, 1986). Ritual is not just a conservator of evolutionary and cultural behavior, it is, as Turner showed, important as a generator of new images, new ideas, and new practices. Reviewing the theories of d'Aquili, Laughlin, McManus, and Lex, Turner was troubled by their failure to deal with play.

[309]

As I see it play does not fit in anywhere particular; it is a transient and is recalcitrant to localization, to placement, to fixation—a joker in the neuro-anthropological act. . . . Playfulness is a volatile, sometimes dangerously explosive essence, which cultural institutions seek to bottle or contain in the vials of games of competition, chance, and strength, in modes of simulation such as theater, and in controlled disorientation, from roller coasters to dervish dancing. . . . Play could be termed dangerous because it may subvert the left-right hemispheric regular switching involved in maintaining the social order. . . . The neuronic energies of play, as it were, lightly skim over the cerebral cortices, sampling rather than partaking of the capacities and functions of the various areas of the brain. As Don Handelman (1977) and Gregory Bateson (1972) have written that is possibly why play can provide a metalanguage (since to be "meta" is to be both beyond and between) and emit metamessages about so many and varied human propensities and thus provide, as Handelman has said, "a very wide range of commentary on the social order" (189). Play can be everywhere and nowhere, imitate anything, yet be identified with nothing. . . . You may have guessed that play is, for me, a liminal or liminoid mode, essentially interstitial, betwixt-and-between all standard taxonomic nodes, essentially "elusive." [1983: 233–34]

For Turner, play is unlocatable because it is quintessentially relational. It is not anywhere "in" the brain (or "in" culture) but everywhere "between."

Turner celebrated the antistructural—the playful, the creative, the artistic—dimensions of ritual. In the antistructural, I suspect, we will find the answer to why ritual and theater are so violent. Turner located the creative dimension of ritual in the creases, knee joints, margins, and cracks of social structure: the elusive "betwixt and between."

As Turner himself notes, there is a contradiction between his theories and the ethological-neurological propositions. To the ethologists and neurologists, ritual is central to behavior and to brain structure/function. But Turner places ritual "betwixt and between," making it more like play than anything else. The ritual process is liminal-liminoid, its operations are unauthorized, antistructural, subjunctive, and subversive. Perhaps this contradiction can be resolved if ritual is viewed separately from ritualizing (the ritual process). The ritual frame—the "cognitive imperative"—is a frame or armature; the experience of ritualizing is destabilizing, liminal, hard to locate or pin down. Ritual organizes, conserves, and narrates; ritualizing stimulates the brain to such a degree that often the "rebound" Lex describes occurs with its resultant oceanic experiences and radical volatility of emotions.

The contradiction can also be seen as expressing the difference between Turner's social perspective and the ethologist's-neurologist's biological one. This difference is a restatement of the old, insoluble argument between determinists and those who assert that human beings are free to make their own destinies.

Turner delighted in the "not-yetness" of human experience, its categorical unfinishedness. Whether performing ethnography in Manhattan, climbing a mountain in Israel, observing Yaqui deer and pascola dances in Arizona, celebrating Carnival in Rio, or conferring with colleagues in Japan or on his back porch in Charlottesville, Turner threw himself into the midst, seeking experience with incredible heart-bursting energy.

For Turner, the ritual process was a living magma upwelling in all human societies: a periodically explosive, hot, and molten creativity. This ritual process is strictly analogous to the training-workshop-rehearsal process where the "givens" or "ready-mades"—accepted texts, accepted ways of using the body, accepted feelings—are deconstructed, broken down into malleable bits of behavior, feeling, thought, and text and then reconstructed into public performances (Schechner 1985).

In traditional genres such as kathakali, ballet, or noh, neophytes begin their training early in life. This training involves learning new ways of speaking, gesturing, moving, maybe even new ways of thinking and feeling. New for the trainee, that is, but traditional for kathakali, ballet, and noh. As in initiation rites, the mind and body of each performer are returned to the state of tabula rasa (to use Turner's Lockean image), ready to be written on in the language of the form being learned. When finished with training, the performer can "speak" noh, kathakali, or ballet: she or he is "incorporated" into the tradition as an initiated member. The violence of scarification or circumcision is absent—but deep, permanent psychophysical changes are wrought. A kathakali performer, a ballet dancer, a noh shite each have their genre-specific ways of moving, sounding, and, I would say, being: they are marked people.

Turner went far beyond Arnold Van Gennep when he said that the artworks and leisure activities of industrial and postindustrial societies were like the rituals of tribal, agrarian, and traditional societies. He

[311]

called the arts and leisure activities "liminoid." Liminal rites are oblig-
atory; liminoid activities are voluntary.

The workshops of experimental theater and dance are liminoid lab-
oratories of psychophysical initiation. Some of the transformations accomplished by workshops are temporary—used in the performance at
hand only. But sometimes workshops effect permanent transformations. An aesthetic-ritual initiation can be as consequential and permanent as anything wrought on an Aborigine. The "parashamans" of
experimental theater and dance—Jerzy Grotowski, Peter Brook, Anna
Halprin (to name three of many)—practice aesthetics to yield initiatory
permanence (Grimes 1982: 255–66). It is this explicit intention to
transform people that has led these and other parashamans to inves-
tigate in a most rigorous way the techniques of shamans and other
ritual specialists among non-Western cultures.

The practice of the parashamans turns orthodox ritual on its head:
ethological procedures are mimicked, neurological responses elic-
ited—but in the service of ideas and visions of society that are anything
but conservative. In nonhuman animals ritual is a way of increasing
signal clarity in order to mediate crisis. It is often this among humans
too, but it is also something else: a means of conserving and transmitting traditional cultural and individual patterns of behavior. Turner
knew this, but in his middle and later thought he did not emphasize
it. He focused instead on how ritual process is a machine for introducing new behaviors or undermining established systems. This led
him away from a primary focus on traditional or liminal rituals toward
investigation of the way artists work, the techniques of the parashamans, and to his own practical theatrical work in "performing ethnography" (Turner 1982).

It is precisely when this creative/subversive function of ritual dom-
inates, spills over its usually well-defined boundaries, that art separates
from—and sometimes opposes—religion. The maskers of Carnival,
Hopi mudhead clowns, and Yaqui pascolas are also antistructural, but
almost always in the service, ultimately, of reinforcing traditional ways
of doing and thinking. A period of licence is permitted, even required.
Things are "done backwards," excesses are celebrated, promiscuous
sexuality and drunkenness flourish. But then Ash Wednesday termi-
nates Carnival, and the subversive shenanigans of Mardi Gras are put
away for another year. Among the Yaquis, the ritual clowning of the
masked Chapayekam continues right through to Holy Saturday. This
clowning is mixed in with their role as pursuers and persecutors of

Jesus. But finally, also, the Chapayekam reinforce Yaqui-Catholicism. There is never an Easter when they are not defeated. The people know what to expect of them, what their actions represent. In art, experimental art especially, things are different. The subversion is continuous. The avant-garde is art's permanent revolution.

V

The violence acted out in performance is no mere "symbol," sapped of its ability to wound, frighten, and astonish. It is rather a mortgaged actuality, awaiting while indefinitely postponing future catastrophe. Ritual violence is not a remembrance of things past. As outlined in my theory of "restoration of behavior" (Schechner 1985: 35–116), the present moment is a negotiation between a future and a past, both always in flux. The future is death and the past, a sudden thrusting onto the stage of life. To salve too direct a realization of this, individuals who will die are assimilated into groups or ideologies which are presumed to be ongoing if not immortal. But the story these groups tell, their ritual enactments, concern death or death-rebirth. Sacrifices and symbolic wounds stave off but do not erase impending doom.

The ancient Greeks always sent a messenger onto stage to report the violent acts performed out of sight of the spectators. Actually, of course, these acts were never performed—they existed as reports only. But did the fictitious atrocities inflicted on Pentheus or Oedipus reflect a historical time when such actions were performed? I think not. Rites come and go, but there is no unilinear pattern leading from ritual to theater or away from violence to mimesis. The fictive violence of the stage refers to the future—to what threatens if the aesthetic-ritual enterprise crashes.

Throughout history, there has been a big place reserved for a theater of violence such as those of the Elizabethan-Jacobean period, the Grand Guignol, or today's horror or vengeance movies. Sometimes this violence is participatory. In the sadomasochistic theaters of New York, minor violence—spanking, whipping, pinching, dripping hot wax on naked flesh—is performed not only on actors but on eager spectator/participants who pay fancy prices for the privilege. Are these people perverts or neo-initiates undergoing ordeals? Or are they just ordinary people out for kicks? Is *King Lear* less effective than *Oedipus* because Gloucester has his eyes put out on stage? Semiotically there is scant difference between "reported" and "pretended" actions. Spectators at *Lear* know they are seeing tricks. Skillfully staged actions, like the messenger's words in Greek tragedy, refer to a violence deferred. But the minor violence of the sadomasochistic theater is similarly a violence deferred. As Belle de Jour, the proprietor of one such theater, told me, "A good sadist or masochist wants to experience giving/getting pain every night. To do that you have to be careful not to injure yourself or your partner." The violence *imagined* at Belle's theater is many times more intense than the violence performed.

Actual violence is all around. Today's American television news tries to get as close to the action as possible. Everyone has seen video images of murder, warfare, terrorism, natural disasters, and personal tragedies. The victims are not actors in the aesthetic sense, even if the reporters are. These images arouse appetites that cannot be satisfied by more of the same. Actual violence framed as aesthetics or sport—like the eroticism of pornography—transforms bits of actuality into fantasy. The omnipotence of thought is given free rein. What would television be like—that is, what would the public imagination be feeding on—if, as in Greek tragedy, all violence was reported instead of being seen? Or am I crediting videotape with too much "actuality"? Is a photograph, or a film, or a tape of an event more real than a verbal description or a written report? Are we headed toward reestablishing the gladiatorial games of the Colosseum?

What about the violence of ritual—human and animal sacrifice, cannibalism, flesh-piercing, initiatory ordeals—on through a very long list? Do these practices tame the violence they simultaneously actualize and represent? Girard believes they are homeopathic—that a little ritual violence inoculates a society against more general, and destructive anarchic violence. This is close to what I say about ritual violence mortgaging death. Or perhaps ritual violence is a vestige of earlier, bloodier "primal rituals."[2] But who can specify the process transforming such rituals into make-believe, into theater? In Papua New Guinea, intertribal warfare and head-hunting have been outlawed. Today Papua New Guinea tribespeople gather at Mount Hagan and other "sing-sings" to perform for each other and for tourists. Some of the dances appear to be transformations of earlier, bloodier encounters (Schechner 1988). But this modulation of warfare into theater hardly seems a general model.

VI

It is no accident that in Asian all-night performances the demons appear in the hours just before dawn. Demons—like the devils of the great medieval European cycle plays—are both horrific and farcical. Appearing as they do at the "witching hour," they participate in both the performative and the dream worlds. Children awaking to the roars of the demons stare wide-eyed, not really knowing if they are "seeing" or "dreaming." Parents too experience the performance while they are in the twilight zone between waking and sleeping. This is not only a matter of clock-time. Japanese say that the proper way to "watch" noh is in a state between waking and sleeping. Among the noh audience are many whose eyes are closed, or heavy-lidded. These experts are "paying attention" by relaxing their consciousness, allowing material to stream upward from their unconscious to meet the images/sounds streaming outward from the stage. In this state of porous receptive inattention, the spectator is carried along in noh's dreamlike rhythms (Schechner 1988). Often images and sounds are shared by shite, chorus, and musicians so that the principal character is distributed among a number of performers. The spectator's own reveries blend in with what is coming from the stage. As Kunio Komparu notes, "the viewer participates in the creation of the play by individual free association and brings to life internally a drama based on individual experience filtered through the emotions of the protagonist. The shared dramatic experience, in other words, is not the viewer's adjustment of himself to the protagonist on stage but rather his creation of a separate personal drama by sharing the play with the performer. Indeed, he becomes that protagonist" (1983: 18).

Ehrenzweig sensed the similarity between this liminal state of half-sleep and artistic creativity. He termed this state "poemagogic" and recognized that it assimilates violence to creativity: "Poemagogic images . . . of suffering, destruction, and death . . . in their enormous variety, reflect the various phases and aspects of creativity in a very direct manner, though the central theme of death and rebirth, of trapping and liberation, seems to overshadow the others. Death and rebirth mirror the ego's dedifferentiation and redifferentiation" (1970: 189–90). In the life of the imagination dreams are the paradigm of liminality, existing in a world totally "as if"—between the clarity of reasoned thought and the confusion of events forced on the dreamer.

It is at the deepest level of dreaming—a level as cultural as much as it is individual—that the strongest connections exist between tragedy, violence, sexuality, and farce. Look at the cartoons little children watch on Saturday morning television. Compare these to the classics of silent film: Chaplin, the Keystone Cops, Laurel and Hardy. Connect this tradition of slapstick clowning to the circus, Grand Guignol, the commedia dell'arte, Punch and Judy shows, and medieval, Roman, and Greek mimes. In the triadic relation of laughter to violence to sex, one corner of the triangle often is hidden. Slapstick connects laughter to violence, romantic comedy connects laughter to sex, sadomasochism connects violence to sex. Sometimes all three corners are visible, as in Aristophanic comedy or in the antics of Hopi mudhead clowns who are obscene, cruel, and funny. The Hopi example could be multiplied the world over.

Milan Kundera nicely frames the progression from laughter to excitement to violence:

> There they stood in front of the mirror (they always stood in front of the mirror while she undressed), watching themselves. She stripped to her underwear, but still had the [bowler] hat on her head. And all at once she realized they were both excited by what they saw in the mirror.
>
> What could have excited them so? A moment before, the hat on her head had seemed nothing but a joke. Was excitement really a mere step away from laughter?
>
> Yes. When they looked at each other in the mirror that time, all she saw for the first few seconds was a comic situation. But suddenly the comic became veiled by excitement: the bowler hat no longer signified a joke; it signified violence. [1985: 86]

The progression can originate anywhere in the triangle and proceed in any direction—from violence to sex, from sex to laughter, and so forth.

The dreaming I am talking about is not limited to fantasies of the night. Dreaming can be trained as a technique of the mind that dissolves boundaries between unconsciousness, consciousness, and public representation (as ritual, theater, dance, visual arts, and so on). What is dreamed is "seen." Quotation marks are necessary because the precise quality of this seeing cannot be known except by some kind of secondary elaboration. A dream is the quintessential private event. But what has been dreamed, or images/actions made from or in reaction to what has been dreamed, can be represented later to others. In art these representations are relatively harmless. But art extends toward other modes of human expression: ritual action, spells and curses, and "acting out" in the clinical sense. The representations of art are relatively harmless, even homeopathic, because they are generally recognized as representations. But other manifestations of dreaming may be very destructive. A military action or a rape (and how often the two go together) at each level of their actualization from planning to battlefield combat/consummation can be interpreted as the acting out of desirous, violent fantasies.

These actualized dreams conform to the theatrical trope of tragi-farce. Tragi-farce because in the unconscious—that is, as dreams—distinctions among the genres collapse. Each theatrical genre expresses a particular mood. But in dreams, and actions modeled on dreams, moods are wildly mixed, the differences between happiness, sadness, terror, and joy are erased; one feeling becomes another without warning. Girard rightly fears chaotic undifferentiation. Yet the lure of undifferentiation is extremely compelling—and not only to artists and shamans. The less differentiated the fantasies are—the more they collapse genres and categories—the more powerfully they operate on people. That is why rituals, like television commercials, obsessively repeat a few basic themes: jingles, tunes, rhythms, catch lines. Repetition collapses distinctions between the idiosyncratic dream images/actions of individuals and the stereotyped/archetypal images/actions of cultures. The play of the illusion of difference is what keeps individualism afloat. But the truth is there are no givens or primaries, no originals or firsts, not even the mind itself.

Do not underestimate the power and actuality of illusion. For animals, illusions may not exist on a par with getting through another day of hunting, mating, and marking/defending turf. But for humans, illusion—what the Hindu philosophers call maya/lila—is, as Shakespeare also knew, the very stuff living is made of.

What is it that makes a person human? A nexus of circumstances: speech, bipedal locomotion, brain size and complexity, social organization. Let me suggest another quality. Dreams are desires, erotic and violent. When dreams were consciously actualized—not only dreamed and remembered but danced, sung, and acted out—a definite threshold was crossed. A performance of a nightmare, or of a vision of paradise (whose violence is the suddenness of loss upon awakening), is, in Jacques Derrida's phrase, the "presence of an

[317]

absence." The dream can never actually be shown—it is, like the violence of Greek tragedy, forever offstage, reported or represented through mimesis. Even what the dreamer remembers of the dream is involuntary, filtered through unconscious censorship. Shamans and artists are "dream-trained"—skilled in focussing their dreams, retaining and retelling them. This retelling may be in any medium: words, actions, pictures, sounds. Dream-trained people are also able freely to combine their dream-images with items from ordinary life and tradition.

Once a dream is performed, it changes its character entirely. It can be taught by the dreamer to others. It enters the social realm, the ritual and aesthetic sphere. It is revised, combined, and transformed to accord with—or radically break from—tradition. The great dreamers are those who can tolerate the most porosity—the greatest elision of what was dreamed with what is combined from other realms—while being able to call on a strict discipline when it is time to rehearse and perform the resultant dream-work.

Thus, three classes of events become performatively possible: what was, what is imaginary (dreams, fantasies, fictions), and events between history and imagination. This third class of events, that of virtual actuality, an actuality that shares the authority of recollection with the play of imagination, is sublimely powerful. Human creativity works the field betwixt and between the ethological, the neurological, and the social. These artful elaborations have been decisive in human history since paleolithic times. They appear always to have been fundamentally erotic and violent.

The future of ritual is actually the future of the encounter between imagination and memory translated into do-able acts of the body. Ritual's conservatism may restrain human beings sufficiently to prevent nuclear or ecological extermination, while its molten, creative core demands that human life—social, individual, maybe even biological—keep changing.

Notes

1. Flow as defined by Mihaly Csikszentmihalyi is "the merging of action and awareness. A person in flow has no dualistic perspective: he is aware of his actions but not the awareness itself. . . . The steps for experiencing flow . . . involve the . . . process of

delimiting reality, controlling some aspect of it, and responding to the feedback with a concentration that excludes anything else as irrelevant" (1975: 38, 53–54).

2. An early theory concerning the emergence of theater from a "primal ritual" was proposed in the first decades of the twentieth century by the "Cambridge anthropologists," scholars of ancient Greek culture who followed the lead of Sir James G. Frazer. See Harrison 1912, 1913, Murray 1912, and Cornford 1914; see Schechner 1988 for a critique of their thesis.

REFERENCES

Bateson, Gregory. 1972. "A Theory of Play and Fantasy." In Bateson, *Steps to an Ecology of Mind*. pp. 177–93. New York: Ballantine Books.
Cornford, Francis. 1914. *The Origins of Attic Comedy*. London: Edward Arnold.
Csikszentmihalyi, Mihaly. 1975. *Beyond Boredom and Anxiety*. San Francisco: Jossey-Bass.
D'Aquili, Eugene G., Charles D. Laughlin, Jr., and John McManus. 1979. *The Spectrum of Ritual*. New York: Columbia, University Press.
Ehrenzweig, Anton. 1970. *The Hidden Order of Art*. Frogmore, St. Albans, Hertsfordshire: Paladin.
Fischer, Roland. 1971. "A Cartography of the Ecstatic and Meditative States." *Science* 174: 897–904.
Freud, Sigmund. 1962. (1913). *Totem and Taboo*. Trans. James Strachey. New York: W. W. Norton.
Girard, René. 1977. *Violence and the Sacred*. Baltimore: Johns Hopkins University Press.
Grimes, Ronald L. 1982. *Beginnings in Ritual Studies*. Washington, D.C.: University Press of America.
Handelman, Don. 1977. "Play and Ritual: Complementary Frames of Metacommunication." In A. J. Chapman and H. Fort, eds., *It's a Funny Thing, Humour*. London: Pergamon.
Harrison, Jane Ellen. 1912. *Themis: A Study of the Social Origins of Greek Religion*. Cambridge: Cambridge University Press.
——. 1913. *Art and Ritual*. New York: Henry Holt.
Kafka, Franz. 1954. *Wedding Preparations in the Country and Other Posthumous Prose Writings*. London: Secker and Warburg.
Komparu, Kunio. 1983. *The Noh Theater*. New York: Weatherhill/Tankosha.
Kundera, Milan. 1985. *The Unbearable Lightness of Being*. New York: Harper Colophon.
Lex, Barbara W. 1979. "The Neurobiology of Ritual Trance." In d'Aquili, Laughlin, and McManus, eds., 1979. Pp. 117–51.
Murray, Gilbert. 1912. "An Excursus on the Ritual Forms Preserved in Greek Tragedy." In Harrison 1912.
Schechner, Richard. 1973. *Environmental Theater*. New York: Hawthorn.
——. 1985. *Between Theater and Anthropology*. Philadelphia: University of Pennsylvania Press.

———. 1988. *Performance Theory*. London: Routledge.

Thompson, Robert Farris. 1974. *African Art in Motion*. Berkeley: University of California Press.

Turner, Victor. 1969. *The Ritual Process*. Chicago: Aldine.

———. 1974. *Dramas, Fields, and Metaphors*. Ithaca: Cornell University Press.

———. 1982. *From Ritual to Theatre*. New York: Performing Arts Journal Press.

———. 1983. "Body, Brain, and Culture." *Zygon* 18, 3: 221–46.

———. 1986. *The Anthropology of Performance*. New York: PAJ Publications.

Epilogue:
Creative Persona and
the Problem of Authenticity

Edward M. Bruner

The theme of this volume, that the creative persona has the power of transformation and transcendence and can change a culture, is both obvious and subtle. We know that there have always been charismatic prophets, political leaders, and intellectual giants who move peoples and nations, and who change the scholarly directions of an historical era. One thinks of Newton and Einstein, Alexander the Great and Napoleon, Jesus and Mohammed, Joyce and Proust. Such exceptional individuals even have a place in superorganic theories of culture. But in the theory held, for the most part, by the contributors to this volume, even little people in the routine and the everyday construct their lives as they live their lives. Changes initiated by persons of power or by elite groups do have a higher probability of being more widely accepted by the larger society, but change occurs among all social classes and segments. Transformation and transcendence are especially marked in cultural performances, in what Victor Turner has called putting experience into circulation, for it is in performance that a society is most articulate and powerful in giving expression to its key cultural symbols, paradigms, and narratives.

Look at it this way:

> If we believe that culture is heavy, ponderous and static,
> If it's a slowly changing beast,

[321]

If there is nothing new under the sun,
If culture is a burden, even oppressive, a weight to bear,

THEN:

It takes a giant to move the world, even a little.

BUT:

If we see culture as always in production, as constituted and reconstituted in every act,

If we agree with the American pragmatists, with Dilthey, and with the hermeneutic tradition that meaning is not prior to an event but is emergent in the event,

If we agree with the French poststructuralists that events do not simply trigger or release a preexisting meaning buried in the text, underlying surface manifestations, behind them or beneath them, and if we see meaning as uncontrollable, as radically symbolic,

If we see culture as alive, in constant movement,

If we agree that every cultural expression is different, however slightly, from the previous expression, if only because the context is different,

If we agree that the various domains of culture are not congruent and do not replicate one another, but rather that there is a dynamic tension between domains,

If we acknowledge that cultural codes, rules, and norms never encompass all of the situations in which individuals find themselves, so that improvisation is a cultural imperative,

If we believe that cultural transmission is not a mechanical replication or reproduction of the heavy heritage of the past,

If we believe all these things, and if we believe in an anthropology of experience, practice and performance,

THEN:

One does not have to be a Napoleon to change a culture.
The little guy has a chance.
It's not only easy to change culture, but we do it all the time.
And if this is so, then creative personas have a wide-open field. She and he, can do anything—if not move the world then, at the very least, they can move themselves and their culture. What Shostak found for the !Kung is actually universal;

"creative expression takes place almost anywhere, during any segment of the day."

That change is inherent in social life is not news. We have had enough critiques of static views of society over past decades to question the separation between homeostasis and transformation. Nevertheless, as Barbara Babcock and others suggest, we somehow feel compelled to "explain" change by reference to the gifted genius, the marginal individual, the charismatic prophet, or we evoke special features of the context, such as historical forces, unsettled times, or even the proverbial raiders from the north. It is as if the initial condition of man, or to borrow a term from computer terminology, the default setting, is one of no change, and every instance of change or innovation is an aberration from that comfortable initial state. The image that comes to mind is of society, somehow, settling down in an overstuffed easy chair, and so reluctant to depart from that idyllic condition that every movement becomes a special event demanding an explanation.

All creative activity, in this view, is attributed to some extraordinary person, time or place. Even Victor Turner, who did more than anyone to open up anthropology by focusing our attention on process and on reflexivity, privileged the liminal and the liminoid, at least in some of his writings (1969, 1974), to such an extent that creativity was relegated to the "extra" ordinary, which diminished the everyday. It is ironic that in his lifelong struggle against formalism and structuralism, Turner so stressed the exceptional—the social drama, the betwixt and between, and the marginal—that, in effect, he abandoned ordinary social life to Radcliffe-Brown. Society became a rather dull place regulated by jural rules and structural principles, a place from which one departed temporarily for a flourish of excitement, creativity, and change, only to return, transformed but exhausted, to a dronelike existence. Turner, of course, was well aware of this criticism and did change the emphasis in his later writings.

How frequently have we read ethnographic accounts in which change was attributed to extraordinary conditions, and particularly to situations of interaction between two or more cultures, to contact between peoples, revolutionary times, or to the coming of the white man, the missionaries, the traders, the settlers, or even the tourists. Yet, we well know that societies have long had to contend with other tribes, with religious proselytizers, with trade, migrations, and probably with strangers, as part of the very conditions of human existence.

As Marjorie Shostak notes, creativity is not a rare occurrence to be placed in a special category without which cultures would stagnate, nor is primitive society necessarily slow to change. We do, certainly, have periods of conquest and empire as well as epochs of more rapid change, but this does not imply that the periods in between are characterized by an absence of innovation or by a condition of stasis.

The essays in this volume struggle with ways of describing innovation, creativity, and change. The aim is twofold: to see process as part of structure rather than to view the two as in opposition (Wagner 1975, Giddens 1979); and to see the context as part of the text, rather than to view one as penetrating as an outside force upon the domain of the other. What is so difficult about these efforts is that built into our Western metaphysics (Derrida 1974) is the notion of a privileged original, a pure tradition, which exists in some prior time, from which everything now is a contemporary degradation. This is what James Clifford (1986) calls the pastoral allegory including the search for origins, the ethnographic present, and the idea of the vanishing primitive taken as a disappearing object, as a trope. It is what I call the problem of authenticity.

The pastoral has been attacked on all fronts (Fabian 1983), an attack that the essays in this book powerfully reflect. But there is irony here. At the time that ethnography is changing, we have an increase in international mass tourism. Just when ethnographers have given up the quest for the exotic, authentic original—the source, hordes of tourists are demanding it, and getting it, all over the world as cultural performances are constructed to fulfill tourist expectations. Ethnographers want thick description; tourists, thin description. Ethnographers seek a processual historical world; tourists, the timeless, ethnographic present. Ethnographers demand complexity; tourists, ready accessibility.

I studied tourism with Barbara Kirshenblatt-Gimblett, and if there is one thing we learned, it is not to underestimate the power of the tourist quest for the authentic savage. Tourists are searching for "experience" and for their "origin" through the rural, the primitive, the childlike, the unpolluted, the pure, and the original. They are returning to the Garden. In the past, travel accounts (Pratt 1985) were the major genre through which Western peoples were exposed to the primitive world, but these days affluent Westerners take organized tours and explore that world on their own. Now, tourists can even choose exactly how much authenticity they want. Smadar Lavie tells of a fake Bedouin tourist village in the Sinai, but for those with less time or a more delicate disposition there is, just outside Jerusalem, a fifty-minute presentation at an ersatz Bedouin encampment. Tourists can find whatever degree of Bedouin-ness they want.

In a sense, ethnographers and tourists are in competition, for both go to foreign lands and return with representations of their experience. The ethnographic product is primarily written, but tourism differs in the fascinating respect that it translates experience into image and object, that is, into photographs and souvenirs. Writing, photos, and objects are equally "representations," but the key difference is that the ethnographic experience is primarily verbal, occurring through language (although it also contains images), whereas the tourist experience is primarily nonverbal and visual, expressed through images and objects (Fernandez 1986). In the Third World countries we visited—Indonesia, Kenya, and Egypt—tourists generally do not speak in a meaningful way with anyone except other tourists, tour guides, or with those locals who are part of the tourist industry. They relate to the local people by looking at them, photographing them, and by purchasing whatever objects, as well as slides and postcards, that are presented for sale. Objects, as material mementos, encapsulate the tourist experience and reduce it to size.

Aside from whatever economic exploitation may be involved—an issue which has been dealt with in the literature—there is a moral dimension that we may not yet have come to terms with. Balinese and Maasai and Bedouin are being transformed into signs of themselves, culturally specific ones to be sure, but, nevertheless, they are becoming objects, like the souvenirs they sell. From the tourist perspective, indigenous peoples come to stand for African-ness or primitiveness although, from the native perspective, the performances have cultural meaning. What should be the moral position of anthropologists on this issue?

Authenticity, then, has become problematic. Ethnographers are rejecting the quest for authenticity and are examining the ethnographic process (Clifford and Marcus 1986), a theme that has shaped these essays; tourists, however, are still seeking authenticity with a vengeance; and the peoples we study are now questioning their own authenticity. Indeed, the papers by Kirin Narayan and Lavie are essentially about authenticity. Is this guru genuine or a fraud? Swamiji not only tells his disciples how to distinguish between a real guru and a charlatan, but he mocks the Western fascination with India. During

[325]

a moment of cultural self-doubt the Mzeina Bedouin, concerned about how to maintain their own tradition of hospitality given the influx of visitors and tourists, ask if they themselves are any longer real Bedouin! And in a curious turn so characteristic of this postmodern era, Smadar Lavie, half Yemenite and half Lithuanian, an Arab Jew, an Israeli studying at Berkeley, finds herself assuring the Bedouin that their traditions are still "alive and well."

For ethnographers, tourists, and indigenous peoples the question is not if authenticity is inherent in an object, as if it were a thing out there to be discovered or unearthed, but rather, how is authenticity constructed? What is the process by which an ethnography, a tourist performance, or any item of culture or practice achieves an aura of being authentic? What are the processes of production of authenticity? Just as ethnicity is a struggle (Fischer 1986), authenticity, too, is something sought, fought over, and reinvented.

As Renato Rosaldo shows, the unpredictability, variability, ambiguity, and indeterminacy in culture provides the "social space within which creativity can flourish." People construct culture as they go along and as they respond to life's contingencies. No one denies the importance of rules and codes, but we will never understand how culture works, or how it changes, unless we take account of the human capacity for improvisation and creativity. Rather than ask what culture is, ask how culture is achieved, produced, and made believable.

Narayan's essay highlights the continuing dialectic between creativity and tradition, between person and persona, as Swamiji actively constructs his role as guru. He plays with his audience and comments on his culture. If there were no person but all persona, then we would have a fastidious performance but no change. If it were all person and no persona, then we would have social chaos. If, however, the person participates in the construction of a persona, if it is role making rather than role taking, then there is the potentiality for creativity.

Richard Schechner describes how dramatic narrative, ritual, and theater are so often explicitly violent and sexual, themes which are simultaneously the most serious and the most playful. Aggression and sex are the stuff of serious play, cross-culturally, in theater as varied as the Ramayana, Japanese noh, and sadomasochistic shows in New York. What is cruel and what is obscene capture the imagination, and Schechner suggests there is a human "need" for representations in play of these potentially destructive, and creative, impulses. The sheer

[326]

amount of human creative energy that has gone into the play of aggressive and sexual themes is probably beyond calculation.

Shostak strikes a note of caution here. Her essay explores what creativity means to the !Kung, and shows how the !Kung artist must strike an egalitarian balance between creative expression and social expectation. The creative person in !Kung life must not claim self-importance or superiority, but within these limits, creativity flourishes. The general point is that there are always cultural constraints, not only on improvisation itself but on the general acceptance of an innovation by others.

This book both questions the ethnographic process and takes a radical turn in how it deals with subject-object relations. Those we had previously called our "informants" have been rescued from anonymity. We are talking about Ceferino Suárez, Swamiji, Jimmy, Helen Cordero, Induan Hiling, Américo Paredes, and the others. They are not absent from the text. They are presented in our ethnographic texts as historically situated persons, with voices, names, and presence. It is hard to call them informants anymore or even by the trendy term "consultants." They emerge in these papers as full-fledged personalities, and our new way of dealing with them has changed us, as ethnographers. We, too, have become less anonymous, less the objective scientific recording machine.

Names are significant, in that by giving names we locate our informants contextually, acknowledge their history, and position them in a particular social setting. In the past, we constructed an anonymous informant, the generalized Hopi or the Bushman, which enabled us to assert our dominance in the relationship (Pratt 1985). To provide names is to demystify the ethnographic process and to expose its mechanisms of construction. To name an informant is to give up some measure of our own power, and paradoxically, to the extent that we yield control we are free to become more creative. Also, providing names unmasks the assumed homogeneity of primitive peoples, that never-never land where one informant was, more or less, like any other. Ethnographers have always had names; now that our informants do, the gap between subject and object is further reduced.

It is ironic that the "new" new ethnography which celebrates the informant also runs the risk of celebrating the ethnographer. Michel Foucault asks, "What is an author?" (1977). He might have been surprised by the answers provided by those experimental ethnographies that deal with subject-object on the level of interpersonal relations more than on the level of discourse. The current critique of these ethnographies is that they are self-indulgent, too introspective, and even narcissistic. But as my colleague Alma Gottleib has remarked, the problem is to distinguish between narcissism and reflexivity. As we have paid increasing attention to the construction of the ethnographic text, we have put the ethnographer back into the text, and it may be that in some cases the ethnographer's role has become too prominent, or as James Fernandez writes, we may not have paid enough attention to voices on the ground. Of course, we must do so. The crucial point is to have both voices, multiple voices, in dialogic interplay.

I like it when the involvement, the stance, and even the commitment of the ethnographer are apparent in the text. The delight and the joy that Edith Turner evokes when she tells the story of the pilgrimage to the tomb of Bar Yohai clearly stem from the Turners' long-standing interest in ritual and pilgrimage, but also reflect the fact that the Turners are Catholic converts. Barbara Myerhoff shows that the ethnography takes shape through our own understanding and our own experience, and we, too, become the objects of our own inquiry. That Lavie is an Israeli with an Arabic-speaking Yemenite grandmother, who sees her own predicament reflected in the Bedouin, helps me to understand her account better. Narayan, the anthropologist/folklorist, describes herself as "a demure sari-wearing daughter of Nasik," whose grandmother is an orthodox Brahman. Her ethnographic project may be part of her personal effort to determine what is genuine and what is spurious in Indian and in Western tradition.

I even see similarities between the ethnographers and the informants they have selected, although I recognize this may be an outrageous presumption on my part. But Narayan is as droll as Swamiji. Don Handelman is as thoughtful and reflective as Henry Rupert. Anna Tsing is as innovative as Induan Hiling, Barbara Babcock as creative as Helen Cordero. José Limón is another Américo Paredes. Schechner is a parashaman. Fernandez, like Ceferino Suárez, is playful, poetic, and ironic. If I am correct in these perceived similarities between the ethnographers and their informants, it may be because both are engaged in what is essentially the same enterprise. Swamiji, Ceferino, and Helen Cordero, like Narayan, Fernandez, Babcock, and the others, are all storytellers, struggling to express themselves, to comment on their society and their times, and to establish their own position in the larger scheme of things. Ethnographers have always constructed their ethnographic texts, but now the ethnographers are entering the world they have constructed, living in that world, looking around, finding others to have conversations with, and reporting on the dialogue. Lavie's informant asks, "So who are the Bedouin and who are the guests?" I ask, "So who are the subjects and who are the objects?"

Ethnography is getting much more interesting than I, for one, had ever imagined.

The voices in these papers not only include those of the ethnographer and the informant but extend to the world system within which they are embedded—Cuba, the Camp David accords, the Anglo art market in the southwest of the United States, native texts saying "made in China," and to Sephardic pilgrims in an Israel dominated by an Ashkenazi political elite. These voices from afar have always been present in ethnographic encounters, but until recently we have not considered it worthwhile or appropriate to record them. The essay by Fernandez is especially sensitive to the dialogic in its attention to Ceferino's "particular voice" and its place among other voices from the village and beyond. Fernandez is also attentive to the "ambiguous interplay of forces coming into being and forces passing away," so that dialogic narration is seen as continually in construction and as moving with currents of history. Ceferino's voice is not just there, or once found, forever fixed; he constantly struggles to find his voice. It is fragile, ever changing. James Boon (1984) is correct; the world is a wayang, a Mardi Gras, a mélange, always in motion.

Handelman calls our attention to other voices that are absent from the text. Some individual informants have dealt with a series of ethnographers as well as with journalists, photographers, and assorted seekers of the exotic other. There is a history of their relationship to outsiders. Helen Cordero's grandfather was an informant to Adolph Bandelier, Edward Curtis, and Ruth Benedict; her mother was Esther Goldfrank's main informant; and Helen is working with Barbara Babcock. We have extended families and entire lineages of information givers! Handelman reports that Henry Rupert had had contact with six other ethnologists before him, and that Rupert was very aware that Handelman was one of a series. The point is that such informants not only have an active role in constructing their culture, they not only edit themselves to use Handelman's phrase, but they have an active role in constructing us and our discipline. One sees so clearly now that there are two active selves in the ethnographic process, them and

[329]

us, both interpreting themselves as they are interpreting the other. We have long realized that all ethnographers approach the field with a prior agenda—there are no naive ethnographers—but neither are there naive informants.

Handelman points to the importance of discursive practices, to what we might call the political economy of the text, that is, the restraints imposed on our ethnography by the conventions of the discipline, by our career orientation, by our claim to "authorship" and originality. Consider, for example, a bibliography in comparison with a preface. We have paid attention to prefaces (Nelson 1976, Pratt 1986, Clifford 1986) and to the entry stories they contain. But what of the bibliography, to the claims of authority it makes? Prefaces appear at the beginning of the text, but they are usually written last; bibliographies appear at the end of the text, but they are probably written, or known, first. Or at least we know in advance the body of literature to which we shall refer. What a bibliography does is to locate the author within the wider anthropological community. A bibliographic citation is very much part of the text but is not just an objective reference; it is also a political statement that stakes the author's claim to a position within a particular scholarly tradition. But as Handelman notes, the voices of other ethnographers are allocated a very narrow space in the discourse.

These essays call attention to political issues, to questions of authority and the politics of creativity. The point is not creativity in opposition to politics but creativity in the service of politics. The theme runs through Babcock's paper. It is not just the association of corn and pottery and fertility, but it has to do with what is men's business and with women's business. The paradigm had been symbolic power for women and political power for men, but Helen Cordero is changing that. The narrative focus also emerges in Babcock's paper, where we see storytelling as reproduction and as a mechanism of power, as well as of meaning. The profoundly political question becomes the following: who has the right, by what means, to tell what stories? It will be interesting to follow these developments along the Rio Grande.

Anna Tsing, like Babcock, deals with creativity in expression and politics, and shows how women's work can revise a male-dominated tradition. What women do is to incorporate the dominant conventions at the same time as they invert them, resist them, and transform them. Change occurs more through an end run than a frontal attack. Tsing stresses improvisation and deals with the cutting edge of resistance, showing how a female activity can be a commentary on male shamanism and an exposé of male practice. The crucial issue, again, is who has space in the discourse and the right to politically significant, expressive models. Tsing notes that women are disadvantaged "not so much by what was said but by who got to speak."

Voices again, active selves, and a balance between authoritative tradition and original knowledge.

Limón, too, deals with power, politics, and narrativity. He tells the story of Gregorio Cortez, based on events in 1901: a migrant journeys from the border, has a confrontation with the Anglos, and returns to reestablish links with his native community. It is a resistance narrative (Bruner 1986), one retold in the 1958 book by Américo Paredes, in the life story of Paredes as reconstructed by Chicano activists, in the paper by José Limón included here, and in the events of Limón's life as implied in the text. Cortez, Paredes, and Limón all sing the same corrido. But every time the story is told, it resonates with individual experiences of discrimination, which revitalize and personalize the narrative, and make it more vivid. What is remarkable in Limón's paper is how a folk ballad becomes an anthropological text, which in turn is transformed into a ballad again in a new historical era of activism in the 1960s, and in Limón's able hands, is retold as text in the 1980s for an audience of interpretive anthropologists. Which is the etic and which is the emic? Where is the difference here between subject and object? The distinction between "them" and "us" has dissolved; it appears that we are them and they are us.

An interesting question becomes, what happens to old stories? With each retelling in the present the original is transformed, for the past is never just recalled; it is always constructed. The original events of 1901 were changed by Paredes in 1958, modified by the Chicano movement, and again by Limón's current text. Old stories are like data entries in a computer spreadsheet. Each new entry changes the other totals in the spreadsheet, instantaneously, as all data and formulas in the spreadsheet are completely interactive. Computers have no consciousness, so the analogy is flawed, but the point is that old stories are never just stored in memory nor are they ever really recoverable, for they change with each telling. We can recover the words of the story but never the same context or the prior interpretation, if only because the world has changed and we are different. There are no authentic originals, only a process of authentication.

Edward Schieffelin's elegant essay on mediums in Papua New

Guinea shows us how authenticity is constructed in Kaluli séance, or more generally, how people experience a ritual and how the performance becomes compelling, believable, and transformative. We see how the medium commits the participants to the construction of the performance, and how, while searching for clarification of the spirit's message, the people "create the meaning they discover." How could we ethnographers have ever described any performance, either ritual or narrative, without dealing with the audience as creative agents who engage in acts of interpretation? Schieffelin sets our priorities straight when he writes that it is the performance that accounts for the belief system rather than the other way around. Meaning is not in the text but is emergent in the performance. And Schieffelin, like Rosaldo, shows how the open spaces and indeterminacies in social life lead people to reach for meaning and thereby to construct themselves and their societies. This essay celebrates the revolutionary potential in ritual and demonstrates that change is inherent in structure.

Myerhoff's essay, probably her last, is poetic, personal, and profound. It communicates the excitement of a journey into the anthropology of experience, connects the inner and the outer worlds, and shows how culture is made "real and immediate to each person." We see that only in performance are we made the embodiment "of the stories we tell." Because the essay is incomplete, constructed by Edith Turner from notes, it reminds us that all ethnography is partial and incomplete, and the very incompleteness of text and life requires that we constantly strive for understanding. Authenticity is a struggle, not a given. Myerhoff demonstrates how individual persons become invaded by persona, how a private life partakes of a collective tale, and how a bridge is constructed between biography, culture, and history.

Edith Turner tells the story of the pilgrimage to the shrine of Meron in the northern Galilee in 1983, showing that just as Bar Yohai's legacy is renewed and refashioned in contemporary Israel, so the legacy of Barbara Myerhoff and Victor Turner, both of whom participated in that pilgrimage, reaches out "beyond their own deaths." Creative personas do outlive themselves and there is a diachronic chain of poetic selves.

It is appropriate that this volume be dedicated to the memory of Victor Turner, for we are writing about him. He is our subject matter, as these papers are about the creative persona, and he is the archetype of the creative spirit in anthropology. His power, whimsy, and spark inspired so many of us and encouraged us to actualize our own creative potential. There is a chain of poetic selves, from Victor Turner to us. I conclude by paying tribute to creative personas, to:

a village poet in northern Spain
a Hindu guru
a !Kung musician
a Pueblo potter
a Meratus shaman
the Bedouin in the Sinai
a Washo healer
a Sephardic holy man in second-century Palestine
a Chicano scholar and activist
and to Victor Turner, the personification of the creative spirit.

And I pay tribute to us, to the creative persona in all of us.

REFERENCES

Boon, James A. 1984. "Folly, Bali, and Anthropology, or Satire across Cultures." In Edward M. Bruner, ed., *Text, Play, and Story: The Construction and Reconstruction of Self and Society.* 1983 Proceedings of the American Ethnological Society. Washington, D.C. Pp. 156–77.

Bruner, Edward M. 1986. "Ethnography as Narrative." In Victor W. Turner and Edward M. Bruner, eds., *The Anthropology of Experience.* Urbana: University of Illinois Press. Pp. 139–55.

Clifford, James. 1986. "On Ethnographic Allegory." In Clifford and Marcus, eds., 1986. Pp. 98–121.

Clifford, James, and George E. Marcus. 1986. *Writing Culture: The Poetics and Politics of Ethnography.* Berkeley: University of California Press.

Crick, Malcolm. 1985. " 'Tracing' the Anthropological Self: Quizzical Reflections on Field Work, Tourism, and the Ludic." *Social Analysis* 17:71–92.

Derrida, Jacques. 1974. *Of Grammatology.* Trans. Gayatri C. Spivak. Baltimore: Johns Hopkins University Press.

Fabian, Johannes. 1983. *Time and the Other: How Anthropology Makes Its Object.* New York: Columbia University Press.

Fernandez, James W. 1986. "The Argument of Images and the Experience of Returning to the Whole." In Victor W. Turner and Edward M. Bruner, eds., *The Anthropology of Experience.* Urbana: University of Illinois Press. Pp. 159–87.

Fischer, Michael M. J. 1986. "Ethnicity and the Post-Modern Arts of Memory." In Clifford and Marcus, eds., 1986. Pp. 194–233.

Foucault, Michel. 1977. "What Is an Author?" In Donald F. Bouchard, ed., *Language, Counter-Memory, Practice: Selected Essays and Interviews by Michel Foucault.* Ithaca: Cornell University Press.

Giddens, Anthony. 1979. *Central Problems in Social Theory: Action, Structure and Contradiction in Social Analysis.* Berkeley: University of California Press.

Kirshenblatt-Gimblett, Barbara, and Edward M. Bruner. n.d. "Tourism: Performing Ethnographic Tropes."

Nelson, Cary. 1976. "Reading Criticism." *PMLA* 91: 801–15.

Pratt, Mary Louise. 1985. "Scratches on the Face of the Country; or, What Mr. Barrow Saw in the Land of the Bushmen." *Critical Inquiry* 12: 119–43.

——. 1986. "Fieldwork in Common Places." In Clifford and Marcus, eds., 1986. Pp. 27–50.

Turner, Victor. 1969. *The Ritual Process.* Chicago: Aldine.

——. 1974. *Dramas, Fields, and Metaphors.* Ithaca: Cornell University Press.

Wagner, Roy. 1975. *The Invention of Culture.* Englewood Cliffs, N.J.: Prentice-Hall.

Contributors

Barbara A. Babcock is Professor of English and of Comparative Cultural and Literary Studies at the University of Arizona. She has also taught at the University of Texas and Brown University, where she was Director of the Pembroke Center for Teaching and Research on Women. Her publications include *The Reversible World: Essays in Symbolic Inversion* (1978), *Signs about Signs: The Semiotics of Self-Reference* (1980), *The Pueblo Storyteller: Development of a Figurative Ceramic Tradition* (1986), and *Daughters of the Desert: Women Anthropologists and the Native American Southwest, 1880–1980* (1988). She is the editor of *Inventing the Southwest* (1990), a collection of essays on region as commodity, and *Pueblo Mothers and Children: Essays by Elsie Clews Parsons, 1915–1924* (1991).

Edward M. Bruner is Professor of Anthropology and of Criticism and Interpretive Theory at the University of Illinois. He was past president of the American Ethnological Society and of the Society for Humanistic Anthropology. He has done fieldwork among American Indians and in Indonesia. His edited volumes include *Art, Ritual, and Society in Indonesia* (with Judith O. Becker); *Text, Play, and Story: The Construction and Reconstruction of Self and Society;* and *The Anthropology of Experience* (with Victor W. Turner). He is currently writing a book on tourist performances.

Contributors

James W. Fernandez is Professor of Anthropology at the University of Chicago. He has worked in various parts of Africa and Northern Spain. His essay in this volume treats material taken from "A Life History of Ceferino Suárez, A Countryman Discussed," which is itself part of a long-term research project on social change among cattle-keepers and miners in the Spanish province of Asturias.

Don Handelman is Professor of Sociology and Anthropology at the Hebrew University of Jerusalem, Israel. His fieldwork was carried out in the Great Basin in the United States and in Newfoundland, Sri Lanka, Israel, and India. His theoretical interests include symbolism, rituals, play, and bureaucracy. His most recent book, *Models and Mirrors: Towards an Anthropology of Public Events*, was published in 1990.

Smadar Lavie teaches anthropology and critical theory at the University of California, Davis. She is the author of the award-winning book *The Poetics of Military Occupation: Mzeina Allegories of Bedouin Identity under Israeli and Egyptian Rule* (1990) and co-editor of the forthcoming *Diaspora, Displacement, and Geographies of Identity*. She is currently working on a book manuscript about Third World Israelis writing in the race/gender border zone of Zionism.

José E. Limón is Professor of English and Anthropology at the University of Texas at Austin. He is the author of *Mexican Ballads, Chicano Poems: History and Influence in Mexican American Social Poetry* (1992).

Barbara Myerhoff, who died in 1985, was Professor of Anthropology at the University of Southern California. Among her writings are *The Peyote Hunt: The Sacred Journey of the Huichol Indians* (1974) and *Number Our Days* (1978). The latter book was the basis for a documentary film, which won an Academy Award.

Kirin Narayan teaches at the University of Wisconsin–Madison. She is the author of *Storytellers, Saints, and Scoundrels: Folk Narrative in Hindu Religious Teaching* (1989), which was awarded the Victor Turner Prize for Ethnographic Writing (1990) and the Elsie Clews Parsons Prize for Folklore (co-winner, 1990). Her novel about cross-cultural experience will be available in 1993, and currently she is working on women's songs and folk narratives from Kangra, Northwest India.

Renato Rosaldo teaches at Stanford University. He has conducted field research among the Ilongots of northern Luzon, Philippines, and the Zinacantecos of southern Mexico. Currently he is working among Latinos in San Jose, California. His writings include *Ilongot Head-hunting, 1883–1974: A Study in Society and History* (1980) and *Culture and Truth: The Remaking of Social Analysis* (1989).

Richard Schechner is a University Professor at the Tisch School of the Arts, New York University, where he teaches performance studies. A theater director who has worked in the Americas, Europe, Asia, and Africa, Schechner is artistic director of East Coast Artists (New York) and editor of *TDR: A Journal of Performance Studies*. Among his books are *Between Theater and Anthropology* (1985), *Performance Theory* (1988), and *The Future of Ritual* (1993).

Edward L. Schieffelin received his B.A. from Yale University in physics and philosophy and his M.A. and Ph.D. from the University of Chicago in anthropology. He has conducted field research in the Southern Highlands Province of Papua New Guinea since 1966. His writings include *The Sorrow of the Lonely and the Burning of the Dancers* (1976) and *Like People You See in a Dream* (1991) (with Robert Critlenden). He has taught at Fordham University, the University of Pennsylvania, and Emory University. He is currently lecturer at University College, London.

Marjorie Shostak is Adjunct Assistant Professor of Anthropology at Emory University. She is the author of *Nisa: The Life and Words of a !Kung Woman* and co-author of *The Paleolithic Prescription* (Eaton, Shostak, and Konner). She is currently working on a book about her return to Nisa during 1989.

Anna Lowenhaupt Tsing teaches anthropology at the University of California, Santa Cruz. She is co-editor, with Faye Ginsburg, of *Uncertain Terms: Negotiating Gender in American Culture* and author of *In the Realm of the Diamond Queen: Marginality in an Out-of-the-Way Place*.

Edith Turner teaches anthropology at the University of Virginia. Her major interests are symbolism and ritual, anthropological writing, the Ndembu of Zambia, and the Inupiat of northern Alaska. She is the author of *Experiencing Ritual* (1992); "Poetics and Experience in Anthropological Writing," *Steward Journal* (1987–88); *The Spirit and the Drum* (1987); and *Image and Pilgrimage in Christian Culture: Anthropological Perspectives* (with Victor Turner, 1978). She is at present finishing a monograph on what the Inupiat call "Eskimo Spirituality."

Index

Abraham, 214, 225, 228
Adam, 214. *See also* Adam Kadmon
Adam Kadmon, 234, 235, 238
Adang, Uma, 102, 104, 106, 123
Aliya, 230, 235, 238
Alkabez, Solomon, 235
Allegorical type, 231, 237, 238
  among the Mzeina Bedouin, 156,
    174–76, 180n.20
  Shimon Bar Yohai as, 225–26, 239
  and symbolic type, 250n.1
  See also Allegory
Allegory, 153, 156, 180n.19, 180n.21,
    249
  as critique, 173–74
  as interpretation, 176, 180n.15
  and irony, 177
  pastoral, 324
"Allegory and Representation" (Green-
    blatt), 153
Angels, 214, 219, 226, 228, 231, 235,
    236
Animals, 298, 314
  behavior of, and ritual, 296–97, 301,
    312
  as familiars, 299
Animism, 305

Anthropos, 238
Anti-Semitism, 230, 235
Ardener, Edwin, 87
Arquero, Juanita, 78
Art
  and dreams, 315–18
  Freud on, 305–6
  as liminoid activity, 311–12
  linked with neurosis, 307–8
  and violence, 297–99, 302
  See also specific art forms
Artists
  and !Kung cultural requirements, 55–
    56
  as liminal personalities, 67–68, 69
  and Shamans compared, 306, 307
  See also Art; *specific artists*
Ascetics, 38–39, 40, 42
Athabascan hunters, 262–63, 264
Auschwitz, 216, 300–301
Authenticity, 324–26, 328
Autobiography, ethnic, 204–5, 206

Ba'al Shem Tov, 230, 235
Ba-at, 257, 259
Babcock, Barbara, 4, 323, 328, 329, 330
Babylonian captivity, 235

[339]

Ilongots (*cont.*)
and social grace, 263–64, 268
talk of hearts, 260–61
visitors' arrival scenes, 258–60, 266–67
Indeterminacy, 155, 254, 255–56, 305, 326, 332
Indian Time, 255
Individual and communal identity, tension between, 12, 20–23, 26–27
Indonesian Borneo, 100, 102. *See also* Meratus Dayaks
Informants, 3, 327, 328–30. *See also specific individuals*
Initiation rites, 219, 246
Inquisition, Spanish, 229, 235
Institute for Religion in an Age of Science, 238
Interreference, 205
Intertextuality, 204–5
Islam, 226
Israel
Jews' return to, 227, 230, 232, 235, 236, 238
political and community structure of, 239, 250–51n.3, 251n.5
Iyakiku, 85

Jerusalem, 212, 227, 228
Jews
history of, 211–12, 228, 229, 235
Moroccan, settlement in Israel of, 230, 232, 250–51n.3, 251n.5
return to Israel, 227, 230, 232, 235, 236, 238
See also Hasids; Judaism; Kabbalah; Sephardim
Jimmy, 57–60, 67, 68, 69, 327. *See also* !Kung San
Juan de Juanes (Suárez), 16
Judaism, 212, 215
sacred time in, 216–17, 221
symbolism in, 211, 213, 217–20
tradition of zaddiks in, 226
See also Bar Yohai; Bar Yohai's tomb, pilgrimage to; Kabbalah
Jungian psychology, 238, 249

Kabbalah, 212, 214, 221, 231
creation myth of, 232–34, 235

doctrine of "the Breaking of the Vessels," 234, 235
and Judaic religious protohistory, 235
secrecy of, 228–29, 248
and the Shekhinah, 233, 235–36, 245, 248
and Tikkun, 234
world tree diagram of, 228
Kabbolos Shabbos, ceremony of, 235–36
Kabir, 217
Kafka, Franz, 308
Kalimantan. *See* Indonesian Borneo
Kalu hungo:, 282–83, 291
Kaluli. *See* Séance, Kaluli
Kapferer, Bruce, 109
Karwat aḍ-ḍeif. *See* Hospitality, Bedouin code of
Kathakali, 311
Kegel, 274–75, 280, 284
Kennedy, John F., assassination of, 300
King Lear (Shakespeare), 27, 302, 313–14
Kiva membership, 85, 86, 87
Komparu, Kunio, 315
Kundera, Milan, 316
!Kung San, 54
bead weaver, 65–67, 68
egalitarianism of, and artistic accomplishment, 55–56, 68, 327
musician, 57–60, 67, 69, 327
roles of healer, 61–62
types of creative expression among, 55, 56–57
woman healer, 57, 61–65, 67, 68
Kushner, Lawrence, 217

Lag B'Omer, 211, 213, 215, 218, 219–20, 239
Lange, Charles H., 92n.13
Laughlin, Charles D., Jr., 308, 309
Lavie, Smadar, 4, 226, 324–25, 326, 328
Leach, Edmund, 92n.11
Lentricchia, Frank, 206–7
Levels of Communication and Taboo in the Appreciation of Primitive Art (Leach), 92n.11
Lévi-Strauss, Claude, 181n.22
Leviticus, 219
Lex, Barbara, 309
Life history typification, 138, 139

Anthropology of Contemporary Issues

A SERIES EDITED BY

ROGER SANJEK

Library of Congress Cataloging-in-Publication Data

Creativity/anthropology / edited by Smadar Lavie, Kirin Narayan, and
   Renato Rosaldo.
          p.   cm. — (Anthropology of contemporary issues)
       Includes bibliographical references and index.
       ISBN 0-8014-2255-8 (cloth : alk. paper). — ISBN 0-8014-9542-3 (paper : alk. paper)
       1. Creative ability–Cross-cultural studies.   2. Symbolism—Cross-cultural stud-
   ies.   3. Ethnology—Philosophy.   4. Turner, Victor Witter.   I. Lavie, Smadar.   II. Narayan, Kirin.   III. Rosaldo, Renato.   IV. Series.
   GN453.C74   1993
   306.4—dc20   92-52765